RELIGION AND THE
WAR IN BOSNIA

AAR

American Academy of Religion
The Religions

Editor
Paul B. Courtright

Number 3
RELIGION AND THE
WAR IN BOSNIA

edited by
Paul Mojzes

RELIGION AND THE
WAR IN BOSNIA

edited by
Paul Mojzes

Scholars Press
Atlanta, Georgia

RELIGION AND THE
WAR IN BOSNIA

edited by
Paul Mojzes

© 1998
The American Academy of Religion

Library of Congress Cataloging in Publication Data
Religion and the war in Bosnia / edited by Paul Mojzes.
    p.   cm — (AAR the religions ; no. 3)
    Includes bibliographical references.
    ISBN 0-7885-0428-2 (pbk. : alk. paper)
    1. Yugoslav War, 1991– —Religious aspects. 2. Yugoslav War,
1991– —Bosnia and Hercegovina—History—1992–   I. Mojzes,
Paul. II. Series.
DR1313.7.R45R46 1998
949.703—dc21   97-49123
                                                CIP

Printed in the United States of America
on acid-free paper
∞

Dedicated to all those religious people
who did not succumb to the forces of
hatred and destruction.

TABLE OF CONTENTS

PREFACE

The wars in the former Yugoslavia (1991-1995), particularly in Bosnia and Herzegovina, one of its former federal states, have agitated the minds and hearts of countless people around the globe. Explanations and descriptions have abounded in the press, media, diplomatic meetings, scholarly analyses, and conversations among the learned as well as average people. Many were conscience-stricken as they watched helplessly the most massive devastation of populace and dwellings in Europe since World War II, looking for interpretative tools as well as plans for action to stop the war. At no point in my long academic career was I more in demand as a speaker; groups--academic, civic, and religious--sought someone, anyone, to help them understand and respond.

During my service on the *Ad Hoc* Committee on International Connections of the American Academy of Religion, I was given the opportunity to organize a Special Forum, under a similar title as this book at the Annual Meeting of the AAR in Chicago in November 1994. Dr. Barbara DeConcini, the executive director of AAR, suggested that a book dealing with the subject might be of interest to the Scholars Press. Upon consultation with many colleagues who are knowledgeable in the field, I undertook this project. Many of them became contributors to this volume--a price frequently paid for volunteering an opinion! My projection that the book would be completed in a year and that it would be a small volume was unrealistic.

I sought out all the scholars whom I knew to have an understanding of the religious dimension of the war in Bosnia, both in the USA and in the countries of the former Yugoslavia. The response was astonishing. Only two people who I originally hoped would respond did not. But, others responded to my call for papers as to who could shed light but not heat on this ultra-sensitive topic. Not only did they respond, but most of them produced very thorough, lengthy analyses which I decided not to reject for brevity's sake.

A number of manuscripts were submitted in the variants of the southern Slavs. These caused considerable delays as I had to translate them into English. Others arrived already translated into English, but in need of very extensive editorial work. The result of that translating work is frequently unsatisfactory in terms of effective English communication. Academics are known to have cumbersome writing styles; European academics have the additional tendency of inordinately long and complex sentences. Turning these texts into crisp prose was nearly impossible, especially since I myself inherited this European trait. While the stylistic form of some of the papers may leave something to be desired, the content seems exceptional and some of the viewpoints rarely encountered in the West. However, not the entire spectrum of opinion is represented here. I did not invite, and in one case rejected a solicited essay if the authors viciously attacked a side not their own. Conversely, I encouraged internal criticism, i.e. the critical reflections of abuses and mistakes by members of one's own ethnoreligious group. The degree of rationalization and justification of certain attitudes and actions do vary from author to author.

The nineteen chapters are subdivided into three parts. Part I contains the works explaining the context. There is no single work that summarizes all issues leading to this tragic warfare, but such works are now easily available in a large number of languages.

Part II contains the bulk of this book as it presents analyses of the religious component of the war. Chapters 4 to 8 provide the most general approaches. Chapter 9 provides a Muslim perspective (two of the expected but undelivered papers were to be offered from the Muslim perspective). Chapters 10 to 13 deal with the Serbian Orthodox Church's role, all written by Serb authors. This perspective happens to be the most neglected aspect in the general literature, because while Serbs have been the frequent target of critical analyses, one rarely locates analyses by Serbs other than those written in Serbia for other Serbs. Chapters 14 and 15 are from a Roman Catholic perspective, although chapter 15 by its intention and style could just as easily have been placed in the more general subsection of Part II. Chapter 15 also provides a good transition to Part III which contains chapters dealing with proposed ways for religions to become agents of reconciliation rather than to fuel the war of which they stand accused in Part II.

I continued to be in contact with all of the contributors by mail and by telephone and with many of them in person at various conferences. Nearly all the essays were written in 1994 or 1995; a few were written earlier and only one or two later. All of the authors requested that I emphasize the context of the time period when the essays were written, namely at a time when the war in Bosnia had not yet ended and when it was impossible to foresee in which direction war and/or peace might develop. As I re-read these essays at the time of their final submission, it became obvious that the analyses are remarkably on target although many of the authors, if they had a chance to make minor corrections, would do so. I am thankful to them for their patience during the extended period of collecting, translating, editing, and formatting the texts, the task of which was extended by my transition from teaching religious studies to academic administration as academic dean. These exceptional testimonies of a specific war may become a paradigm for future ethnoreligious conflicts around the world. They help us to understand the confusing conflict in Bosnia and Herzegovina but also help us discern patterns of the kind of wars that may replace the great power Cold War rivalry with incessant ethnoreligious conflicts.

My colleague, Dr. Mary Ann Macartney, who teaches literature and writing at Rosemont College, deserves my greatest gratitude for sacrificing her summer 1996 vacation by taking on the unenviable task of trying to give these diverse pieces a certain stylistic continuity. Much more could not be done short of rewriting them, and although she has little professional interest in the area, she spent many days trying to make sense of passages that yielded little in the way of clues as to what the author meant to say. The responsibility for possible misinterpretation of the authors' views rests, however, on me. Additional thorough copy editing was done by Ms. Holy Martin, a graduate student of Emory University, through a kind service provided by Dr. Paul Courtright, editor of the series "Religion in Life." I thank him for having encouraged the submission and subsequently the acceptance of this collection. My son, Bernard Mojzes, offered me the assistance that one's offsprings tend to be so able to do in the technological field. However, the most tedious and thankless job of typing in the corrections, careful reading, and finally making the entire manuscript camera-ready according to the publisher's specifications was accomplished by my secretary, Ms. Rosemary Sheehan and the faculty secretary, Ms. Carmella DiMartino. They did this task with infinite patience and good cheer (at least when I was around). Thus, my three Rosemont College friends deserve the greatest accolades for whatever readability this collection has.

Paul Mojzes

Rosemont College
September 28, 1997

PRONUNCIATION GUIDE

A, a   =   car

C, c   =   hats

Ć, ć   =   mutual

Č, č   =   chapter

Dj, dj = ginger

Dž, dž = just

E, e   =   pen

G, g   =   go

H, h   =   loch

I, i   =   deep

J, j   =   yard

Lj, lj   =   million

N, n   =   no

Nj, nj =   new

O, o   =   dormitory

Š, š   =   ship

U, u   =   broom

Ž, ž   =   treasure

All other letters generally correspond to the conventional English equivalents.

1

THE BOSNIAN MUSLIM NATIONAL QUESTION[1]

Francine Friedman

The contemporary plight of the Bosnian Muslims is almost incomprehensible if we ignore historical, political, and social aspects of their position in the Balkans before the current fighting began. Many analysts, of course, point to the Bosnian Muslims as an anomaly in the middle of Christian Europe and imply that the collapse of Communism meant that other threats to European stability--such as the menace of Muslim radicalism--needed to be dealt with. Furthermore, they describe current hostilities in Bosnia as merely one more in a long battle between the fractious, multireligious and multiethnic South Slavs, who are, somehow, different in their contentiousness from other Europeans. However, these analysts have overlooked long years of cooperation, if not harmony, among the South Slavs in multiethnic Bosnia and Herzegovina as well as the former Yugoslavia as a whole. Thus, religious/national differences in Bosnia and Herzegovina and other parts of the former Yugoslavia are merely an excuse used by former Communist leaders to maintain power in post-Communist Yugoslav regions, not the reason for the atrocities suffered by the Bosnians and other Yugoslavs of all religious persuasions.

Fighting for its sovereignty within internationally recognized borders now at the end of the twentieth century, Bosnia and Herzegovina spent very little of its history as an independent entity, although it survived Ottoman and Austrian rule as an integral, administrative unit. In 1929, the Yugoslav Kingdom was divided into *banovinas*, but Bosnia and Herzegovina was able to retain its borders; in 1939, however, parts of Bosnia and Herzegovina were given to Croatia under the *Sporazum* (Agreement) fashioned between the Yugoslav government and Croats who demanded significant autonomy from the Serb-dominated Yugoslav government. During World War II, the Nazis awarded the whole of Bosnia and Herzegovina to the Independent State of Croatia.

---

[1]This chapter based on findings reported in Francine Friedman, *The Bosnian Muslims: The Denial of a Nation* (Boulder: Westview Press, 1996).

Europe's western-most Islamic community has occupied a controversial status politically, as well as juridically, in the twentieth century, the controversy partially stemming from differing interpretations of the history of the Bosnian Muslims. Throughout their history in Bosnia and Herzegovina, the Bosnian Muslims were not particularly forceful in expressing a sense of national self-determination. The short-lived independent medieval Kingdom of Bosnia was replaced by Ottoman tutelage during which time the Bosnian Muslims, as ruling Muslims do throughout the world, controlled the territory and its policies. Thereafter, the Bosnian Muslims were forced into a more subordinate role. However, Austrian rule at the turn of the twentieth century was not particularly onerous for Bosnian Muslims, nor was Serbian domination in the Yugoslav Kingdom in the interwar period, perhaps because the Bosnian Muslims were masters of system manipulation when involved in a multinational entity and maintained communal security by cooperating with whomever conquered them.

Yugoslavia suffered grievously during World War II, but Bosnia and Herzegovina was the scene of particularly terrible carnage. Belying their previous long history of mutual religious toleration, Serbs, Croats, and Muslims wreaked horrible religiously-inspired atrocities against each other on this land, killing many Yugoslav inhabitants.

In the post-World War II period, Communist Yugoslavia attempted to utilize federalism to ameliorate the national hatreds which had congealed as a result of the war's atrocities. As a good Communist, Yugoslav President Josip Broz Tito probably would have preferred to simply nullify all national self-identification and replace it with class identification. However, he was also a Yugoslav, who knew that it would not be easy to separate the South Slavs from their memories of past glories and communal dreams of future success. Therefore, he attempted to foster elite consensus, hoping that federalism, controlled by a strong, centralized Communist Party, would attenuate the bitterness wreaked by World War II, particularly in the nationally mixed and, thus, sensitive region of Bosnia and Herzegovina.

The history of Bosnia and Herzegovina reflects its mostly pluralistic and tolerant nature, long inhabited as it was by members of many religions (after World War II increasingly classified also according to corresponding national group--Croatian Roman Catholic, Serbian Orthodox, etc.). For many Bosnians, living in such a mixed area, neither national nor religious identification was important, particularly during the secularizing years of post-World War II Yugoslavia. In such surroundings, until 1969, the Bosnian Muslims were not considered, and largely did not consider themselves to be, a precisely national group in the Yugoslav meaning, which meant that most of the nation was located in and formed a large proportion of a discrete Yugoslav republic, like the Serbs in Serbia or the Croats in Croatia.

It is clear, however, at least from the post-World War II censuses, that the Bosnian Muslims thought of themselves as a separate group from the Serbs and Croats. Many Bosnian Muslims defined themselves as no more than a religious minority or, for those secular Muslims, part of the Yugoslav nation. When called upon to declare a national identification for census purposes, Bosnian Muslims designated themselves as "nationally undetermined" or as "Yugoslavs," when that option was available. Only a minority declared themselves to be nationally Serbs or Croats, the other numerically dominant groups in Bosnia and Herzegovina. Indeed, current Bosnian President Alija Izetbegović underlined the tenuousness of the Bosnian Muslim national identification in Yugoslavia during the postwar period in a 1991 interview in *Borba* when he said that "thanks to the policy of the last forty some years [Muslims] have not sufficiently affirmed themselves as a nationality, they have not been sufficiently aware, and their interests have not been articulated in any manner whatsoever."[2]

TABLE 6.1. POPULATION OF BOSNIA AND HERZEGOVINA BY CENSUS

Year	Muslims	Serbs	Croats	Yugoslavs	Total Pop
1948	788,403*	1,136,116	614,142	--	2,563,764
1953	--	1,264,372	654,229	891,800**	2,847,459
1961	842,248ᵃ)	1,406,057	711,665	275,883	3,277,948
1971	1,482,430	1,393,148	772,491	43,796	3,746,111
1981	1,629,924	1,320,644	758,136	326,280	4,102,783
1991	1,905,829			239,834	4,364,574

*called nationally "undetermined" Muslims
**called "Yugoslav undetermined"

a) Steven L. Burg suggested this number might be too low in reality since there were many self-identified Serbs, Croats, Yugoslavs, etc., who adhered to Islam. "The Political Integration of Yugoslavia's Muslims," p. 39.

Sources: Atif Purivatra, *Nacionalni i politički razvitak Muslimana* (Sarajevo: Svjetlost, 1970), p. 33; Mushtak Parker, *Muslims in Yugoslavia: The Quest for Justice* (Toronto: Croatian Islamic Centre, 1986), p. 15; "The National Composition of Yugoslavia's Population, 1991," *Yugoslav Survey* (1992), pp. 4-5.

---

[2]Željko Vuković, "Kompromisi u dva poluvremena," *Borba* (9-10 June 1990), p. 5.

Since the late 1960s, the Bosnian Muslims were officially regarded as a Yugoslav nation, which meant that they were considered to be equal in status within Yugoslavia with the Serb, Croat, and other Yugoslav nations, with whom they share common Slavic origins. This recognition of the Bosnian Muslims as a nation was a recognition of their gradually developing need for self-realization. But it was also a political decision taken by the Yugoslav leadership to solve conflicts among the Yugoslav nations as well as to enhance Yugoslavia's international prospects and prestige with the largely Muslim nonaligned world. The manipulation of the Bosian Muslims, therefore, met a wide variety of needs. The implication of this decision for the unity of Yugoslavia and Bosnia and Herzegovina in the post-Tito period, of course, belied the motives for which this move was apparently undertaken.

When Tito recognized the Bosnian Muslims as a national group in 1969, they became politically and juridically a Yugoslav nation. While their historical roots had not changed, their standing in society did, as economic, political, and social resource distribution within post-World War II Yugoslavia was largely based on nationality. Yugoslavia was a pluralist system, but one in which national groups were recognized as legally constituted entities, and resources and personnel, etc., were distributed according to quota systems and the "national key." The Serbs and Croats had historically sought Bosnian Muslim loyalty so that one or the other by virtue of a majority could control the republic, each advancing a plethora of arguments and counterarguments surrounding the circumstances of medieval religious practices in Bosnia, as well as important demographic and political circumstances of the region, to imply a stronger claim than others to control the region.

With their new status, the Bosnian Muslims could more strongly and capably demand access to decision-making prerogatives while they rejected Serb and Croat blandishments to cleave to one or the other national grouping. Furthermore, the adjustment in Bosnian Muslim status within Yugoslavia not unnaturally produced an alteration in their own self-identification. Official recognition of their nationhood contributed a new element to their identity, enhancing their differentiation from the other Yugoslav nations by other than religious criteria. The Bosnian Muslims, thus, became a nation because they were so treated officially after 1969, and because they came to believe it of themselves.

In the wake of their official acknowledgement as a nation, Bosnian Muslim historians sought to demonstrate the validity of the contemporary, Bosnian Muslim nation as the legitimate successor of the independent, medieval Bosnian state. Nationalistic Serbs and Croats, on the other hand, dismissed the existence of deep-seated Bosnian religious identification as the basis of national self-identification and continued to insist that the Bosnian Muslims were, more or less, lapsed Serbs or Croats, respectively, who simply followed a different religion.

The Yugoslav leadership's attempt to liberalize the Yugoslav system following the nationalistic upheavals of the preceding years led to the creation of a confederation in the 1974 Constitution. This action merely legitimized the corporate pluralism of Yugoslavia and underscored the artificiality of Yugoslavia's much-vaunted "brotherhood and unity" by weakening the center's decision-making capabilities. The rules of the game now required republic unanimity for decision-making, virtually impossible to achieve on most important issues. Furthermore, the loss of Tito in 1980 irrevocably shattered one of the few remaining centralizing agents remaining to Yugoslavia. The field was, thus, given over to the republics, many of which were dominated by nationalistic leaders advocating narrow rather than all-Yugoslav agendas. Instead of attempting to integrate the Yugoslav economy with an eye to closer bonding with Western Europe, republic elites chose the road of narrow political preference, i.e., ethnonationalism, instead.

Tito had carefully crafted a set of institutions to take his place after he was gone. The institutions were created to ensure as much continuity and as much pressure to maintain the unity of Yugoslavia as Tito could build in without undermining his own power. But Tito, although President-for-life, could not guarantee after his death that the institutions he so carefully fashioned would do their jobs.

Indeed, after Tito's death, the working of the institutions had begun to encourage ethnonational rather than Yugoslav aspirations. The complexities of the issues and the ramifications of the decentralization and liberalization of the League of Communists of Yugoslavia (the former Yugoslav Communist Party), the burgeoning economic discontent between the poorer and richer republics, and the fissures developing in the political system were only just becoming apparent to some extent at Tito's death.

The position of the Bosnian Muslims apparently improved in some ways during the 1980s. Muslims simultaneously seemed to have been integrated into Yugoslav life while developing a new sense of either religiosity or national consciousness. Recognition and elevation to national status within the Yugoslav federation was an important step for the Bosnian Muslims. The Islamic religious community was now accorded recognition similar to that of the leaders of other religious communities representing national groups. It no longer appeared to be without influence in the decision-making spheres of the government and seemed to be attaining a new self-confidence and even activism on behalf of its constituents.[3] However, some federal elites were concerned about this new activism as early as 1984, considering the Muslim question in Yugoslavia one of the "chief axes of nationalist disequilibrium."[4] Ultimately, in the wake of federal moves to limit perceived Bosnian Muslim nationalism, such as the trial in 1983 of eleven Bosnian Muslim intellectuals (including Alija Izetbegović) on the charge of promoting chauvinistic nationalism,[5] the gains of the Bosnian Muslim community proved in reality to be more limited than they appeared to be.

As political and economic exigencies became intermixed, exclusivist nationalistic feelings of both those who felt economically deprived (the poorer areas in Yugoslavia) and those who felt economically robbed (the wealthier areas in Yugoslavia) were exacerbated. The system increasingly undercut the accessibility to power of people who had a stake in the continuation of Yugoslavia as a whole--those who thought of themselves as just Yugoslavs without hyphenation. Many of these Yugoslavs lived in Bosnia and Herzegovina and, coincidentally, were Bosnian Muslims. When political and economic decision-making and personnel decisions became wholly based on national identification and the "national key," "Yugoslavs" became an unrepresented group. It was potentially more rewarding, then, to declare themselves Croat, Serb, Bosnian Muslim, or other recognized nation than to hold fast to any obviously undervalued self-identification as "Yugoslav." The political dynamics of the post-Tito era were, thus, a far cry from what Tito intended when he altered the system in the 1970s, as this dynamic forced many people who considered themselves simply Yugoslavs, Bosnians, or just members of a religious community to opt for self-identification in one of the available national groups. However, during the 1980s and early 1990s, these groups increasingly adopted distressingly nationalistic rhetoric and postures.

Gradually throughout the 1980s, the dynamics of the Titoist machinery not surprisingly produced policies based on distinctions among nations (and nationalities). When the political unit for economic and political decision-making (the republic or the autonomous province) coincided fairly well with national boundaries, it was inevitable that economic and political decision-making would be infused with ethnonationalism to the detriment of both the

---

[3]Sabrina P. Ramet, *Balkan Babel: Politics, Culture, and Religion in Yugoslavia* (Boulder: Westview Press, 1992), pp. 173-174.

[4]See, for example, Ramet, *Nationalism and Federalism in Yugoslavia, 1963-1983* (Bloomington: Indiana University Press, 1984), p. 144.

[5]"The Trial of Moslem Intellectuals in Sarajevo," *South Slav Journal* 6 (Spring 1983), pp. 55-89.

economic and political systems as well as to various republics at various times.[6] Throughout the 1980s, this situation worsened until it culminated in the 1990s with the ultimate breakdown of Yugoslavia into constituent parts and the mutual bloodletting among formerly cohabiting South Slavs. The Bosnian Muslims, given access to decision-making levers, were relatively unsuccessful in creating lasting coalitions with other Bosnian groups which might have stabilized the political scene there. Without Tito to quell nationalistic outbursts, and with the political monopoly of the League of Communists of Yugoslavia unchallenged by the failure during the 1960s and 1970s to introduce in Yugoslavia truly democratic institutions within which to work out conflicts, recognition of human rights, and economic liberalization, the Bosnian Muslims had no political cover when the Titoist institutions, including the Communist Party and the Yugoslav army, meant to protect the integrity of Yugoslavia and the peoples of Yugoslavia, failed.

The elite consensus in Yugoslavia was revealed to be as artificial as the Tito-created internal borders of Yugoslavia. The federal system and its successor confederal system could not totally ameliorate this artificiality since all Yugoslav politics, access to resources, and decision-making was based on national identification. Serb and Croat arguments over to which of their nations belonged the Bosnian Muslims and which nation should, thus, control multiethnic Bosnia and Herzegovina (with the majority status the Bosnian Muslims would, thus, create), were on-going but inconclusive, as no one was able to advance unequivocal geographic or ethnographic claims on today's Bosnian Muslims to the exclusion of all other counterclaims. The resistance by Bosnian Muslims to considering themselves as Serbs or as Croats despite increasing Croat and Serb pressures stimulated among Bosnian Muslims a stronger communal solidarity in order to increase their abilities for defense of the Muslim community.

In Bosnia and Herzegovina itself, the Bosnian Muslims, who were mainly of secular orientation, found themselves pitted against Bosnian Serb and Croat nationalists who resisted creation of a secular, multinational Bosnia and Herzegovina divorced from the rest of the former Yugoslavia. The nationalists, in fact, desired union with Serbia and Croatia respectively in relative homogeneity and rejected the secular ideal championed by Bosnian President Izetbegović in the early 1990s.

Even during the contemporary carnage visited upon Bosnia and Herzegovina by rampaging Serbs and Croats as well as Muslims, many Bosnian

---

[6]*Danas* reported a severe degeneration in the Yugoslav economy in every republic, with Bosnia and Herzegovina showing the least precipitous declines and Montenegro the worst. (4 December 1990), p. 18.

Muslims have persisted in clinging to the idea of a multinational, secular, European country. The following anguished statement by a Bosnian Muslim when faced with the evidence of Bosnia's betrayal by its own--Bosnian Serb-- inhabitants reflects both that hope and the beginning of its deflation:

> Born 15 years after the war ended, I belong to the second generation of post-war Bosnian Muslims, for whom our Muslim identity was a quaint aspect of family heritage, something to marvel at rather than immerse oneself in. Islam as a religion represented our past rather than our future. I identified myself as a Muslim by nationality, which meant I had ties neither to Serbia nor Croatia, but saw my social and cultural identity as a part of an ethnically-mixed Bosnian tapestry, from which I drew all my cultural and emotional experiences, and in which I belonged together with all other non-Muslim Bosnians . . . . [However] the truth is that the worst and most abhorrent acts of violence are being committed by yesterday's friends and neighbours.[7]

Observing the targets of Bosnian Serbs, it appears that Muslim-free areas is only one of the goals. What British journalist Michael Nicholson termed "elitocide"--the destruction of the educated Muslim strata--also seems to be an objective pursued by the Bosnian Serb forces,[8] the leadership of which did not credit that many inhabitants who identified themselves as Bosnians of Muslim and other religions. The Bosnian Muslim community was to be bereft of any kind of leadership when the fighting finally ended.

In conclusion, official recognition of the Bosnian Muslims made them vulnerable to Serb and Croat pressures because neither would accept the Bosnian Muslims as anything more than a religious, certainly not a national, entity. The protective coloring they had maintained throughout many years and under many regimes of religious minority status was stripped away and replaced by the legitimacy of political and juridical recognition as an equal nation within Yugoslavia. The result of this politically motivated decision was that the Bosnian Muslims began to act like an equal nation because *de facto* and in practice the behavior of all the actors in Yugoslavia was predicated on the belief that the Bosnian Muslims officially constituted a nation. The outcome was that the Bosnian Muslims became vulnerable to those who now considered them rivals for power and resources. At the same time as the national and religious identifications of the Bosnian Muslims were forcibly commingled, leaving no other outlets for political expression for the unattached, nationalistic Serbs and Croats denied the truth of the historical separateness of Bosnian Muslims from Bosnian Serbs or Croats respectively. The confusion extends today as

---

[7]Indijana Harper, "Unwanted, Unarmed and Under Attack," *East European Reporter* 5 (November-December 1992), pp. 64-65.

[8]David Rieff, *Slaughterhouse: Bosnia and the Failure of the West* (New York: Simon & Schuster, 1995), p. 113.

Izetbegović, the President of Bosnia, is variously and sometimes simultaneously treated both in the lands of the former Yugoslavia as well as internationally as the head of the Bosnian state, which contains citizens of various national self-identifications, but also as the leader of the Bosnian Muslims, presumably with only their interests at heart. A young Bosnian Muslim soldier expressed the bewilderment of many Bosnian Muslims at the turn of events in Bosnia in this way:

> I never thought of myself as a Muslim. I don't know how to pray, I never went to mosque, I'm European, like you. I do not want the Arab world to help us, I want Europe to help us. But now, I do have to think of myself as a Muslim, not in a religious way, but as a member of a people. Now we are faced with obliteration, I have to understand what it is about me and my people they wish to obliterate.[9]

One wonders how long Izetbegović will be able to resist casting himself primarily in the role of Bosnian Muslim leader, instead of Bosnian President, when most of the South Slav leaders persist, despite his arguments to the contrary, in regarding him as pursuing the agenda of creating a Bosnian Muslim state in the middle of Europe.

---

[9]Ed Vulliamy, *Seasons in Hell: Understanding Bosnia's War* (New York: St. Martin's Press, 1994), p. 65.

2

THE GENOCIDAL IMPERATIVE:
THE SHADOW OF RELIGIOUS-POLITICAL BONDING

John Dourley

Carl Jung's understanding of the psyche centers on the individual but is never without its social and political dimension. Of the relation of personal to social psychopathology, crucial to his discussion of the psychology of genocide, Jung writes, "But there is one simple rule you should bear in mind: the psychopathology of the masses is rooted in the psychology of the individual."[1] His core conception of individuation itself contains a social component. Individuation describes a psychic *telos* that moves simultaneously toward progressive personal integration and to an increasingly empathic embrace of the world beyond the individual. The experience of a personality increasingly integrated in itself and imbued with an expanding universal sympathy, Jung equates with the experience of grace and of the divine.[2]

Jung identifies the compelling experience of the self, thus described, with the psychogenesis of religious experience and so of the world's religions. And, yet, such experience has its shadow side. In our epoch, argues Jung, this same archetypal experience informs national and political communal bonding whether such bonding has an explicitly religious referent or not. The profound paradox of this view centers around the implicit contention that the psychic basis of religion itself works in these communities to create those opposing, often murderous, allegiances which made and make the twentieth century the century of genocide.

Jung's analysis of the psychology of genocide rests on four foundational but closely related notions in his work. Two of these foundational notions he drew from the anthropologist Levy Bruhl. They were Bruhl's conception of the

---

[1] All citations from C.G. Jung are from *Collected Works,* (Princeton: Princeton University Press). Citations will cite volume no. (CW), paragraph and page. "The Fight with the Shadow," CW 10, par. 445, p. 218.

[2] "Transformation Symbolism in the Mass," CW 11, par. 396, p. 261.

participation mystique and the *representations collectives*. The third is Jung's conception of the "isms," archetypal bonding powers which work "psychic epidemics" and "mass psychoses." The fourth is his understanding of the collective shadow, the tendency of those bonded by one archetypal configuration to demonize those who are differently bonded and, in turn, to be demonized by them. Let us look briefly at how these Jungian conceptions illuminate the possibility if not necessity of genocide between archetypally bonded groups, especially when they relate in geographical contiguity.

Jung's Appropriation of Levy Bruhl's *Participation Mystique*

Jung's appropriation of Bruhl's *participation mystique*, which Bruhl and the ethnological community were eventually to disown,[3] is ambiguous. Although ambiguous, it is predominantly positive and informed by a wistful regret that contemporary Western consciousness has lost the possibility of such experience. The lost experience is that of the continuity, if not identity, of the individual with the surrounding world of nature and of humanity worked by the dynamic "all oneness" of the underlying unconscious.[4]

Jung both appreciates and criticizes the sense of community as communion that such an experience generates. He identifies the primary function of the *participation mystique* to be the creation of that tight cohesiveness characteristic of archaic societies.[5] At the same time, Jung sees the *participation mystique* operative in a wide range of human activities and relationships. It is at work in Rousseau's later and more sophisticated, though romantic, understanding of universal relatedness.[6] It works the unities between analyst and client in transference[7] and between child and parent to the possible detriment of both the analytic process and of the autonomy of the child.[8] Ideally, Jung would understand the role of education to be in large part the dissolution of the *participation mystique* between child and parent in favor of the child's growing

---

[3]*Mysterium Coniunctionis*, CW 14, fn. 662, p. 250; "General Aspects of Dream Psychology," CW 8, p. 265, fn. 12; "Psychological Commentary on 'The Tibetan Book of the Great Liberation'," CW 11, fn. 28.

[4]*Psychological Types*, CW 6, par. 430, p. 255.

[5]*Ibid.*, par. 12, p. 10; "On Psychic Energy," CW 8, par. 127, p. 65; "The Structure of the Psyche," CW 8, par. 329, pp. 153, 154; "General Aspects of Dream Psychology," CW 8, par. 507, pp. 264, 265.

[6]*Psychological Types*, CW 6, par. 123, p. 82.

[7]*Psychological Types*, CW 6, par. 146, p. 93; "The Psychology of the Transference," CW 16, par. 376, pp. 182, 183, fn. 27.

[8]"Mind and Earth," CW 10, pars. 69, 70, p. 37.

independence.[9] The *participation mystique* is operative in any form of projection in which an archetypal reality is identified with an object which can then be divinized as mana[10] or vilified as the other, now a denier and so a threat to one's own sacred truth. [11]

Jung's ambivalence about the *participation mystique* lies in his ability to appreciate the power of such experience to unite the individual, community, and nature even as he deplores the "state of identity in mutual unconsciousness . . ." such a state so easily breeds.[12] The *participation mystique* can foster the most intense sense of mystical communion with all that is as well as the "mass intoxication" or "psychic epidemics" of group possession.[13] While such experience enables the height of mystical communion, it forces Jung to wonder in the end if critical consciousness and morality are compatible with it.[14] Jung extends the operation of the *participation mystique* to post-Enlightenment religious and political communities.[15] In certain ways, these communities are much more highly developed consciously and technologically. However, their very consciousness renders them dangerously unconscious of their manipulation by archetypal powers still operative in the collective unconscious as the source of their disparate and conflicting bondings. The holy soil of the father or motherland, the home of the ancestral spirits, the preferred religion, political system, or movement remain for Jung but thinly disguised forms of the *participation mystique*.[16] In short, Jung is depicting contemporary religious, political, nationalist, and ethnic bonding as little more than remnants of unconscious tribalism with the ever-present danger of tribal warfare.

Jung and the "Representation Collectives"

As he develops Levy Bruhl's related idea of the *representations collectives*, Jung's thought becomes explicitly societal. He identifies these major motifs as grounded in archetypal powers and as bearing the psychic equivalent of a magical salvation to modern societies under the guise of "religions and

---

[9]"Child Development and Education," CW 17, pars. 107, 107a, pp. 54 - 57; "The Significance of the Unconscious in Individual Education," *ibid.*, par. 253, p. 149.

[10]"The Structure and Dynamics of the Psyche," CW 8, par. 127, p. 65.

[11]"Archaic Man," CW 10, pars. 130, 131, pp.64, 65.

[12]"Mind and Earth," CW 10, par. 69, p. 37; *Symbols of Transformation*, CW 5, par. 504, p. 327; "Anima and Animus," CW 7, par. 329, p. 206.

[13]"Concerning Rebirth," CW 9i, pars. 225-227, pp. 125-127.

[14]"Psychological Commentary on 'The Tibetan Book of the Great Liberation'," CW 11, par. 817, p. 504, fn. 28.

[15]"Commentary on 'The Secret of the Golden Flower'," CW 13, pars. 66, 67, p. 45.

[16]"On the Relation of Analytical Psychology to Poetry," CW 15, par. 128, p. 82.

political ideologies."[17] Again, there is the same ambiguity in Jung's appreciation of these bonding symbols and their mythology which so readily become ideology. Admittedly, they can be "therapeutic,"[18] because they arise to consciousness from that dimension of the unconscious common to "mankind in general."[19] As such, they appear in the distant past in more primordial form and in the present wherever societal absolutes are held by contemporary cultures. There are few cultures without them.[20] More over, where they do appear, they carry with them an emotional power, making them irresistable to individuals and societies whose lives they can permanently possess and transform.[21]

In the insane, the *representations collectives* are heard as the voice of God.[22] Elsewhere they create as wide a range of phenomena as the religions themselves:[23] personal religious figures such as messiahs, prophets and shamans,[24] good poetry, and the lowly slogan.[25] In the deeper sense Jung gives to them, they connect the individual throughout human history and currently with the unconscious and its vitalities.[26] They are the basis of the living substance of whatever truth is transmitted through esoteric teaching.[27] While Jung here is speaking of such transmission among primordial peoples, he elsewhere implies that Christian dogma, and by extension all dogma, once carried the energies of such archetypal experience.[28]

Possessive and dangerous though they may be, where they fail to reconnect or reroot individual and society with the unconscious, the mind is cut adrift and "in practice is susceptible to psychic epidemics."[29] As such, the impact of the *representations collectives* create historical epochs with their successive revelations and are, for Jung, the deepest healing resources when

---

[17]*Symbols of Transformation*, CW 5, par. 221, p. 156.

[18]*Ibid.*, par. 683, p. 442.

[19]*Psychological Types*, CW 6, par. 692, p. 417.

[20]*Ibid.*, CW 6, par. 692, p. 418; "Fundamental Questions of Psychotherapy," CW 16, par. 247, p. 120.

[21]"Psychological Factors in Human Behaviour," CW 8, par. 254, p. 122.

[22]"Analytical Psychology and Education," CW 17, par. 207, p. 116.

[23]"The Philosophical Tree," CW 13, par. 478, p. 347.

[24]"Psychological Factors in Human Behaviour," CW 8, par. 254, p. 122.

[25]"The Assimilation of the Unconscious," CW 7, par. 231, pp. 145, 146.

[26]"Fundamental Questions of Psychotherapy," CW 16, par. 247, p. 120.

[27]"Archetypes of the Collective Unconscious," CW 9i, par. 6, p. 5.

[28]"The Archetype in Dream Symbolism," CW 18, pars. 551, p. 240 and "The Healing Split," *ibid.*, par. 579, p. 253.

[29]"Concerning Rebirth," CW 9i, par. 227, p. 127 and "Conscious, Unconscious and Individuation," *ibid.*, par. 496, p. 278.

consciously assimilated available to therapy.[30] And yet, like the *participation mystique* they foster, they can destroy the autonomous consciousness and moral responsibility of societies they possess. Writes Jung in 1936:

> There is no lunacy people under the domination of an archetype will not fall a prey to. If thirty years ago anyone had dared to predict that our psychological development was tending towards a revival of the medieval persecutions of the Jews, that Europe would again tremble before the Roman fasces and the tramp of legions, that people would once more give the Roman salute, as two thousand years ago, and that instead of the Christian Cross an archaic swastika would lure onward millions of warriors ready for death--why that man would have been hooted at as a mystical fool. And to-day? Surprising as it may seem all this absurdity is a horrible reality. . . . The man of the past who lived in a world of archaic "representations collectives" has risen again into very visible and painfully real life, and this not only in a few unbalanced individuals but in many millions of people.[31]

Jung's ambivalence toward the *collective representation* as the agent of archetypal bonding is nowhere more evident when he attributes to it the origins of such morally opposite movements as Hitler's regime in the twentieth century and the witch hunts in fifteenth century Germany as well as the rise and spread of Christianity in the second and third centuries and Islam in the seventh.[32] Although of contradictory nature, these movements proceed from the same source and under identical archetypal impulse.

In their capacity to deprive their victims of conscious discrimination and moral autonomy, a connection exists between Jung's understanding of Levy Bruhl's *representation collective* and his use of Pierre Janet's *abaissement du niveau mental*. Both describe states of loss or deliberate surrender of conscious control to unconscious forces.[33] Such loss can be worked involuntarily by the power of archetypal attraction.[34] When this occurs, the total personality, possessed by one form of archetypal power, is reduced to the status of fanatic single-mindedness.[35]

In linking the *collective representation* to the *abaissement du niveau mental* the profile of archetypally informed religious or political faith as a diminishment of the individual and as a danger to surrounding society becomes much clearer. Where humanity has lost sight of the origins of religion in the psyche, and, here, Jung usually has Enlightenment rationalism in mind, religion

---

[30]"Editorial (1935)," CW 10, par. 1043, p. 549.

[31]"The Concept of the Collective Unconscious," CW 9i, par. 98, p. 48.

[32]"Techniques of Attitude Change Conducive to World Peace," CW 18, par. 1389, p. 607; *Symbols of Transformation,* CW 5, par. 221,p. 156.

[33]*Psychological Types*, CW 6, pars. 199, p. 123 and par. 765, p. 451.

[34]"Synchronicity: An Acausal Connecting Principle," CW 8, par. 841, p. 436.

[35]"Concerning Rebirth," CW 9i, par. 214, p. 120.

has been transformed into politics, resulting in mass murder on an unparalleled scale.

Jung and the "isms"

The unconscious religious-political unities and communities formed by the *participation mystique* and its *representations collectives* are the target of Jung's thought on the "isms." Such unconsciousness he likens to ". . the demons and gods of primitives or the 'isms' so fanatically believed in by modern man."[36] For Jung, the ism becomes a "magic word," effectively a new religion,[37] which possesses those uprooted from their deeper human instincts and wholly immersed in mass collective consciousness.[38]

Not infrequently, notes Jung, religious mentors themselves extol such loss of consciousness as a commendable faith commitment to what is from his perspective a parochial revelation seeking universal acceptance.[39] As such, the modern political "isms" are but ". . a variant of the denominational religions . . . ." Yet no one, for Jung, is exempt from the influence of a dominant "ism" in one's individual psyche.[40] It is to this personal "ism," the inner capacity and necessity to commit to archetypal suasion, that the political and social "isms" appeal, even as they dull individual autonomous consciousness and moral responsibility in doing so.[41] Jung would here align himself with thinkers like Paul Tillich in identifying a dimension of faith in the very constitution of humanity. In Jung's formulation, no one can lay aside faith without assuming another one.[42] The paradox is then restated. Humanity cannot be without faith even as it becomes increasingly aware that faith threatens its future.

The Collective Shadow

Jung's understanding of the collective shadow is in direct continuity with what has been said about religious and political bonding worked by the archetypal dimension of the psyche. In such bonding, a direct correlation exists between the cohesiveness of the bond and the loss of individual consciousness of those bonded. Once individual responsibility is lost, the power drive of the

---

[36]"On the Nature of the Psyche,", CW 8, par. 366, p. 175.

[37]*Ibid.*, par. 405, p. 206.

[38]"Epilogue to 'Essays on Contemporary Events'," CW 10, par. 469, p. 231.

[39]"On the Nature of the Psyche," CW 8, par. 425, p. 219.

[40]"Concerning the Archetypes and the Anima Concept," CW 9i, par. 125, pp. 61, 62.

[41]"A Study in the Process of Individuation," CW 9i, par. 617, p. 349.

[42]"Concerning the Archetypes and the Anima Concept," CW 9i, par. 129, pp. 62, 63.

bonding archetype is unleashed.[43] In a society unconsciously bonded by an archetypal force, called by such various names as "faith," "loyalty," or "patriotism," any differently bonded society becomes its shadow, a threat to the "truth" of its bonding power, an insult to its God and culture. Religiously, this creates such inflated assertions as the contention, for example, that the "soul is naturally Christian," implying non-Christian souls are somehow less than fully human. The only response for a society, thus, bonded in relation to a differently bonded society is to convert or kill it or both as has happened to vast segments of the North and South American aboriginal peoples at the hands of their European conquerors.

These options are particularly evident where differing religious bondings inform geographically contiguous societal orders as in Ireland or where the differently bonded share the same geography as in the Middle East or Yugoslavia. Ethnic cleansing then becomes nothing less than a religious, political, and even "rational" necessity based on the psychodynamics of archetypal bonding.

Jung's Response to the Psychology of Genocide

There are grounds for a well-founded suspicion that Jung's analysis of the psychology of genocide describes accurately in some depth a problem to which he offers no real solution and for which there may be none. Put succinctly and reduced to its essentials, the problem is this: archetypally based bonding is necessary in the building of a cohesive society, but archetypally based bonding is in and of itself certainly potentially and possibly necessarily genocidal. To date, humanity has produced no society without some form of archetypal bonding. Such archetypal bonding is religious in its nature even when disguised in political form where it currently functions with the power of religion or as religion formerly functioned when in power.[44]

Jung suggests that the demonization of the differently bonded can only be overcome when the collective shadow is withdrawn from the hated other and becomes the basis of the introversion of war. But how many are likely to take seriously his implication that, for instance, the evil of fascism lives within oneself and the fight against fascism must first begin there?

Jung's counter to psychically necessitated genocide is, thus, fragile but may be useful to the survival of the species. This counter rests on two principles.

---

[43]"The Fight with the Shadow," CW 10, par. 455, p. 224.

[44]"Epilogues to 'Essays on Contemporary Events'," CW 10, par. 474, p. 237.

The First Principle: The Permanence of Religion

The first counter to religiously necessitated genocide is the realization that religion is an intractable element in the human spirit, because it is a product of the psyche. Consequently, a strategy to eliminate genocide by eliminating religion or its modern political equivalents is a dated and futile strategy. Jung pays implicit tribute to the Enlightenment's fight against religion and the consequent freeing and enhancement of reason it worked. But, he insists that the discrediting of religion at the conscious level did nothing to restrain the unconscious in its role of producing religious conviction and community now in secular guise.

Consequently, the unconscious left to its own religious devices came to possess the Western mind with competing political ideologies which functioned with the same or greater genocidal zeal as had informed specifically religious genocide in previous centuries. In fact, because the Enlightenment mind became increasingly unaware of the unconscious, it was even more susceptible to that religious mass-mindedness which breeds genocide as demanded by reason itself when reason is severed from its connectedness with a wider and deeper empathy.[45]

The Second Principle: The Rerooting of Modernity in its Common Ground

It is difficult to read Jung at length without coming to the conclusion that his psychology is an apology, if not for religion, then at least for a sensitivity which would reconnect the individual with his or her deeper truth. Connection with this truth becomes for Jung the ultimate bastion against those psychic epidemics which breed genocide. Jung identifies severance from this truth, the truth of the self, as a major factor in the German consciousness which preceded the Holocaust. At times, he calls such deep disjointedness a removal from "instinct," leaving its victims without a sense of personal responsibility.[46] Hitler was only too happy to take on responsibility for the uprooted around him.[47]

But Jung's contention that genocidal consciousness can only be effectively parried by the individual's cultivation of the self puts so great a demand on the individual that one is forced to wonder if it is realistic. The stark demand of such an imperative is most evident in these not atypical lines addressing the problem. "Resistance to the organized mass can be effected only by the man

---

[45]"After the Catastrophe," CW 10, par. 431, pp. 210-212.

[46]*Ibid.*, par. 413, p. 200; "Fundamental Questions of Psychotherapy," CW 16, par. 251, pp. 122, 123.

[47]"After the Catastrophe," CW 10, par. 413, p. 201.

who is as well organized in his individuality as the mass itself."[48] How many individuals are that well organized? In Jung's program, it would seem that the next holocaust can only be avoided through the transformation of one Nazi, or true believer, at a time. This assumption is reinforced when Jung more than once affirms that only the grace of inner transformation or personal spiritual renewal would stand as the ultimate resource against the genocidal proclivity of possessed collective consciousness.[49]

The importance of the organized individual is again assumed when he speaks of processes of anticipating or "intercepting" archetypal powers that could overwhelm society. In these passages, he seems to have in mind therapies with profound societal consequence that could discern the archetypal nature of incipient political movements and aid in their more pacific integration by the individual and through the individual by society.[50] Such a process of interception would demand much from any therapist who might be assumed to be deeply involved in the political and social milieu in which archetypal forces appear as was Jung in the pre-Nazi period. To ask a therapist to be immersed in and yet somehow to transcend such social forces in the interests of their more gracious personal and societal integration is to ask as much or more of the therapist as of the individual who is to be as well organized as the unconscious masses he or she might face.

Although the foregoing response to genocide may be fragile and even romantic, the question arises as to what alternatives are available? Jung's consistent critique of ecclesial consciousness would contend that the major denominations sponsor rather than eliminate their own forms of collective consciousness.[51] Even so liberal a twentieth century theologian as Paul Tillich could speak of Christianity as vested with the "final revelation,"[52] a phrase too close to the idea of the "final solution." In the wake of the Holocaust, Jung comments that someone looking at Europe from beyond would ask, "Are the death camps a part of Christian culture?" In these passages, he extends Europe's

---

[48]"The Undiscovered Self," CW 10, par. 540, p. 278.

[49]"After the Catastrophe," CW 10, par. 441, p. 216, and par. 443, p. 217; "Epilogue to 'Essays on Contemporary Events'," *Ibid.*, par. 486, p. 243.

[50]"Epilogue to 'Essays on Contemporary Events'," CW 10, par. 461, p. 229 and par. 473, pp. 236, 237.

[51]"The Undiscovered Self," CW 10, par. 533, pp. 271, 272 and par. 536, pp. 275, 276.

[52]Paul Tillich, *Systematic Theology* , vol. 1, (Chicago: Chicago University Press, 1951) part I, sec. II, B, 6. p. 132f.

collective guilt to the Christian Church.[53] After the Holocaust, he was to ask his fellow Swiss, "Who are we to imagine that 'it couldn't happen here?'"[54]

If institutional religion has little to offer in overcoming collective genocidal consciousness, do other agencies such as those of education, communication, and various forms of international rapport have more? The problem here is that many of these agencies are children of the Enlightenment, and so are themselves removed from the Jungian sense of those archetypal depths from which religion and its genocidal tendencies reach consciousness. As such, they are not usually equipped to analyse the deeper currents at work in genocidal activity which they may encounter. Moreover, such agencies are frequently involved in forms of collective response themselves and so become bearers of their own ideology. Such ideology is frequently timid to point to the religious basis of genocidal reality because of a dubious faith in reason to overcome genocidal response or because it remains still politically incorrect to identify the link between religion and genocide in the extended sense of religion which Jung gives to the term.

In the end, the turn inward to an allegiance to the self which can never be given to reality beyond the self might serve to create a sounder personal faith by relativizing its external concretions and prohibiting idolatrous total personal investment in collective commitments with their ever-present genocidal threat. It would be the ultimate irony if humanity were to destroy itself in the name of the variants of archetypal good news meant to save it. But this is just what Jung feared as he approached death. In the end, all he had to offer were the more inclusive empathies of the self. However tenuous, the cultivation of these fragile empathies may be humanity's ultimate resource against its destruction by the very religious and political bondings it itself generates. Such empathies may play a role in bringing about, if it is to be brought about, that vision beyond political-religious conflict Jung wrote of in his later years, "The afternoon of humanity in a distant future, may yet evolve a different ideal. In time, even conquest will cease to be the dream."[55]

---

[53]"After the Catastrophe," CW 10, par. 404, p. 196.

[54]*Ibid.*, par. 412, p. 200.

[55]"Psychological Commentary on 'The Tibetan Book of the Great Liberation'," CW 11, par. 787, p. 493.

3

LIBERATION MYTHOLOGY
THE ROLE OF MYTHOLOGY IN FANNING WAR IN THE BALKANS[1]

Mitja Velikonja

Any research into the history of collective conceptions must always include both an historical and sociological perspective. Whilst the former reveals the sequence of occurrences, the latter reveals their position in the stormy firmament of social conception and the ways in which authority repeatedly tries to manipulate them. Accepted historical facts are not indispensable, necessary, or even important in the construction of social conceptions. The function of society "is possible" merely if it believes in its own story, and to do that it isn't even necessary for it to be familiar with that story.

Time worn myth and an ideological vulgarization of history are all too frequently encountered in the Balkans: a partisan historical memory, political amnesia, concealed defeats, the glorification of past tragedies, are all topped-off by an unreasonable pride in times gone by. Current occurrences are, as a rule, mixed with and mistaken for mythical elaborations of past events. It was during the period of national awakening, which itself began in the nineteenth century and, to an even greater degree over the past few years, that actual events were manipulated in such a way that they were made to adopt or absorb mythological elements. The bloody Balkan conflict, unfolding before a bewildered world audience, is a sinister example of where and how far an ideologized abuse of historical fact and ancient mythology can lead.

From within the historical chronologies of the southern Slavic nations currently involved in this conflict, it is possible to detect certain shared characteristics. Despite a large number of differences, distinctions, and

---

[1]This text is an abbreviate version of Chapter VIII from the book *Masade duha-- Razpotja sodobnih mitologij* [Masadas of the Mind--Crossroads of Contemporary Mythologies] (Ljubljana, Slovenia: Znanstveno in publicistično središče, 1995).

peculiarities of the present imaginative ideological order of those warring Balkan states, they all retain some major and quite significant common traits and images of themselves and their southern Slav neighbors.

American religiologist Paul Mojzes speaks of four myths common to the collective memory of the Balkan states. The first is the "myth of land and blood." Native soil is sacred, and the contemporary state maintains the continuity of the original and righteous medieval state. There is a constant danger coming from foreigners who are the ones responsible for the present problems. The second myth is the "crucifixion and resurrection syndrome," by way of which defeats are turned into victories. The third is a "mythological perception of time," the mythicized events of ages past are often mixed with the present ones, by way of which the current enemy becomes permanent--the eternal enemy. The final common myth is the "glorification of war and violence as the best way to keep or reclaim one's freedom." This also includes the veneration of war "heroes," together with their heroic feats and accomplishments.[2]

I have used the method of structural analyses of myth, devised by Clause Levi-Strauss in his book *Structural Anthropology*, to research clusters of variants as successive elements in a broader mythological corpus. I have divided the mythical experiences of the southern Slavonic nations (with the exception of Bulgaria and Slovenia, which I discussed in a previously mentioned book)[3] into four mythems: "the golden age," "defeat by a stronger neighbor," "the Yugoslav phase," and "the final liberation."

"The Creation and the Golden Age of Statehood"

The fundamental mythical story is one of birth and origins. It is concerned with the arrival on present-day territories from an undefined wilderness, which was supposedly followed by a utopian and paradise-like era of national unity and independence, youth and purity of society. The first state is established, the mythical king emerges, and the nation's "ethnic and historical borders" are defined.

The above remains as the basic political myth, the cosmogony, the story of creation. In spite of obscure and vague historical details, the arrival of the southern Slavs into the Balkans has acquired the mythical characteristics of a transition from chaos to cosmos. During the sixth and seventh centuries AD, the southern Slavs splashed across the Danube river and trekked across the Pannonian Plains from their, somewhat nebulous and undefined, former homeland which existed "behind" the Carpathians Mountains and "beyond" the

---

[2]Paul Mojzes, *Yugoslavian Inferno* (New York: Continuum, 1994), pp. 39-41.

[3]*Masade duha - Razpotja sodobnih mitologij.*

Pripet Marshes. On reaching the eastern Alps, these peoples conquered and settled the entire Balkan peninsula (with the exception of the larger coastal towns which remained Roman or Greek). They had moved from an absolute wilderness to the very bosom of the civilized world. The history for the southern Slavs begins after their crossing of the Red Sea of the Danube and with their arrival in the mountainous Dinaric Canaan.

The mythical order only acquires its full value with the second part, namely with the mythological founder of statehood--the "holy king," i.e. with the formation and consolidation of the first state and religious conversion. A characteristic common to all the early Slavic states in this territory was that they were "jammed into the vice" by the interests and religions of their larger and more powerful neighbors. One by one the early Slavic states were born, prospered fleetingly, and then disappeared or withered away.

In comparison with other Slavic nations and neighboring ethnic groups, the southern Slavs found themselves restricted within the spheres of influence of the older Mediterranean cultures relatively early on. Consequently, the southern Slavs' early conversion to Christianity lead to an almost total lack of testimony as to the structure of their former pantheon. Conversion to Christianity was connected with conflicting political tendencies and occurred in a special way. A huge number of pre-Christian doctrines were incorporated into the new religion and its rituals, particularly in rural areas, where the Christian novelty became just a part of the entire older body of mythology.

The glorious era of the medieval Serbian state began at the end of the twelfth century with Stephen Nemanja, the Grand Zhupan of Rashka (1151-1196), who united the Serb tribes and established the Nemanjid Dynasty. His sons, Stephen "the First Crowned" (1196-1228) and Rastko, "the Saint Sava," threw off Byzantine sovereignty and won the state its absolute political, and with the formation of the Serbian Orthodox Church, religious independence. The period of rule by Dushan the Mighty (1331-1355) was the culmination of the medieval Serbia,--its golden age. During the first half of the fourteenth century Serbia became the greatest power in the Balkans, and in 1346 Dushan the Mighty was crowned Tsar of Serbs and Greeks. After his death, Serbia underwent the fate of its predecessors: there was decentralization, internal conflict, and political disintegration as the dynasty fell apart into a collection of feuding principalities (despoties). The nation's fate was sealed in 1389 by the defeat that Lazar of Rascia and a Serbian army suffered at the hands of the Turks on the "Field of the Blackbirds" (Kosovo Polje).

Medieval Bosnia was founded as an independent state (Banate) by Ban Kulin (1180-1204). During his reign, the Bogomil (friends of God) religion spread throughout the state. Bogomils were one of the variants of the

Manichaean sect, which was fairly common across southern Europe during the High Middle Ages. For political and social reasons, the Bogomils and their church received support from Bosnian rulers; however, it was repudiated by both eastern Orthodoxy and western Catholic Christianity. Despite the struggles with (Hungarians, Serbs, Croats, and Venetians) neighbors, which occurred on the grounds of heresy, the dominion enjoyed enormous good-will from all of Bosnia's social classes, even among the nobility. Bosnia, together with the Bogomil sect, was the largest and most powerful during the reign of Tvrtko I (Kotromanich, ca. 1338-1391), who enlarged the state and was crowned the "King of Bosnians and the Serbs." After Tvrtko's death, the kingdom rapidly declined due to the self-will of feudal lords, infighting amongst the dynasty and the main noble families as well as the crusades of Sigismund, King of Hungary and Poland. Later on increasingly strong Turkish interference lead to the Ottoman conquest and subjugation of Bosnia (1463) and Herzegovina (1483).

The first independent ruler of a Croatian state was Prince Trpimir who ruled during the mid-ninth century; later, in 925, the Croatian Prince Tomislav was crowned a king by the Pope. An intermediate period of Byzantine overlordship was thrown-off by Peter IV Kreshimir during the second half of the eleventh century, after which Croatia rose to become an economically prosperous and politically strong Balkan state. Peter's successor, Zvonimir, received his coronation from the Pope (1076), so strengthening Croatia's orientation towards the Roman Catholic Church and western culture. Soon after Zvonimir's death in 1089, Croatia fell under the rule of Ladislas I, King of Hungary. His successor, Coloman I, entered into a personal union with Croatia, and, thus, it was finally annexed by Hungary in 1102 (*Pacta Conventa*).

So much for the history of these nations. The southern Slav peoples of the High Middle Ages, together with the formational dynamics of states they created were not always logical, nor were they straightforward or self-explanatory. However, there are those in the successor Balkan republics who would wish to simplify things by portraying a mythical consciousness, and an ideological pretension of an idyll, of which their states are, of course, a natural continuation. Statehood, national consciousness, and a sense of belonging were comprehended very differently in the Middle Ages than they are perceived today.

Comparison of the historical data, given above, with its subsequent adaptation and modification shows that these states "in those times" (*in illo tempore*), had neither natural enemies nor natural allies. The present-day Balkan hell, thus, cannot be explained or justified through the existence of some inherent animosity.[4] Balkan states continually acquired and lost territory on account of their neighbors, entered into coalitions, and waged wars against each other. During their halcyon eras of greatest prosperity and influence, all of these states gained control of a large swathe of territory to which all their successors, including the present-day republics, have referred to and aspired towards.

According to Roland Barthes, "a myth is a depoliticized speech"[5] which transfers human activities into a sphere which cannot be reached. The discourse in the Balkans concerning naturalness (the natural *status quo*, natural adversaries, natural transitions and natural orientation) is, more than anything else, a mythical strategy.

"The Defeat by a Stronger Neighbor"

The essence of the second mythem is the subjugation by a more powerful adversary, in the form of a opportunistic neighbor who, in the main, was able to exploit the situation because of treason or disloyalty amongst one's own. Both grounds imply far-reaching and wide-ranging consequences. Invariably, such a defeat ended a turbulent period of considerable or limited, longer or shorter independence. Despite the political defeat and the loss of statehood, the continuity of the national, religious, and cultural nucleus was, supposedly, preserved. The military and political disintegration in the face of a stronger or more powerful enemy is not perceived as final in national mythology. The essence of the nation, its consciousness, and continuity of existence has been preserved in the collective folk memory and tradition (e. g. songs, folk tales, etc.). Defeats, in particular, left a profound scar on the collective memory of these nations. The deepest and most profound wounds were suffered by the Serbs since the myth surrounding Kosovo (the "Field of the Blackbirds" where they were defeated by the Turks in 1389) has to a great extent determined the later perception and understanding of "Serbianism."

The paradox of every war--including the present-day war in the Balkans-- lies not only in the fact that any party at war merely defends themselves, responds to attacks, and guards their own people, but above all else is the fact

---

[4]Croats, Carantanians, Carniolans, and Serbs participated in the early ninth century revolt led by Ljudevit Posavski. During certain periods, medieval Serbia enjoyed very good relations with Rome, even so far as for the Pope to confer and crown Serbia's early rulers. It is also true that Serbia's Stephen Nemanja offered German Emperor Frederick I Barbarossa an alliance against the Byzantines, further to which in these efforts he received support from the Venetian Republic. Dushan the Mighty sought allies at the Papal curia as well with the Venetians for his Serbian campaign against Constantinople (Byzantium), which only failed to materialize due to Hungarian opposition. The Bosnians fought alongside the Serbs against the Turks, etc.

[5]*Mythologies*, pp. 142-145.

that each warring party, one way or another, wins. Or to put it another way: the mythology always triumphs--a defeat can be turned to its own benefit by turning it into a victory. There are several eloquent historic examples of this: the Field of the Blackbirds (Kosovo Polje); the *Pacta Conventa* in Croatia; the fratricide and bloody fighting that took place inside individual southern Slavic nations during, and immediately after, the Second World War--as well as all those incidents that have occurred since 1991.[6] It is particularly indicative that such defeats turned into victories leave an even deeper trace of the bygone golden age in the mythical tradition than the true high-points. The Serbs, thus, celebrate the loss of independence that followed their humiliating defeat at the Field of the Blackbirds, their mythical place, their cradle, rather than the admirable and historically proven prosperity of the Nemanjid Dynasty and state.

Such a turning towards a mythical trauma is always connected with current political interests. The rejuvenation of old tales and their nostalgic revival occurs when a society is caught in a difficult situation of conflict. Here one can find the reason for the perseverance of the national myth: in its structure the national myth preserves the system's void, the unsolved question from the past, which in itself always implies new answers for the present. A painful defeat following on after the end of a golden age opens up a wound which through time acquires different mythical elaborations. Every passing dilemma is translated into this discourse so that the current ideology can respond to the challenge. It offers its own conclusions and "permanently" closes the traumatic openness of the old myth. The ancient defeat becomes decisive in the national mythology: all the other phases encounter it and in some way try to solve it. Myth is, therefore, not a "complete" story, as it leaves the essential issue open-- and it is this which precisely generates its actualities. Myth is a super-historical constancy, within which the differences between yesterday, today, and tomorrow are erased,[7] and at the same time it accomplishes group identification for all the future generations, united in a pitiful search for the answers to the open mythical wounds of the past. Mythology enlists this contingent event into the realms of eternity, and thus mythologized, it became a good companion and support for all the future attempts at liberation.

The long and exhausting battle of the Field of the Blackbirds took place on St. Vitus' Day, 15th June 1389 (28th June according to the new calendar),

---

[6]The election campaign posters of the HDZ (Croatian Democratic Union) party, of the year after the culmination of the 1991 war with the Serbs in which the Croats lost one third of their territory, proclaimed that the Croats were moving "From Victory to Prosperity."

[7]Aleš Debeljak, *Twilight of the Idols*, p. 19.

a date which itself became mythical for the Serbs. It claimed innumerable casualties on both sides, including both leaders. Serbian "Prince" Lazar of Rascia was captured and decapitated whilst the Turkish Sultan Murat was reputedly cunningly killed by a Serbian nobleman, Milosh Kobilich (better known as Obilich, the letter "K" only being omitted in the eighteenth century). It was Kobilich who used an act of "heroic deception" in order to kill Sultan Murat and wash off the shame that had occurred earlier. The Turks had won the battle but, nevertheless, withdrew from the field on account of their losses. Their withdrawal and the death of Murat left the impression that the united Christian army won the day.

Parallel to the legend surrounding the heroic Milosh and his tricking the enemy, the story concerning the treason of Vuk Brankovich developed; it was he who was blamed for the defeat because of his alleged flight from the battlefield. However, in actual fact, it was Brankovich who was to fight on against the Turks, by way of which he actually acted against the interests of Milica, Prince Lazar's widow, who was in favor of making a compromise with the Turks. Brankovich, together with his Serbian and Hungarian allies, continued to wage war against the invaders until he was finally defeated by the Turks. He died in their prison.

In the meantime, the Serbian Orthodox Church proclaimed Lazar a saint and, thus, bestowed the legitimacy of succession to the throne on the Lazarevich branch. In 1396, most of Serbia became a Turkish vassal state although active resistance against them did continue for an additional fifty years. Nonetheless, the occupation of the rump-nation's capital of Smederevo represented the nation's final and complete loss of independence. In 1459, Serbia was incorporated into the Ottoman Empire and feudal law was introduced, however, the Serbs did manage to preserve a high degree of autonomy.

Over the following centuries, a considerable number of Serbia's Orthodox population retreated northeastwards, across the Sava and Danube rivers towards Hungary (i.e. in 1690 from Kosovo to Vojvodina) as well as west across the Drina river into Bosnia and Croatia. Evacuated territories in what is referred to as "ancient Serbia," including Kosovo, were populated by Albanians. Kosovo, therefore, again becomes a central mythical focal-point, the sacred place of the Serbian nation. At the same time, the battle on the Field of the Blackbirds becomes a great collective drama, an inexhaustible point of reference and source of mythical material, which goes on to provide the framework for all the great Serbian mythological production that was to follow.

Some of the most prominent mythological stories are connected with events that took place on that June day over 600 years ago: the story about the Mother of the Jugovich's, the Kosovo Maiden, the Kosovo Peony, Brankovich the traitor, and Lazar the hero, who, in mythical tradition, was exalted to the rank of "prince," etc. These associatively heavy ingredients were then fitted into constantly new mythological arrangements. This was especially true during those periods which offered difficult and historical challenges such as at the times of insurrection against the Turks at the dawn of the nineteenth century as well as during the Balkan wars and current conflicts with the Croats, Bosnians, and Albanians. In popular belief, spurred by myth, even the *hajduks* (highwaymen and robbers) gradually acquired the distinction of fighters for national liberation by way of which plundering the Muslims was perceived as a patriotic fight for the "holy cross and golden freedom." Many of Serbia's national leaders and statesmen sprang from the ranks of *harambashas* and *chetovodjas*--the chieftains of the so-called *hajduks*.

Over the centuries, the Serbian Orthodox Church has played a pivotal and decisive role in preserving the concept of Serbianism, a role which was particularly important during the period of Turkish rule. The spirit of *"Svetosavlje"* (after "Sveti Sava," i.e. Rastko--the "Saint Sava," founder of the independent Serbian Church) became a cohesive membrane during the Turkish subjugation. According to Paul Mojzes, this praising and glorification of the Serbian Christian identity served as its protection under a cloak of mystery, especially during difficult times. The martyrdom of Saint Sava supposedly conveys the suffering that the Serbs endured over the centuries.[8] The Orthodox Church created the myth about Serbs being a heavenly, chosen, divine people, a nation of martyrs, who during their entire history were nothing but humiliated, abused, and injured. Yet such a plot implies a triumphant ending. It is yet one more "suffering" myth, which like the Kosovo one, leaves the essence open: some day the story is going to end well.

The Orthodox Church itself is organized as a state or a national church. Religious and national identity are entirely equal in the mythical self-perception (hence the significance of the edict "God saves the Serbs" together with all the claims concerning the concord between the Church and the state). In the case of the Serbs and Montenegrins, this is indicated by a specific politico-religious syncretism: biographies of Serbian rulers were transformed into saintly chronicles (known as "zhitiye"--the medieval written legends about the lives of saints). Church interests were merged with ruling interests. When one takes this into consideration, it is possible to understand all the various instigations and incitements, or at best the loquacious silence, on the part of the highest dignitaries of the Serbian Church concerning the present goings on and atrocities that are occurring in the Balkans.

---

[8]Mojzes, *op.cit.*, p. 18.

Of the 130 cults that have existed in the religious culture of Serbian Orthodoxy from the tenth century to the present day, forty appertain to the five largest ruling noble families. At the same time, omnipotent power is attributed to the saints and their relics, hence the custom of "sunbathing" bones.[9] An intriguing fact remains that despite the role which the Serbian and Montenegrin people attribute to the Orthodox Church in preserving their national essence, it was, during all those centuries of subjugation, that very same church which cooperated with Turkish authorities and, occasionally, even acted as its extension.

Specific to Montenegrin mythical history is that they considered themselves to have remained independent of the Turks and, by way of this, the only insubordinate Christian nation in the Balkan region. But the fact remains that their leader, Ivan Crnojevich, who originally ruled over the country as a Venetian duke, recognized Turkish rule after 1479. Over the ensuing centuries, the Montenegrins, like their neighbors the Serbs, lived as Turkish vassals under a system of local "ducal" self-government in a type of two-tier system of administration. Montenegrian national identity hardened through repeated rebellions. From 1521 until 1851, the Montenegrins observed theocratic order by way of which the ruler was also a bishop--the so-called *vladika*. The main mythical point in Montenegrin history occurs with the expulsion of the Turks and Turkicized Slavs, an occasion which was immortalized in Peter Petrovich Njegosh's epic poem "Mountain Wreath."

The second "defeat by a stronger neighbor" phase on the territory of present-day Bosnia and Herzegovina evolved in an entirely different manner. Strong Islamization of the Slavic population took place, especially of those segments of society who had belonged to the Bogomil church organization. To the Bogomil sect, Islam represented an escape from the universal ostracism into which they were pushed and the attacks which they suffered, during the thirteenth and fourteenth centuries. To the Bosnian Muslims, who are nowadays accused of being "Turks," the new religion (which was quite different from orthodox Arab Islam and distinct even from its Osman-Turk version), represented just one qualification for their identity as a group. Most of the converts settled in the towns whilst the countryside remained mainly Catholic.

The Croats came under the Hungarian crown in 1102 with the *Pacta Conventa* treaty[10] by way of which they "consented" to the ceding of power to their stronger neighbor although they were able to preserve their own nobility

---

[9] During Serbia's most recent national-religious "revival," which began during the late 1980s, Lazar's remains were exhumed and sent on a tour of the country.

[10] Recent studies have indicated that the actual document itself is of a later date.

and enjoy a special status. In the decades that followed the battle of Krbava in 1493, a large portion of Croatian territory came under Turkish rule. It was only at the end of the seventeenth century that the Croats, in collaboration with the Hungarians, finally defeated and drove off the Turks once and for all.

In 1527, and seeking protection, Croatian delegates elected Archduke Ferdinand of Habsburg as their king. From that time on, the destiny of Croatia was more connected with the Austrian and Central European states than with the Balkans. Territories which were historically Croatian became populated by large numbers of expelled and exiled Serbs. The Habsburg court incorporated these ethnic Serbs into their defence plans for the Empire, using them on their southern flank as a bulwark against the Turks. Between the second half of the sixteenth century and 1881, the so-called Military Frontier Region (*Vojna Krajina*) became a special Austrian administered unit under direct supervision from Vienna and, thus, in political sense separated from the rest of Croatia. So during those 250 years, there were two Croatias in existence, the Principal and the Krajina. Also during that period, the Serbian Orthodox Church spread its activities and organization into those parts of Croatia where the Serbs had come to live. The once glorious Croatian Kingdom had been reduced to the "remains of the remnants" (*reliquiae reliquiarum*).

Apart from aristocratic-feudal autonomy, the Catholic faith was presumed to be a recognizable force with the help of which the Croatian people were supposedly able to attain and preserve their national identity. Linked to this was also the centuries-old tendency towards the revival of the ancient Slavonic or "Glagolithic" liturgy, which reaches to the present day, as well as the mythicization of Grgur Ninski (the tenth century Bishop of Nin, considered to have been a staunch defender of the Glagolithic movement). The Virgin Mary became a kind of national and mythical being for the Croats; above all, she symbolized a martyr(-like) mother (the "Croatian Mother;" "Blessed Mary, Queen of the Croats").[11]

Because of the specific historical circumstances occurring in the Balkans, nation states were never able to establish themselves here. In fact, just the reverse occurred. Invariably, the established church played a significant role in the constitution of a nation and, by way of this, a kind of religious ethnocentrism was instituted.[12] The importance and pivotal role of the church in society, thus, remained intact and inextricably linked with the concept of a nation. This together with the regional fragmentation and diaspora of the peoples

---

[11]See Ivan Cvitković, *Katolička crkva i nacija*, pp. 33-34.

[12]Maxims like "God save Croatia," "God saves Serbs," or "Saint Sava and God save the Serbs," are indicative.

of the three religions and traditions created the characteristic Balkan jigsaw puzzle.

The territories of Bosnia and Herzegovina, Montenegro, Albania, Sandzhak (the Novi Pazar region of Serbia) as well as some parts of Croatia severely complicated the establishment of nations along the lines of the western models. In the Balkans, religion, together with the religio-cultural difference between neighbors, later became the basis of national identity, and, therefore, affiliation.[13] As a result of this, religious tradition became an integral part of national mythology.

In this, the second mythem, historical fact negates the desired image of a mythicized past. After its aforementioned defeat, Serbia became a vassal state, and Serbian armies lead by their own nobility fought alongside the Turks.[14] Until the sixteenth century, the Christian feudal lords of the Ottoman Empire played an important role within the Turkish army (for example in the conquest of southern Hungary). During the second half of the seventeenth century, protagonists of Croato-Hungarian conspiracies against the Habsburgs (Nikola Zrinski and later Petar Zrinski, Franjo Krsto Frankopan and Franjo Rakoczy) sought help from the French, Venetians, Poles, and even the Turks (Croatia was supposedly in vassal relationship with the Great Porta). During the war of 1683-1699, Serbian-Albanian troops assisted the Austrian army against the Turks.

"The Yugoslav Phase"

Characteristic of this, the third mythem, is the decline and fall of the powerful neighbors. After being liberated from foreign rule, the southern Slavic nations, with the exception of the Bulgarians, surrendered their sovereignty to

---

[13]Dinko Tomašič, *Osebnost in kultura v vzhodnoevropski politiki* [Characteristics and Culture in Western European Politics], p. 187; Marko Keršervan, *Nacionalna identiteta in religija v Jugoslaviji*,[National Identity and Religion in Yugoslavia], pp. 816-817. The authors points out the different degrees of importance of the church in the formation of national identity. Supposedly, the importance of the Church has been higher in the case of the Serbs than it has with the Croats.

[14]In 1395, Stephen Lazarevich, a son of the defeated Lazar of Rascia, was also defeated at the battle of Rovinari, during a Turk-Serb military campaign in Wallachia. Marko Kraljevich, mythical hero of several southern Slavic nations, was killed in this same battle. At the battle of Nicopolis, a year later in 1396, Stephen Lazarevich's cavalry played a decisive role in the Turkish victory over the badly organized crusader army under the Hungarian King Sigismund. Stephen, together with Vuk Lazarevich and alongside the Turk Sultan Bayazit, fought in Asia Minor against Tamerlane (Timur) and his Mongol Empire. The Christian Serbian rulers were also later to contribute to the triumph of central authority within the Osman-Turkish state and help the Turks fight off internal threats as well as those that came from abroad. Also see Ignacij Voje, *Nemirni Balkan*, [Restless Balkans], pp. 115-117.

a common state in good faith and with great expectations. They entered into this new common nation from differing backgrounds and in different manners by way of which these peoples drew different conclusions and expected different benefits from their being joined together.

The Serbs and Montenegrins liberated themselves from Turkish rule during the first half of the nineteenth century. In the following years, both nations were able to enlarge their states at the expense of the waning Ottoman Empire. The Serbs, thus, perceived Yugoslavia merely as a logical consequence of their natural expansion although in fact this new state was some ten times larger in territory than the initial Belgrade principality which, after an uprising in 1817, received its first genuine autonomy from Turkey.

The Serbs considered themselves the saviors of this territory, the southern Slavic "Piedmont," looking to unite a Slavic "Italy" subjugated by foreign powers. It was for this reason that they attributed their king, Petar I. Karageorgevich, the epithet of the "Great Liberator" and bestowed on his son, King Alexander, the title of "Unifier." The Serbs developed a complex mythology concerning their sacrifice for Yugoslavia and their undeserved suffering in this. Both Serbs and Montenegrins also mythicized their rebellions and liberation from the Turkish yoke. Particularly strong was the "Bonapartistic-Garibaldian" myth concerning the Karageorgevich dynasty who were described as being "people's monarchs," and "crowned plebeians" coming from the peasant class. As such they were considered true democratic representatives of the nation.[15]

Such Serbian concepts were an anathema to the Croats and their perception of a "Greater Croatia." The most extreme Croatian ideas were based on the concepts of Ante Starčević, according to whom all the southern Slavic nations, including the Slovenes (who were denoted as being merely "Alpine Croats"), were of Croatian descent. The Nemanjid dynasty was supposedly an "eminent Croatian dynasty" whilst Marko Kraljevich and Milosh Obilich were also supposedly Croats. The Croatian nation apparently stretched "from the Socha to the Focha" rivers, which generally corresponds to the territory of the Greater Croatian Kingdom which existed during the second half of the eleventh century. Josip Juraj Strossmayer, a Croatian bishop and the founder of the Yugoslav Academy of Arts and Sciences, held a quite opposite viewpoint. He stressed the need for the cooperation among the southern Slavs and also warned about the danger of hegemony by Vienna and the Vatican.

---

[15]They were supposedly different from the Romanovs, Hohenzollerns, and Habsburgs. Lev Kreft, *Estetika in poslanstvo*, [Esthetics and Mission], pp. 82 and 86.

During its seventy-three years of existence, Yugoslavia developed many integrative mechanisms with which it was able to justify its legitimacy. The Yugoslav spirit had, supposedly, extended back for centuries, and history was portrayed as a logical process and the progressive route to a just society. Glorification of the status quo together with the adaptation to current intentions and conditions and the concept of the "permanent present" became the constant mythical companions to current events. The existing was, at every phase, presented as a stable, harmonious, safe, consistent, and non-contradictory unity. It was the final fulfillment of the natural cycle of the history, in effect the ultimate phase and the realization of all that had happened previously. Everything inside that present, as it existed, was "necessary;" within Yugoslavia itself, it was self-understood that the Slavs from this territory could live only together and only inside Yugoslavia. Ancient dreams of nationhood had come true, and oppressed peoples who for centuries had been forced to live beneath the double-headed Habsburg eagle and under the Ottoman crescent moon had been freed.

The paradox arose later when the transition into a new, national phase, labeled as "liberation," began. The self-conceptions of the new states wallowing in the present euphoria of vulgarized nationalism overlook, conceal, and even feel ashamed by the fact that the Yugoslav idea was a liberating ideology in which these same nations were released from the former multi-national empires and their "back-yard" spheres of influence. Even before World War I, the Yugoslav concept had its followers among the three largest southern Slavic nations. However, they did not have a unified or concrete conception of how to realize it,[16] but it was the Great War which finally provided the key.

The existence of Yugoslavia cannot be simplified and explained away through its having a "continually cruel and repressive apparatus" or its being able to achieve a state of "general terror" amongst the population. Indeed, the Yugoslav idea did function and, in its time, the state was supported by the majority of its subjects.[17] The mythology of Yugoslavia was based on certain consecrated elements. One such element in the first Yugoslavia was undoubtedly the Karageorgevich dynasty and its being the symbolic founder of the common descent. Following World War II, it was the persona of Marshal Josip Broz Tito (who was a triple leader: the state, Communist Party, and the army) that left an indelible mark upon the second Yugoslavia.

---

[16]Peter Vodopivec, *Srednja Evropa, nekdanja Jugoslavija in Balkan: Novi ali stari nacionalizmi?* [Middle Europe, Former Yugoslavia, and the Balkans: New or Old Nationalisms?], p. 8.

[17]Mojzes, *op. cit.*, pp. 2 and 84.

Tito's split with Stalin's Soviet Union in 1948 caused him to be known in world circles as something of a "Communist Luther." It was Yugoslavia's own "devilish" neighbors who allegedly tried, but were not able to succeed, in disuniting the nation's constituent republics and peoples through attempts to inflame ethnic hatred between them after which they could once again dismember the country (Yugoslavia was surrounded by "BRIGAMA."[18] Tito's Yugoslavia was desirous to break with the old pattern of subjugation and exploitation and went about achieving this through an unparalleled socioeconomic revolution (factories were given to the workers, land to the peasants, and work to all). The mythology surrounding this multinational, socialist, self-managing, independent, and non-aligned state also purposefully excluded any explicit manifestation of the religious traditions of any individual constituent nation. The new self-perception did not tolerate many of the old components.

In the Kingdom of Yugoslavia, which in effect existed between 1918 and 1941, the theory of Yugoslav nationhood was represented by the Yugoslav version of the unifying myth. It was a theory of the fraternity and unity of equal nations which was battle-hardened during World War II into the unity of the Federation. Through all of this, the state portrayed itself as a harmonious community of fraternal nations: compatriots and relatives. The first Yugoslavia brought about some temporary solutions to ethnic-relations within the Balkans; for example those concerning the Serbian question received an answer since under the umbrella of Yugoslavia all the Serbs were actually able to live "in one country."

The post-war Yugoslav Federation (referred to as "Titoland" by Sir Winston Churchill) was based on federalism. It recognized Macedonians as a distinct community and nation; at the same time, it curbed the territorial aspirations of the Serbs and Croats with regard to Bosnia and Herzegovina. The latter was achieved mostly by establishing borders between the constituent Republics as well as through the use of an ill-chosen and politically incorrect name for the major ethnic group living inside Bosnia: the "Muslims." The mythology surrounding partisan resistance and the heroic "National Liberation Struggle" represented one of the major bases for the acceptance of the new order and government. According to Lev Kreft, this was the only mythology which,

---

[18]A Serbo-Croatian word meaning 'troubles', also an acronym composed of the initial letters of Yugoslavia's 'troublesome' neighbors: Bulgaria, Romania, Italy, Greece, Albania, Madjarska (Hungary), Austria.

particularly in the early 1950s, was able to precipitate the legitimacy of the authorities in the public eye, as well as relate the then leadership to the masses. It also conferred a moral right on the ruling class and justified the subordination to the representatives of the revolution who could not be said to speak on behalf of the working class, but rather in the name of their own previous merits.[19]

Nonetheless, the Yugoslav reality was in Monarchy as well as in Federation rather different from that which was affirmed. Inside Yugoslavia, there was a permanent and ongoing conflict between those with a centralist-unitaristic political orientation and those who had a more federalist-autonomistic viewpoint. Within what should have been (in principle) neutral and balanced key state institutions, such as government, public administration, the military, and police, there was always disproportionate ethnic representation. The state was, in fact, a brotherhood of big and smaller brothers, and at the same time, there was a brutal settling of accounts with disobedient or undesirable minorities (which led to the exodus of Germans, Italians, and Turks following World War II) and the repression of ethnic Albanians in Kosovo. There also existed the ideology of "Yugoslavhood" in the sense of a national melting-pot ("one nation with three tribes that had been separated by fate"), statistical ethnogenics (of the Muslims and the Yugoslavs), and ethnocides. The problems and tensions which arose from a high rate of unemployment and economic migration should also not be forgotten.

"The Final Liberation"

If the particular level achieved does not acknowledge the possibility of alternatives, then it considers that it has reached the end of the history itself. The fourth mythem represents the "final emancipation"--the last chapter in the history of a nation. Final emancipation through independence was considered the "inevitable" culmination of dissatisfaction and humiliation--when the threats and the destruction of the essence of individual nations had, allegedly, reached their intolerable peak. It has been asserted that each and every Yugoslav nation allegedly underwent one disappointment after another, that they experienced nothing but exploitation, torture, misery, and genocide.[20]

---

[19]Kreft, *op.cit.*, pp. 144-146.

[20]Consider the frequency of the reiteration of the Jasenovac myth (Jasenovac was a Croatian concentration camp run by the *Ustasha*--Croatian fascist sympathizers) and the story of the Jewish fate of the Serbian nation (Jovan Rašković). Also consider Stjepan Radić, the symbol of the Croatian suffering during the war; or the Bleiburg incident (which occurred immediately after the cessation of hostilities in World War II); the topics of political discourse within Croatia and Serbia.

Yugoslavia was, supposedly, only a coercive formation artificially created for the convenience of the major world powers and in later years was kept together through a reign of terror, executed by the secret police and its Communist Party master. In effect, the seventy-three year long Yugoslav experience was nothing but a "dark era" during which the reigns of power were always held by another, neighboring nation, and never by one's own. According to Dobrica Ćosić, a Serb novelist and later politician, whatever it conquered in war, Serbia lost in peace, and that the bitter experience of the fratricidal war, which took place between 1941 and 1945, was followed by another vain and futile attempt at living together in a common state.

In Yugoslavia old differences and disagreements didn't vanish, quite the contrary, new ones accumulated. "Objective circumstances" and "increasing complexity" supposedly dictated changes "on their own accord." In such mythological self-perceptions violence and war became inevitable necessities. Despite the admonishments, tensions, and bloody fighting which as a rule accompany the process of disintegration, the decision for independent sovereignty and statehood had supposedly been proven to be justified.

Here one can speak about "vaccination" (Roland Barthes), one of the common mythical conceptions which can be used to justify every momentary evil, for the reason that it saves the community from an even greater evil. Such logic is obscene to the extreme. It perceives that no matter how great the present torments are, they are small, even negligible, when compared to those which would have been generated had nothing been done and had everything continued as before. This philosophy also maintains that the entire tragedy of war and devastation is easy to endure as, in every respect, it is better to be "on one's own." The re-formation of these Balkan national states was to fulfill a thousand years of dreams.

In the fourth mythem, one returns to the first one--"to the good old days of national unity." This is the point from which everything is supposed to originate--myth is a deterministic discourse par excellence--and where everything is supposed to return. The most puerile and idiotic of theses and caricatures of history live to see their acceptance because of this searching for or, better, finding ethno-national genealogies which at times resembles the cheapest form of science fiction. This quest concerns itself with going back, with reattaining the golden age, and achieving the Renaissance of the nation, and within such states, national identity becomes a new reference point. In the imaginative Balkan mythical orders, the myth surrounding the decline and fall of the golden era provides fertile grounds for a rematch: i.e. the present war and the struggle of the righteous, good and great, against the evil.

The authorities always draw on, or more precisely ideologize, only those stories, legends, teachings, and identifiers from the storeroom of society's collective mythical memory which are useful in the current situation. Pragmatically, they close the ancient mythical dilemmas. In recent years, the excessive vulgarization of mythology indicates how old stories can unambiguously serve present interests. Ernst Cassirer claims that contemporary political myths do not grow up freely; rather they are created according to a plan and are artificial products manufactured as a weapon by skilled and cunning artisans.[21] However, one way or another they have been made to dovetail into the old myths, even when such a connection may be contradictory or inconsistent.

Mythology becomes the source and starting point of political option. Current political and national problems, dilemmas, and decisions are enriched with entirely mythical extensions. Thus, for example, the ancient Serbian nation once again fights for its just cause (Kosovo); only the enemies are new: the Albanians, desecrating sacred Serbian land; and Croats and Moslems who bear the "historical guilt" for that humiliating defeat 600 years ago. The struggle against these people is perceived as a repetition of an original act in which mythicized adversaries perform. Thus, the violence accumulated in society becomes channeled outwardly against these enemies. The official propaganda unceasingly circulates stories about Serbian military dominance over these territories and about how the Serbs have always fought "on the right side" and "for just causes." The Serbian "*vozhd*" (leader) is, just like his Croatian counterpart, attributed many virtues which have mythical extensions (the drawing together of personal and national destiny, visionary powers, messianic qualities, etc).

Each of the Balkan nations created a myth about its being a "defensive wall against barbarian invasion," about its "bordering the savage East." However, at the very same time the Turks also consider themselves to be such a buffer state whilst the Greeks are convinced it is they who are plugging the dam. The Serbs also consider themselves to be a bulwark of Christianity (although they also enjoy playing their other role at the threshold of the Moscow-Belgrade-Athens Orthodox axis, preventing the eastward spread of Catholicism). Since the sixteenth century, the Croats have deemed themselves to be the wall of Christianity, the "*antemurale Christianitatis*."

The more strained the situation becomes within any of the individual Balkan societies, the more the new national mythologies depend on convenient links with the transcendental to traditional religious values and the multi-tiered

---

[21]*Myth of the State*, p. 282.

church tradition which allegedly proves the ancient status of the nation. Through helping to create a new national mythology, the churches also try to recreate and acquire anew their "ancient" privileged positions in what are changed circumstances which is why they have been encouraging and have gladly welcomed such processes occurring in their environment. The churches have stirred up not only national conscience but also nationalist feeling.[22] Hence, the presence of religious elements in entirely secular, political, or even military matters and ceremonies as well as in the everyday life of citizens (e.g. the consecration of buildings and the holding of religious services on national holidays). Within the mythologies of southern Slavic nations, religion is equated with national identity and affiliation, as a result of which people's religious feelings are exploited politically. The religious monopoly is closely connected with the phenomenon of militant "secular religions" and strengthens the tendency towards a political monopoly.[23]

In this whole process, every new successive phase is presented as a direct opposition to the preceding one. The newly-founded states on the territory of former Yugoslavia constantly try to justify their withdrawal or abandonment of the previous state and at the same time prove how organic and harmonious their present situation is. According to Ćosić, it was only through the people's democratic revolt, better known as the "anti-bureaucratic revolution," that the Serbs were again embodied as an historic nation. The political discourse became transformed into an altogether mythical one by way of which vulgar mythological determinism prevailed.[24]

In the mythology of the "unfinished war," this means that the quarrels and disputes from all the previous wars have to be settled. Thus, "*janissaries*" fight against "*hussars*;" Islamicized Slavs "*poturice*" against "*hajduks*;" knights take-on cavaliers; "*Spahijas*" do battle with Dukes; and the sixth "Lika" and the seventh "Banija" partisan divisions wage war on Ustasha troops. In obituaries, killed Croatian soldiers are referred to as "Croatian knights" whilst Krajina becomes a Serbian Sparta, and the detachments of Serbian volunteers who came

---

[22]Mojzes, *op.cit.*, page 126. In Mojzes's opinion, the most recent war has brought the inhabitants of former Yugoslavia back into the churches and mosques. This has been facilitated by the erasure of the differences which at one time existed between the national and the religious. On page 170 Mojzes also maintains that the bigger the dilemma that a given ethno-religious group faces, the more radical it becomes.

[23]Marjan Smrke, *Pozabljena obletnica*, p. 13.

[24]This encompasses all spheres of life and society, even sporting achievements. When "Red Star" of Belgrade won the European Champions' Soccer Cup in 1991, it was celebrated as a victory over fascists and secessionists who dared stand up against Serbia, as well as a tangible proof of the power of a united Serbia and strong Yugoslavia.

to its aid perceive that they are the warriors of Dushan the Mighty. The responsibility for national well-being erases all other responsibilities. In the on-going war, slaughterers enjoy the status of national heroes; they receive exalted titles and become the stars of new epics, and their actions are described in comic books (e.g. Kapetan Dragan). The Serbs ground their territorial claims with the rights of "Serbian graves," i.e. every plot of land on which a Serbian warrior has trod should, according to their own mythology, belong to Serbia.

As in all the previous ones, the present Balkan War is concerned with depriving and humiliating the enemy and violating its mythical self-perception.[25] Only this can explain the methodical destruction of the symbols of the previous regime and the objects sacred to the enemy nation. More consequential than the blowing-up of shrines, churches, and mosques was the besieging and shelling of the strategically unimportant town of Dubrovnik.

In certain parts of the former federal state, the population was so well integrated that their nationality was not distinguishable, and in such places former brothers became "eternal" enemies. By way of this Croats became "genocidal *Ustasha,*" Bosnians are "Islamic *mujahedin*" fighting a "*jihad,*" and the Serbs are born *Chetniks*, and the Slovenes, Austria's stable-hands. Such defamation is confronted by what is seemingly, at first glance, a more conciliatory remark which is, in fact, even more discriminatory. Here we are talking of the use of the adjective "honest" (in conjunction with an Albanian, Serb, Moslem, or "southerner") which quietly implies that, apart from the denoted exception, all the other members of that nation are far from honest. Thus, synonymity is established between, for example, an Albanian and the adjective dishonest--implying there is something wrong with that particular person's "Albanianism" if he/she is honest.

The principal community needs an enemy against which it can establish itself as the radical opposition and, by way of this, defines its complementary imaginative mythical order. For the enemy to play its role effectively, it also has to assume some metaphysical dimensions. The quarreling southern Slavic states are surrounded by "enemies," the fatality and evil power of which stretch in proportion to their distance. The nearest enemies, geographically speaking, are merely emanations of the hellish intents of the more distant, larger, and powerful enemies. Allegedly, these enemies (in the form of national minorities) are already teeming within the borders of the state, and it is they who are perceived as merely the "extended dirty fingers" of their principal nations.

---

[25]Also see Renata Salecl, *Zakaj ubogamo oblast?*, pp. 185-189.

Danger is, avowedly, omnipresent and lurks from each and every corner. By way of this a paranoic feeling of being besieged is created.[26] The Serbs, for example, consider the Pope to have been a permanent malignancy from time immemorial, even though the man who sat on the throne of St. Peter during the medieval period invariably collaborated with the Serbs. The second "enemy" are the Muslims. "Christian" Serbia and Montenegro try to present themselves as defenders of the faith against the "Istanbul-Tirana-Sarajevo green crescent of Islam" and the "Macedonia-Bulgaria-Romania-Albania-Bosnia axis of Turkish affinity." Earlier, some quite contrary examples were cited such as pro-Hungarian and pro-Turkish Serbs fighting each other for control over the early and mid-fifteenth century Serbian vassal state.

The third of Serbia's "historical" enemies are the Germans together with their "*Drang nach Osten*" (eastward push) project (not to mention Austrian-German "meddling" in Serbia's affairs which directly led to World War I). Also the modern school of "Serbian thought" prescribes that a union between the USA and Serbia would, supposedly, present an obstructing element to the unification of Europe "under the heavy German baton." Historical evidence, however, concerning the Serb-German relationship much of the time provides a different testimony and demonstrates how weak the historical memories of these new apologists are.[27]

This perception relates to a conspiracy in which an abstract enemy is made real. An abstract, metaphysical enemy becomes metamorphosized into an actual conspirator, operating within organized, clandestine bands. The imaginative mythical order that exists within the Balkan detritus has brought a huge number of such fabrications to the surface: Vatican intrigues, the conspiracies of Islamic fundamentalists, and the machinations of the Fourth

---

[26]Giving the interview to the Slovene weekly, *Mladina* in February (18th) 1992, Dr. Branko Kostić, vice-president of the Presidency of SFRJ (the Federation that was the former Yugoslavia), described the situation in following way:

> Germany and Austria have achieved their goals although the process is not over as yet. Just consider the demands of Hungary for the protection of its minority in Vojvodina, the behavior of the Bulgarians as well as the activities of Albanians in Kosovo and Moslems in the Sandzhak region . . .

[27]An efficient pro-German quisling regime reigned over Serbia during World War II. In endeavoring to conclude a separate peace treaty with the central powers in 1917, Serbia even put on trial and sentenced the organizers of the assassination of Archduke Franz Ferdinand in Sarajevo (the Salonika trial). Prior to that, two dynasties (the pro-Russian Karageorgevichs and pro-Austrian Obrenovichs) had been contesting the Serbian throne for a hundred years, spilling a lot of Serbian blood in the process. Between 1691 and 1739 the Serbs, encouraged by and with substantial help from the Habsburg monarchy and its Austrian army, successfully rebelled against the Turks and even succeeded in liberating Belgrade (1717).

Reich. Some of these are particularly contradictory and demonstrate the unlimited mythical acrobatics of the new order. Innovative buzz words, which also include such expressions as "Bolshevik-Chetnik army," "Vatican-Comintern conspiracy," or "Udbomafia" (the "mafia" of the former secret police who are able to use their previous exalted positions for their own benefit). The vocabulary of the "Serbian antibureaucratic revolution" consists of neologisms such as "differentiation of ideas" and "stabilization of the situation."

"Hereditary" allies supposedly protect these countries against the "hereditary" enemies. The Croats seek such allies in the west where they themselves presume they, in a "historic and cultural" sense, belong. The Serbs look towards the Russians and Greeks-- their brothers in Orthodoxy. This has lead to the "Boshnjaks" (Bosnian "Muslims") to count on the support and empathy of their more "wealthy" fellow-believers from near and far. Historiography offers a string of examples which could demonstrate just the opposite; however, such facts are far from helpful to official mythology and cast shadows over the concept of the proclaimed permanent adversary.

The Illyrian movement and the Illyric idea of "nativity," the ancient common origin of all southern Slavs, thrived in Croatia between 1835 and 1848. It is also interesting to note that during the nineteenth century the so-called "Cyril-Methodius idea," which contained distinct political dimensions, sprang-up amongst believers in the two largest southern Slavic nations. Apart from perceiving the unification of the Catholic and the Orthodox, it also espoused the idea of attachment and brotherhood among the Slavic nations and of the necessity of emancipation from the foreign yoke. For centuries, predominantly Orthodox "*Uskoks*" had defended the Habsburg monarchy and Venetian estates against Turkish raids. Serbian troops from the Military Region joined Napoleon on his ill-fated Russian campaign and self-sacrificingly fought against Mother Russia. Experience acquired since 1991 show that it is really a struggle of everybody against everyone else, a situation in which even the worst enemy can become an ally and vice-versa.

The "national hero" is the second part of the mythological opposition of good against evil, the black and the white, which cannot embrace the concept of shades of gray. The national hero is the mythological figure who appears in all the mythems since he undergoes new reactualizations which are often ambivalent. With the incarnation and persona of a national hero, an abstract social and political force acquires embodiment. The leader, founder, savior is eulogized and attributed superhuman abilities which surpass the abilities of the human frame and the intelligence and artfulness of the common man. Such was the figure of the holy king from the golden era, previously mentioned. He is succeeded by equally prominent successors, the prophets, who with the help of their "avant garde of the righteous," lead the exhausted into the promised land. Here contemporary ideology and old myth intertwine. In recent years, Croatia conspicuously remembers Ante Starčević, the martyr Stjepan Radić, and the Archbishop, and later Cardinal, Alojzije Stepinac.

The mythical self-perception of Yugoslavia emphasized similarities between the southern Slavic nations; it focused on everything that united them whilst the imaginative orders of the successor states exclusively stressed the differences and heightened and aggravated everything which directly divided them. Finally, one can ascertain that unless we are familiar with the mythical imaginative orders of the nations involved in this war, we are unable to understand what is going on in the Balkans. These imaginative orders consist of four successive elements which together form a "logical" circle: from the golden era into the periods of subjugation and oppression and on through the "Yugoslav intermezzo" to "final" freedom and independence. The mythological system is circular; the end always brings one back to the beginning.

Bibliography

Barthes, Roland. *Mythologies*. London: Vintage, 1993.

Cassirer, Ernst. *The Myth of the State*. New Haven, CT and London: Yale University Press, 1967.

Cvitković, Ivan. "Katolička crkva i nacija " *Pogledi* (Split), April 1983, pp. 32 45.

Debeljak, Aleš. *Twilight of the Idols: Recollections of a Lost Yugoslavia*. New York: White Pine Press, 1994.

Kerševan, Marko "Nacionalna Identiteta in Religija v Jugoslaviji," *Teorija in praksa* (Ljubljana) July 1987, pp. 810-820.

Kreft, Lev. *Estetika in Poslanstvo*. Ljubljana: Znanstveno in publicistično središte, 1994.

Levi-Strauss, Claude. *Strukturalna Antropologija*. Zagreb: Stvarnost, 1989.

Mojzes, Paul. *Yugoslavian Inferno: Ethnoreligious Warfare in the Balkans*. New York: Continuum, 1994.

Ovsec, Damjan J. *Slovanska Mitologija in Verovanje*. Ljubljana: Domus, 1991.

Salecl, Renata. *Zakaj Ubogamo Oblast?* Ljubljana: DSZ, 1993.

Smrke, Marjan. "Pozabljena Obletnica," *Razgledi* (Ljubljana), 12(1043) 1995; pp. 12-13.

Tomasić, Dinko. "Osebnost in Kultura v Vzhodnoevropski Politiki," *Nova Revija* (Ljubljana) 93-94, 1990; pp. 176-199. (Translated chapters from "Personality and Culture in Eastern European Politics," New York, 1948.)

Velikonja, Mitja. *Masade Duha: Razpotja Sodobnih Mitologij* (Masades of the Mind: Crossroads of Contemporary Mythologies) Ljubljana: Znanstveno in publicistično središte, 1995.
Vodopivec, Peter. "Srednja Evropa, Nekdanja Jugoslavija in Balkan: Novi ali Stari Nacionalizmi?" *Glasnik Slovenske Matice* (Ljubljana) 1-2, 1993; pp.1-14.
Voje, Ignacij. *Nemirni Balkan.* Ljubljana: DSZ, 1994.

Translated from Slovenian by Mojca Tarko

4

BOSNIA'S "TRIBAL GODS": THE ROLE OF RELIGION IN NATIONALIST POLITICS

Lenard J. Cohen

As it went on, the war in our country became more and more a religious matter.
   - Roman Catholic Father Anton Brajko (Mostar)

In time of war religion always attracts more followers....It is very important for us to motivate the people in this way.
   - Bosnian Muslim Army Chief-of-Staff, Rasim Delić (Sarajevo)

I have profited very much from my firm connections with the Church.
   - President of the Bosnian Serb Republic, Radovan Karadžić (Pale)

Introduction

The role of historical and cultural influences in recent Balkan warfare has been the subject of considerable debate among commentators both within and outside the former Yugoslavia. For example, some observers, who might be considered members of the *primordial hatred school*, have emphasized the cyclical role of "ancient enmities" and atavistic impulses in the Balkans. In contrast, another group of analysts, who have subscribed to the *paradise lost approach*, focus on the long periods during which populations of different languages, religions, and other facets of Balkan ethnic identity, managed to peacefully co-exist. This second perspective downplays historical factors and attributes the violence and savagery of recent years to nationalist leaders who whipped up antagonisms to suit their own political agendas.

Unfortunately, both views, especially cast in their starkest forms, tend to miss the mark. Thus, impatient or dogmatic commentators often fail to consider the way in which modern history and elite action have combined to shape the recent Balkan conflict. Indeed, such simplistic explanations may lead to inaccurate, unrealistic, and potentially dangerous expectations. For example, in the course of a relatively short period during 1995, official Washington underwent a paradigmatic shift in its policy assumptions from knee-jerk historicism (the extreme primordialist view) to a historical over-optimism (paradise lost/paradise regained). Thus, divisions between Bosnia's three ethnoreligious groups, which were only recently viewed as intractable facets of a hellish "quagmire," suddenly became amenable to rapid resolution by the international community. The Dayton peace agreement, signed in the fall of 1995, represents a very important breakthrough in the Balkan crisis. But the Clinton administration's suggestion that a multi-lateral "Implementation Force," including 20,000 American troops, can transform the nature of Bosnian society and politics in only one year, underscores the danger of over-selling and exaggerating expectations based upon political expediency.

Examining the role played by religious factors in recent Balkan politics and warfare can help to illustrate the complex interplay between historically conditioned attitudes and more recently evident elite strategies of ethnopolitical mobilization. Differences in customary confessional identity or theological beliefs, as such, have not been the prime factors motivating the violence in the Balkans. However, particularly in Bosnia, ethnocultural divisions, and especially negative historical memories linked to episodes of religiously-based violence among the various confessional communities during the first half of the twentieth century, have played a significant and indirect role in generating the recent war. The religious dimension of the conflict has, moreover, assumed increasing importance as the warfare dragged on between April 1992 and November 1995. Thus, religion's main impact on South Slav discord and conflict, as one analyst correctly observed, has been in "shaping culture and custom, which in turn influenced political loyalties."[1]

This study will examine religion's impact on the recent pattern of aggressive nationalism in Bosnia-Herzegovina. Three main issues will be of special concern: (1) the association between ethnic and religious sentiments in the Balkans, and the changing role of religious belief in the former Yugoslavia

---

[1]Aleksa Djilas, "Fear Thy Neighbor-The Breakup of Yugoslavia," in Charles A. Kupchan (ed.), *Nationalism and Nationalities in the New Europe* (New York: Council of Foreign Relations, 1995), 87. For an excellent survey concerning the impact of religious factors in historical and recent Balkan ethnic conflicts see, Josip Kumpes, "Religija i etnički sukobi na prostorima bivše Jugoslavije," in Ivan Grubišić (ed.), *Konfesije i rat* (Split: Centar za religijska istraživanja, 1995), 257-280. The same author has also prepared the most comprehensive bibliography on the subject. "Religija, politika, etničnost: selektivna bibliografija," *Migracije teme*, Vol. 10, No. 3-4 (1994), 251-280.

prior to 1991; (2) the influence of religious factors on the violent disintegration of Yugoslavia and the emergence of the Bosnian conflict; and (3) the growing role that religion assumed during the almost four years of the Bosnian war.

Ethnoreligiosity and Trends in Secularization

The Ethnoreligious Nexus

It is a commonplace that religious identification and ethnic affiliation have been very closely linked in the Balkan setting. Thus, each of the major nations and nationalities cohabiting in the first (1918-1941) and second (1943-1991) Yugoslav states was highly homogeneous with regard to both ethnic identity and confessional orientation. Moreover, confessional affiliations have been closely associated with the formation of distinct national groupings in the Balkans, although as a rule inter-religious conflict and antagonism have been the outgrowth, not cause, of nationalist sentiments.[2] Naturally, the extent of religious commitment exhibited by members of each ethnic group and the strength of the association between religion and nationalism has tended to wax or wane, depending on the particular period and prevailing policies under consideration.

Bosnia-Herzegovina provides a particularly good illustration of the close linkage between ethnic and confessional identities. In the 1953 census--the last enumeration in socialist Yugoslavia which included such data--88.9 percent of the population of Bosnia-Herzegovina (approximately 2.8 million inhabitants) indicated their confessional orientation.[3] Among such "believers," 99.5 percent of the roughly one million "Orthodox" of Bosnia declared themselves as Serbs, while 98.1 percent of the over 600,000 Catholics in Bosnia claimed to be Croats. The adherents of the Islamic faith in Bosnia exhibited a somewhat less straightforward position on the matter of ethnic identification than either their Orthodox Serb or Catholic Croat neighbors. During both the interwar period and prior to the 1960's in socialist Yugoslavia, the designation "Muslim" was a religious category, and Muslims (who as a group in Bosnia generally descended from Serbs and Croats who had converted to Islam) were officially unrecognized as an ethnic or national group. Even so, in the 1953 census, 93.7 percent of those self-declared as Islamic believers were listed for ethnic or national purposes as "Yugoslav undeclared," that is, the then prevalent euphemism for

---

[2] John Lampe, "Nationalism in Former Yugoslavia," in Paul Latawski (ed.), *Contemporary Nationalism in East Central Europe* (New York: St. Martin's Press, 1995), 146-148.

[3] 10.9 percent of the citizens in Bosnia claimed they were "without a religion," "religiously undeclared," or "indifferent." Roughly 0.2 percent gave no answer. *Popis stanovništva 1953, Knjiga I, vitalna i etnička obeležja* (Belgrade: Savezni zavod za statistiku, 1959), 278-279.

those who would be described after the mid-1960's as "Moslem in the ethnic sense."

Elsewhere in Yugoslavia during 1953, the overlap of confessional identification and ethnicity was equally pronounced. For example, in Serbia, 95.2 percent of the republic's predominant Orthodox religious group declared themselves to be Serbs; in Croatia 94.6 percent of Catholic believers were self-identified as Croats. Such figures were not surprising in view of the significant role played by historically fashioned denominational identities in the Balkans and the fascinating pattern of interaction among the different ethnoreligious groups in multi-confessional areas such as Bosnia and Croatia. Notwithstanding these trends, during the nearly forty year period between the 1953 census and socialist Yugoslavia's violent disintegration during 1991-1992, relatively little importance was attributed by either Yugoslav or foreign analysts to the potential political repercussions that might arise from the strong linkage between ethnic affiliation and religious orientation. For example, during the Titoist period, most commentators on religious affiliation in Yugoslavia stressed the allegedly negative or anti-modern features of denominational affiliation and also pointed to the evident decline of religious sentiment in the country.

Several reasons account for the under-estimation or unfavorable treatment of religiosity throughout most of the Tito period. Most important perhaps was the initial hostility of the Communist authorities toward religious belief. Thus, Yugoslav Marxists saw religious sentiment as a vestige of traditional society. The official view of the one-party regime was that modernization and the development of a new socialist Yugoslav mentality would gradually erode religious and ethnic commitments. During the fifteen years which followed the 1948 Tito-Stalin rift, the Yugoslav brand of Marxism shed most of the cruder aspects of the Marxist-Leninist-Stalinist ideological system, and the Belgrade regime adopted a rather pragmatic approach to the persistence of religious belief.[4] But even after the Titoist one-party state underwent yet another decentralizing and essentially liberal face-lift in the mid-1960's, and overtly repressive treatment of the country's religious communities was abandoned, the authorities and their allies in academic life continued to emphasize the fundamentally regressive impact of religion on inter-ethnic relations. Thus, religious belief and established religious communities were unenthusiastically tolerated, not condoned, and any signs of religiously-inspired nationalist expression were severely proscribed. For example, in 1973, one of Yugoslavia's

---

[4]For an excellent survey of this period see Robert F. Miller, "Church and State in Yugoslavia: Exorcising the Spectre of 'Clerico-Nationalism'," in R.F. Miller and T.H. Rigby (eds.), *Religion and Politics in Communist States* (Canberra: Australian National University, 1986), 64-93.

most prominent establishment scholars observed that "when the church was the fundamental ideological force and the most important spiritual force in society, religion divided people into relatively narrow, exclusive, endogenous groups." "Up to World War II," he continued, "the church exacerbated national conflicts," and "represented a destructive force in the Yugoslav state." As a result, it was further noted, the new Communist state had introduced "religious tolerance and strict separation of church from state."[5] In addition to Yugoslav Marxism's basic antipathy to religion, many scholars outside the Balkans, particularly those politically enamored with the alleged potential of "workers' self-management," tended to downplay residual religious belief in Balkan society or to view religion as fundamentally associated with traditional and authoritarian attitudes that were reportedly losing their significance.

Secularization Ascendant: The 1960's and 1970's

Detailed studies by a few Yugoslav social scientists reported that for most citizens religious identity and ethnic identity continued to be "virtually synonymous."[6] For example, the prominent Sarajevo sociologist of religion, Esad Ćimić, observed in a 1966 study that "in Herzegovinian conditions nationality is obviously one of the pillars of religion.   And among our respondents the identification of the national with the religious is nearly the rule." With regard to the Muslims of Herzegovina, Ćimić observed that "ethnic separateness from the Croats and Serbs was increasing."[7] But if Yugoslav scholarship in the 1960's and 1970's concluded that confessional affiliation and ethnicity remained symbiotically linked, most analysts also enthusiastically reported that a striking trend toward secularization was underway in Yugoslav society.

Empirical research and trend analyses by Yugoslav scholars in the early 1970's, for example, suggested that religiosity was increasingly becoming a marginal aspect of citizen belief and a phenomenon which appeared to survive mainly in rural areas and among the less educationally advanced and older segments of the population. In relative terms, religious belief seemed to be less intense among the traditionally Orthodox portions of the population such as the Serbs, Montenegrins, and Macedonians than in Roman Catholic areas such as Slovenia and Croatia or among the Islamic population of Bosnia. However, the overall reported trend was a weakening of customary religious commitments.

---

[5]Najdan Pašić, "Varieties of Nation-Building in the Balkans," in S.N. Eisenstadt and Stein Rokkan (eds.), *Building States and Nations* (Beverly Hills: Sage Publications, 1973), 128.

[6]Ruža Petrović, "Etno-biološka homogenizacija Jugoslovenskog društva," *Sociologija*, Vol. 10, No. 2 (1968), 25.

[7]*Socijalističko društvo i religija* (Sarajevo: Svjetlost, 1966), 123.

Indeed, country-wide survey research of adults revealed that in the fifteen years after the 1953 census, the number of citizens expressing religious belief had plummeted to less than half of the population, while atheists, non-religious respondents, and those indifferent to religion had collectively undergone a five-fold increase.[8]

Moreover, beyond their empirical verification of growing secularism, Yugoslav analysts found that although ethnicity and religious belief continued to be closely associated, the religious facets of national identities had become less important than in the past. This view was said to be especially characteristic of the Muslims of Bosnia, whose nationhood in an "ethnic sense" was officially promoted, but who were discouraged from any commitment to Islam as a faith. As a 1971 analysis surveying the evolution of Muslim ethnic identity put it, "religion did provide the initial basis on which the Muslims constituted themselves as a nation," but religious factors were "losing their former significance in giving way to other spiritual and material factors, not unlike the process characteristic of other Yugoslav peoples."[9]

Survey findings which reported the steady secularization of Yugoslav society during the two decades after 1953 seemed to support views which downplayed the significance of religiously based cleavages and conflicts in Yugoslavia. Interestingly, scholars found evidence that a portion of the population attributed their rejection of religion to the terrible inter-ethnic blood-letting during World War II. Representative answers from Esad Ćimić's 1966

---

[8]The sources for Table 1 are: *Popis stanovništva 1953, Knjiga I, vitalna i etnička obeležja*, 278-279; Ljiljana Bačević, "Neki aspekti stanja religijskog fenomena u našem društvu," in *Jugoslovensko javno mnenje o aktuelnim političkim i društvenim pitanjima* (Belgrade: IDN, 1964), 109-145; *Svet* (December 7, 1968), 8; Dragomir Pantić, "Neke vrednosne orijentacije omladine," in S. Joksimović, *et al.*, *Stavovi i opredeljenja Jugoslovenske omladine* (Belgrade: Mladost, 1974), 25-53; Srdjan Vrcan, "Omladina osamdesetih godina religija i crkva," in Srdjan Vrcan, *et al.*, *Položaj, svest i ponašanje mlade generacije Jugoslavije* (Zagreb: IDIS, 1986), 150-168; Dragomir Pantić, "Religioznost gradjana Jugoslavije," in Ljiljana Bačević, *et al.*, *Jugoslavija na kriznoj prekretnici* (Belgrade: IDN, 1991), 243; and Dragomir Pantić, "Prostorne vremenske i socijalne koordinate religiozonsti mladih u Jugoslaviji," in S. Mihailović *et al.*, *Deca krize* (Belgrade: IDN, 1990), 207 and 222.

[9]Atif Purivatra, "On the National Phenomenon of the Moslems of Bosnia-Herzegovina," in Koča Jončić (ed.), *Nations and Nationalities of Yugoslavia* (Belgrade: Medjunarodna Politika,1974), 313.

study of religion in Herzegovina provided fascinating evidence of this association.[10]

A 57-year-old Muslim farmer with an elementary school education:

"I lived in poverty during the war. I saw all sorts of things. People said: 'Kill the man. God will, forgive you; then take his possessions and you will be rich.' I thought if God really existed he would not have permitted this."

A 46-year-old Serbian Orthodox farmer with an elementary school education:

"The events of 1941 and after the liberation convinced me that there is no God. I saw and am seeing that those who committed the most atrocities are not expelled from the church. It goes just as well for those who don't believe as for those who do believe."

A 64-year-old Catholic with no schooling:

"Under the cloak of God people were liquidated in 1941. If God is the father why did he permit the slaughter of his children?"

Evidence of an increasing trend toward secularization also appeared prevalent among young people who had not experienced the trauma of World War II, but who accepted the anti-religious or non-religious views of their parents and the Titoist state. Most Yugoslav studies of religious trends during the 1960's and 1970's accepted the notion that political socialization to the norms of self-management had resulted in a substantially secularized or secularizing society.[11] A question not raised in such studies was whether beneath the contrived conformity of the one-party regime, latent religious commitments and yearnings still existed, not to mention intolerant revanchist attitudes toward neighbors of other ethnoreligious origin and belief. Rather, scholarly attention during this period, both within and outside Yugoslavia, was devoted to the organizational uniqueness and alleged democratizing potential of socialist self-management. That focus tended to overshadow any concern for the possibility that deeply held and residual religious beliefs remained politically salient or that the latent transgenerational transmission of religious values and identities might prove significant under changed circumstances. There was also almost no consideration of what impact might derive from the reduced strength of religious

---

[10]*Socijalističko društvo i religija*, 167-169.

[11]Dragomir Pantić, *Neki aspekti religijskog fenomena u našoj zemlji* (Belgrade: IDN, 1967).

injunctions in the post-1945 period.[12] For example, might the diminished role of religious ethics in society remove an important barrier to violent inter-personal behavior? And could such an ethical vacuum have a deleterious influence should another civil war or military conflagration erupt in the Balkan region?

Religious Revitalization

If a sizeable portion of the Yugoslav population, for one reason or another, described itself as secularized or non-religious during the first three or four decades after World War II, the same surveys indicated that large numbers of citizens still subscribed to traditional confessional identities. Moreover, as the Yugoslav communist regime began to encounter serious economic, political, and inter-ethnic problems during the twilight of Tito's rule and the first half-decade of the post-Tito period, Yugoslav analysts began to identify new tendencies toward the slowing, and possible reversal, of the secularization process. For example, as early as 1974, the Split-based sociologist of religion, Srdjan Vrcan, observed that strongly held forms of "traditional consciousness," together with the disruptive effect of rapid modernization, and also the regime's failure to achieve its goals, could stimulate the eventual upswing of religion in Yugoslavia.[13] Indeed, according to Vrcan, many Yugoslavs had already accepted a "skeptical and resigned mood" toward regime-sponsored values.
In the years following Vrcan's perceptive insights, numerous surveys by Yugoslav scholars confirmed his prediction.[14] Some of these studies indicated that the secularization process appeared to have halted, or temporarily reached its limits, while other analyses suggested that a renaissance or revitalization of religiosity was taking place. As always, there were important regional variations in these trends. Thus, "retarded" secularization and an increase of religiosity was most extensive in traditionally Catholic and Muslim regions of the country. The growing interest in religion among Yugoslav youth was one interesting

---

[12]An interesting exception is the work of Michael Petrovich, which emphasized that the churches in Yugoslavia, as cultural institutions, helped to define national identities and also reinforce "local national patriotism at the expense of a larger Yugoslav nationalism." This did not mean, Petrovich concluded, that religion would "necessarily continue its disintegrative role," as long as awareness developed of the need for "a new spirit of oecumenism," and of inter-ethnic cooperation. "Yugoslavia: Religion and the Tensions of a Multi-national State," *East European Quarterly*, Vol. 6, No. 1 (1972), 135.

[13]"Religija kao oblik tradicionalne svijesti," *Sociologija*, No. 2 (1974), 211-235.

[14]Dragomir Pantić, *Klasična i svetovna religioznost* (Belgrade: Centar za politikološka istraživanja i javno mnenje, 1988), 23-45.

aspect of this new trend although it was reported that the majority of younger people continued to express a non-religious outlook.

As political, ethnic, and socio-economic problems multiplied during the decade after Tito's death in 1980, research indicated growing momentum toward "desecularization" and increasing religiosity. By 1985, for example, surveys of young people throughout Yugoslavia carried out by Srdjan Vrcan, showed a high degree of religious belief. A country-wide study of citizens employed in the social sector, conducted the same year by Dragomir Pantić at the Institute of Social Sciences in Belgrade, indicated that the trend toward enhanced religiosity might actually be stronger among younger people than among the older generation.[15] The end of Tito's personal control and the mushrooming of conflicts concerning the accumulated problems of the one-party regime (e.g., Albanian nationalist demonstrations in Kosovo during 1981, more overt nationalism in the Serbian intelligentsia during 1985-1986, festering dissatisfaction in Croatia with Tito's earlier crack-down of nationalism in that republic), undoubtedly partially accounted for a major shift in public attitudes regarding religion. The rather rapid shift in survey findings on religiosity suggest, however, that earlier conclusions reached about ascendant non-religiosity and atheism may actually have been inaccurate and failed to recognize deeper value configurations in Yugoslav society. As one Yugoslav scholar would later suggest, secularization did not prove to be a very "lasting phenomenon," and earlier findings on non-religious sentiments "may have been dealing with a superficial and ephemeral conformism."[16]

In any case, by the end of the 1980's, an important country-wide survey of young people, *Children of the Crisis*, conducted by the Institute of Social Sciences in Belgrade, revealed that an entirely new and potentially disturbing complex of attitudes was present in Yugoslavia.[17] The religious aspects of the *Children of the Crisis* study are particularly interesting because the data was collected roughly two years prior to the disintegration of the Yugoslav socialist federation when the full-blown appearance of nationalist sentiments and nationalist mobilization was taking place in political life. It was also a period when the religious sentiments of citizens were being overtly encouraged and courted as part of the ethnomobilization strategy of leading politicians in the country such as Serbia's Slobodan Milošević and Croatia's Franjo Tudjman.

---

[15]Srdjan Vrcan, "Omladina osamdesetih godina religija i srkva," 150-168 and Dragomir Pantić, *Klasična i svetovna religioznost*, 36-38.

[16]Sergej Flere, "Denominational Affiliation in Yugoslavia 1931-1987," *East European Quarterly*, Vol. 25, No. 2 (June 1991), 163. See also his "Explaining Ethnic Antagonism in Yugoslavia," *European Sociological Review*, Vol. 7, No. 3 (December 1991), 189, 191.

[17]S. Mihailović *et al.*, *Deca krize* (Belgrade: IDN, 1990).

Milošević had been using his official political position in Belgrade to fan Serbian nationalism since at least 1987 while Tudjman was beginning to openly play the nationalist card as part of his bid for power in Croatia. The growing revitalization of religion that had been occurring over the preceding decade undoubtedly contributed to the ability of such nationalists (and their counter-parts in other ethnic communities and regions of Yugoslavia) to offer programs which resonated with their respective ethnic constituencies.   Once the nationalists had legitimatized their roles in Yugoslavia's republics, discussion of religious values, appeals to traditional religious symbols, and a growth of religious feeling noticeably increased in the country.

In his analysis of the *Children of the Crisis* survey data collected in early 1989, Dragomir Pantić observed that though the absolute majority (57 percent) of young people in Yugoslavia declared themselves to be "irreligious," this figure was considerably reduced compared to twenty years earlier. Together with traditional sources of religiosity, Pantić noted that an erosion of the "ruling self-management ideology" appeared to have stimulated the interest of young people in religion. In ethnically mixed areas of Yugoslavia such as Croatia and Bosnia, religiosity was considered to have "a certain compensatory and nationally defensive function," especially when a small segment of one ethnic group found itself surrounded by a "greater nation."   Among the factors suggested by Pantić for the growth of religiosity in Yugoslavia was the use of religion for "manipulative purposes" by nationalistically oriented politicians.

> The trend toward desecularization among Yugoslavia's younger generation is partially a spontaneous and elemental response to the crisis, but in part it is directed, not only from the circles of religious organizations which are naturally interested and also have worked for such a turn of events, but also from the ranks of leading political forces which obtain the help of religion in order to exercise authority and control over young people by offering them indirectly seemingly absolute, eternal, and tested values.[18]

Interestingly, Pantić found that in Bosnia-Herzegovina, (Table 2) religious belief was most marked among the republic's Croats (53 percent), who were far above the country-wide average (34 percent). Religious belief was precisely on average for the Bosnian Muslims and well below average (21 percent) for the Serbs of Bosnia. For the younger generation of Bosnian Croats at least, the data illustrated that the religious component of the important ethnoreligious symbiosis was predominant. Formulated in another way, nationalist appeals to the young citizens of Bosnia that included a religious component would appear to have the best chance for reception among Bosnian Croats and, in country-

---

[18]Dragomir Pantić, "Prostorne vremenske i socijalne koordinate religiozonsti mladih u Jugoslaviji," 227.

wide relative terms, have an average level of reception among Bosnian Muslims. Meanwhile, Serbs appeared least receptive to the religious facets of nationalism. In fact, Bosnian Serbs showed the lowest level of religiosity when compared to the Serbs of Serbia proper (26 percent), Vojvodina (29 percent), Croatia (26 percent), and the extremely high level of such religious beliefs manifest by Serbs in Kosovo (43 percent).

Survey data for adults in Yugoslavia collected by the Institute of Social Sciences in the spring of 1990, not long after the *Children of the Crisis* study was carried out, revealed that 84 percent of the country's adult citizens expressed a confessional identity or roughly the same amount as reported in 1953 (87 percent).[19] Among the country's republics, the citizens of Bosnia-Herzegovina as a whole registered the highest level of respondents who did *not* declare a confessional orientation (29 percent)--a finding that can undoubtedly be attributed to the large contingent of self-declared "Yugoslavs" in Bosnia who exhibited a high aversion to religious feeling. However, the data also indicated that throughout Yugoslavia those declaring a Catholic and Muslim confessional orientation were far more religious than those of the Serbian Orthodox confession. Thus, Bosnia stands out not only as an area of religious heterogeneity, but also as an area whose population included some of the most fervent believers (particularly younger Croats, who as a group exhibited a very high level of ethnic distance toward other ethnic groups)[20] and also some of the least religious inhabitants of the country (the republic's "Yugoslavs"). Viewed from a different perspective, Bosnia included clusters of citizens who might have served as a bridge of co-existence and inter-ethnic cohesion in socialist Yugoslavia, but also included significant elements of the population exhibiting very militant religious beliefs.

The preceding data also suggests that cultural factors, including but not predominantly the religious facet of identity, were most responsible for the commitment of Bosnian Serbs to nationalism while the religious facets of ethnicity were more prevalent in the nationalist outlook of Bosnian Croats. In the case of the Bosnian Muslims, religion represented a core facet of overall identity, but in relative terms as a group in Bosnia, Muslims exhibited only an average or moderate level of religious commitment.[21] Moreover, other data indicated that just prior to the dissolution of the second Yugoslavia, more

---

[19]*Ibid.*, 252-253.

[20]Dragomir Pantić, "Nacionalna distanca gradjana Jugoslavije," in Ljiljana Bačević, *et al.*, *Jugoslavija na kriznoj prekretnici* (Belgrade: IDN, 1991), 178-179.

[21]For a good discussion of the "gentle" and "unmilitant" character of Islam in Bosnia before 1991, see Andrei Simić, "Where Cultures Meet: The Slav Muslims of Yugoslavia," *The World and I* (September 1990), 639-649.

Bosnian Muslims (88 percent) valued their affinity with that state than either the republic's Serbs (85 percent) or Croats (63 percent).[22] A surge of pan-Islamic nationalism with important religious overtones was taking place in certain quarters of Bosnia's Muslim intelligentsia during the 1980's, but the Muslim population's overall loyalty to the Yugoslav idea remained steadfast. How long the preference of the Bosnian Muslims for the territorial configuration of the second Yugoslavia would last, and in what way the religious dimension of their national identity would influence their political preferences, remained rather unclear at the onset of the 1990's. Unfortunately, the overall findings of the 1990 survey analysis revealed that the "escalation of national conflicts and antagonisms" had reached a high level, and that inter-ethnic relations in the country, and particularly in its most multi-national regions, were "at the edge of national and religious war."[23]

Prelates and Politicians: Evoking the Tribal Gods

Nationalist politicians and some religious leaders bear considerable responsibility for the mobilization of radical nationalist sentiments in Bosnia during the early 1990's. One aspect of the ethnonationalist mobilization that took place in Bosnia involved a direct appeal to religious themes by nationalist leaders who were well aware of the deep historically shaped divisions and latent antagonisms that existed among Bosnia's different confessional communities. Nationalist leaders often proved successful in enlisting the support of religious leaders in their cause while in other instances members of the clergy enthusiastically participated in the formation of nationalist organizations. Overt appeals to religious feelings and divisions in Bosnia and the connection between religious leaders and politicians gained momentum as the fragmentation of the Yugoslav League of Communists as a country-wide organization unfolded at the end of the 1980's.

The Orthodox Church and Serbian National Renaissance

The particular features and consequences of the relationship between religion and nationalist politics in Bosnia during this period naturally differed from one confessional community to another. For example, by the end of the

---

[22]Dragomir Pantić, "Širina grupnih identifikacija gradjana Jugoslavije: Vrednovanje pripadnosti od lokale do mondijalne," in Ljiljana Bačević, *et al.*, *Jugoslavija na kriznoj prekretnici*, 237.

[23]Ljiljana Bačević, "Yugoslavia at a Turning Point in Crisis," in Bačević *et al.*, *op. cit.*, 320.

1980's, the Serbian Orthodox Church (SPC) throughout Yugoslavia had already assumed a quite active role with regard to the Serbian nationalist cause. Although guardianship of Serbian national interests had historically been viewed by the SPC clergy as one of their central tasks in relation to secular matters, Orthodoxy's Byzantine traditions also cast the church in a loyal and subordinate role vis-a-vis state authorities. By the end of the Tito era, however, having endured a long period of manipulation and suppression by the Communist one-party state,[24] the strongly anti-communist SPC began to seek greater influence with respect to the position of Serbs throughout Yugoslav society. The alleged grievances of the Serbian community in Kosovo (with Serbs and Montenegrins constituting roughly 15 percent of that province's population in 1981), as well as the position of Serbs in Croatia (12 percent in 1981) and Bosnia (32 percent), were particularly important to the younger and more militant faction that emerged in the SPC clerical hierarchy.[25]

During the last years of control by SPC Patriarch German--who headed the church from 1958-1990--the younger group of Orthodox leaders represented a sort of "clerical-political underground,"[26] working to enhance the influence of the church in Yugoslav society and also to advance the interests of the Serbian nation. Strongly conservative on religious and political matters, the younger clique of SPC leaders welcomed the nationalist renaissance taking place within Yugoslavia's Serbian community. The SPC and its younger zealots also viewed the growing delegitimization of the self-managing Titoist state and the emergence of a more nationalist course by the Milošević regime in Serbia as opportunities for advancing their various positions. Thus, although naturally suspicious of Milošević--an attitude reciprocated by the rising new Serbian political leader--the Orthodox hierarchs were, nevertheless, very willing to take advantage of the new and more accommodating policies of Serbia's state authorities (e.g., support for the long-awaited completion of the massive Serbian Orthodox Cathedral of St. Sava in Belgrade that had been halted by the Communist regime). Most importantly, the SPC leadership and Milošević shared common ground regarding the grievances of the Serbian diaspora in Kosovo, Croatia, and Bosnia.

---

[24]Radmila Radić, *Verom protiv vere: država i verske zajednice u Srbiji 1945-1953* (Belgrade: Institut za noviju istoriju Srbije, 1995).

[25]Radmila Radić, "Srpska pravoslavna crkva u poratnim i ratnim godinama 1980-1985," *Republika*, Vol. 7, No. 121-122 (August 31, 1995), 1-24. See also Sergej Flere, "Rasprostranjenost i prihvatanje pravoslavlja danas," in *Religija i društvo* (Zagreb: Centar za idejno-teorijski rad GKSKH, 1987), 112-121.

[26]Marinko Čulić, "Pastir svih Srba," *Danas*, No. 386 (July 11, 1989), 25.

Indeed, at the 600th anniversary of the Battle of Kosovo, which took place in June 1989 at the shrine of Gazimestan, Patriarch German, together with the members of the group of his more aggressively nationalistic fellow clerics, joined with Milošević and Serbia's political and cultural elite in an emotional celebration of Serbian history and national feeling. Thus, on the eve of the celebration, Patriarch German commented that "the present changes in the attitude of the Serbian [political] leadership toward the Serbian Church and its people...is the beginning of good cooperation, that will benefit everybody."[27] For his part, Milošević reminded the enormous crowd that six centuries after the Battle of Kosovo, Serbs were again engaged in "battles and facing battles." Indeed, he further observed ominously that although the struggles confronting the Serbs were "not armed battles...such things cannot yet be excluded."

Milošević's incendiary rhetoric was in no way uniformly endorsed by the SPC. The mainstream leadership of the SPC, for example, took a moderate, albeit concerned, position regarding the growth of nationalist militancy in Yugoslavia. Thus, in November 1991, Patriarch Pavle, who succeeded Patriarch German at the end of 1990 (German died in August 1991), suggested that if the nationalities which had formed the Yugoslav state in 1918 decided they must separate, they should do so "as reasonable people, calmly and in agreement with each other."[28] But the Patriarch also expressed his strong support for the idea of Serb solidarity and self-determination, i.e., Milošević's idea that all Serbs should be allowed to live together in a single state if they so wished. To a large extent, SPC support for Serbian national interests was a reaction to developments in Croatia which occurred at the end of the 1980's. The year following the Gazimestan celebration in Kosovo coincided, for example, with the rise of a strong Croatian nationalist movement headed by Franjo Tudjman. After Tudjman achieved electoral victory in Croatia in May 1990, and among other inflammatory nationalist remarks, suggested that Bosnia was naturally in the Croatian sphere of interest, the SPC became more vigorously concerned with the grievances of the diasporic Serbs. Albanian nationalism in Kosovo had concerned the SPC hierarchy since the early 1980's; the new threat was from Croatian nationalism.

For the most nationalistic Orthodox clerics, Tudjman's political movement (the Croatian Democratic Union) represented the rebirth of the World War II ultra-nationalist Ustasha organization that had massacred thousands of Serbs in Croatia and Bosnia-Herzegovina. Such SPC concerns seemed to be confirmed

---

[27]Patriarch German interviewed in Milo Gligorijević, "Kosovo lekcije iz istorije," *NIN*, No. 2008 (Special Supplement), June 25, 1989, 5.

[28]Patriarch Pavle interviewed in Milorad Vučelić (ed.), *Conversations with the Epoch* (Belgrade: Ministry of Information of the Republic of Survey, 1991), 13.

by the Tudjman government's support for the rehabilitation and honoring of Croatian Cardinal Alojzije Stepinac, Croatia's leading cleric at the time of the World War II Ustasha-inspired ethnic cleansing in Croatia and Bosnia (in which more than a few Franciscan and other Catholics clerics had participated).[29] After the war, Stepinac was subjected to a grotesque Communist show trial, and based upon unfounded charges that were designed to discredit the Catholic church, he was jailed for ten years. In fact, Stepinac had never approved of the Ustasha killing, and as time passed, his sympathy for the Ustasha state had declined. But the Croatian cleric had also not openly and directly condemned the Ustasha's activities. In any case, by the 1980's, Stepinac's ordeal at the hands of the Communists had turned him into a nationalist and religious figurehead among Croats. For Serbs and the SPC, however, praise for the Cardinal by Tudjman and the HDZ symbolized a revival of "Serbophobia" and threatened the very existence of the Serbian ethnoreligious community. The Stepinac issue tended to overshadow the fact that the Catholic church hierarchy in Croatia had been positively influenced by the modernizing religious trends of the Second Vatican Council in the mid-1960's, generally expressed moderate perspectives on inter-religious matters, and also resisted establishing a close linkage with Croatia's non-Communist nationalist politicians.

Islam and Electoral Ethnopolitics

Although enthusiastically supported by the Serbian diasporic communities in Yugoslavia, the perspectives advanced by Milošević and the Serbian national-cultural renaissance in the second half of the 1980's, engendered a very negative and reactive nationalist response among the country's other ethnoreligious groups. For example, in 1989, SPC clerics and Serbian leaders from Bosnia (including local Communist officials) held a local celebration of the Battle of Kosovo anniversary. Top Communist officials in Bosnia cautioned that the celebration was the tip of a growing ethnoreligious iceberg that could become a direct threat to inter-ethnic relations in the republic. For example, Nijaz Duraković, a university professor serving as the president of the Central Committee of the League of Communists, denounced what he called a "national-religious euphoria" in the republic and offered a glimpse of what was occurring beneath the seemingly calm surface of Bosnian political life.

> As never before in postwar history a massive politicization and indoctrination is occurring on a religious basis, passions have been revived, divisions, counting of heads, distrust and suspicions stirred up. Likewise a

---

[29]Yeshayahu Jelinek, "Clergy and Fascism: The Hlinka Party in Slovakia and the Croatian Ustasha Movement," in Stein Ugelvik Larson, *et al.* (eds.), *Who Were the Fascists: Social Roots of European Fascism* (Oslo: Universitetforlaget, 1980), 369-372.

reinforcement of such politicization is occurring which advances the thesis that now, more than ever, Muslims throughout Yugoslavia must close ranks, return to the bosom of Islam because once again they are being threatened by Christian repression, and particularly by Serbian and Montenegrin vengeance. Many perceive the celebration of the Battle of Kosovo as an intentional provocation that implies a 'new extermination of the semi-turks,' and the annihilation of everything Islamic, including Muslim culture and heritage. In this context, some Muslim nationalists have overtly joined forces with the Albanian nationalists and have wholeheartedly supported their irredentist claims, and the counter-revolution [in Kosovo].[30]

As relations between the republic's Muslims and Serbs deteriorated, a group of aggressively pan-Islamic oriented clerics in the Bosnian Muslim community stepped up their efforts to ensure that all members of the Islamic faith demonstrated solidarity with the Muslims of Kosovo. For Bosnian Muslims, who shared a common faith with most Albanians (even though the two groups were ethnically distinct), Kosovo was a religious issue. Meanwhile, many Serbs felt, or could be persuaded to feel, that a pan-Islamic coalition was uniting against them. Bosnian Muslim support for the Kosovo Albanians put a serious strain on Serb-Muslim relations in Bosnia and demonstrated the inter-dependence of events taking place in different parts of Yugoslavia.

Inter-ethnic tension among Bosnia's three major religious communities escalated in 1990 as the republic prepared for its first multi-party elections since 1938. The fact that a distinct political party emerged to represent each of Bosnia's principal ethnic communities was itself a politically divisive factor for the republic. Inter-ethnic harmony among Bosnia's three major ethnic groups was further threatened as each ethnopolitical party leadership fostered extremely close links with the religious leaders of its respective community. For example, in the case of the Party of Democratic Action (SDA), formed in the spring of 1990, not only was its membership and leadership overwhelmingly Bosnian Muslim, but many of its top leaders were also directly involved in Islamic religious activities. Thus, the SDA's forty-odd founding members included practically all the major representatives of the pan-Islamic current in the religious structure of the Islamic Community of Bosnia-Herzegovina.[31] Moreover, the head of the SDA, Alija Izetbegović, was a devout Muslim conservative who, if not accurately described as a religious fundamentalist, was definitely perceived by most members of the republic's other ethnoreligious communities as a religious nationalist and a man whose political mindset included devotion to Islamic principles.

---

[30]Xavier Bolgarel, *Le Parti de l"Action Democratique: de la marginalite a l'hegemonie* (Paris: DEAIEP, 1993), 50-51.

[31]*Ibid.*, 59.

Imprisoned in the 1940s for his religious nationalism, and prosecuted again by the Communists in the early 1980s for similar views, Izetbegović was the author of the 1970 *Islamic Declaration, (A Programme for the Islamicisation of Moslems and Moslem Peoples)*, a document which offered a general blueprint for the organization of a state along Islamic lines. The *Islamic Declaration* was interpreted by many foreign observers as a program for an essentially modern, democratic, multicultural state devoted to civic rather than religious values. But for most Serbs and many Croats in Bosnia who believed that Izetbegović had developed a manifesto for political activity based on the precepts of radical pan-Islam, the document was perceived to be extremely threatening. In terms of political analysis, what is most important are not the details of the *Islamic Declaration* itself, but rather Izetbegović's authorship of the manifesto and his leadership of the SDA at a time of rising inter-ethnic tensions in Bosnia. Few people in 1990-1991 had actually read the *Islamic Declaration*, but most non-Muslims in Bosnia were very concerned about the possible political ascendancy of a leader associated with an Islamic blueprint for state organization. Assurances to non-Muslims in Bosnia from both Western observers and some Bosnian Muslims that there was nothing to fear from the electoral victory of the predominantly Muslim SDA, which represented the largest ethnic group in the republic headed by the author of the *Islamic Declaration*, meant very little in the atmosphere of anxiety and tension associated with Yugoslavia's disintegration. One Serbian author has correctly described it:

> Even if by some chance the Serbs and Croats were mistaken when they understood the *Islamic Declaration* as a threatening manifest of Islamic fundamentalism, their hermeneutic principles should have been taken into account. Politically and later militarily, they behaved in accordance with their own, rather than Western convictions, and this fact proved to be decisive in determining the course of events and deterioration of circumstances in Bosnia-Herzegovina.[32]

Moreover, in view of the demographic growth of the Bosnian Muslim population before 1992, many non-Muslims felt insecure, not reassured, when Izetbegović remarked in one of his speeches during the early 1990's that "for the time being," the establishment of an Islamic republic was out of the question for Bosnia because the Muslims of the republic were not an absolute majority.[33]

In contrast to the vast majority of citizens in the Bosnian Muslim community who were highly secularized and devoted to Yugoslavia's unity prior

---

[32]Darko Tanasković, "Why Is Islamic Radicalization in the Balkans Being Covered Up?" *Eurobalkans*, No. 15 (Summer 1994), 35.

[33]Esad Ćimić has suggested that from such remarks it "isn't difficult to conclude," that the creation of "some kind of Islamic, Muslim state . . . is not rejected but simply postponed." "Okrugli stol-'Što je vjerski rat'," in Ivan Grubišić (ed.), *Konfesije i rat*, 294.

to 1991, Izetbegović and the leadership of the SDA had a different vision of Bosnia's future. The SDA's initial political platform was not an exact replica of the program advanced in the 1970 *Islamic Declaration*, but neither was it incompatible with the Muslim manifesto.[34] Given the well-known pan-Islamic views of the SDA elite, it was not entirely irrational for members of Bosnia's non-Muslim ethnoreligious communities to perceive the new Bosnian Muslim party in a negative light. Anxious non-Muslim citizens of the republic did not stop to either consider or feel reassured by the fact that the majority of Muslim voters who supported the SDA in the 1990 election were less religiously or ideologically fervent than the leadership nucleus of their preferred party. From May 1990 to April 1992, the SDA gradually evolved into a broadly based national Muslim political movement, and the party also cultivated a more moderate and pluralistic image. But the existence of a religiously oriented pan-Islamic core group in the SDA's founding leadership--who continued to exercise considerable influence in Bosnia's predominantly Muslim government throughout the first half of the 1990's--provided a convenient target for militant Serb and Croat nationalists, and also allowed them to persistently exaggerate the religiously fundamentalist character of the Bosnian Muslim community.

As the SDA became more directly involved in governing Bosnia, differences of opinion emerged between the more secular and the more religiously inclined members of the Bosnian elite concerning Islam's relationship to political life (e.g., the "politicization of Islam" or the "Islamicization of politics"). Indeed, in December 1991, SDA chief Izetbegović commented that "we are not a religious party but a political [party]."[35] However, many of Izetbegović's public statements about such distinctions had in previous years appeared to be rather vague. For example, when asked by Sarajevo's leading newspaper in September 1990, whether the SDA was a lay party or a religious movement, Izetbegović responded, "neither the one, nor the other...it is a Muslim party, which resembles the nation from which it recruits its partisans. It is a religious nation. In its scale of values, faith represents the summit. It is impossible for these features not to leave their mark on the general atmosphere which prevails at SDA rallies."[36] In fact, during its first years of existence, the SDA appeared to be a party preeminently based upon the ideology of religious nationalism, and it was difficult to determine which component, the religious or the nationalistic, would predominate in its subsequent policies and impact. For most non-Muslims, such debates and distinctions were highly academic,

---

[34]Xavier Bolgarel, *op. cit.*, 62.

[35]*Ibid.*, 67.

[36]*Ibid.*, 68.

particularly as the lines of division among the ethnoreligious communities in the republic sharpened, and eventually became military fronts rather than merely psychological barriers. The frequent observation by Western commentators that Bosnian Muslims have had a traditionally secular and European outlook and have tended to "wear their faith lightly" is essentially correct.[37] But those outside Bosnia often failed to recognize that, owing to the attitudes advanced by most nationalist and many religious leaders within the Muslim community during the 1980's and 1990's, and also in view of the modern history of Bosnia, most non-Muslims did not take the political aspirations of the Islamic faithful quite so lightly.

The influence of religion on growing ethnic conflict in Bosnia is also illustrated by the activities of the two other ethnically based parties which contested the fall 1990 elections. In both cases--the Serbian Democratic Party (SDS) and the Croatian Democratic Union (HDZ)--nationalist politicians attempted to use the established church of their respective ethnic communities as a means of garnering support and legitimacy. Bosnian Serb leaders were politically mobilizing and appealing to a population in which religious belief *per se* was far less salient than a general ethnocultural form of identity. Nevertheless, the Orthodox church enjoyed tremendous respect among the Bosnian Serbs as a cultural institution that had historically labored for the protection and preservation of Serbian interests and that also served as a major link among Serbian communities throughout Yugoslavia. Moreover, by 1990, most SDS leaders, including its head, Radovan Karadžić, were non-Communist or anti-Communist in outlook. Although dependent on support from the powerful Belgrade-based national Communist leader, Slobodan Milošević, the Bosnian Serb political elite was also fundamentally suspicious of the Serbian president. Thus, by associating themselves with the Serbian Orthodox church, Bosnian Serb leaders saw a way to enhance their position as political-cultural representatives of their people while also gaining a certain amount of leverage in dealing with Milošcvić. This posture was reciprocated by the Serbian Orthodox hierarchy, and especially its more militant nationalist and non-Communist faction, who viewed Milošević as a necessary evil and who regarded vigorous backing for the Serbian diaspora as a core facet of their clerical-political mission. During the second half of the 1980's and early half of the 1990's, the Orthodox church, as onc Serbian author has observed

> fostered national continuity, a cult of the national and religious grandeur, and
> also national history, national literature and traditional customs and

---

[37]A Bosnian Muslim view of "Bosnian Islam" cited approvingly by Fouad Ajami in Elaine Sciolino, "What's Iran Doing in Bosnia Anyway?" *New York Times*, December 10, 1995, Section 4, 4.

values....It rejected every reproach concerning the politicization of the church, but early on part of the clergy and bishopric, together with part of the intelligentsia, set in motion the problems and offered solutions to the Serbian national question, the organization of the state, the position of the church in the state, relations toward the West and the East, etc. In that way an ideology was formed which deepened the crisis and opened new fronts....The fact is that the political actors would not have been able to carry out their successful homogenization of the Serbian ethnos, were it not for the support of the church.[38]

Catholicism: Dinaric Men Versus A Universal Deity

The relationship between the Roman Catholic church and the principal political party of the Bosnian Croats, the Croatian Democratic Union (HDZ)--in essence a branch of President Franjo Tudjman's Croat-based HDZ that had come to power in 1990--was also one of close cooperation. For the religiously fervent Bosnian Croat community, faith and Croat nationalism were inextricably linked. Thus, Tudjman's success in developing a nationalist platform aimed at breaking with the Communist past, reconciling Croats of differing political viewpoints and past experience, and urging a return to Christian values, was greeted very approvingly by the Bosnian Croat community. As noted above, the traditional religiosity of Bosnian Croats had persisted and stood out in relative contrast with other confessional groups during the years when the process of secularization in Yugoslavia was most pronounced. However, Bosnian Catholic religious commitment received additional stimulus in June 1981, after youngsters praying in the town of Medjugorje, located in western Herzegovina near the Bosnia-Croatia border, claimed to have seen an apparition of the Virgin Mary. The claim by the children and others of subsequent daily appearances of the Virgin turned Medjugorje into a Roman Catholic shrine which, by the early 1990's, had been visited by millions of pilgrims from all over the world.[39]

Support for the Medjugorje phenomenon was particularly strong among the members of the Franciscan order in Bosnia, an organization which by 1992, had been active in Bosnia-Herzegovina for some 700 years and had long played a prominent role in ministering to Bosnia's Catholic inhabitants. Operation of

---

[38]Radić, "Srpska pravoslavna crkva u poratnim i ratnim godinama 1980-1985," 24.

[39]Gerald E. Markle and Frances B. McCrea, "Medjugorje and the Crisis in Yugoslavia," in William Swatos Jr. (ed.), *Politics and Religion in Central and Eastern Europe* (Westport: Praeger, 1994), 197-208. The Croatian-American sociologist, Stjepan Meštrović, has argued that the central message of Medjugorje is peace, an expression of Croatian culture that is "still Gothic" and non-expansionist. He claims that any Croatian brutality committed following Yugoslavia's disintegration in 1991 is simply reactive nationalism to Serbia's "expansionist 'civilization'." *Habits of the Balkan Heart* (College Station: Texas A&M University Press, 1993), 128-129.

the church at Medjugorje, and most other Catholic churches in Bosnia, is the responsibility of the Franciscans. Preaching a message of "evangelical poverty," the Franciscans of Bosnia have had serious differences over church doctrine and resources with the more secular Catholic hierarchy of both Bosnia and Croatia. Thus, while some members of the non-Franciscan church hierarchy endorsed the authenticity of the Medjugorje phenomenon, others were more skeptical. The contrast between the reserved approach of the Catholic hierarchy and the emotional populism of the Franciscans was also apparent in their different perspectives toward the aggressive Croatian political nationalism advanced by the Bosnian branch of the HDZ. Thus, while the Roman Catholic hierarchy in Zagreb exhibited a generally sympathetic, but arms-length posture toward Tudjman's HDZ--as a secular organization promoting the interests of Croatia and Croatians--many of the local prelates in Bosnia, and the Franciscans in particular, became more directly engaged in the surge of Croatian ethnoreligious nationalism in their midst.

Indeed in Bosnia, emotional conviction regarding the events at Medjugorje stimulated support for Croatian nationalism and reinforced what has been termed "a militant Marian ideology united with conservative political forces."[40] The Bosnian Serbs' SDS leaders had quickly realized the political advantages of maintaining closer ties with the SPC, even though most Bosnian Serbs were only nominally religious. However, the HDZ Croat leaders of Bosnia were appealing to a community that was deeply imbued with traditional religious sentiments. But if the HDZ leadership in Bosnia benefitted from the religiosity of its constituency and the nationalist enthusiasm of the Franciscan order, they also had to routinely contend with a chain of religious command centered outside Bosnia and, indeed, outside the Balkans. Thus, while many Bosnian Catholic clerics enthusiastically supported Croatian nationalist ideology and nationalist ideologues in their republic, a less locally colored and pragmatic perspective was advanced by the Catholic hierarchy in both Zagreb and Rome.

For its part, the Catholic hierarchy in Zagreb was pleased with the defeat of Communism in Croatia and also with the victory of the center-right and pro-Christian HDZ, but the church also wished to preserve its hard-won autonomy. As Zagreb's Cardinal Kuharić pointed out at the end of 1990, "the Church will guard its autonomy, and respect the autonomy of [state] authority in its area. Ceaseropapism can no longer be respected. However that doesn't mean that the Church can't engage in specific, primarily spiritual moral areas of societal life, and also in this regard adopt a critical attitude toward public authority where it

---

[40]S. Zimdars-Swartz, *Encountering Mary* (Princeton: Princeton University Press, 1991), p. 19, cited in *ibid.*, 203.

is necessary."[41] Kuharić's views illustrated the intention of the Roman Catholic hierarchy not to become the captive of any political party or political viewpoint. It also revealed a strong contrast with the traditional views of the Serbian Orthodox hierarchy in the Balkans. Thus, most leaders of the Serbian Orthodox church, who belonged to a "national" rather than a "universalistic" clerical institution, traditionally exhibited enthusiastic support for the political leaders of the Serbian people (although many Orthodox prelates favored maintaining a healthy distance from non-religious or anti-religious state authorities). Concerned with its own autonomy as part of a "universalist" church (whose international policies were coordinated by the Vatican), the Roman Catholic hierarchy in Croatia took a reserved stance toward the militant nationalism exhibited by the Catholic clergy and Croatian flock in Bosnia.

One of the leading spokesman for the Zagreb Catholic establishment provided an interesting insight into the internal divisions within Croatian Catholicism when asked about the problems between the republic's Roman Catholic hierarchy and the aggressive religious and political Bosnian Croat nationalists. In brief, he was asked, were Bosnia's Catholics more attracted to a "tribal god" than to a universal Christian deity?

> It isn't only the [Catholic] Hercegovinians. The whole dinaric region still has a very strong all pervasive tribal mentality....I am thinking of the part of our national development that is closer to the tribal than the national state end of the spectrum. In terms of the overall well-being of Croatians, these people are very devoted, you can always count on them, but you can't be sure that their opinions will succeed in contemporary political conditions. They are prepared to lose everything. Sometimes I'm afraid that they are proudest to die in order to take pride in a victory. I've even known them to say from the church altar: 'I'm sick of Croatian martyrs, heaven is full of them. Show me winners!'...Through the domination of such a mentality the Christian God degenerates into various tribal gods.[42]

War and the Political Role of Religion

Prior to the outbreak of hostilities in Bosnia, aspects of revitalized religiosity and the nationalist views advanced by many religious leaders had provided fertile soil for ethnopolitical mobilization. That mobilization, in turn, stimulated the overall desecularization that had been occurring for some years.

---

[41]Kuharić interviewed by Marinko Čulić, "Nismo u naručju vlasti," *Danas*, No. 461 (December 18, 1990), 22.

[42]Živko Kustić interviewed by Davor Butković, "Iz komunističke tiranije upali smo u još stariji tip primitivizma!" *Globus*, No. 140 (August 13, 1993), 32.

Once the war was underway, nationalist politicians, most of whom had first made their public appearances in the 1990 elections, were under increased pressure to utilize religion as an instrument for generating elan and political support. As for the soldiers on the front line, the simplistic religious symbolism touted by their nationalist leaders and some clergymen often served to provide a rationale for the ongoing violence and the complete break-down of inter-ethnic rapport: "This is a holy war," said one Serb conscript. "I'm an atheist but the important thing is that I'm not a Muslim....The world needs to open its eyes to our struggle--we are fighting Europe's battles."[43] A Croatian soldier visiting Medjugorje connected the war's origins with the failure of religious devotion: "We have not done what the Virgin Mary asked....She asked for conversion [to Catholicism] so that peace would come. We haven't converted the non-believers and so we have war."[44] For the battling troops, religious symbols offered a framework of belief or psychological comfort. But as the war dragged on, and as conflicts arose within each nationalist camp over strategy and tactics--as well as over responsibility for set-backs, failed alliances, and other mistakes--the interface between religion and nationalism acquired many forms.

Catholic-Muslim Schism: The Religious Dimension

The case of the Roman Catholic church and Croatian nationalist politicians in Bosnia is a case in point. Initially during the war, Croats and Moslems worked closely together to resist the ferocious onslaught by Serbian forces who were backed by both remnants of the Yugoslav People's Army and various Serbia-based paramilitary groups that crossed into Bosnian territory. The historically conditioned tendency of many Bosnian Croats to view the Muslims as Islamicized Croats who could not be fully trusted, or as junior partners at best, led to a certain tension in the Muslim-Croat alliance from the very outset. Negative Croatian attitudes toward Bosnian Muslims were particularly prevalent in the political leadership of Herceg-Bosna, the semi-autonomous Croatian political entity established in June 1992 and led by Mate Boban. Boban and other leaders of the Bosnian HDZ were closely linked by origin and outlook to several leading members of the Tudjman HDZ government in Zagreb, often referred to as the "Herzegovinian lobby."

The most prominent member of that lobby was Croatian Minister of Defense, Gojko Šušak, who had lived in Canada for many years and was also linked to members of the large Croatian diaspora around the world. Boban and Šušak, as well as Tudjman himself, tended to see the Bosnian Croat community

---

[43]*Globe and Mail*, December 9, 1995, A11.
[44]*San Francisco Chronicle*, August 11, 1995, A1.

and its territory, as well as the Muslims of Bosnia, as part of the traditional Croatian sphere of influence, or what some considered to be "Greater Croatia." For example, in mid-1992, Boban observed that he had strong reservations about the Muslims' claim that they were a constituent nation in Bosnia and also their ability to defend the Bosnian state. "I'm not supposed to say this," Boban confessed to one interviewer, "and I'm neglecting their rights, but a lot of Moslems think they will get a state by praying for it...they always take sides too late." "Personally," he added, "I see no future in basing a nationality on faith."[45] Such perspectives on Bosnia and Bosnian Muslims were opposed by many other Croat leaders and citizens, who believed that Tudjman had harmed Croatia's moral and political position by allegedly making a secret deal with Milošević to partition Bosnia between Croatia and Serbia. Opponents of such a carve-up scheme believed that it was essential to preserve the Croat-Muslim alliance, and the unity of Bosnia, if there was any hope that Zagreb would obtain international support for the recovery of Croatia's Krajina region that had been lost to Serbian rebels in 1991-1992.

During early 1993, the ongoing friction between the predominantly Muslim Bosnian government and the Croatian leadership in Bosnia led to a breakdown of the Muslim-Croat alliance and fierce fighting between the two former allies (including the murder of a number of Franciscan priests by Muslims and the massacre of Muslim villages by Croats).[46] The conflict was precipitated to a great extent by the effort of Croat forces in Bosnia to extend the territory under their control following the Serbian rejection of the Vance-Owen peace plan. The Muslim leadership of Bosnia blamed the rupture on the "Greater Croatia" mentality prevailing among the Croatian leadership of Herceg-Bosna and particularly on President Tudjman's imitation of the ethnic cleansing

---

[45]*Globe and Mail*, July 27, 1992, A1.

[46]The war in Bosnia led to wide-spread destruction of churches, church property, and even the murder of clergymen by extreme elements of all the warring sides. Most acts of church destruction were carried out as part of an effort to establish ethnically pure zones of control, particularly by Serbian and Croatian forces. Claims about the nature and magnitude of such activity became a regular component of the heated propaganda battle during the conflict. While such destruction and atrocities obviously illustrate a religious aspect or by-product of the warfare in Bosnia, it is extremely difficult to comprehensively evaluate the complex of motives and circumstances that account for numerous particular cases. Not surprisingly, the various antagonists often make claims that their side's particular religious beliefs account for a higher level of ethical conduct in the fighting. For a Croatian presentation of this position with regard to Croat-Serb fighting in Croatia, see Miroslav Vujević, "Utjecaj vjerskih normi na ponašanje u hrvatskom domovinskom ratu," *Politička misao*, Vol. 131, No. 4 (1994), 147-153.

tactics earlier employed by the Serbian side.   Once again, the religious dimension of the Bosnian conflict, although by no means the prime cause of hostilities, assumed heightened importance.   Thus, Croat leaders attributed the new ethnopolitical schism to radical Muslim fundamentalists and the efforts of Muslim politicians to create a "unitary civil state" without due regard for Croatian interests.   As one Croat observer commented in April 1993, "the Muslims hold the real power in all sectors--state administration, diplomacy, economics, social activities, television, etc....This has created the psychology that the Muslims have an exclusive right in Bosnia-Herzegovina....Unfortunately, the Muslims find it difficult to accept the fact, especially in the conditions of this war that Bosnia-Herzegovina can only exist as a community of three constituent peoples."[47]   Monsignor Vinko Puljić, the Catholic Archbishop of Sarajevo, expressed concern that, in central Bosnia, Catholic priests "live under house arrest and the faithful are afraid to go to church." He added that "if Bosnia goes down the road to become a Muslim state I fear the tendency toward theocracy. For Muslims religion and state are bound closer than they are for us."[48]

Concern over the escalation of Croat-Muslim fighting prompted Zagreb's Cardinal Kuharić to assert a more public role on Bosnian affairs.[49]   He did so by reiterating the Vatican's support for a united Bosnian state and indirectly criticizing the essentially anti-Muslim policies being pursued by President Tudjman and the Bosnian Croat leadership.   During the summer of 1993, in an only slightly veiled attack on Mate Boban and the radical Bosnian Croats, Kuharić condemned the atrocities committed by Croats in Bosnia and suggested that the reputation of Croatia and all Croats would be harmed by such activities. Boban reacted sharply to Kuharić's intervention, accusing the church leadership of meddling in affairs that were not its concern.   Spokesmen for Kuharić suggested that Boban's counter-attack was actually prepared by Herzegovinian Catholic clerics who were pursuing their own differences with the Catholic hierarchy in Zagreb.

Kuharić's condemnation had prudently been directed at the radical Bosnian Croats rather than at President Tudjman personally.   However,

---

[47]Martin Udovičić, "Hrvatska Travnička Zajednica-Travnička Provincija," in Marko Karamatić (ed.), *Rat u Bosni i Hercegovini: uzroci, posljednice, perspeketive* (Zagreb: Franjevačka teologija, Sarajevo, 1993), 80.

[48]*Independent,* October 5, 1993, 3.

[49]Cardinal Kuharić had earlier stated his views on the nature of the war in Bosnia: "One needs to clearly realize that the [Roman Catholic] Church didn't proclaim the war in the Church and that this war has completely other motives, absolutely political, that these are aggressive pretensions, and that people who are simply not open to advice from any religious community have their goal, they wish war, a war of exclusivist nationalistic policy. What can the churches do now?" *Novi danas,* August 31, 1992, 17.

upholding Vatican policy, Kuharić rejected the division of Bosnia-Herzegovina through the use of force. The Cardinal's concerns appeared well-founded when bitter Muslim-Croat fighting escalated during the second half of 1993 and the tide turned against the Croatian side. This debacle led to extensive Croat civilian casualties and the displacement of thousands of Croats from their homes in central Bosnia. Faced with defeat in Bosnia, the threat of international sanctions for having committed so many Croatian troops to the Bosnian front and strong carrot-and-stick incentives from the United States, Tudjman decided to change course. Less than six months after the Kuharić-Boban affair, Tudjman reversed his policy on Bosnia, renewed the Muslim-Croat alliance, and sacked Mate Boban from his leadership role in Bosnia (he was given a plum job in a leading Croatian petrochemical firm). The attitude of the Catholic church hierarchy on Bosnian matters had not been the decisive of Tudjman's *volte-face*, but undoubtedly had been a significant factor influencing his views.[50]

War and the Growth of Islamic Consciousness

The enormous pressures and trauma caused by the war and suffering in Bosnia also had a major impact on the role of religion in Bosnian Muslim affairs. Thus, the imperatives of self-defense vis-a-vis the Bosnian Serb onslaught as well as fighting with their former Croat allies stimulated forms of radical religious consciousness and behavior that were quite unusual for the traditionally secular and moderate Muslim population. Under assault and siege from their ethnoreligious neighbors, and feeling abandoned by the international community--except for the Islamic world--many Muslim military, political, and religious leaders encouraged greater reliance on the spiritual aspects of their community's heritage as a means of developing solidarity and raising moral. This approach was reflected in the introduction of religious teaching in the school system and also religious indoctrination in the military.

For example, the Black Swans, a 600-man elite unit of the Bosnian army, garrisoned in the mountains near Sarajevo, adopted Islamic law as its code of conduct, including daily prayer and religious training by Islamic chaplains (two hours a day); no alcohol or contact with women; and exemplary personal hygiene. Similar procedures were also introduced into other units of the Bosnian armed forces. By early 1995, Bosnian television carried images of a celebration of the 3,000-man Seventh Muslim Brigade with soldiers wearing bright green headbands and chanting Islamic slogans. Public airing of the religious indoctrination that had, in fact, been underway in the armed forces for

---

[50]In January 1994, Kuharić had issued a more direct criticism of Tudjman's policies in Bosnia, and also called for better relations among all nationalities. *British Broadcasting Corporation Shortwave Broadcast/EE/1903/C*, January 24, 1994.

some time, created a political firestorm in the Bosnian government. Five members of the multi-ethnic seven-person Bosnian presidency--four Croats and a Serb--jointly wrote to President Izetbegović objecting to such a clear departure from the multi-religious ethos often proclaimed by the Bosnian government. The five presidency members claimed that the Bosnian military was undergoing a process of "ideologization and the negative instrumentalization of religion."[51] Members of Bosnian opposition parties attributed this development to efforts by the ruling SDA to control the military machine as part of a drift toward totalitarianism. Critics claimed that the trend toward the fashioning of an Islamic state also represented a victory for the views of long-time Muslim nationalists and fundamentalists who had benefited from the fact that during the war Bosnian Muslims had had their "backs against the wall" and were now compelled to turn to religious values.

The Serbian members of the multi-ethnic presidency acknowledged that the Islamic community had endured the most suffering during the war, but decried a "trend toward exclusiveness." Izetbegović brusquely rejected such complaints: "Those that want to talk about the ideology of the Bosnian army should first count the graves,"[52] he retorted, alluding to the fact that Muslims had suffered the greatest casualties in defending the Bosnian state." Izetbegović had the enthusiastic backing of the Army of Bosnia-Herzegovina, an organization with a 90 percent plus Muslim majority, whose non-Muslim officers had essentially been marginalized. For example, Bosnian army chief-of-staff, Rasim Delić, observed that during the war Muslims had been seeking "their roots in religion. They find additional motives for their struggle in their religious commitments. And it is very important to us that a man be motivated in that way to take part in the defense of Bosnia-Herzegovina."[53]

Wartime efforts by radical clerics such as Mustafa Cerić, the powerful Imam of Sarajevo and head *(reis ul-ulema)* of the Islamic Community in Bosnia-Herzegovina, to advance Islamic religious beliefs and practices and to limit the rights of non-Muslims (promoting a ban on such things as playing "Serbian" music on the radio, the sale of pork, mixed marriages, etc.) offended many non-Muslims and secular Muslims in Bosnia. Members of the Bosnian political elite were divided over the question of an Islamic religious revival, but the war clearly tilted the Bosnian Muslim community in a more religiously nationalistic direction. For example, during mid-1995, President Izetbegović demanded and

---

[51] Foreign Broadcast Information Service-Eastern Europe-95-032 [hereinafter FBIS-EEU], February 16, 1995, 29-30.

[52] Paul Hockenos, "Shreds Remain of Multicultural Bosnia," *National Catholic Reporter*, Vol. 31, No. 20 (March 17, 1995), 8.

[53] *FBIS-EEU-95-071*, April 13, 1995, 30.

obtained a temporary amendment to the Bosnian constitution, guaranteeing a Muslim successor in the event of his death during wartime. The move sparked a political battle with Prime Minister Haris Silajdžić, who regarded the president's action as a violation of the Bosnian government's multi-ethnic image and who threatened to resign. Izetbegović persuaded Silajdžić to stay, but the reality of ethnoreligious criteria in elite recruitment was becoming more routine in Bosnian society. "You have to be (a) a Muslim and (b) a member of the SDA to be a director of a company these days," observed the head of one of Sarajevo's independent radio stations in September 1995.[54] Many secularly oriented members of the government and intelligentsia were resisting the trend toward creating an exclusively Muslim state, but at the time of the signing of the Dayton accord in the fall of 1995, it was unclear whether Bosnia would be able to establish genuine religious pluralism.

The SPC and Intra-Serb Politics: Dayton as a Defeat

War-related pressures on the Serbian side of the Bosnian triangle also heightened the impact of religious factors on nationalist politics. As previously mentioned, prior to the break-up of socialist Yugoslavia in 1991, the SPC exhibited strong support for the national interests of the Serbian communities in Croatia and Bosnia and also maintained a tolerable working relationship with the nationalistically oriented Milošević regime. But, though Orthodox church leaders were pleased by various accommodations to the SPC proffered by Milošević, they were fundamentally hostile to the socialist orientation of his regime. After witnessing the bitter warfare in Croatia during the second half of 1991, the onset of the war in Bosnia during the spring of 1992, and the imposition of painful international sanctions against rump Yugoslavia (Serbia-Montenegro), the SPC decided to adopt a more critical stance toward Milošević. Thus in May-June 1992, the Orthodox leadership publicly attacked Milošević's policies and demanded that he relinquish his leadership. Patriarch Pavle accused Serbia's leaders of "closing their eyes to crimes," an illusion to atrocities committed by Serbian paramilitary forces in Bosnia.[55] Joining with members of the opposition parties, and the anti-Milošević segments of the middle-class and intelligentsia, some SPC leaders hoped to unseat Milošević and find a more internationally acceptable and moderate non-Communist leader to advance Serbian interests (such as Prince Alexandar Karadjordjević, who visited in Belgrade in June 1992). The church's efforts at displacing Milošević proved

---

[54]*Boston Globe*, September 22, 1995, 1.

[55]*Independent*, June 15, 1992, 9.

fruitless, and the Serbian leader went on to handily triumph in the fall 1992 Serbian election.

While most Orthodox religious leaders were rather distrustful or skeptical about Milošević and his policies, the younger and more militant faction of SPC theologians also believed that official state support for the interests of the Serbs across the Drina in Bosnia was essential and, indeed, should be intensified. For example, during Christmas 1992, the highly nationalistic and controversial Bishop Amfilohije Radović, the Metropolitan of Montenegro, met with and allegedly blessed the notorious Željko Ražnatović (Arkan), the Serbian paramilitary chief whose forces had taken part in attacks on Muslim civilians in Bosnia during April 1992. In any event, failing at their effort to influence the distribution of power in Serbia during 1992, SPC leaders turned their attention to assisting the struggle of the diasporic Serbs. Indeed, over the next three years, the SPC, particularly its most militant clerics, would maintain close and supportive ties to Bosnian Serb president Radovan Karadžić and the leadership of the Republika Srpska headquartered at Pale.

The SPC was particularly sympathetic to the non-Communist orientation of the Bosnian Serb regime and also its willingness to support traditional church goals. In the Republika Srpska, for example, the national anthem is entitled "God of Justice," religious instruction in the schools is mandatory, the history of the World War II Chetnik movement is treated respectfully, there is strong support for the Serbian monarchy, and the church hierarchy enjoys high esteem.[56] The partial political benefits for the Bosnian Serb leadership in maintaining such a pro Orthodox posture became evident during 1994 and 1995 when Slobodan Milošević decided to throw his full support behind the international community's Contact Group peace plan for Bosnia and, more importantly, to severely restrict his previous tangible backing for the Karadžić regime and the Bosnian Serb army. Friction between Karadžić and Milošević had been evident for years (e.g., a last minute decision by the Pale Serbs not to support the Vance-Owen plan in 1993 had greatly embarrassed Milošević), but in taking stiff measures to isolate the Bosnian Serbs in 1994 and 1995, the Belgrade regime precipitated a major intra-Serb conflict.

Disturbed by the break-down in Serbian solidarity at a time when the international image of the Serbian ethnic community was already at an all-time low, Orthodox church leaders attempted to repair the Milošević-Karadžić rupture. The isolated Karadžić, who has described himself as the defender of

---

[56]*FBIS-EEU-94-178*, September 14, 1994, 57.

the Serb "tribe and our church,"[57] was effusive in his gratitude for the SPC's mediation effort.

> We think the Serbian Orthodox Church is the most important connecting tissue that has preserved the unity of the Serbian people through centuries....It is an honor for us that they are with us, that they assess the steps we take and support us...I have profited very much from my firm connections with the church. I have heard many useful pieces of advice and received support for my decisions....Only those who are intolerant and are not interested in the opinion of the whole nation can fear the church.[58]

Once again, as in its effort to support opposition elements in Serbia during 1992, the SPC hierarchy failed to have any appreciable impact on Milošević. In August 1995, after facing Croatian and Bosnian Muslim military successes, as well as intense NATO bombing, Karadžić and the Bosnian Serb leadership were pressed to sign over authority for diplomatic negotiations on Bosnia to Milošević.[59] In order to impress the international community with the contractual sanctity of his special status regarding Bosnia, Milošević asked SPC Patriarch Pavle to sign the authorization given by the Bosnian Serbs.

Having manipulated Bosnian Serb interests for a half decade to serve his own political purposes, Milošević proceeded to trade away the major interests of the Pale leadership during the Dayton peace negotiations in return for the lifting of sanctions on Serbia proper. At a holy synod of the SPC held on December 22, 1995, militant Orthodox bishops condemned the Dayton agreement and declared that the church's earlier endorsement of the authorization for Milošević to represent the Bosnian Serbs at the peace conference was null and void.[60] The synod also argued that President Milošević had "taken advantage" of Patriarch Pavle and that the church leader should resign for not having opposed an "unjust" peace. However, after years of having cooperated with the pursuit of Serbian nationalist goals, the Serbian religious elite found itself politically marginalized. Devoted to preserving his power at almost any price, Milošević was unmoved by the plight of the Bosnian Serbs he had once encouraged and even less willing to accommodate the demands of a Serbian Orthodox hierarchy that had called for his removal and derided his rule of a

---

[57]Karadžić interview in *Svetigora* as reported by Paul Mojzes, "Confessions of a Serb Leader," *The Christian Century*, August 16, 1995.

[58]*FBIS-EEU-95-009*, January 13, 1995, 43.

[59]On August 7, 1995, after Croatian troops recaptured the Krajina area, Patriarch Pavle and the Holy Synod of Bishops of the Serbian Orthodox Church condemned the Milošević regime: "With its power-hungry actions and self-serving attitude, this same leadership trampled on all promises and guarantees it gave to the Serbian Krajina, and led the nation into a blind alley."

[60]*Agence France Press*, December 23, 1995.

"godless regime." Even more than his counterparts in the political leadership of Zagreb and Sarajevo, who also took an inscrutably pragmatic approach regarding the role of religion in nationalist politics, Milošević was exclusively focused on the imperatives of temporal power. For the immediate future, at least, it appeared that a phalanx of NATO generals would have precedence over Bosnia's tribal gods.

5

THE CAMOUFLAGED ROLE OF RELIGION IN THE WAR IN BOSNIA AND HERZEGOVINA

Paul Mojzes

It continues to be puzzling that very few authors in the many articles and books that have now been written about the war in Bosnia prior to this volume deal seriously with religion in connection with the war except to note that the once multireligious communities have generally become homogeneous after ethnic cleansing. Entire issues of independent periodicals such as *War Report, Erasmus* and others fail to deal with religion. A partial explanation for that omission is that many of the journalists and scholars who are doing the analysis do not have interest in religion nor do they have a fine-tuned nose for it. Those who do mention religion generally deny that religion has a significant role to play, often thinking that when one mentions the word "role" that it has to mean a war-supporting or advocating option, and this they wish to deny. Some do not see that to deny that religion played any role in the war is in itself a damning indictment of religion, because religion should be playing a role in the lives of at least its own members, and also war is certainly not a minor event in people's lives. Thus, unless religion were to be involved in reconciling the warring parties--which might be judged as a positive role for religion to play--all other options would potentially be negative, even if they consisted of passivity. My contention is that while religion did not play a primary or overt role in the war in Bosnia, it nevertheless made a substantive, though camouflaged, impact. If this thesis has merit, it may diminish the puzzlement over the seeming inattention to the role of religion by many scholars and journalists who have been analyzing this war.

One person who had a chance to view the war from proximity was Tadeusz Mazowiecki, who served as the UN Human Rights rapporteur in the Balkans. Mazowiecki was a prominent Roman Catholic layman, editor of an influential Catholic periodical *Wiez*, and a dissident intellectual who was invited to become the first post-Communist Premier of Poland in August 1989. He had excellent credentials to assess the role of religion. He stated that his reports to the UN demonstrated that the war in B&H was not a religious war, "[b]ut the religious differences have played a part as elements of national identity, and have been frequently exploited from within or attacked from the outside."[1] Mazowiecki saw the churches as blocking efforts for interfaith cooperation and specified that the Serbian Orthodox, for instance, were successful in convincing their people that they were victims of a Catholic and Islamic anti-Serbian conspiracy. He noted that the leaders of the Serbian Orthodox Church (hereafter SOC) cooperated closely and supported the national extremist Radovan Karadžić more than Slobodan Milošević. He also pointed out that while some of the top Roman Catholic clergy behaved responsibly, a number of priests, especially in Herzegovina, behaved nationalistically and kept stressing only the damage done to the Croats but overlooked entirely the malevolent behavior of Croats in their conflict with the Muslims. While Mazowiecki disagreed with the Muslim claim that the international community was slow to intervene on their behalf on account of their religion, he did acknowledge that this perception among Muslims was increasingly affecting their perception that "Christian" Europe treats them differently than other Europeans.[2]

It is not necessary to agree with every detail of Mazowiecki's conclusions, but he surely testifies that religion **is** playing a role in aggravating the conflict. In this chapter, I will attempt to demonstrate that religion played an integral role even more destructively than Mazowiecki observed. The negative role of religion was implicit, yet structural and deliberate.

To begin, one needs to look at the nature of religion in the Balkans, which is a definitional issue. Anyone who knows the field of the study of religion realizes the obstacles which exist in defining religion, and, therefore, it should not be surprising that unclarity in defining religion obfuscates the role of religion in this conflict. Many observers state that this is not a religious war, because they are looking for overt religious justifications of the kind that were provided during the crusades, *jihads*, and other religious wars where the religion played an explicit role, sometimes even camouflaging political, social, and economic reasons. However, religion is not only capable of hiding other factors, but it can be a hidden or camouflaged factor by being covered up by other, more visible factors. For many modern people, religion has been so marginalized that they cannot fathom its role in statecraft in the late twentieth century.

---

[1] Jonathan Luxmoore, "Former UN envoy accuses churches of blocking cooperation," Ecumenical News International," September 14, 1995.

[2] *Ibid.*

In our contemporary setting, we tend to see religion as a private and individual, but extraordinary and self-aware experience. Both Communist and non-Communist societies nurtured the conviction that religion is a conscious act of the individual which impacts the thinking and behavior of persons who know themselves to be religious. Catherine Albanese divided religion into ordinary and extra-ordinary, pointing out that the ordinary religious mode is traditionalist, unself-conscious, and conformist while the extra-ordinary is the one in which a person's religious commitment is so sharply defined that for the sake of religious values he or she might be willing to become non-conformist and break tradition.[3] As examples of ordinary religion, she cites the experience of many Catholics to whom religion is imbedded into their culture and everyday life; as examples of extra-ordinary religion, she cites the case of Jesus (one may add other religious founders and reformers), the monastic communities, and many Protestants.

Today, it is the latter that is generally regarded as "religious," not only by those who themselves fall into this category, but even by those who are critical of or neutral to religion because they think that religious people are "different." Even those who are practitioners of "ordinary" religion are often unaware of how the "ordinary" aspects function, for they have been alerted to the function of extra-ordinary religion which they also have come to regard as being synonymous with the entire religious spectrum.

But perceiving religion only in its extraordinary form robs us of fathoming the forms of religion prevalent, not only in the past, but surviving today in this implicit form among the majority of the world's population, particularly in societies where modern individualism has not become dominant as it has in the countries from which most modern religious scholars come.

For many people today, religion is a separate sphere of the individual's experience which one can choose to join, or not to join, and to change when desired. Although religion may impact upon other spheres of human activities, many people think that the religious sector is a clearly defined set of feelings, beliefs, rituals, commitments, etc., and with the increasing sense of separation of church and state, many disconnect religion from all other human activities. The general **perception about** religion in the former Yugoslavia, including B&H, is this more individualistic, separate, extra-ordinary view, but the contention here is that this is not how religion frequently **is being experienced** in that area.

---

[3]Catherine L. Albanese, *America: Religions and Religion.* (Belmont, CA: Wadsworth Publishing Co., 1992), 6-9.

Traditionally, religion was enmeshed with all other cultural and civilizational aspects of life to the degree that it was not possible to clearly delineate where religions ended and politics, art, or science began, and vice versa. Among the great world religions, Islam to this day most closely maintains this model. Muslims frequently will say that Islam is not a religion, but a way of life. Indeed, religion is or should be a way of life. It is not surprising that early Christians before the word "Christian" came into use called their experience of salvation or wholesomeness, "the way." The "*Tao*" in Taoism also means "the way". Religion is, then, a collective as well as an individual experience that infuses all cultural factors of private and public life, attending to questions of family relationships, healing, dietary regulations, social structure, criminal law, and entertainment just as surely as a belief in afterlife or in angelic visitations. There are simply two ways, "the way of God" (or the equivalent notion) which is always ultimately good and victorious, and "the way against God" which is ultimately against one's best individual or collective interest. Each community (family, tribe, nation) attempts for the sake of its own survival to follow the way of God, and often the ways of the group are equated with the way of God.

Another typology has been frequently used in the study of religion: priestly and prophetic. The priestly function is the maintenance of the community or the institution. It is care-taking and nurturing, and it is protective of the continuation of communal life, including its flaws. The only unforgivable sin from the perspective of the priestly community is the splintering of the community either by desertion or by alleged harm to others in the community which then necessitates excommunication. The priest is envisioned as a pastor or a shepherd of an endangered flock that is preyed upon by "big bad wolves," powerful enemies who can devour the flock.

The prophetic function is focused on the fundamental purposes of the community and the willingness to criticize, not only the behavior of leaders and of groups within the community, but even the entire community for departing from the life-giving fundamental premises. The prophet believes that the community can be lost, even if it is physically preserved, when the community loses its soul and its original purpose. In the ancient Hebrew scripture, the conflict between the priestly and prophetic elements in the leadership reached classical proportions, both ultimately making their contribution to the identity of the Jewish community.

But not all communities develop the prophetic element, sometimes, it is non-existent or minimal. In the Balkans, the prophetic element in the community is rare, while the physical preservation of the community tends to be always paramount. In all three major Balkan religious communities, Eastern

Orthodoxy, Roman Catholicism, and Islam, the emphasis is not on the religious behavior of the individual, but on the collective. Unlike the individualistic Protestant question, "Brother or sister are **you** saved?" The stress is on "**the people** of God." The entire community is God's, and the individual is either more or less active in his or her awareness and contribution to the community. Religiously inactive or even alienated individuals are still, by virtue of their family or national history, group members who will potentially, given time and right circumstances, acknowledge their belonging and even contribute faithfully. The ultimate sin is defection, that is the conversion to another faith. This is why the penalties for conversion were so drastic, including the death penalty. For the group, it is not important that some members are passive (they might be activated in a crisis or when properly nurtured).

A group of people have been earmarked in the community to fulfill the function of the community's relation to God. In Eastern Orthodoxy and Roman Catholicism, this is obviously the priesthood, hierarchically organized, upon whose ordination, holiness, rightness, and devotion hinges the very nature of the church that is coextensive with the community. One should note that in the Balkans, entire groups of people (tribe/nation) became Christianized in mass conversions, so that one dates the conversion usually to the conversion of the king, who then more or less by command brings his entire people under the leadership of the clergy, many of whom stem from royal or noble households. One might think that it is different with Islam, but in the Balkans it is not. The Islamic community was headed until the twentieth century by the caliph, or *sheikh-ul-Islam,* who was the Turkish sultan. While there is no official clergy, the Balkan Muslims, having converted to Islam from hierarchical priestly communities, maintained a clerical structure of their own with the *Reis-ul-ulema* as the supreme leaders of the Islamic religious community and with the *imams* and *hodzhas* as the local religious leaders whose task it was to administer the Muslim law.   The *dervishes* (members of various Sufi orders) were the equivalents of the monastic communities, such as the Franciscans, keeping religious devotion among the populace to as high a level as possible.

Much has been written about the degree of overlap between belonging to an ethnic community and a religious community in Eastern Europe. Although Communists tried to loosen or even dissolve this century-long symbiosis, it is obvious that they failed to do so, and that both ethnic and religious leaders in many parts of Eastern Europe tried to strengthen these links and reinforce the identification. Such a symbiotic union between nationality and religion does not make sense if religion is seen in its more modern, individualistic sense. Nor would it make sense to see the present war in B&H as a war between Orthodox, Catholic, and Muslims. But if we are correct in defining religion in the Balkans as being predominantly of the ordinary, traditional, collective type, then the reality of *ethnoreligiosity*, a concept that I used in my book, *Yugoslavian Inferno: Ethnoreligious Warfare in the Balkans*,[4] inevitably allots a significant role to religions in the Bosnian conflict. To differentiate Serbs, Croats, and Muslims simply by their religious differences[5] is inaccurate. Here, religion is part of a conglomerate of characteristics which are so fused that when, for instance, Serbs go to war or make alliances, religion is inevitably part of the package. They nurture friendship with countries where the Orthodox religion is part of the fusion, just as they are suspicious and hostile toward non-Orthodox nations. The Croats are more inclined toward alliances with other Roman Catholic states and harbor animosities to Orthodox or Muslim countries. And finally, the Bosnian Muslims, though in a unique position due to their European heritage, do find it easier to cooperate with Muslim collectives and fear both types of Christian communities that surround them. All this is taken as completely natural and self-evident in the Balkans; it produces no serious dissent. If it were entirely for explicit, extra-ordinary religiosity, such perennial conflicts and sympathies could not be factually supported, but since it is a collectivist ethnoreligious enmeshment, one can understand how socio-political and other concerns can quickly engage the services of the religious community as their religious leaders want to protect their community from all dangers, even in realms seemingly unrelated to religion.

How closely the ethnic designation is with the religious can be easily noticed in the everyday conversation of people where they use the ethnic and religious terminologies interchangeably, being unaware of having switched from one to another. Since the Orthodox Church continues to use the Julian calendar, there are discrepancies in the dates of major religious holidays. Thus, people use interchangeably the term Catholic and Croat Christmas and Easter, or Orthodox and Serb Christmas and Easter. When Serbs talk about their animosity to Croats and vice versa, which is actually of very recent date since the two nationalities did not fight wars against each other prior to the twentieth century, they really talk about the animosities springing from the Great Schism, usually dated in 1054 when the Eastern Orthodox and Roman Catholics split from each other, each claiming to be the one, true, apostolic, and holy church and, thus, engaged in a millennium of rivalry and attempts to upstage each other's jurisdictional lines. Hence, it **feels** as if Serbs and Croats have been eternal rivals. Since the national and religious designations were co-extensive for the above two groups, the people thought that it naturally applied also to

---

[4](New York: Continuum, 1994).

[5]As for instance in Noel Malcolm, *Bosnia: A Short History*. (London: Macmillan, 1994).

Muslims. Islam was brought to the Balkans by the Turks, and consequently, there has been a tendency to regard the native Balkan people (Bosnians, Montenegrins, Albanians, etc.) as Turks, though they clearly are not. The Bosnian Muslims were in a particularly confusing situation, because the Slavic population that followed Islam, at least culturally, had to reject their genetic ties to Serb or Croat ancestors since that would immediately connote that they are either crypto-Christians or potential Christians. When a Muslim, even an entirely non-religious Muslim, converts to Christianity, she or he thinks of her or himself as having **returned** to the ancestral faith as well as to her or his people (*narod*). Even atheistic Muslim nationals consider such a decision as traitorous to Islam and to the Muslim peoplehood although they do not consider their atheism--otherwise anathema to Muslims--as betraying the Muslim community. If a Serb were to accept Catholicism--a rare occasion, indeed--most people would consider this person as having abandoned not only Orthodoxy but as having betrayed the Serb nation and as having become Croatized. The reverse is true if a Croat were to accept Orthodoxy. Until the onset of Communism and mass urbanization, the number of intermarriages was relatively small. Only the Communist antinationalist and antireligious propaganda and wholesale mixing that was encouraged by the state in schools, the army, living quarters, and the work-place has resulted in the abandonment of the ancient taboos against intermarriage (unless a Muslim was to take a Christian wife, which was permissible by Islamic rules).

This, then, is a structural, unavoidable role that religion plays, and in so far as there are ethnic conflicts in the Balkans, they inevitably have a religious dimension.[6] But let us go into greater specifics.

Without charting the degree of religious liberty for the religious communities which I have done elsewhere[7], let it be noted that the Yugoslav government subjected the religious communities to an intense pressure and surveillance, even outright persecution, in the immediate post-World War II years and then slowly after 1953 granted greater freedoms. Nevertheless, it was not until the actual collapse of Communism in the late 1980s that the religious communities experienced a genuine feeling of liberation from interference by the

---

[6]Insofar as Western policies were directed at weakening Communist power by promoting anti-Soviet polycentrism based on nationalism of the various Communist parties, these policies unconsciously contributed to resurrecting this symbiosis. When "basket three" of the Helsinki agreement was being fostered, especially in regard to religious liberty, again an ethnoreligious symbiosis was being unconsciously encouraged because it was very easy for some activists to move from being a religious dissenter to also supporting nationalist interests.

[7]*Religious Liberty in Eastern Europe and the U.S.S.R.: Before and After the Great Transformation* (Boulder,CO: East European Monographs, 1992), 339-382.

government. This process of greater freedom for religious communities coincided with the greater political freedoms which ultimately resulted in the creation of a multi-party system and the loss of power by the Communist Party (and the Communist parties of the republics).

Most of the political parties identified themselves to a greater or lesser degree with one of the nationalities and quickly sought to bolster their nationalistic image by expressing support for the established religion of their nation. This produced a fairly rapid growth in the public importance and image of the religious leaders and institutionalized religions. From being marginalized, controlled, and even oppressed, they suddenly found themselves courted by politicians, the media, and even by academics. It is fair to say that most of them were not used to this limelight, and it made most of them prone to being manipulated by all this attention and flattery. In addition, the political platform of the nationalist parties coincided more closely with the traditional aspiration of these ancient religious communities rather than with the former Communists or with those who were interested in a civil society. So, they gave initially enthusiastic support to leaders such as Tudjman, Milošević, Karadžić, and Izetbegović.

Paradoxically, as warfare advanced, there was on the one hand an increasing political involvement of the religious leaders in the cause their nation followed, at least in the case of the higher clergy of the Roman Catholic and Orthodox Churches, and on the other hand, a certain cooling toward the concrete policies of Tudjman and Milošević, stressing that the religious communities would not provide an across the board support of a particular party program. One can note, however, massive support of the Catholic clergy of Bosnia and Herzegovina for the Croatian Democratic Union, of the Orthodox clergy for the Serbian Democratic Party, and of the Muslim clergy for the Party of Democratic Action. This support consisted in both open and veiled appeals to religious people of their denomination to support the respective party with their vote in declarations that provided sanctification of the specific programs or actions, in attending meetings and being available for photo opportunities with prominent politicians, and finally by actively lobbying on behalf of specific concerns of their nationalist leaders with the international community. As to the question whether the religious leaders manipulated the politicians or the other way around, one may say that both took place, but it seems that the politicians were more skilled manipulators and took greater advantage of this relationship. Perhaps it should again be noted that by and large there was an age-long symbiotic union of church and nation (or sometimes state) with extremely few instances of open dissent against state leaders (the Communist leaders may have received the least support when compared with leaders prior to and after Communist rulers.)

Another religious contribution to the fostering of war psychosis was the increasing vocalizing of very pronounced and even strident national memories and myths. This was done for the benefit of whomever would listen: tourists, church members, pupils, theological students, etc. For instance, visitors to monasteries or medieval Serbian Orthodox churches would be given tours and lectures by monks who passionately recounted horrors perpetrated by Muslims and Catholics upon their buildings and the populace, some of which would be historically, blatantly inaccurate. A non-religious Muslim from Tuzla, Imamović, recounts the astonishment and recoil when he encountered in a Serbian monastery a vociferous indictment of Turks/Muslims.[8] Roman Catholic clergy in B&H and Croatia stressed the alleged total domination of Serbs in all areas of life (which was only partially true). They vastly exaggerated the role of that domination by attributing the low birthrate and the somewhat higher emigration rate of Croats, although other more plausible reasons can explain these phenomena. Most Catholic clergy were unwilling to own up to Yugoslavia; they always stressed the Croat dimension. Muslim clergy glamorized the alleged superiority in tolerance of the Ottoman period and the achievements of the Islamic civilization and frequently demonized Christians as crusaders and oppressors of Muslims, staunchly denying the oppressive elements of the Ottoman regime. Many Muslim clergy and academics promoted a new interpretation, proclaiming that it was the Muslim population of Bosnia that was not only the "constitutive" nation, but also its earliest and most indigenous. One should note that in the Balkans it is widely believed that primogeniture establishes exclusive contemporary rights to territory and to rule. However, if there are prior claims, such as those of Albanians that they are the Illyrian aborigines of the Balkans, then such claims are quickly denied by their Slavic neighbors. Speeches, sermons, church literature, great gatherings, and celebrations were all used to enhance the importance of the contribution made by the church as defender of the nation, and conversely, as the reinforcer of enemy images, some of them latent and some largely forgotten during the Tito era.

The greater degree of freedom of expression, including freedom of the press, was used and abused not only by the general press, but also by religious publications. Articles, editorials, essays, and books appeared, explaining the alleged victimization of one's own group and asking for restoration of full rights

---

[8]Jasmin Imamović, *Ubijanje smrti* (Tuzla: Radio Kameleon, 1995), 15-17. Personally I heard a very similar bending of history by a monk during a visit to a monastery in Nikšić, Montenegro, in 1995.

according to the maximalist demands of each group. Sometimes, formerly suppressed thinkers from another era or those who lived abroad were now published in the land. Some of those were clearly extremists. Others may not have been explicitly threatening other groups but were perceived by readers of the rival faiths as making claims or demands that they deemed injurious to the interests of one's own community. Thus, a series of editorials in the Islamic religious community's periodical *Glasnik* (*Messenger*) published material written by non-Bosnian Muslim writers, ancient and contemporary, who describe an utopian Islamic vision of a world under the governance of Allah as understood by the classical sources of Islam. It is hard to know how they were understood by the average Muslim reader, but they certainly caused consternation among those who felt fear of and animosity to Islam. Of course, it was not unusual for such readers, even those who claimed purely scholarly intentions, to present quotations out of context and to provide a worst-case interpretation of the text. The famous "Islamic Declaration" of Alija Izetbegović, written during his dissident years, was used adversely for the Muslim cause, despite later qualifications issued by the author when he assumed political importance.[9] A frequent tool in the propaganda war was to uncritically claim, despite much contrary evidence, that Bosnian Muslims are fundamentalists. The generalized charge of fundamentalism was being used fairly indiscriminately to describe the position of rival faiths, which is surely an appropriate designation of some extremists in each group, but is not (yet) a truthful presentation of the over-all community.

Another threatening role of religious communities was the unconcealed military activities of a segment of the clergy. Following a long-standing tradition of being of the people and for the people, a number of priests and imams became not just military chaplains who gave blessing and justification even to war criminals, but with arms in their hands, participated in the fighting, giving it always a defensive rather than aggressive interpretation. The highest clergy in their appeals have occasionally condemned criminal behavior of troops of all three sides, but almost never specifically condemned those crimes that were clearly perpetrated by their own side. There is no case of disciplining or defrocking, much less of excommunicating, priests for participating in armed

---

[9]This author witnessed first hand such misuse when a small group of Bosnian Serb Orthodox monks distributed in Kecskemét, Hungary, at an international conference on "Christian Faith and Human Enmity" in August 1995 a hand-out that provided a single quotation from the lengthy declaration with no contextualization or referencing, not even the mention of the origin of the hand-out, presumably in order to create among the Christian participants a fear of Muslim intentions in Europe and more sympathy for the Serbian Orthodox struggle against Islam.

actions by any of the three hierarchies. Evasive generalization was the usual response to specific inquiries about the violent behavior of a clergyman. At no point in the history of the three communities was there ever a document issued admitting guilt like the Barmen Declaration of German Christians.

A further contribution of the warfare was the use of religious symbols by soldiers and civilians to bolster their cause. When one hears "*Allahu Akbar*" [God is great] as the fighting cry of Muslim soldiers, and "*Bog čuva Srbe*" [God protects the Serbs], and sees Croatian guardists using prayer beads to designate their loyalty to Jesus and Mary, along with hearing "*Bože čuvaj Hrvatsku*" [May God protect Croatia], then it becomes clear that religious iconography is called into service of the war god, and that each group appeals not to the One Universal deity but to tribal gods.

The Serbian Orthodox Role

The leadership of SOC seems to have played the most harmful role as compared to the other two major religious communities. Both prior to and throughout the war, its leadership underscored the threat--real and imaginary-- from the two rival faiths and continually linked this war with World War II and previous threats to Serbians as if all of these were perpetrated not by the ancestors, but by the presently living, who were now the declared enemies. They promoted a collectivist concept of responsibility and a fusion of the past and present in which the past is perpetually the present.

Throughout the 1980s, Orthodox publications and speakers started transmitting the views of two deceased writers--Bishop Nikolaj Velimirović and the theologian Justin Popović--who espoused anti-ecumenical and narrow, even chauvinistic, views regarding their belief in the superiority of Serbian Orthodoxy.[10]

The Serbian Orthodox Episcopal Synod completely endorsed the notion that all Serbs must live in the same country and distanced themselves from Slobodan Milošević only when it became obvious that he no longer, for very pragmatic reasons, supported his own initial stand. In their pronouncements, they made exaggerated claims of Serbian losses and considered Serb defeats "apocalyptic." "The Church bears her Cross and ascends Golgotha with Her afflicted people."[11] The Church and "Her people" are referred to as "crucified" and it is repeatedly stated that the Serbs were subjected to genocide physically

---

[10]Geert van Dartel, "Nikolaj Velimirović (1880-1956)," *Glaube in der 2. Welt*, Vol. 21, No. 4 (April 1993), 20-26. Anne Herbst, "Tod und Verklärung: Die Orthodoxe und die Katholische Kirche im südslawischen Konflikt," in *ibid.*, 14-18.

[11]"Message of the Holy Assembly of Bishops, Serbian Orthodox Church, Belgrade, August 1995.

during World War II and morally during the Communist period. Church leaders pleaded with the leadership of various Serb 'states' "not to succumb to the enticements and dishonorable demands of the world powers who encourage them to betray their own people,"[12] a clear reference to attempts by the international community to bring about a cease-fire in Bosnia and Croatia.

Democratically oriented observers in Belgrade criticized SOC for "fervent nationalism" that became "the self-proclaimed guardian of national interests" of Serbs on both sides of the Drina River.[13] The SOC was also criticized in the World Council of Churches, of which SOC is a member, by other member churches, notably some Swiss, German, Scandinavian, and Dutch churches and agencies, some of which accused the SOC of a similar sin as that of the so-called *Deutsche Christen* who gave support to Hitler's nationalistic policies, namely of too closely identifying the Church with the Bosnian Serb war cause.[14] There were some who demanded the suspension of SOC from WCC because of its uncritical support of the Bosnian Serb cause, an unprecedented measure. In response, Bishop Lavrentije, a member of the WCC's Central Committee, defended his church, stating his belief that the decades under Communism were responsible for the genocide, pointing out that the SOC has condemned war in the name of religion, and accusing the Roman Catholic Church of aggressiveness toward Serbs.[15] At earlier meetings, Patriarch Paul gave assurances to European ecumenical leaders that SOC was doing all in its power to bring about a peaceful solution to the problem,[16] but such general appeals were not consistent with the specific actions, locally and generally, that tended to blame the international community for the incitement and intensification of the war while the Serbs were described as simply protecting their ancient homeland.[17] Calls for the unity of all Serbs, issued by SOC, can be interpreted as the voice of concern for the fate of their people in a difficult hour--that was the way the

---

[12]*Ibid.*

[13]"Support for Greater Serbia," *The Christian Century*, Vol. 112, No. 25 (August 30-September 5, 1995), 808-809.

[14]"Serbian church criticized as world church gathering opens," *Ecumenical News International*, September 14, 1995. Konrad Raiser, the General Secretary of WCC expressed his personal conviction of such collusion.

[15]"Serbian bishop blames communism for aggression," *Ecumenical News International*, September 18, 1995.

[16]"Serbian church calls for international support," *Ecumenical News International*, May 3, 1995.

[17]E.g. "Public Statement Regarding NATO's Recent Military Activities Against the Serbian People," Belgrade, September 7, 1995.

Church self-interpreted it.[18] But many of the SOC statements resemble more military fact-finding reports than religious statements.[19] The church frequently maintained that the Serbs were accused of the sins of others rather than admitting and chastising the brutalities of Serb actions. Rather, they criticized President Milošević for "imposing a shameful blockade against their brothers on the other side of the Drina River" when the 'government' at Pale was unwilling to accept the Contact Group's cease-fire plan.[20]

While some bishops tried to present the Synod as speaking with a unified voice (Bishop Lavrentije of Šabac), there were clearly bishops who took a more uncompromising hard-line stand and who may have manipulated the elderly Patriarch Paul I who is generally regarded as a saintly, ascetic man who prefers to highlight equal responsibility of the three nations for the fratricidal civil war--which is how he sees this conflict.[21] The two hierarchs who excelled in their diatribes against the other two faiths were Bishop Atanasije Jeftić of Herzegovina and Metropolitan Amfilohije Radović of Montenegro. To illustrate the extremism of their positions, one needs to mention the criticism of Amfilohije by the President of Montenegro, Momir Radović, who opined that the Metropolitan tried to "compel the people to something they do not want. Instead of reconciliation he causes altercations between people . . .he divided more than he conciliated . . . what hatred is in this man who does not listen to the voice of reason . . . . "[22]

Individual priests may not have always shared the views of the hierarchy, but none of them protested publicly. Other priests certainly surpassed the hierarchy in fueling the war. For instance, Rev. Djordje Ilica of Ilidža (a town near Sarajevo that was under Serbian control) volunteered this theological principle: "The one who forgives is worse than the one who did the bad thing in the first place,"[23] an abominal principle certainly not derived either from the Holy Scripture nor from the writings of the Church Fathers. The same priest proceeded, "I would like us to live with any nationality except the Muslims and

---

[18]"Statement from the Bishops' Consultation of the Serbian Orthodox Church," Belgrade, March 3, 1995.

[19]E.g. "Sveti arhijerejski sinod srpske pravoslavne crkve, saopštenje za javnost, Jasenovac posle Jasenovca," *Glasnik*, Vol. LXXVI, No. 6 (June 1995), 98, 102-103.

[20]"The Holy Assembly of Bishops of the Serbian Orthodox Church," Message to the Public No. 70, May 1995.

[21]Letters of Patriarch Pavle to Cardinal Franjo Kuharić and *Reis-ul-Ulema*, Jakub Selimoski, in *Glasnik* (Belgrade), Vol. LXXIII, No. 8 (August 1993), 130-131.

[22]"O mitropolitu Amfilohiju," *Politika Ekspres*, (Belgrade), (August 25, 1995), 2.

[23]Barbara Demick, "Bosnian Serbs nurture anger," *Philadelphia Inquirer*, September 26, 1995, A9.

Croats. Even the children, they will grow up to kill Serbs again." Priests like Ilica became the spiritual counselors to their troops. The blessing of weapons and soldiers was a common occurrence engaged in by all levels of the clergy.

Another unique policy of SOC during the war in Bosnia was to withdraw all their bishops and nearly all the clergy from those cities and villages not held by Serbs. Two SOC priests with whom I talked, who on their own decided to stay in lands not held by the Serb army, expressed bitterness in regard to this departure of the long-observed practice that the clergy stay with the people and remain in their monasteries and churches.[24] It was their opinion that the bishops who fled had no longer the ability to accurately assess the situation nor to issue statements in the name of those who remained.

To get an appreciation of the degree of interaction between Serbian Orthodoxy and the political leadership of the *Republika Srpska BiH* (self-styled name of the Bosnian Serb territorial unit), one needs to read an interview which its leader, Radovan Karadžić, gave to a Montenegrin Serbian Orthodox periodical, *Svetigora*. Here we shall excerpt only the most pertinent quotations:

The interviewer asked, "Are we to understand that Communism was only a cover-up for Islamization?" Karadžić responded: "Absolutely correct. Communism was used by non-Serb peoples to keep the Serbs in subordination, while elsewhere the national and religious programs of the Roman Catholic Church and Islam were being promoted."[25] Further, Karadžić maintains that the proportion of atheists was not larger among Serbs, but that it only appeared so because "Serbs could be devoted to their God and their own soul only in their own homes and in their solitude."[26]

Further, Karadžić discussed the fate of Muslims who regard themselves Serb by nationality. Karadžić claimed that those who had greater religious interests turned to Islam and, thereby, became lost or "failed" Serbs, while those who retained a collective memory of the Serbian past functioned as Serbs whose family had turned Muslim. While these did not practice an Orthodox spirituality, they did have "an Orthodox anguish with God."

> It is clear that the path to salvation of Serbs of the Muslim faith is the return to Orthodoxy. I am saying this completely responsibly; I know that not everyone can do this and that it is not easy, but I know that it is the only way to overcome the dualism in their soul. They were temporarily--in respect to

---

[24]The two Serbian Orthodox priests were Father Jovan Nikolić of Zagreb and Fr. Krsto Bijeljac of Sarajevo. Metropolitan Nikolai Mrdja celebrated his first liturgy in government-held Sarajevo on January 8, 1996, after having taken up residence during the war years in a particularly nationalistic Serb stronghold in Republika Srpska.

[25]*Ibid.*, 15.

[26]*Ibid.*

eternity what is a few hundred years--of another faith either because of the
pressure of the occupiers or personal comfort . . .it does not mean that they do
not have in them much of what is Serb, Christian, and Orthodox. As it is
now, they will be neither Muslims nor Serbs.[27]

Then, Karadžić reveals his plan for all Bosnian Muslims:

Therefore I think that the Serb people will recuperate entirely and wholly only
when the majority or all of them--I am speaking in the sense of a peoplehood
(*narodnosnom*)--including Serbs who are of the Islamic religion, experience
healing of their soul and enter into the wholeness of their being. This of
course, must and cannot be coerced.[28]

Karadžić claims that politically he and his political party, the Serbian
Democratic Party, can be proud that they restored freedom to the people,

all else is God's work. And God probably brought us freedom because he
taught us what to do, and the Holy Spirit whispered to us what we should say,
of which I am personally convinced because frequently I went to gatherings
without a prepared concept--actually this is so always with the exception of
three-four important historical gatherings--and I always went according to the
Gospel "Do not worry what you will say. The Spirit alone will tell you what
should be said."[29]

Karadžić then claims that the intention of the Communists was to keep the
Serbs in servitude by being tricked to promote "brotherhood and unity."[30] Now
the Serb transfiguration is generally most fervently fostered by the very same
people who fell victims to the Titoist propaganda, which--here Karadžić the
psychiatrist claims--is entirely understandable because they are angriest at having
been most deceived. He states that most *chetnik*-like (i.e. aggressively
nationalist) behavior is displayed by the children of Tito's *partisans*.

In regard to Roman Catholics, especially Croats, he feels that they were
clever when they turned defeat in World War I to their advantage by embracing
the Serbs only to at once wish to break up the country, taking with them all that
the Serbs had won in the war. The same happened in regard to World War II.
"And this [current] war was conceptualized in the same manner, a politics that
came under the same flags, same emblems and heraldry, same rhetoric, same
desires and aspirations, but God wanted this time for us to stop being misguided
and to be ready."[31]

---

[27]*Ibid.*, 16.

[28]*Ibid.*

[29]*Ibid.*

[30]The implication here is that Tito's Communist system kept Serbs in servitude;
"brotherhood and unity" was a favorite slogan of Tito promoting interethnic harmony.

[31]*Ibid.*, 19.

Karadžić sees himself as the defender of "our tribe and our Church hoping to God that we used only as much force as was necessary." As to his own historical role and burden he said,

> God graced me to do something in my life that is significant, so significant that I think it was worth being born, live, and die to help my people. . . . God gave me good health . . . . It is only difficult to make a decision--then I ask many people even children and even more importantly we ask our Church. Not a single important decision was made without the Church.[32]

Karadžić rejects the charge coming from Serbia that the Bosnian Serbs are clericalists, saying that the Orthodox Church simply cannot be clericalist, but rather that they are blessed with having an outstanding metropolitan [probable reference to the Bosnian metropolitan Nikolaj Mrdja] and bishops [e.g. the hard-line Atanasije Jeftić] who do not impose their views but wait to be asked. Since the Serbs had suffered for centuries for Orthodoxy, Orthodoxy is now their defense and way of salvation; the Church is with the Serbs.

A greater concern to this author is not whether to believe Dr. Radovan Karadžić's religious claims, but why an official Serbian Orthodox publication such as *Svetigora* would carry an interview in which the interviewer is coaxing Mr. Karadžić to make provocative and menacing ethnoreligious claims (not that he needed much prompting!) and that the editors nowhere indicate any reservations about the views expressed. To the contrary, the other articles in *Svetigora* are equally strident. There seems to be an emergence of an Orthodox fundamentalism and militancy usually not unveiled to ecumenical visitors. I believe that the main stream of Orthodox believers and other church communities needs to become aware of the rise of such militancy within the Orthodox Churches.

The Croatian Roman Catholic Role

According to a cliche, the Serbs are brutally open about their intentions while the Croats play their cards closer to their vest, as in poker. There is a good deal of truth in this cliche. Consequently, it is not as easy to find explicit claims of the Roman Catholic complicity with the war efforts of the Croats. It is clear, however, that the Catholic leaders were most effective in producing an enormous amount of informational material, with their interpretation of events, that was made more widely available than what the Serbs and Muslims produced, and thereby, tended to make the Croat slant on the Balkan war the most widely shared among Western shapers of public opinion. The Serb Orthodox propaganda attempted to ward off some of these effects by its own barrage of pronouncements of the Holy Synod, usually trying to use the

---

[32]*Ibid.*

channels of the World Council of Churches, but it could not match the amount and effectiveness of the Catholics.

To start by summarizing observations made in my book, *Yugoslavian Inferno*, there is first of all the too close structural identification of the Catholic Church with Croatdom. While the Church for canonical reasons cannot call itself the Croatian Catholic Church, it has used quite deliberately the term "The Church among Croats" as if there are no Catholics of other nationalities living on the territories predominantly inhabited by Croats. And, indeed, one finds no sign of any pastoral care by the Catholic Church of Italians, Hungarians, Slovenians, Czechs, Poles, and others who may dwell along with Croats. The leadership of the Roman Catholic Church in Croatia and B&H seem to be exclusively concerned with the fate of Croats. Their statements about the identification of Croats with the Catholic Church leaves out the minority option of Croats who are either Protestants or non-religious.

The second problem stems from the prewar period when Franjo Cardinal Kuharić, the archbishop of Zagreb and the head of the Catholic Bishop's Conference, seeing the possibility of the imminent collapse of Communism, massively supported the activities of the Croatian Democratic Union (HDZ). He did so not only on the territory of the republic of Croatia, but also strongly urged the creation of a Croat national party in B&H. Granted that in the late 1980s the defeat of the Communists at the election was not self-evident, it is, however, clear that anyone who understands the delicate interethnic relationships in B&H and supports the organization not of civil society but of ethnoreligious political arrangement, may well be advancing the narrow religious and, perhaps, even the nationalistic advantages of his own group. The Roman Catholic bishops of the former Yugoslavia, headed by Kuharić, showed little foresight of the destructiveness of nationalistic politics. They also fell prey to the slogan, "let's first defeat the Communists (including the reform-minded Prime Minister Ante Marković) and then we'll settle accounts among ourselves." So, they did! The fuse was lit and exploded in everyone's faces.

The Catholic bishops and clergy of B&H started distancing themselves from the policies of the HDZ both in Croatia and in B&H, but only when they saw that this would lead to such a partitioning and "ethnic cleansing" that the Croats might take possession of their self-proclaimed state of "Herzeg Bosna" with the capital in Mostar but be expelled from Bosnia proper. The Croat population in B&H was relatively small (17 per cent), and this would mean that their presence from areas where Croats dwelled for centuries would now be devoid of them while retaining questionable control of Herzegovina where they would continually be challenged regarding their sole possession of it by Muslims and perhaps even Serbs. Thus the Catholic bishops of B&H and Croatia decided to give support to the policy of a single B&H. If that single B&H were to stay in a federation with the Muslims, this might be of such advantage to the numerically weaker Croats that they could come to play either an equal or even superior position in the federation, especially if the federation was confederated with Croatia. The Croats could well come out of the war in B&H as the clearest winners (in so far as there are winners in wars). This may not have been lost to the Catholic leaders of Croats--nor to their enemies.

Lastly, one needs to single out the behavior of some Catholic clergy in Herzegovina whose allegiance to extremist Croatian nationalism was well known; Herzegovina was a foremost breeding ground of the *ustasha* movement in the 1930s and 1940s and continues to be that in the 1990s. Herzegovinians have a reputation of being the most ardent nationalists, regardless of whether they are Croat, Muslim, or Serbs. Other Croat Roman Catholic clergy testify to the intransigence of many of the Herzegovinian clergy when it comes to dealing with people of other faiths. Many of these clergymen openly support the secession of Herzeg-Bosna from B&H and its annexation by Croatia. *Some* are undisguised advocates of Croatian extremist politicians and urge their flock to support the policies of these politicians. A number of them, like some of the Orthodox priests and Muslim leaders, took guns into their hands and participated in the armed struggle.

After the Serb forces were driven out of Mostar, a bloody war between Croat and Muslim extremists ensued. The city was partitioned, and the Croat part came to be dominated by the "ustashas." The clergy was beset by their own conflicts between the Bishop and the local Franciscans in Medjugorje as to whether the alleged visions were a deception or a miracle. "We hoped that the Church will have a positive influence. But there came for us a tragic conflict between Herzegovinian Franciscans and Petrinists. This conflict weakened the influence of the Petrinists, which radicalized the Catholic clergy. Among the clergy the separatistic extremists won."[33] Some declared that they can no longer coexist with Muslims.[34] At that point, there was a need to protect the churches and mosques, but instead, one of the old Orthodox churches was totally demolished and many minarets were destroyed on mosques. An old Catholic church and the Franciscan monastery were also destroyed, along with the famous old bridge that gave the city its name (the latter by Croat artillery). In 1993, Martin Planinić, a Franciscan friar, found the time in his book to exonerate the

---

[33]Editors of *Erasmus*, "Razgovori na dvije obale," [Conversations on two river banks], *Erasmus*, No. 16 (March 1996), 29.

[34]Said Rev. Ante Marić, a village priest near Mostar, "The Muslims have a holy war with us. We cannot accept the Dayton agreement." Mike O'Connor, "Bosnian Croats Resist Peace Accord," *New York Times*. February 13, 1996, A8.

accused war criminal of the World War II era, Fra Tomislav Filipović, who under the pseudonym Fra Miroslav Majstorović, participated in the extermination of Serbs in the concentration camp Jasenovac. If Filipović was, indeed, unjustly accused, it is desirable to set the record straight, but there is something profoundly obscene when in the midst of another war between Serbs, Croats, and Muslims, a Franciscan friar finds no more urgent business than to defend a man who was actually expelled by his own order during World War II for, minimally, being present during killings of Serbs by an *ustasha* unit to which he became a chaplain against the express orders of his superiors.

Successes in the war in 1995 were celebrated widely. The pseudonymous commentator "Maša" ascribed the victories of the Croat armies using the strategy of prayer. Says she, "Prayer beads became the 'trademark' of the Homeland War and Croat defense since 1991."[35]   A Croat in Sarajevo explains that after material goods lost their value, a genetic Catholicism reappeared. "Culture and prayer are in our genes, just as faith is in our genes."[36] These are among the many confirmations that ethnoreligiosity, i.e. Catholicism and Croat ethnicity, is broadly synthesized even in the religious press.

The Muslim Role

Having sustained the greatest losses in the war, it is somehow distressing to write about the Muslim complicity in initiating and waging the war. Regretfully, they, too, contributed to the mayhem, although certainly not to the extent that the SOC did.

The most important factor was the even closer ethnoreligious symbiosis among the Muslims than among the other two groups. Students of Islam have long noticed its claim not to be merely a religion, but a way of life, and certainly as a way of life, Islam tenaciously held on among nearly a half of the population of B&H although frequently the religious dimension was all but suppressed. When the national question of those Bosnians who were of the Islamic heritage was being resolved in the 1970s in such a way that the term Muslim became a national designation of those Bosnians who were neither of Serb nor Croat ethnoreligious designation, then Muslims sought to express their national aspiration in ways that had clear religious dimensions. In other words, the institutions most ready to display their Muslim characteristics were those that had a clear religious function such as the mosque, *medresa* [religious school], religious publications, the rising prestige of the *hodjas* or *imams*, forms of

---

[35]Maša, "Strategija molitve," [The strategy of prayer], *Veritas*, Vol.34, No. 9 (376), September 1995, 13.

[36]"Biti za čovjeka," [To be for the human being], *Veritas*, Vol. 34, No. 1 (369), January 1995, 11.

greetings and so forth. Some religious Muslims claim that they were persecuted by the Communists more than the others,[37] but that is a claim made by religious leaders of all three groups--their common malady being myopic ethnocentrism. Imam Senad Agić of Hrasnica, now leader of Bosnian Muslims in the Chicago area said, "I blame Serbian and Croatian religious nationalism for the failure of pluralism in Bosnia."[38]

During the latter years of Tito's reign when he worked hard at being one of the leaders of the non-aligned movement in which numerous Muslim countries participated, Tito opened the door to the training of Muslim leaders abroad, as well as to visits and aid from Muslim circles abroad to Yugoslav Muslims. These increased contacts brought about an increased Muslim self-awareness and an influx of more traditionalist Muslim ideas that a segment of the Muslim community embraced wholeheartedly. They, like the Christian leaders, wondered what effective and authentic religious and cultural existence meant under reform Communism. Increasingly loud claims could be heard for more explicit and far-reaching Muslim activism to strengthen the Muslim position. Whether or not such activism was designed to intimidate rivals, the result was that Christians and other non-Muslims began to fear the ramification of living in a country where Islam would become a determinative influence.

The students who had been trained in Egypt, Iran, Saudi Arabia, or other Islamic study centers tended to promote more pronounced involvement and renewal of Islamic teachings and practice which large segments of the Muslim population had neglected upon their return. This tended to provoke fear and suspicion by non-Muslims and even among the secularized Muslims who interpreted this minimally as a return to a more conservative life-style. Many also feared that this might spread pan-Islamic ambitions for Muslims to gain an upper hand and rule over others. Indeed, the ambition of the small number of Islamists (a better term than fundamentalists) or traditionalists to revive the role of the *Shariate* law struck terror in the minds of many. Such fears, whether reasonable or not, did exist and could be later exploited particularly by Serbian extremists who forecast darkly a future in which the Islamic yoke would be reintroduced over the Balkans, threatening all of Europe. The world-wide rise in power of Islamic countries, and particularly Turkey's re-emergence as a regional power in the context of Western policies to support a Turkish rather than Iranian model of Islam, raised the specter of Balkan Christians having to be again a buffer zone to Muslim penetration into Europe. It is easy to see how

---

[37]"A Bosnian Muslim Speaks Out. An Interview with Imam Senad Agić," *Christian Century*, August 2-9, 1995, 745.

[38]*Ibid.*, 746.

Muslims would be scared by the secularizing and 'Christianizing' influences of their neighbors, and conversely, the Christian fear that they would be pushed back to live under an Islamic government.

Alija Izetbegović's "Islamic Declaration" has been much maligned and exploited for anti-Muslim sentiments. Izetbegović was from his youth in the early post-World War II period an anti-Communist, Muslim activist who had twice been sentenced by Tito's government for alleged Muslim nationalism. Many have quoted the "Islamic Declaration" out of context and claimed that it provided a manifesto for a Muslim take-over of Yugoslavia or Bosnia. Izetbegović wrote the Declaration long before he got into power and has since on numerous occasions disclaimed any intention to make Islam the official order of Bosnia. There is no reason to present Izetbegović as a fundamentalist; he is capable of compromising and negotiation. However, there are many Muslims who are suspicious in regard to his ability and interest in multinationalism, multiculturalism, and multireligiosity for Bosnia, feeling that he has shown distinct partisanship and desire for monopoly of power for his political party, SDA (Party of Democratric Action), which is nearly completely Muslim. He also did not discourage the creation of Bosnian government army units that are exclusively Muslim in composition and are given intense Muslim indoctrination and who fight, indeed, in the name of Allah as if it were for the victory of an Islamic Bosnia--rather than a civil society. The "Islamic Declaration" is neither as threatening as Izetbegović's enemies allege, nor as benign as his followers and many Western journalists claim. A non-alarmist investigation of the "Islamic Declaration" does give rise to some concerns that Mr. Izetbegović, while never mentioning B&H by name, is promoting a renewal of a world-wide Muslim commonwealth that has a political order very different from democracy to which even non-Muslims who live on that territory will have to submit themselves, since it is allegedly a higher form of human justice and orderliness. He has little regard for non-Muslim educational systems and condemns leaders of Muslim countries who have been Westernized. His personality has been described as mystic, and he has closely identified himself with the *kismet* or fate of B&H. "Some local Muslim imams are even spreading the story that Izetbegović is the next after Muhammad, who will tell and realise final truth."[39]

Muslim publications, periodicals, and books featured statements that appeared to be militant calls to common action on changing B&H into a Muslim-dominated state, a kind of an Islamic republic. In Bijeljina (or Prijedor), a group of Muslims drew up in 1990 a local constitution in which

---

[39]Miroslav Jančić, "Behind the Split," *War Report* (London), No. 36 (September 1995), 7.

they wanted to introduce drastic *Shariate* punishments for offenses, and it was also in Bijeljina where a group of Muslims drew up a list of Serbs who should be executed when their plan is implemented. Muslim paramilitary units directed their guns upon Serbs who came to negotiate, provoking angry Serb reprisal.[40]

As the war progressed, the predominantly Muslim Bosnian army units increasingly resorted to Islamic religious phrases and symbolism. Though outgunned by Serb units, they would attack with their initially meager weapons shouting, *"Allahu akbar!"* Later, elite commando units were formed such as "The Black Swans," an 800-man brigade who lived according to Islamic law, having daily prayers, abstaining from alcohol and women, and maintaining an exemplary personal hygiene. They claim not to be fundamentalists; in fact, many of them have followed no religious practices until recently, but now find inspiration in Islamic practices. Such groups have up to two hours of religious training a day from a *hodja*, a religious leader who now serves as a military chaplain. One of them says, "First they learn the rules of Islam and follow them, then comes faith."[41] With about 90 per cent of the Bosnian government army units being made up of Muslims, the claim that they went to battle for a multiethnic, multireligious state continued to be made for the benefit of the international community, but an increasing number of them turned into purely Islamic units defending a Muslim nationalist ideology. The government first denied, then played down the existence of such units, but gradually they came to the surface, shocking not only outsiders, but even many Bosnian Muslims with a different orientation. The 3,000 strong Seventh Muslim Brigade, sporting green headbands with Islamic insignia and saluting in Arabic, was a sign of the increasing involvement of the religious element in the military.[42] The existence of foreign volunteer *mujahedeen* fighters who came to defend a Muslim state (though not numerous--estimated at about 3,000) present a fairly radical Islamicist element (which plays an unknown but in my estimate minor role) and the discovery of the existence of a training school for terrorists, all represent a worrisome increase in the more radical Islamic religiously nationalistic strain in Bosnia.

Publications like *Preporod*, published by the *Mashihat* of the Islamic Community of B&H, and *Glasnik* and *Takvim* published by the Supreme Islamic Leadership in Sarajevo, tended to publish both ancient and recent writings of prominent Muslim thinkers who stressed the unity of the religious and political

---

[40]Interview with a refugee Bosnian Croat who used to work in the Department of the Interior in B&H, Philadelphia, February 27, 1996.

[41]Paul Hockenos, "Islam is a Growing Rallying Cry for Bosnian Army," *Religious News Service*, July 27, 1995.

[42]*Ibid.*

system in Islam and its superiority over all other systems, while the editorial boards did nothing to distance themselves from these views, but rather praised the authors as authentic expressions of Islamic thought.[43]

The above simply attempts to point out that the Muslims were not simply the passive recipients of unprovoked Serb aggression, but have added a number of tiles to the mosaic of violence. When a group is 44 per cent of the population or more, and is demographically expanding, and some of its leaders say that after they become 51 per cent they have the right to establish a traditional Islamic state with Islamic laws with no regard to the will of the minority or even the majority, that, indeed, presents an extreme threat to other enthnoreligious groups.

Positive Contributions of Religious Communities

The positive contributions of the religious communities were few, and the negative were many. There were a few well publicized meetings between the Patriarch and the Cardinal who were then joined occasionally by the *Reis-ul-Ulema*. These declarations against the war were beautifully worded and received a limited exposure abroad but were not effectively disseminated in war territories.

As a fine example of these declarations, we can cite the most forceful text that emerged out of the 1992 Geneva meeting between Patriarch Pavle and Cardinal Franjo Kuharić partially reproduced here as follows:

> Following our prayers and conversations, we appeal with one mind and voice to the faithful of our churches, to the responsible organs of the state, to military commanders and troops, to all peoples and men and women of our common geographical and spiritual area, as well as to all international forums and institutions engaged in the search for a solution or in the provision of aid to our region and in our states; and we do not only appeal but demand, on the basis of our spiritual position and moral responsibility:
>
> 1. Immediately and without condition to cease all hostilities, all bloodshed and all destruction, in particular to stop the blasphemous and insane destruction of places of prayer and holy places, Christian and Muslim alike; and that negotiations between the warring parties be initiated without delay.
>
> 2. Immediately and without condition to liberate all prisoners of war and hostages, as well as to close all prison camps and to free all those incarcerated in this evil war.
>
> 3. Immediately and without condition to cease the inhuman practice of ethnic cleansing, by whomever it is being incited or carried out.
>
> 4. To permit all refugees and deportees to return to their homes and to ensure all bishops and priests of our churches as well as Islamic spiritual leaders free access to their flock and undisturbed exercise of their office.

---

[43]In *Preporod* of April 15, 1992, a *fetva* or judgement was rendered declaring the war in Bosnia a *jihad* and stating that betraying the war effort is tantamount to betraying the religion.

5. That normal communication and unrestricted circulation be re-established, as well as the possibility of free movement and settlement for all people, whatever their religious or national affiliation, and

6. That all suffering people be assured undisturbed and equal access to humanitarian aid.

Equally with one mind and voice we condemn all crimes and distance ourselves from all criminals, irrespective of which people or army they belong to or which church or religious affiliation they claim. We especially express our horror at the perpetration of extremely immoral misdeeds, at the mistreatment of older and younger women and girls, which only monsters can perpetrate, no matter what name they give themselves.

Before God, before humanity and before our own conscience we pledge that we will use all evangelical means and the full influence of our office and responsibility in church and society to work, in our own states and peoples, decisively and openly for peace, justice and the salvation of each and every one, for the dignity and inalienable rights of every individual and every people, for humanity and tolerance, for forgiveness and love.

We ourselves call, individually and together, for repentance before the God of love, for conversation and for service to him, that we can live anew as neighbours, friends and brothers,

Peace to all![44]

Higher clergy like Vinko Cardinal Puljić of Sarajevo and Bishop Franjo Komarica of Banja Luka spoke eloquently about the need to defend their own people from the effects of "ethnic cleansing" and spoke on behalf of the right of all autochthonous peoples to remain living next to each other. Initially, the leaders of all three religious communities issued reservations and criticisms of the Dayton Agreement but later agreed that despite flaws, as they looked at these documents, that it was the best that could be achieved and minimally the agreement interrupted or ended the war-making.

There were lower clergy who probably courageously fought for peace and concord, but their voices rarely reached beyond their own communities. One can only surmise that some who were most conciliatory were possibly opposed by the nationalists in their own community. There are numerous stories of local battles during the war where the only people sufficiently trusted by the embattled Muslim and Croat parties were the clergy of the two groups who would be permitted to escort negotiators into the 'enemy' territory to work out cease-fires or evacuations of civilians. While many clergy fled with retreating civilians, there were also those who stayed on the ground with those too sick or too old to leave. Some of those paid for their pastoral care with their lives, because rampaging, vengeful warriors would rarely respect these men of good will. Basically, one can stress the positive role of all religious leaders in their

---

[44]Full text in *Occasional Papers on Religion in Eastern Europe*, Vol. XII, No. 5 (October 1992), 50-51.

role of bandaging the literal and metaphorical wounds of their injured communities.

But some succeeded in continuing the tradition of communal tolerance and even dared to dream of a time when the passive forms of former social acceptance of each other may grow into active interfaith dialogue and cooperation. For instance, a small group, *Zayedno* [Together], consisting of Jewish, Muslim, Catholic, and Orthodox clergy and intellectuals valiantly continued to promote the ideals and practices of pluralism in B&H as well as among emigrants abroad. They planned the establishment of a department of interreligious dialogue at Sarajevo University with the assistance of sympathetic foreign academic, ecclesiastic, and individual contributors. The ability of the *Zayedno* group to work harmoniously across religious boundaries is both untypical and generally not appreciated by their own respective religious leaders, although in principle these leaders tend to stress their general belief that one must nurture interfaith contacts and cooperation.

The religious leaders of B&H tend to emphasize that the humanitarian agencies associated with their religious community assist needy people without regard to religious affiliation. Church groups that do not have adherents in B&H likewise have become active in providing relief and repatriation assistance, the most notable being the United Methodist Committee on Relief that was selected as a lead humanitarian agency by the U.N. High Commissioner for Refugees since they have shown that they are able to distribute aid equitably and efficiently.

While it is not easy to cite too many positive roles played by the religious communities, it does not mean that it has to remain indefinitely so. The healing and reconciling role of religion is potentially so, and can and must become actualized if B&H is to have a promising future. It is with this hope, despite the above cited divisive roles of religion, that I chose to end this account. Those who genuinely love and know their religious history and living community know that there is a font of inspiration at the beginning of each of these great religious traditions that commits adherents to work for peace, justice, and healing. If the present followers are to remain authentic to the original message, they must be transformed into agents of reconciliation, showing loving kindness and concern for the well-being not only of their co-religionists and co-nationals, but to all individuals and groups, because they share the same God-given humanity.

6

BOSNIA: A CASE STUDY IN RELIGION AND ETHNIC CONFLICT

N. Gerald Shenk

Background and involvements

Because personal identity and origins, language and religion mean everything for clarity of human interactions in the Balkan region (and elsewhere as well!), I will identify myself briefly at the outset, even though this is not really my own story. I belong to the Mennonite Church, a small evangelical group among Protestants committed to peaceable solutions to conflict. Born of ethnic roots that were mostly Swiss and South German in the United States, I have no direct ties to any of the nationalities that made up the former Yugoslavia. But between 1977 and 1989, I spent nine years as student, church worker, teacher, and friend of local Protestant communities in that land. Since 1989, I have returned each year for several weeks of lectures in the Evangelical Theological Faculty now located in Osijek, Croatia. My work is in the sociology of religion, and I have studied especially the changing role of religion within Yugoslavia in the 1980s.

Two years of my study were in Sarajevo at the Philosophy Faculty of its university. (The Dean of our faculty at that time has recently been identified in international reports as the minister of foreign affairs under Radovan Karadžić in the Serbian separatist forces in Pale, Bosnia.) My friends were Muslim, Orthodox, Catholic, Protestant, and Marxist. Almost everyone who learned of my interest in religion would make two points in reply: 1) the several religious traditions used to be very important here, and 2) we would not want that era to return because when religion controlled society it made too many conflicts. Besides, some would add, many of us now belong to more than one background; what would people of mixed heritage do in a world of separatism?

A Brief Anatomy of the Conflict

Ethnic History, Main Groups: Slavic settlement in the region began with migrations in the seventh century. Saints Cyril and Methodius and their disciples are credited with the conversion of the Serbs to Christianity in the 800s A.D. Frankish missionaries loyal to Rome brought the Croats into the fold. Regional feudal and nascent political formations further aligned them with the East and West until the Great Schism of 1054 confirmed the framework for a process of differentiation that continues to the present day. It is uncanny to observe the striking continuity of patterns in maps of regional conflicts from one century to the next for the entire millennium. The Krajina in particular, for example, was disputed territory in each of several centuries, a frontline for the Ottoman and Habsburg empires and other regional powers.

The other definitive development for Bosnia was the arrival of Islam with Turkish conquest in the 1400s. Mythology obscures the politically sensitive question of the ethnic identification of today's Muslims prior to the conversion to Islam; whether originally Serb or Croat, most of these Muslims clearly have Slavic and Christian origins. (I am personally intrigued with the sketchy accounts of a previous protest movement, the medieval Bosnian Church which arose between the two branches of Eastern and Western Christianity--especially because its members also refused military involvements. Also linked to the larger Balkan movement known as Bogumils, some trace a direct connection to those who later adopted Islam.) The basic triangular pattern of relationships in Bosnia has not changed ever since, even under the strenuously secular regime of Tito and Communism. In fact, Tito's strategy clearly made this triangle the bulwark in several ways for stability in the middle of multiethnic Yugoslavia. I resided in Sarajevo during the lengthy period of his final illness and death; it was an objective observation that displays of mourning remained in shop windows longer there than in any other region of Yugoslavia.

The Tito legacy is complex and would deserve an entire study to evaluate it anew in light of current developments. That is beyond the scope of this essay. Both blame and credit would attach to various elements of his policies on religion, on minorities, on regional concerns, on human rights, etc. In retrospect, it seems that an effective policy of repression on national, minority, and other expressions can prove most costly at the demise of the enforcer. The explosion of conflicts in this case is due, perhaps in large part, to the failure to develop other methods of dealing with normal conflict under the single-party state.

Not One War, But Several: Even in good times, Yugoslavia was known as "the despair of tidy minds." This complicated war may be seen first of all as a war of definitions. Some of the suggestions include civil war versus war of aggression; war of succession to the property and powers of a federal state in disintegration; wars of ancient tribal animosities and ethnic repression; and wars of the dissolution of a federal military into various regional militias and further into little more than thuggery and roving gangs of banditry. A further war is the multifaceted struggle for and against outsider opinion, the battle for the power to define things correctly on CNN or SkyNews, etc.

Most of us could somehow come to comprehend these tragic events, settling for one definition or another. But there is another level at which these struggles have come into our consciousness, and perhaps this should be called the war for our own souls. Reports of beastly atrocities have burned across the distances, which do not turn out to be such great distances after all. Against our will, we are drawn into this maelstrom; we are hooked by our own fascination with brutal violence in its worst forms, and we stand indicted by our collective failure to find an effective response to the slaughter of the innocents, the rapes, the wanton destruction of undefended civilian populations. This raw evil is far beyond military calculation. These are crimes against humanity.

Bosnia Is Unique: The political leadership and the general population of Bosnia were not more bellicose than other parts of the former Yugoslavia. In fact, its leadership along with that of Macedonia played a moderating role in the larger conflicts over the eventual break-up of the federal order. Slovenia and Croatia made their moves for independence in mid-1991, with recognition by Germany and the European Community about six months later. Open warfare in Slovenia was brief (about ten days). Croatia's independence was immediately complicated by resistance from a large part of its Serbian population gathered in mostly rural regions to the east and along the inside of its southern flank. Warfare over these regions lasted about six months until a ceasefire in January 1992. Again, a larger study should review the significant impact of the Yugoslav Federal Army in its interventions, its withdrawals, and its collaboration with irregular formations, notably Serb militias in various regions receiving military hardware to such an extent that later conflicts were substantially exacerbated. Looking back, it seems as if Slovenia were playing with matches, the Serbs and Croats with dynamite, and in Bosnia the world was toying with atomic weaponry.

Both within Bosnia and from outside, most observers regarded it as the worst-case scenario if fighting should spill over into a complex three-way struggle for control of Bosnia. Whether from denial or wishful thinking, many internal and external factors combined in a failure to prepare for the eventuality of open warfare and a failure to effectively prevent it. The elected government had virtually no time to acquire weaponry for the fledgling state; but not having weapons did not allay the fears and suspicions on the other side. Many critical observers count the EC recognition of Bosnia's independence on 6 April 1992 a precipitating factor in the eruption of deadly strife. This took place on the anniversary of Hitler's bombardment of Belgrade, playing right into the view that the West was colluding in a renewal of aggression against Serbs. The Serbs of Bosnia, in undisguised close cooperation with Serbs elsewhere in Croatia and Serbia, had held their own referendum in late 1991 to justify a refusal to go along with a prospective move by Bosnia's Croats and Muslims to withdraw from Yugoslavia.

But everybody knew that what made Bosnia really Bosnia was not the simple sum of its various parts. What always made Bosnia specific was its often tense interaction at the conjunction of two major religious worlds (Christian and Islamic) and three connecting faith communities (Muslim, Orthodox, Catholic). None was in an overall majority, but each had its own regions of predominance. The Muslim population of Bosnia was usually given around 40%; the Serbs had a bit more than 30% and the Croats under 20%. The simple figures are by themselves misleading, however. Landholding patterns before the outbreak of hostilities were significantly different from the ethnic proportions: due largely to differences in settlement patterns, Serbs in Bosnia held something more than 50% of the lands in private ownership. Muslims dwelling more typically in towns and cities had a smaller share.

The inadequacy of general population statistics is especially evident in the finding that of Yugoslavia's twenty-three million inhabitants before this warfare about seven million were the children or grandchildren of ethnically mixed marriages. A simplistic division into "cantons" for each ethnic group would clearly leave large numbers of people without an obvious "bantustan" to which to belong. Where would they find refuge? Which ethnic identification would they have to select? None of the maps in the various fateful "peace plans" ever showed a territorial answer to this stubborn problem.

As of this writing, the Dayton Accord brokered by heavy US involvement and backed by significant NATO and European assistance for implementation had recently overcome an otherwise relentless pattern of failures in diplomacy and international (UN) interventions. On all sides, even those most committed to struggle for peaceful solutions had expressed deepening dismay over sanctions and arms embargoes, ineffective responses, and confusion in contradictory strategies that only complicated the basic task of bringing the hostilities to a close.

Religion in the Social Crisis

Religion as Marker: Religion had always been one way of symbolizing the boundaries between various communities. Its symbols, loyalties, and differences have been the stuff of basic human interaction at the level just beyond the individual. Each group's heritage is rich with history and memories understood in terms of faith. In the long sweep of centuries, this becomes more and more mythical, but for any given individual, it has been an unavoidable defining question. "What are you?" was almost always part of a get-acquainted conversation in Bosnia. The answer could take two forms: ethnic or religious.

To illustrate: when my Muslim landlord in Sarajevo was trying to understand me in our early encounters over coffee, he once asked whether we celebrate Christmas. Not particularly interested in the careful nuances of my description, he pushed on to inquire, when? If January, he would place my curious (unknown) version of Protestantism within the Orthodox orbit; if December, then obviously I belonged to the Catholic world. Categories matter. Not having any of the traditional religious markers, one could only be left with Marxism, but that was rarely asked.

Key Players, Strategic Choices: Leaders of religious communities in the collapse of Yugoslavia could be forgiven if they saw in it and rejoiced over an end to state suppression of religious life, a release from the repression of minority groups, a chance to reassert ancient claims on collective life. For many clerics, an atheist regime had prevented proper social recognition, even devaluing their education and work history in calculating retirement pensions. As elsewhere in socialism, there were claims over properties long since confiscated.

Furthermore, and tragically, as it turned out, some religious leaders also saw in resurgent nationalism a clear opportunity for affirmation and vindication of a long-neglected role for religion in public affairs and in the general cultural life of their respective peoples. Sooner or later, most did recognize the demonic hostilities awakened by resurgent nationalist separatism, and moved against the hatred, mistrust, and manipulation of fear which fed it. Slowly, the statements and declarations came forth with some effort even in ecumenical frameworks. But all too little could be done in prevention of hostilities. The traditional religious structure did not encourage independent initiatives at the local or regional levels. Especially in times of crisis, major action depended on the central figures. Yet the crucial tests would often arise out at the fringes, where contesting groups met at local levels.

Collapse of Civility: The growing hostility of the clashes had a contagious effect, often magnified by hysterical propagandist treatment in the mass media. Symbols of civilization itself became the target of deliberate destruction. Little remained of traditional exclusions from "civilized warfare": hospitals and schools and museums and especially places of worship were often selected for attack. Religion as marker was a conspicuous casualty. Nothing was sacred, at least if it belonged to the enemy.

One key component of controversy and inter-ethnic hostilities was the charge that a Muslim-led state in Bosnia would mean the establishment of a radical Islamic fundamentalist regime. Suspicion centered on the figure elected in 1990 to the Bosnian presidency, Alija Izetbegović. He had been put on trial in 1983 by the Communist authorities on political charges, stemming primarily from his unpublished manifesto circulating since 1970 as *The Islamic Declaration.* Issues raised in the trial and swirling in the overheated separatist fervor of the early 1990s continue to match the scope of current polarization over the nature and future of life in mixed or barely separated communities in the Balkan area.

Some read the manifesto as a charter for radical Islamic control, even a totalitarian threat against others under its domination. Others attempt to downplay this danger, due to the broadly secular character of most Bosnian Muslims. Tito's Yugoslavia had carved out the Muslim ethnic identity as a nationality on a par with the larger groups (Serb, Croat, Slovene, etc.), mostly for political purposes. Many political figures who survived a transition away from socialist rule took up an ethnic, nationalist identity, making at least a show of embracing the traditional religious garb that comes down through the legacy of history.

Izetbegović, however, showed little interest in Islamic theology or its traditional thought. His manifesto was rather a protest at various Muslim societies in their accommodation to modern values and institutions (others might call them moderate regimes). Not a return to religious dominance in society, but a retrieval of Islamic social and political thought into current practice by Muslim peoples everywhere seemed to be his overarching goal. The scope of this renaissance for Islam would be "a great federation from Morocco to Indonesia, from tropical Africa to central Asia."

The deepest offense which critics take at the claims of *The Islamic Declaration* centers on specific lines, regarding "the incompatibility of Islam with non-Islamic systems. There can be neither peace nor coexistence between the Islamic religion and non-Islamic social and political institutions." Islam, the manifesto declares, is only strong if it completely rejects accommodation to modern (Western) socio-political norms and structures. Religious renewal is primary, but closely followed by political revolution, whereby Muslims recover their own original Islamic character.

The rhetoric of the manifesto does not appear directed in any specific sense to the multiethnic, religiously diverse circumstances of contemporary Bosnia. Not a single feature unique to that reality (in 1970 or 1983 or 1990 or 1996) is mentioned; in fact, the social specifics which do crop up seem to come from other places and other times. "Harems must be abolished." The "tendency should be to curb polygamy," writes Izetbegović, "to eventually eliminate it completely from practical life," even though it had not been sanctioned in

Bosnia for decades. Islam should also not be used "as a reason to keep women disenfranchised; abuse of this kind must be brought to an end"--just as Tito and the Partizans had accomplished in Yugoslavia a quarter century earlier!

Other religious groups and minorities within Islamic societies are merely mentioned in passing. *The Islamic Declaration* can hardly be taken as a text for these questions; if offers far too little reassurance on the nature of minority protections and political rights. Renewed Islam may be perceived as a threat by its neighbors unless civil and political freedoms are spelled out in much greater detail on constitutional grounds elsewhere.

As I have observed elsewhere,

> With regard to Christianity, the declaration expresses a clear preference for Christ's teaching, which it distinguishes from the church, 'an organization which, with its inevitable hierarchy, politics, wealth, and interests, has become not only non-Islamic, but anti-Christian.' In other words, this program for the 'desecularization' of Islam hopes for cooperation with a 'depoliticized' Christianity. There is irony here, but it may be too subtle, especially for Christians long influenced by their proximity to Islam. Restoration of Christianity's fundamentals, it clearly suggests, would make the Christian community less political and, therefore, easier to live with.[1]

It is easier to imagine that radical intensification of the political character of Islam for Muslim peoples might spark a similar politicization of faith among their Christian neighbors. Both Christians and Muslims must clearly rethink the implications of their faith and political visions for life in close proximity, indeed for life in a minority position, and for treatment of other minorities on their own turf, if civility is to survive as a plausible virtue into the new century.

Social Crisis in Religion

I have deliberately refrained from assigning blame in clear proportions to the parties to this conflict. In various ways, at various levels, we are all guilty and complicit in the horrors I have had to describe. The question of how and where these conflicts originated is important although almost impossibly complex. Collective responsibility for the terror and trauma is not evenly divided among all parties, least of all the children of this war, who will be paying the price for decades to come.

The task of affixing blame may itself be a detour, avoiding the deeper struggle to assess the impact of such incivility and irreligion on morality, character, and human dignity at large. Especially in the failure of outside interventions, we sense the untenable nature of easy moralizing postures. Quick condemnation leads us to overlook the despair and futility of our own ineffective

---

[1]Shenk, *God With Us? : The Roles of Religion in Conflicts in the Former Yugoslavia* (Uppsala: Life & Peace Institute, 1993), 28.

response. Like many others here, I have agonized in deep and often speechless dismay, verging on chronic depression over Bosnia. Multiply this sense of futility in individual response into the scale of sporadic and fickle diplomacy, and you have the formula to turn Bosnia into Lebanon (fifteen years of strife) or Northern Ireland (twenty-five years). Bosnia is a test for our resistance to total dehumanization. This is a question of faith.

An Early Research Project on Religion in the Conflicts

For the most part, religion has received very bad press in the decline and fall of Yugoslavia. It is an easy target both in the active warfare and in the game of affixing blame from outside the situation. But some of us were persuaded there must be more than meets the eye; perhaps some of the better evidence is being overlooked. We set out to find the contrary evidence, where religiously motivated actors in the struggle had taken real action to stem the tide of violence, to resist the hatred, to empower what is noble, to heal the wounds, and to seek "the things that make for peace," as Jesus put it. With support from church agencies and directed by the Life & Peace Institute (of Uppsala, Sweden), colleague David Steele and I began in mid-1992 and intensively in the first six months of 1993 to journey from one embattled region to another, seeking out the best examples we could.

Many accounts were simply sad beyond measure; we spent hours listening to laments. But here and there, people knew of instances where someone had gone beyond the obvious duty to care for one's own, reaching out to victims also on the other side. Collecting these accounts, we were able to share them as inspiration for others along the way. Eventually, we got support for a gathering on neutral ground where some who had been laboring in isolation could take courage from direct encounters with those who have been seeking and making peace on the other side or sides. This represented a qualitative conceptual breakthrough since the net result more than reinforced confidence that lonely peacemakers do not labor in vain. Some of those accounts are presented in the participants' own words in the video entitled "Beyond the News: Hope for Bosnia."

Further research efforts have included seminars and workshops to train for conflict resolution at local and regional levels in various parts of the former Yugoslavia. David Steele and others have pursued these activities with diligence, even amidst considerable uncertainty and hazard while the conflicts continue. There is serious work to do in preparation for peace. Any solid future solutions to the present conflicts will necessarily include the most constructive role for religious communities that we can imagine.

Conclusion

A few guiding theses are being offered in place of summary here:

1) We must not regard as inevitable the clash of civilizations. Bosnia in all of its chapters has included the confidence that differences can be lived with and that the tensions can be constructive.

2) We must resist the view that the latest news of tragedies is the real story of Bosnia. Both the future and the past have a claim on our understanding that resists the tyranny of the urgent.

3) The complexity of the current conflict and its backgrounds in Bosnian history defies any precise assignment of blame and responsibility for each of the parties involved. Both victims and perpetrators (but not alike) have claims on our capacity to comprehend the enormity of evil which has befallen us in intractible hostilities during recent years there.

4) Nevertheless, in the wake of atrocities, finding the truth and doing justice are both essential steps in recovery and building peace.

SOURCES

Balkan War Report (journal edited by Anthony Borden), published by Institute for War and Peace Reporting, London.

Cviic, Christopher. *Remaking the Balkans*. London: Royal Institute of International Affairs, 1991.

Forrester, Duncan. *Beliefs, Values and Policies: Conviction Politics in a Secular Age*. Oxford: Clarendon Press, 1989.

Glenny, Misha. *The Fall of Yugoslavia: The Third Balkan War*. New York, London: Penguin Books, 1992.

Johnston, Douglas and Cynthia Sampson, eds. *Religion, the Missing Dimension of Statecraft*. Oxford: University Press, 1994.

Kotkin, Joel. *Tribes: How Race, Religion and Identity Determine Success in the New Global Economy*. New York: Random House, 1993.

Mojzes, Paul. *Yugoslavian Inferno: Ethnoreligious Warfare in the Balkans*. New York: Continuum, 1994.

Religion in Eastern Europe (journal edited by Paul Mojzes), published by Christians Associated for Relations with Eastern Europe.

Shenk, Gerald and David Steele. *God With Us? The Roles of Religion in Conflicts in the Former Yugoslavia*. Uppsala: Life and Peace Institute, December 1993.

7

THE RELIGIOUS FACTOR AND THE WAR IN BOSNIA AND HERZEGOVINA

Srdjan Vrcan

I

The role of the religious factor in shaping the three monotheistic religious confessions (Catholicism, Orthodoxy, and Islam) in the current war in B&H may be analyzed from the standpoint of the sociology of religion either as a contemporary case with high symptomatic relevance or as an obvious anomaly with no symptomatic relevance at all. However, it may be argued that it is a case which could disclose in a very manifest and drastic way some of the structural trends and situational constraints as well as some contemporary religious potential for conflicts that are present in other situations as well, but remain latent and hardly discernible. If there is truth, as there is, in Karl Popper's description of the historically structured situation in East and Central Europe as a product of ethnic migrations and collisions of cultures, resulting in a linguistic, ethnic, and cultural mosaic mishmash, a mixture which could not be disentangled again, then this is quite accurate for B&H. The relevance, pluriculturality, and plurinationality in B&H has been a fact persisting for centuries and not a result of some very recent migrations. Therefore, Catholicism, Orthodoxy, and Islam in B&H are to be considered equally autochthonous.[1] Furthermore, there is no doubt that it is a society struck by a grave social crisis and radical changes, afflicting all levels of social life from the systemic one to the everyday one. Therefore, it is a case which may exhibit conflicting potential of the religious factor to emerge with force into the open, mainly in situations of grave social crises and social breakdowns. In this sense,

---

[1] This is to be distinguished from multiculturalism analyzed by John Rex in Western Europe and it concerns not the status of a minority or of minorities in a stable society but the very basis of the society as such. John Rex, "The Political Sociology of Multiculturalism and the Place of Muslims in West European Societies," *Social Compass*, 41, 1994, 1, 79-92.

B&H may be seen as a kind of a contemporary testing ground to explore the possible consequences of some recent developments and trends of wider interest for contemporary sociology of religion.

There is no need to argue extensively to demonstrate that the actual war in B&H has something to do with its plurireligious, pluricultural, and plurinational nature and its possible survival retaining these features. There is less need to argue long in order to show that the actual war did not break out as a totally unexpected and unforseen event, just exploding like a thunderbolt from clear skies.[2] Minimally, there is no need to argue in order to indicate that the actual war has not been an accidental war, caused by the purely contingent and unpredictable conjunction of rather casual events which could have been easily avoided.

First, the war in B&H is to be approached as a highly probable and almost necessary stage of the grave and global crisis in and of former Yugoslavia in general and more particularly of transitional processes from Communism to post-Communism going on so far in the region. In that context, the war is in a direct way the almost necessary and unavoidable consequence of political philosophies and political strategies, having become dominant since the mid-1980's and defining the actual course of transition to post-Communism, basically by trying to impose a very specific solution to the Yugoslav crisis in terms not too far from I. Cristoll's formula for solutions of contemporary crises: free market plus nationalism plus religion. In substance, the war in B&H has been since its very beginning primarily a political war, caused by previously formulated conflicting fundamental objectives of the dominant political strategies, thus confirming fully von Klausewitz' thesis that the war is but a continuation of politics by other means and methods. It may be reasonably asserted that the war in B&H has been an almost necessary result of the pursuit

---

[2]The author of this paper wrote in August 1991, in an essay written for a pacifist conference in Austria eight months before the outbreak of the war in Bosnia and Herzegovina that the war was certainly going to be extended pretty soon to Bosnia and Herzegovina since it would be very unrealistic to presume that Serbs and Croats were going to live in stable peace and coexistence in Bosnia and Herzegovina, while, depicted as arch-enemies, they were fiercely fighting in Croatia. And it would be quite senseless to believe that Bosnia and Herzegovina could survive in peace and continue to persist as a plurinational, pluricultural, and plurireligious state while the on-going deconstruction and reconstruction of the former Yugoslavia was being based, motivated, and legitimated upon the antithetical political philosophy of the so-called fallacy of multiethnicity (the term was used by Tomislav Sunić, "The Fallacy of the Multiethnic State: The Case of Yugoslavia," *Conservative Review*, 1(1990), 9-11.) Srdjan Vrcan, "A European Lebanon in Making or a Replica of Pakistani/India Drama?" in T. Kuzmanić, A.Truger, *Yugoslavia War*, (Ljubljana and Schlaining: Austrian Study Centre for Peace and Conflict Resolution Schlaining and Peace Institute Ljubljana, 1992), 117-130.

of irreconcilable programs for political deconstruction and reconstruction of former Yugoslavia and more particularly of B&H. To put it simply, the war in B&H is the necessary result of nationalist political philosophy and functioning nationalist political strategies, dominating so far in transitional processes with contrasting fundamental political objectives, but basically following the same political ideal best expressed by the formula of G. Mazzini, "Every nation one state. Only one state for every nation." Consequently, it may be even predicted, reversing von Klausewitz' thesis, that even the politics of tomorrow with peace finally imposed from outside would be in substance a continuation of the current war by other means and methods.

Second, it is evident that the actual war in B&H is not a radical historical novelty and a social *novuum* to be presumably interpreted simply as a heritage or a tail of Communism, interpreting dominant nationalism not as an alternative to Communism but as its last stage, to use A. Michnik's words. It is easy to show that the actual war bears too many signs of something *deja vu* and of a partial repetition of something that already happened although now in the most exacerbated, drastic, and cruel way. Therefore, it is a war more in accordance as a probability than in radical discordance with the matrix of long-term developments in B&H and its potentiality with Communism or no Communism involved. There are evident connections or similarities, for instance, with events in 1941-1945, in 1918, in 1914 and so on. Consequently, the actual war in B&H may be plausibly seen as the latest stage of long-term historic-social developments since the Austro-Hungarian occupation and annexation and the beginning of modernization of Bosnian society. It has to do basically with the problem of finding a new and stable (presumably modern and democratic) basis for the very existence or probable survival of a plurireligious, pluricultural, and plurinational society since the breakdown of the traditional Ottoman institutional and cultural arrangements. For centuries there seemed a basis for stable and more or less peaceful existence and persistence of plurireligious, pluricultural, and plurinational life. Such was the system of *millet* and *zimmi* at the official level in the context of a hierarchical pluralism and Ottoman-Muslim dominance and the system of *komšiluk* at the level of everyday life but sustained by the state. It concerns essentially the crucial contradictions or at least permanent tensions emerging since that time between the political structuring and securement of the basis for stable and peaceful persistence of plurireligious, pluricultural, and plurinational Bosnia basically upon the modern principle of citizenship and democracy, guaranteed ultimately by free and active consent and participation of the governed, belonging to different communities and the political structuring, basically upon the basis of communitarism, that is, in short, between ethnicity[3] and citizenship as the principle of crucially relevant political structuring, or between construction of an identity based upon a political community and construction of a political community, based upon ethnic identity. One has to be aware that "the structuring principle of the Bosnian political order is not the citizenship but communitarian belonging: from 1910 to 1990 all the elections in B&H ended in a large domination of national parties."[4] There are other circumstances which underline additionally the symptomatic relevance of the role of the religious factor in the Bosnian-Herzegovinan war. One may mention, for instance, at least Max Weber's prognosis that even in the modern age of *Entzauberung* the old gods may resurrect one day and arise from their tombs to engage again in their eternal struggles since beyond ultimate antagonistic values there remains nothing but violence and force. And B&H may be viewed as the contemporary scene on European soil where this tragic dance goes on. The recent situation has been characterized and welcomed jubilantly by many as an epoch-making historically decisive "victory of God" (John Paul II) or in terms of a religious *reconquista* of the society, that had been long exposed to secularity and secularism.[5] It has also been phrased in terms of a God's revenge[6] and/or in less triumphalistic terms of a massive and penetrating return of the sacred with religion invading and occupying definitively the otherwise naked public square in so many contemporary societies. For illustration of early optimistic expectations, inspired by such a victory and *reconquista*, one may quote a Serbian sociologist of religion writing in 1991, that "owing to the eclipse of the socialist ideology, a social, cultural and spiritual climate has created very favorable conditions not only to a rebirth of Orthodoxy, but for its blossoming" with the Orthodox faith offering "to millions of men love and peace, felicity, and tolerance" as well as the possibility of finding a meaning of life and a reason for living and a feeling of equilibrium and stability, culminating in a lasting emancipation of the inner man in his spirituality.[7] This he certainly would not dare to repeat today after four years of a dirty war. Furthermore, it may be maintained that contemporary B&H is the best testing ground to evaluate the plausibility of the well-known public claim that a religious institution has been primarily an expert on humanity, far better here

---

[3]The terms ethnic and ethnicity are used here as purely technical terms generally used, although misleading as the existing religious, cultural, and national differences in Bosnia and Herzegovina historically developed basically upon the same purely Slavic background

[4]Bougarel, 1994, 7.

[5]Berger, 1986, 21; Voyé 1995, 40.

[6]Kepel, 1991.

[7]Djordjević, 1991, 9.

religious institution has been primarily an expert on humanity, far better here than in Northern Ireland, Lebanon, the Basque region, etc. Finally, there is the fact that it is mostly the Christians (Catholics and Orthodox) mutually and the Muslims and, thus, adherents to the family of the Book (*ahl el kitab*) who have been again killing each other in B&H, and not odd pagans or followers of some wild sect, who obsessed by the sacred, have gone mad. This is confirmed by the undeniable fact that religious symbolism has widely been used by the warriors and the warring sides in B&H.

Consequently, the first crucial question of the analysis appears to be the question *whether the three monotheistic religious confessions have basically been vectors of social divisions, social cleavages, and social conflicts and, therefore, of the commencement and development of the war, or whether they have proven to be vectors of peace, democracy, moderation, and tolerance in a plurireligious, pluricultural and plurinational country par excellence?* To put the same question in other terms, *whether the welcome of God's victory and the proclamation of religious reconquista of society have been creating some crucial conditions necessary for stable intercommunitarian peace and interreligious tolerance based upon fundamental democratic principles, or are they leading to new social, political and cultural polarizations, closures, and exclusions and to a tragic renewal of interfaith conflicts and strife nowadays under the guise of interethnic and intercultural confrontations?* And the second crucial question is, to borrow Franco Ferrarotti's words, *how can a contemporary multicultural society[8] function as a democratic society?*

An answer to the first question has to be plausibly searched in a meaningful context best described by two extreme points of view already formulated. The first one insists on describing the role of religion in positive terms: "One of the typical functions of religion through history has been to unify, to bind peoples, cultures, and civilizations together"[9] and to serve as a means to spiritual unification of continents.[10] The second one emphasizes (e.g. B. Barber) that however much the forms of an enlightened universalism used to glorify the past of such monotheistic religions as Judaism, Christianity, and Islam, in reality many of them in their modern incarnations are paroxysmal and not cosmopolitan, full of hatred and not of love, proselytizing and not ecumenical, fanatical and not rational, sectarian and not deistic, ethnocentric and not universalist with the result that, as the new forms of hypernationalism, they

---

[8]Ferrarotti, 1993, 118.

[9]Muray, 1991, 1.

[10]Voyé, 1995, 42.

are the new expressions of religious fundamentalism, schismatic and secessionist, never integrative.[11]

II

It is possible, of course, to reject such a context for a sociological analysis of the role of the religious factor in war in B&H by minimizing the symptomatic relevance of the current war in B&H for the contemporary sociology of religion simply by taking it as a totally anomalous, contemporary phenomenon outside of the matrix of the twentieth-century European political and religious history and/or having nothing to do with the universal dynamic of transition to post-Communism and/or most conveniently as a case in part generated by so-called Balkanism described long ago as:

> the custom and the system governing the pubic life of the Balkanic people: lack of principles, fighting with irregular and unlawful means, fraud, politically motivated murders, corruption, grab for fast gains, the creeping before superiors, cruelty towards subordinates.[12]

However, one ought to take into consideration some well-known hard facts too such as:

a) That wars have not been such a rare phenomenon in the twentieth century; to the contrary, this century has been a violent and frightening one[13] or even as the most violent one in human history[14] and that, as Hannah Arendt hinted, deprived, displaced, expelled persons and refugees on a mass scale may be taken as a kind of signature of this century,[15] regardless of whether Balkanism is involved;

b) That the invention of total war--and the war in B&H has been waged as a total war primarily by leaving no one outside the conflict in the protected status of civilian population--as "the generalization of the war to the whole of populations" has been a European one, and that "total wars are deliberately conducted not purely against the hostile armed forces but with the deliberate aim to break down and to obtain the total submission of the respective enemy population in general,"[16]

---

[11]Barber, 1992, 844.

[12]Schierup, 1993, ?

[13]Claimed by Anthony Giddens in Giddens, 1992, 3.

[14]As suggested by Charles Tilly (1992).

[15]Quoted by Habermas, 199, 651.

[16]Giddens, 1992, 330.

c)That there have been recently more than thirty wars mostly of ethnic, national, racial, tribal and/or religious nature;[17]

d)That some recent wars, classified by contemporary military theory as conflicts of low intensity, have not excelled in anything similar to a low level in terms of victims, producing since the end of the Second World War more than 15,000,000 of dead in Vietnam, India, Algeria, Angola, and so on with record losses in human life of as much as a half of the population exterminated in 1962 in West Papua and a third in 1975 in East Timor;[18]

e)That there are some trends of wider relevance which, for instance, Alain Touraine has recently identified as "the great return of nationalisms, of particularisms, of integrisms, religious or not, which seem to progress everywhere in the most modern countries as well as in those that have been most upset by forced modernization,"[19] concluding that the contemporary world has been imbued by conflicts even more radical than those of the classical industrial age by being conflicts of cultures and identities, basically non-negotiable and with no possible mediation, no common beliefs and practices, with affirmations of absolute differences and total rejections of others, and warning that "conflicts have never been so global up to the point that the world today has been permeated more by crusade-like wars and life-and-death fights than by conflicts which may be politically negotiated";[20] and

f)That Samuel Huntington offered an intriguing diagnosis of the world cleavages very relevant for B&H, insisting upon the oncoming of a new civilization-centric partition of the world or a new polarization of the world dimensions basically along religious lines turned now into civilizational ones, and that the crucial source of contemporary conflicts and "the longest and the most violent wars" is the essentially different and rarely substitutionable cultural and religious attitudes.[21]

III

The religious factor in the recent tragedy in B&H may be plausibly described in very general terms, used by R. Robertson, as situated within a recent trend of almost world dimensions of "politicization of religion" and

---

[17]Barber ,1992, 843.

[18]Tehranian, 1994, 89.

[19]Touraine, 1992, 14.

[20]Touraine, 1992, 372.

[21]Huntington, 1993.

"religionization of politics"[22] to be basically a predictable result of the recent desecularization of social life and primarily of a delaicization of politics. Evidently such a politicization of religion[23] and religionization of politics have occurred almost in every corner of former Yugoslavia. However, such a politicization of religion and a religionization of politics has occurred in B&H in a very specific historical and social context of a plurireligious, pluricultural, and plurinational society in which it has been the religious factor defining for centuries individual and collective identities and creating different communities or, to put it in another manner, defining the most important "We-s" as well as the most important "Them-s" and their respective relations and confines. In substance,

> making their religious chiefs responsible administrators of their communities, the Ottoman system of *millet* has in some way crystallized the religious confessions as the faithful could get out only by conversion. . . . *Millet* permitted the conservation of religious faith and its affirmation in face of others--basically Muslims--it had shortened the growing awareness of national groups to the point of making undisociable the binoms Greek and Orthodox, Serbs (or Bulgarian) and Orthodox. The history imposed this peculiar weight to the religious factor in elaboration and preservation of their cultures.[24]

At the same time, the politicization of religion and religionization of politics has occurred in B&H within a matrix of transition to post-Communism, politically and ideologically defined by dominating nationalism and nationalist political strategies.

It is important to remember, and to be able to understand the logic of recent developments in B&H, it is important to remember some fundamental characteristics of nationalism. They have been pregnantly described by E. Gellner:

a) that nationalism is

> a theory of political legitimacy which requires that ethnic boundaries should not cut across political ones, and, in particular, that ethnic boundaries within a given state--a contingency already formally excluded by the principle in its general formulation--should not separate the power-holders from the rest[25]

---

[22]Robertson, 1989, 13.

[23]It is interesting to mention that Patrick Michel hints at an inherent connection between politicization of religion and a religious revival as he puts the question: "Politicization of religion, in the perspective that it generates a mission or articulates itself upon it, has not become, nor was it becoming a condition of 'religious revival'?" P. Michel, 138.

[24]Castellan, 1991, 25.

[25]Gellner, 1986, 1.

b)that it tries to put in practice the formula "One nation, one culture, one state" which seems to be an inescapable corollary of the new socioeconomic order so that a close relation between the state and culture--the state giving necessary political roof to a distinct culture--is realized which is the essence of nationalism,[26]

c)that for nationalism,

> culture is no longer merely adornment, confirmation, and legitimation of a social order which is also sustained by harsher and coercive constraints; culture is now the necessary shared medium, the life blood or perhaps rather the minimal shared atmosphere, within which alone the members of the society can breathe and survive and produce. For a given society it must be the same culture[27]

with the exclusion of real cultural pluralism so that "a high culture pervades the whole society, defines it, and needs to be sustained by the polity,"[28] and that "genuine cultural pluralism ceases to be viable under current conditions,"[29] and

d) that in some cases, particularly in Eastern Europe, the implementation of the nationalist imperative is

> bound to involve population exchanges or expulsions, more or less forcible assimilation, and sometimes liquidation, in order to attain that close relation between state and culture which is the essence of nationalism.[30]

Furthermore, it may be added that the fate of minorities facing nationalism has not been rosy since in the best case, as E. Kamenka indicated, "while minorities organized as communities can be subjects, modern history has shown that it is very difficult for them to be citizens."[31]

One has also to take into consideration the fact of contemporary bonds between nationalism and religion, contrary to some assertions, describing nationalism as a fruit of secularization and as a kind of secular alternative to religion or as two basically competing transcendental ideas of superiority and

---

[26]Gellner, 1986, 2. In another analysis, E. Gellner points out that nationalism is to be defined minimally as a political principle and that the only legitimate foundation of the modern state is the nation.

[27]Gellner, 1986, 37-38.

[28]Gellner, 1986, 18.

[29]Gellner, 1986, 55.

[30]Gellner, 1986, 101.

[31]Kamenka, 1973, 15. Tomislav Sunić goes a step further maintaining that democracy in a pluriethnic country is political nonsense while Anthony Giddens warns that "there is no type of nation-state in the contemporary world which is completely immune from the potentiality of being subject to totalitarian rule." Anthony Giddens, *The Nation-State and Violence*, (Oxford: The Polity Press, 1992), 116.

two rival transcendental realms of sublime essences and forces.[32] It means that today, at least in the former Yugoslavia, nationalism does not appear and become more important as secularization allegedly advances and religion somehow declines, but an upsurge of nationalism goes on hand-in-hand with a religious revival. Therefore, nationalism does not function as an alternative to religion, entering into the naked public square when and where religion weakens, but they advance both mutually, reinforcing one another in the wake of the same dynamics and the same trends, penetrating together into the naked public square. Nationalist reawakenings and religious revivals seem to be complementary today.[33]

It is rather obvious that nationalist political strategies could not be applied to B&H without unavoidable recourse to extreme violence on a mass scale and to resort to arms and war with massacres and ethnic cleansing and, ultimately, without threatening the very existence and survival of B&H as a social and cultural entity and not purely a geographic region. Therefore, the most cruel and most brutal aspects of the recent war in B&H are essentially necessary consequences of the respective nationalist political strategies and not some kind of unwanted marginal appendages or excesses to them. And the so-called ethnic cleansing has not been a consequence of war, but one of the objectives of political programs having lead to the war and of the war itself. It was not hatred that produced nationalist politics but nationalist politics deliberately generated and inflamed hatred to a pathological degree.

IV

A number of crucial moments come into the focus of the analysis trying to identify the role of the religious factor in the Bosnian-Herzegovinan war. However, three preliminary points of view should be underlined.

First, there is no more one permanent, monolithic, and unchanging "Islam" or Islamic movement in B&H than there is one, monolithic, and unchanging "Christianity" respectively dominated by sets of relatively enduring and unchanging beliefs and values, directly derived from the respective sacred texts and simply present in B&H. There is basically a historically specific, contemporary Bosnian Islam as well as a Bosnian and Herzegovinan Catholicism (even a Bosnian one and a Herzegovinan one) and a Bosnian and Herzegovinan Orthodoxy, articulated primarily by specific historical experience and traditions

---

[32]Terms are taken from S.N.Eisenstadt, B.Giesen, 1995."The Construction of Collective Identity," *Archives europennes de sociologie*, 36, 1, 89.

[33]Tincq, 1993, 240.

and responding to some specific historical and contemporary challenges, contradictions, and tensions.

Second, all three religious confessions in B&H make the same claim to have been for centuries religions on the frontier with the specific features of religions on the frontier: Catholics on a traditional *antemurrale Christianitatis* and with a modern "experience of frontier facing three ideologizations,"[34] Serbian Orthodoxy at the Western frontiers of Eastern Christianity, and Muslims in the past on the frontier between "*dar-ul-harb*," the home of war and "*dar-ul-Islam*," home of submission to the will of Allah and recently as a bridgehead of the Muslim world and Islamic culture on the European soil.

Third, the role of the religious factor in B&H is currently situated within the matrix of a wider process characterized not by *Vergeselschaftung* but by *Vergemeinschaftung*, not by de-traditionalization but by re-traditionalization, not by *Entzauberung* but by *Wiederverzauberung* of the world, not by privatization of decisions but by collectivization of decisions,[35] and not by a de-totalization but a re-totalization of religion.[36] Also, the processes regarding religions in B&H seem to be more in discordance than in accordance with D. Herveu-Leger's diagnosis regarding religion in Western Europe as a sign of a strengthening of religiosity but at the same time a sign of a deregulation of religious beliefs, producing a type of religiosity weakly connected, or not connected, to religious institutions and to what they proclaim. Therefore, the current reaggregation of religion and the emotional mobilization of memory in this region have been going on so far primarily in favor of the religious institutions which function in a more and more visible way as the exclusive possessors of religious beliefs, values, and norms, as centers of religious reaggregation, and as the guardians of religious memory. This, of course, applies to all three major religious confessions operating in B&H.

V

The role of the religious factor in the war in B&H is to be analyzed by concentrating attention to the following moments.

First, the crucial moment to identify in describing the role of the religious factor in B&H is the impact of religion upon the current political party alignments. In fact, it is the religious factor which stays at the background of the current options and support on a mass scale for different national, political

---

[34]Jukić, 1994, 363-367.
[35]Dobbelaere, 1995, 4-5.
[36]Michel, 1994, 146.

parties. This may be best illustrated by the case of SDA [Party of Democratic Action] which defines itself as a political alliance of citizens, based upon a re-awakening of the Muslim national consciousness and upon taking into consideration its national identity, but the same applies to other national parties too. Therefore, the religious differences appear nowadays as political party differences and vice versa with the resulting direct politicization of religious differences and of their increasing political rigidity, clearly prevailing among the rural or neo-urban population and the population in under-developed areas. Therefore, it is not astonishing that the religious factor, which by its crucial impact upon national identities and political parties identities, has drawn the current lines on the battlefields as preannounced many years ago by James Coleman[37] as well as re-enforced the process of greater political party unanimity (one community, one party, with some minor exceptions mostly in some of the urban areas).

Second, one of the crucial moments for describing the role of the religious factor in the actual war in B&H is to be found in the prevailing attitudes of the respective religious confessions, religious institutions, and confessional communities to the dominant political strategies of manifest nationalist orientations. This is particularly true in the context of transitional processes which have practically raised the existing religious institutions into the politically legitimating institutions of the first order and have given to three major religions practically the status of more or less informal state religions or *quasi* state religions. In substance, the religious factor has been practically involved and deliberately engaged in the current war primarily by giving legitimacy to the dominant nationalist political strategies with some visible distinctions among the three major religions concerned and with the initial exception of Bosnian Islam. None of them, however, with some initial hesitation and oscillation on the Muslim side, has been coherently neutral or firmly reluctant to such strategies in general or has opted for support to some alternative political strategy.

It is necessary to insist upon the specificity of such a legitimacy. Basically, it fuses together different contents but always in superior terms, *numinous* or *quasi*. P. Michel warned that the "Church, as it is known, differs from all other social institutions by invoking ultimately the transcendent" and, therefore, by countering an absolute legitimacy.[38] In this particular case, the religious legitimacy has been given by fusing together *numinous* terms, in so called Grand History on situational terms, but basically extending a protective

---

[37]Coleman, 1956, 46.

[38]Michel, 1994, 136.

sacred canopy to the dominant political strategies of nationalist orientation. The final consequence of such a legitimacy has been in projecting the current political conflicts to a *quasi* ontological and anthropological background, portraying them essentially as conflicts between different and incompatible human, cultural, and civilization types described respectively with negative connotations as Latin or Byzantine or Pan-Islamic fundamentalist. At the same time, all three religious institutions, involved and engaged, did invoke the same doctrine of a just war, all in defense of some fundamental but differently defined rights in peril or allegedly in peril to legitimatize additionally the side in the conflict with which they are aligned.

Third, the reverse side of the legitimacy in superior religious terms is represented not by simply delegitimating the contrary political strategy in purely political terms but by delegitimating it again in superior religious and almost ontological and/ or anthropological and Grand History terms. Therefore, it is the religious delegitimation which has contributed to paving the way to an extreme manicheization of the current political conflicts and to a parallel satanization of the other, hostile side. There is no wonder, consequently, that the war going on in B&H has obtained some attributes of a holy war in which God himself is involved or a religious war as the war in which everybody with a social marker, considered hostile, may be legitimately exterminated, driven away, or converted, and that nationalist political strategies have produced as many murdered victims as persons willing to become murderers, as noted by B. Anderson, these are characteristics of modern, nationalist politics.[39]

Fourth, another crucial moment defining the role of the religious factor in the Bosnian and Herzegovinan war is to be found in motivating the maximal mobilization of all the resources in favor of the nationalist, political strategy, having been legitimated in superior religious terms. And more particularly is the political mobilization of all the resources at the disposal of the respective religious confession, religious institution, and religious community in support of the political strategy legitimatized in superior religious terms. It is a mobilization to be described primarily as an emotional mobilization of memory[40] or "a reactivation of the collective memory" to serve primarily to awaken fears and to alter individual as well as collective expectations.[41] In fact, without such a mobilization of religious resources, the war in B&H should have died long ago from pure exhaustion, and it would not have become "rather a certain

---

[39]Anderson, 1990,120.

[40]Hervieu-Leger, 1993, 76.

[41]Bougarel, 1994-1995, 81.

pathological expansion of hatred than a classical political conflict" as described by a Croatian Catholic sociologist of religion.[42]

Fifth, a defining moment of the role of the religious factor in the actual war in B&H is to be detected in raising, by legitimacy in superior religious terms, the capability of sustaining hardships and sacrifices on a mass scale and of a drastic nature for the respective nationalist, political strategies conditioned by the war going on. In substance, it has resurrected a kind of fascination and glorification of violent death as a voluntary sacrifice. Some examples are illustrative. On the Serbian Orthodox side, most indicative is the recent question of a Serbian Orthodox theologian, starting from the formula "*Semen est sanguis christianorum*," asking whether the alleged historical martyrology of the Serbian people ought to be considered more as a triumph than as a tragedy, more as a victory than as a defeat, and describing the average Serbian Orthodox believer as a person who

> does not partake frequently in communion, he is not a regular Church-goer, he is not very concerned with his religious education, but he knows how to pray with all his soul and with his simple words, which demonstrate a profound, old tradition of living with the truth of Orthodox faith. And, above all, he knows how to die for his faith, to testify to it with his own sacrifice.[43]

The same moment has been stressed recently by frequent Orthodox assertions that a nation which is capable of sustaining enormous sacrifices could never be defeated. A book published recently by the Serbian Ministry of Information asserts in the same vein that "The celestial Kingdom and historical and spiritual message make that a nation compelled to choose between unfreedom and death accepts the death as a regulative idea."[44] On the Muslim side, it is Alia Izetbegović who glorifies martyrs maintaining that

> greatness of the heroic act is not in its utility since it is frequently useless nor in its rationality since it is not rarely irrational. The experienced and lived drama remains the most splendid trace of Divine in this world. In this lies its universal and non-transitory value and significance for all men. More than any prophet and preacher these martyrs are true heralds of the other world.

Sixth, an important moment of the role of the religious factor in contemporary B&H concerns the attitudes of the respective religious confessions, religious institutions, and communities towards the plurireligious, pluricultural, and plurinational nature of the Bosnian and Herzegovinan society. In this particular respect, the role of various religious confessions has been rather different and changing. Serbian Orthodoxy and the Serbian Orthodox Church

---

[42]Jukić 1992, 66.

[43]Bogdanović, 1991, 38.

[44]*Rečnik zabluda*, 1994.

B&H as a plurireligious, pluricultural, and plurinational state and for its partition along ethnic lines and for the ethnic homogeneity of Serbian national entity in the allegedly Serbian lands. Croatian Catholicism and the Croatian Catholic Church have been oscillating more or less with along the oscillations of the traditional Croatia, nationalist politics and the present-day official politics of Croatia. The oscillation between the public support to Croatian, nationalist, political philosophy and strategy, insisting upon the so-called "fallacy of multiethnicity,"[45] and the ideal of the modern state as a homogenous and ethnically clean national state[46] which includes B&H as historically a part of Croatia.[47] Or it oscillates between a necessary partition of B&H, on one side, and, on the other side, support to the political strategy of sustaining the integrity of B&H as a plurireligious, pluricultural, and plurinational state, which would be preferably Catholic/Muslim and would expect that the Republic of Croatia would exercise tutorship and/or hegemony over B&H as a whole. Or, ultimately conceive of the future pluriculturality and plurinationality of B&H in terms of its bantustanization even at the molecular level of society (an example, Mostar today). A temporary divergence in certain Catholic circles in Bosnia from official Croatian politics to B&H, particularly visible in times of armed conflicts between Croats and Muslims, has been based (with some exceptions, like M. Oršolić's) not upon a radically different evaluation of the universal value of pluriculturality and plurinationality or of the integrity of B&H, but upon a rather different evaluation of certain political consequences for Croats living in Central and Western Bosnia by a partition of Bosnia and an evaluation of strategic, political interests of the Republic of Croatia to keep Serbia as far as possible from its frontiers. This distinction has something to do with the distinction between Catholicism in Western Herzegovina which is nationally homogenous and not used to plurireligious, pluricultural, and plurinational living together at the everyday level[48] on one side, and the Catholicism in Central and Eastern Bosnia used to living together at the level of everyday experience on the other. The attitude of the Muslim community towards plurireligiosity, pluriculturality, and plurinationality of B&H has been, since the beginning of the Yugoslav crisis, changing and vacillating between the idea of an independent and integral

---

[45]Sunić, 1990, 11.

[46]Aralica, 1995.

[47]Draganović, Mandić 1991.

[48]One may recall the fact that the districts with almost homogenous Croatian population are located in Western Herzegovina: Grude with 99.76% Croats, Posušje 99.47%, Široki Brijeg 99.22%, Čitluk 98.87%, Ljubuški 92.63%, Tomislavgrad 86.62% to compare with Bosanski Brod 40.99%, Vareš 40.61%, Travnik 36.94%, Kakanj 29.76%, Modrica 27.27%,

Bosnia used to living together at the level of everyday experience on the other. The attitude of the Muslim community towards plurireligiosity, pluriculturality, and plurinationality of B&H has been, since the beginning of the Yugoslav crisis, changing and vacillating between the idea of an independent and integral pluricultural and plurinational B&H and the idea of Muslim state based upon Islamic culture and reckoning with the predictable demographic trends in B&H favoring Muslims. However, it has been evidently changing, owing primarily to the vicissitudes of the war and international intervention and support but also with visible shifts in direction of a growing reluctance to plurireligiosity, pluriculturality, and plurinationality. This has been made clear by Alija Izetbegović. Attacking Fikret Abdić in 1993. he proclaimed that "Muslims have succeeded in becoming a political nation capable to create a state," that is, becoming a political and sovereign nation. In 1994, Izetbegović declared at the SDA Convention:

> Life together is a nice thing, but I believe and I may say honestly that this is a lie, that this is not what our soldiers are dying for. If somebody has nourished illusions about life in common, it has been us. However, realities cannot rest upon lies and we cannot lie to our people. Our soldier on the hills, suffering in mud has not been doing it for living in common but to defend this toprak, this land which they want to take from him. He risks his life to defend his family, his land and his people."[49]

This shift may be the most easily and drastically detected in the official Muslim confessional institutional attitude towards interfaith marriages and to traditional *komšiluk*. Interfaith marriages, very frequent in Bosnia in recent times, particularly in urban centers, have not been interpreted as a normal result of the plurireligious and pluricultural nature of the society, but they have been expressly condemned as a scheme to reduce the Muslim community and a subterfuge to blur and erase its confines and identity. Therefore, *Reis-el-Ulema* Mustafa Cerić declared, comparing rape and interfaith marriages, that "for us these rapes are incomprehensible and never to be forgotten but they are less painful and less difficult to admit than all these mixed wedlocks."[50] Writing about komsiluk as a system of everyday coexistence of different communities based upon rules of strict respect and reciprocity, A. Prijić wrote that "people simply do not want to admit the fact that all this was a lie, a trick, and lost time" and that "Bosnians are going to pass . . . by their *komšija* with a good dose of scorn as they have become a nation, as they have become Bosnians, as they have rejoined Bosnia, Bosnians, and the Bosnian spiritual inheritance."[51] This all could be seen as a direct consequence of the contradiction in the initial

---

and so on. All data are taken from the Census in 1991.

[49]Izetbegović, 1994.

[50]Cerić 1994.

[51]Prijić, 1994 quoted in X. Bougarel, 1994-95, .

attitude of the Bosnian Muslim political party which on one side is in favor of ethnicification of politics and on the other for a civil state. That is on one side proclaiming to be in favor of a Bosnian/ Herzegovinan state to be built as a civil (*gradjanska*) state and upon the fundamental modern and inclusive notion of citizenship, but on the other side favoring practically the political party alignment and organization upon the exclusive principle of one religious confession, one national community, one political party.

Finally, the crucial moment of the actual role of the religious factor in B&H is to be located in attitudes as to what ought to be the basis for constructing the Bosnian and Herzegovinan state as a democracy. This is, of course, of fundamental importance for the survival of B&H in a fourfold manner.

First, it concerns the question whether a Bosnian and Herzegovinan state would be built essentially upon a *pactum unionis* in Thomas Hobbes' words, enabling it to be governed in the future upon the free and active consent of the governed, equal and free as individuals and as members of different communities and upon a stable and fundamental consensus. Or should it be built upon a *pactum of subiectionis*, without such a consent as well as without such a fundamental consensus? Or finally and most probably, should it be based upon a combination of a *pactum unionis* and a *pactum subiectionis;* for some upon a *pactum unionis*, for others upon a *pactum subiectionis*?

Second, it is of crucial importance in view of Bosnian/Herzegovinan history, described by X. Bougarel in these words:

> Terms of 'tolerance' and 'hatred,' of 'coexistence' and 'fear' may equally serve to qualify the Bosnian society: in its context, they fill up respectively or follow rather than to oppose mutually. However, if there is a term which could hardly qualify Bosnian society and its history, it is the term of 'democracy.'[52]

Third, as stressed by Klaus Offe, it is crucial that "at the most fundamental level a 'decision' must be made as to who 'We' are, i.e. a decision on identity, citizenship, and the territorial as well as social and cultural boundaries of the nation state."[53] There are no doubts that former Yugoslavia dominant, nationalist, political strategies have operated with conviction and that, in Offe's words, those basic rules can only be based on unilateral decisions of those who are, due to place of birth, already admitted to the game, or, alternatively, upon the brute facts of international or civil wars, or at best constrained by the fragile web of international law and transnational regimes. Therefore, the "We" who establish and impose on a territory a new constitution, new laws, and new population could not be identical with the "We" of the population actually living there. There is no doubt that such strategies have operated with the crucial, political conviction in legitimacy of a new founding

---

[52]Bougarel, 1994, 7.

[53]Offe, 1991, 886.

"We" as well as, more importantly in legitimacy of exclusion of a section of the previously existing population, being a component part of the former founding "We," the exclusions being effected in the best case deconstitutionalization, desubjectivation, and discrimination of important sections of the respective populations, and in the worst case, by so-called ethnic cleansing.

Fourth, this identity of "We" is crucial since a democratic base for a Bosnian/Herzegovinan state has not been provided or secured so far either by the initial Badinter Commission plan nor by the Juppé /Kinkel plan. The Badinter Commission assumed that a majority vote in a referendum might offer stable and democratic grounds for an independent and democratic plurinational state even if its creation is directly opposed by a very large majority of one of the three major existing communities (36.3 % abstention in referendum, i.e. every third adult citizen being against it), objecting to be forcibly reduced to a minority. Basically, the Badinter Commission

> has raised the principle of electoral majority to the status of a panacea in a region where the permanent anxiety of different national communities has been not to find themselves as minorities as well as in an epoch when the political homogenization of these communities has been such to reduce a referendum of this nature to a confrontation of different unanimities.[54]

This means that it excluded since the beginning the idea of a consociative democracy as a possible democratic solution for the new state in a plurireligious, pluricultural, and plurinational B&H. The Juppé/Kinkel territorial 51% to 49% plan assumed that such a basis may be obtained, reducing the problem of intercommunitarian relations to "a territorial zero game" which is basically in accordance and not in discordance with the matrix of the very logic of the current war and of territorial conquests as well as of ethnic cleansing.[55]

It is more or less evident that none of the religious confessions and religious institutions, legitimatizing basically the dominant nationalist strategies, may claim to have opted for a program of establishing the Bosnian and Herzegovinan state as a coherently democratic one based upon a *pactum unionis* and a free and active consent of those to be governed at least in terms of a consociative democracy and coherently searching for such a *pactum unionis*.

The Serbian Orthodox Church has been the most radical in this sense: its option has been for a partition of B&H along national lines, invoking, at the same time, the right to self-determination as a democratic right and some historic-cultural rights, having nothing in common with democracy and human rights. Consequently, it has deliberately chosen to support a radical, nationalist political strategy, aiming at an ethnically clean and nationally and politically

---

[54]Bougarel, 1994,46.

[55]Bougarel, 1994, 47.

homogenous Serbian state in B&H, associated in some way to Serbia to be legitimated by a *pactuum unionis* of Serbs and their allegedly historical rights to be secured by military conquest but with no rights to non-Serbs and no same rights to be recognized to other communities.

As the war went on into its fourth year, Catholicism in B&H opted for a Bosnian/Herzegovina state and not for a partition of Bosnia.[56] Since the Washington Agreement, in substance it has chosen the option of a state based upon a combination of a *pactum unionis* and a *pactum subiectionis* and legitimized by the right of self-determination as a democratic right but interpreted and applied as a cameleonian right[57] as well as by some historic-cultural and civilizational non-negotiable arguments to be valid today regardless of the will of the people living in some parts of the country and introducing in substance a distinction between two types of citizens, i.e. first class citizens and subjects.

The situation with the Muslim side has been more complex and evidently changing since the beginning of the Yugoslav crisis. There is no doubt that Muslims in B&H have been so far the main victims of the war. At the same time, it ought to be underlined that the Bosnian/Herzegovinan Islam was to be described at the beginning of the crisis as a 'peaceful Islam,' using Ch. Saint Blancat's distinctions of Islam in Europe into a 'secularized Islam,' a 'peaceful Islam,' and a 'reislamizing Islam.'[58]   However, it has undergone a rather important change since the beginning of the crisis. One has to remember that the contemporary Islamic movement in B&H has been historically and personally linked to a Pan-Islamic revival current, appearing in the early forties and basically following the model of the Egyptian Muslim Brotherhood[59] and followed more recently by a movement of *immams*, seeking an Islamic reawakening. It represented at the beginning of the Yugoslav crisis a specific synthesis of Islamic tradition and culture and modernity and democracy with

---

[56]During the Croatian/Muslim war in B&H Cardinal Kuharić declared that "coexistence of Muslims, Serbs, and Croats in Bosnia and Herzegovina is the destiny of that state. Mixing and encounters are inevitable." However, some leaders of Croats in Bosnia and Herzegovina reacted to this by saying that "it is at least indecent to talk about coexistence in the time of war."

[57]Neuberger,1994, 157.

[58]Saint-Blancat, 1993, 324.

[59]The initial programmatic ideas were formulated in this way: 1. ideological edification of individuals, 2. founding of an Islamic society and an Islamic milieu, 3. establishing an Islamic order, 4. political and spiritual liberation and unification of the Islamic world in an immense state or an association of states. Quoted in X. Bougarel, "Un courant panislamiste en Bosnie-Herzegovine," in: Gilles Kepel (Ed.), *Exile ou royaume*.(Paris: F.N.S.P.), 283.

contradictions and vacillations between "a reislamization from above" and "reislamization from below"[60] and inherent tensions between the ideal of an Islamic state and Islamic order and fundamental requests of modern democracy, not of consociative but preferably of the majoritarian type. The shift from reislamization from above to reislamization from below is very clear in Alija Izetbegović. Thus, Izetbegović took the creation of Pakistan as an ideal and as "a fruit of aspiration to the founding of an Islamic order," but he soon realized that "an Islamic order could not be realized but in countries where Muslims represent a majority of population." Therefore, he concluded in 1970, that "an Islamic order without an Islamic society is either a utopia or a tyranny." Consequently, recent signs of oscillations between these two efforts to reislamization may be seen in action against selling alcohol and hog meat in which the initial attempt at reislamization from above has been realistically mitigated when facing resistance. However, the crucial point is that for the Islamic movement, represented by SDA today, sovereignty and indivisibility of B&H come before any free and active consent of the people involved, and they are not grounded upon a negotiable, fundamental, and freely-established consensus and participation of all the communities, but upon some historical facts (tradition of a Medieval Bosnian state, having persisted longer than a similar Croatian state and a Serbian one), some international acts and decisions, changing internal coalitions, etc., required to be recognized in advance by all and eventually imposed by force, preferably international.

Conclusion

Returning to the first question formulated at the beginning of this analysis, it may be plausibly concluded that the religious factor in contemporary B&H has shown that it is inclined more to separate than to unite, more to divide than to link together, more to confront than to cooperate, more to deepen social cleavages than to build bridges, more to inflame conflicts than to mitigate them, and that it is more of a vector of conflict and war than a vector of peace and coexistence.

Returning to the second question, it seems that no religious institution in B&H has given an adequate answer to the crucial problem as to how it is possible for a pluricultural and plurinational society to be coherently organized as a democracy, founded basically upon a *pactum unionis* and as an association of free and equal citizens and not upon a *pactum subiectionis*, for some at least,

---

[60]Terms are borrowed from Henri Tincq, "La monté des extrémismes religieux dans le monde," in Jean Delumeau, *Le fait religieux*, (Paris: Fayard,1993), 729-730. Prevailing was a reislamization from below described as developing a kind of an Islamic Gramscism.

This is, of course, not astonishing. Others, too, have not given an adequate answer to such a crucial question. One may mention that some, at the theoretical level, as for instance E. Grant, consider the formula "One culture one state" as the only viable formula to secure democracy, and they believe that a pluricultural society is viable only under some very specific and limited conditions which certainly are lacking in the case of B&H.[61] Therefore, from that point of view, the crucial dilemma and crucial contradiction seem to be either *homonia* or oppression. It means that there is no democratic solution for the tragic crisis of B&H, but either *homonia*, leading necessarily to partition and ethnic cleansing with some kind of bantustans and appartheid politics, or statal integrity based upon oppression necessary in order to counterbalance the lack of *homonoia*, due to the existing pluriculturality.

However, there are alternative views at a very general level to be taken into consideration. Touraine, for instance, warns that

> when state is defined as an expression of a collective political and cultural entity--a Nation,People--or, what is worse, a God or principle which this People, this Nation and itself are privileged agents to, with the mission to defend it, there is no more democracy even when economic framework permits some public liberties. Democracy is founded upon free creation of the political order, upon people's sovereignty, and, therefore, upon freedom of choice even in regard to all cultural heritage.[62]

and he insists that

> democracy transforms community into society regulated by law, and the state represents the society itself in which power is limited by fundamental laws. Contrary notion which may be called populist, völkisch, recalling that this is the term Nazis used to describe their regime, imposes a fundamental unity beyond any possible choice and which establishes nationalism incompatible with principles of democracy.[63]

---

[61]E. Grant maintains that "multicultural societies are perfectly viable, even entertaining, so long as the main fabric of each subordinate culture consists, and is admitted by its members to consist, of mere collective options, tastes, and idiosyncrasies --of preferences, in short--such as exist even within a single culture. But when such differences are imbued with value, when they are the coordinates of a persons's identity, and especially of his religion-- above all when, as cultural values proper, they not merely differ, but actually conflict--then the overall consensus necessary for peaceful government becomes difficult to find. Societies so plural as to lack any basis whatever for consensus are either ungovernable, or (what is substantially the same thing) can be governed for only by force." R.A.D. Grant, "Freedom for What?" in Gordon L. Anderson, Morton A. Kaplan (Eds.) *Morality and Religion in Liberal Democratic Societies*, (New York: Paragon House, 1991), 25.

[62]Touraine, 1994, 99.

[63]Touraine, 1994, 99.

Daniele Ungaro develops the same view, asserting that democracy
as a formal political formula contains only the following restrictions in respect
to specific values. Human rights should be respected (there is no democracy
with violations of human rights). Pluralism of forms of cultural life, included
in the political order it regulates, should be guaranteed. A democracy which
does not do it becomes totalitarianism, but a democracy which is linked in an
inseparable way to a specific form of cultural life turns into fundamentalistic
integralism.[64]
However, unfortunately, contemporary B&H is very far from a solution of the
crisis in such terms as such a solution presupposes the political defeats of
prevailing nationalism in B&H as well as in Serbia and Croatia.

Bibliography

Anderson, Benedict. 1990. *Nacija zamišljena zajednica.* Zagreb. First published
in 1983 in London by Verso.
Barber, Benjamin. 1992. "Dzhihad proti McWorlda." *Teorija in praksa.* 9-10,
839-848.
Berger, Peter. 1983. "From the Crisis of Religion to the Crisis of Secularity,"
in M.Douglas, S.Tipton (Eds.). *Religion in America. Spirituality in a
Secular Age.* (Boston: Beacon Press), 14-24.
Bogdanović, D. 1991. "Pravoslavna duhovnost na iskušenjima našeg doba."
Gradina. 26, 10-12.
Bougarel, Xavier. "Un courant panislamiste en Bosnie-Herzegovine," in G.
Kepel (Ed.). *Exile et royaume.* (Paris: F.N.S.P.), 275-299.
Bougarel, Xavier. 1994. "Etat et communitarisme en Bosnie-Herzegovine."
Cultures et conflits. 15-16, 7-47.
Bougarel, Xavier. 1994/95. "Voisinage et crime intime." *Confluences
mediterranée.* 13, 75-86.
Castellan, Georges. 1991. *Histoire des Balkans: XIVe-XXe siècle.* (Paris:
Fayard).
Cerić, Mustafa. 1994. *Le Monde.* 28 September.
Coleman, James. 1956. "Social Cleavages and Religious Conflicts." *Journal of
Social Issues.* 12.
Denitch, Bogdan. 1994. *Ethnic Nationalism: The Tragic Death of Yugoslavia.*
(Minneapolis,London, University of Minneapolis Press).
Dobbelaere, Karel. 1994. "Tradizione, secolarizzazione e individualizzazione. Un
riesame di dati e modelli" *Religioni e società.* 9, 20, 4-28.
Draganović, Krunoslav, Mandić, Dominik. 1991. *Herceg Bosna i Hrvatsku.*
(Split: Laus).

---

[64]Ungaro, 1994, 12.

Ferrarotti, Franco. 1993. *La tentazione dell'oblio*. (Roma, Bari. Laterza).
Hervieu-Leger, Danièle. "Un entretien avec Danièle Hervieu-Leger." *Le Monde*. 10 Mai, 1994.
Izetbegović, Alija. 1988. *Islam izmedju Istoka i Zapada*. Beograd.
Izetbegović, Alija. 1990. *Islamska deklaracija*. Sarajevo.
Jukić, Jakov. 1992. "Vjeronauk i nova kultura ravnodušnosti," in *Vjeronauk u duhovnoj obnovi Republike Hrvatske,* (Split: Tajništvo za pastoral Franjevačke provincije Presvetog Otkupitelja) 65-76.
Jukić, Jakov. 1994. "Hrvatski katolici u vremenu postkomunizma." *Crkva u svijetu*. 29, 4, 363-378.
Gellner, Ernest. 1986. *Nations and Nationalism*. (Oxford: Basil Blackwell).
Giddens, Anthony. 1992. *The Nation-State and Violence*. (Cambridge: Polity Press).
Granov, E. 1994. "Kako ćemo se boriti?" in S. Trhulj (Ed.). *Mladi Muslimani*. Zagreb. 122-125.
Grant, R. A. D. 1991. "Freedom for What?" in Gordon L. Anderson, Morton A. Kaplan (Eds.). *Morality and Religion in Liberal Democratic Society*. (New York: Paragon House). 13-26.
Habermas, Jürgen. 1992. *Faktizität und Geltung*. (Frankfurt a/M: Suhrkamp).
Huntington, Samuel. 1993. "The Clash of Civilizations." *Foreign Affairs*. Summer.
Kamenka, Eugene (Ed.). 1976. *Nationalism: The Nature and Evolution of an Idea*. (London: E. Arnold).
Karamatić, Marko (Ed.). 1994. *Rat u Bosni i Hercegovini: uzroci, posljedice, perspektive*. (Samobor: Franjevačka teologija-Sarajevo).
Kepel, Giles. 1991. *La revanche de Dieu. Chrétienes,juifs et musulmane à la reconquéte du monde*. (Paris: Ed. du Seuil).
Michel, Patrick. 1994. *Politique et religion*. (Paris: Albin Michel).
Ministarstvo za informacije Srbije. 1994. *Rečnik zabluda*. Beograd.
Muray, Leslie. 1991. *A Transformative Model of Pluralism*. (Budapest: Eötvös Lorand University).
Neuberger, Benyamin. 1994. "Samoodložba narodov--konceptualne dileme." *Nova revija*. 141-142,142-160.
Offe, Claus, 1991. "Capitalism by Democratic Design? Democratic Theory Facing Triple Transition in East Central Europe." *Social Research*. 58, 4.
Rex, John. 1994. "The Political Sociology of Multiculturalism and the Place of Muslims in West European Societies." *Social Compass*. 41, 1, 7-92.
Robertson, Roland. 1989. "Globalization: Politics and Religion," J. Beckford, Th. Luckmann (Eds.). *The Changing Face of Religion*. (London: Sage). 10-23.
Saint-Blancat, Chantal. 1993. "Hypothèses sur l'evolution de 'l'islam transplanté' en Europe." *Social Compass*. 40, 2.
Schierup, Carl-Urlik. 1993. *Eurobalkanism: Ethnic Cleansing and the Post-Cold War Order*. Umea.

Sunić, Tomislav. 1990. "The Fallacy of the Multiethnic State: The Case of Yugoslavia. " *Conservative Review*. 1,9-11.

Tehranian, Majid. 1994. "World With(Out) Wars: Moral Spaces and the Ethics of Transnational Communication." *Javnost*. 1.

Tilly, Charles. 1992. "War and the International System.1900-1992." Paper presented for the Hannah Arendt Memorial Symposium on Peace and War. (New York: New School for Social Research).

Tincq, Henri. 1993. "La montée des extrémismes religieux dans le monde." J. Delumeau. *Le fait religieux*, (Paris: Fayard). 715-740.

Trhulj, Sead (Ed.). 1992. *Mladi Muslimani*. Zagreb.

Ungaro, Daniele. 1994. "Identità e differenza," L. Martini (Ed.). *Mare di guerra, mare di religioni.Il caso mediterraneo*. (Firenze: Forum per i problemi della pace e della guerra). 105-126.

Voyé, Liliane. 1994. "Molteplice e identitario. Immagini contrastanti del cattolicesimo europeo." *Religioni e società*. 9, 20, 29-48.

8

THE BOSNIAN CROSSROADS

Esad Ćimić

Considering the roots of the war in B&H, I am inclined to accept the interpretation which takes into consideration the *inherited* social-spiritual condition as the essential determinant of these dramatic events. History teaches us, if nothing else, that changing political systems are not a guarantee, but only a condition for more radical social shifts.

Is The Conflict In Bosnia-Herzegovina Basically A Religious War?

No matter how much it might be considered as evasive, the question as to whether the war in B&H is a religious one may be answered by saying *both no and yes!*

It can be categorically said *'no'* for the simple reason that here two religions (Christian and Islamic) and three faiths (Catholic, Orthodox and Muslim), or, speaking sociologically, three churches, three religious institutions and communities, are involved. Seen from the outside, one and the same religion or its members (of two churches) respectively would be in conflict, out of which one (Catholic) is allied by an entirely different religion (Muslim). If it had started out as a religious war, the polarization would be more clean cut. That the term "religious war," in this case, is a *contradictio in adiecto* is obvious since the above mentioned religions, in spite of all differences, have a common moral basis which ardently insists upon the dignity of human persons, freedom, and equal treatment of humans as being intrinsically human, without regard to their religious affiliation. The discrepancy between religious ideals and reality is due to the historical context to which the religious communities all succumb although some of them resist this process of self-degradation more than others. If we compare this assumption against declared programs of all three churches or religious communities respectively, we shall not discover any elements which require the religious community to defect from its primary religious principles. In other words, the extreme destructive conduct is exclusively the action of this or that member of a religious community and, by no means, of a religious community as a whole. Consequently, neither the motive nor the impulse for this war resulted from religions or faiths respectively and, even less, can the religious communities be accused of waging the war.

There is nothing contradictory in my observing that an affirmative answer can be conditionally given as well. Why? While this war developed due to completely different reasons and has other causes, nevertheless, it is true that the war has been dressed in religious clothing in order to disguise its real motives. Simply said, although it is not a religious war, still this war looks like one to a superficial observer. Politicians are certainly trying to present it in these terms, and, regretfully, a part of the hierarchy of religious communities are doing likewise, especially those of the Serbian Orthodox Church. These are the allegedly God-fearing people who with their attitudes, behavior, and actions offer excuses to the "masters of war," supplying them with acceptable justification and reason for this conflict. It is obvious that sacral objects have been destroyed and eradicated in monstrous proportions in this war. However, it is significant that, for example, in all places where Croatian people were in the majority, all or almost all objects of the Catholic church have been destroyed, but on the other hand, as a rule, where the Croats were in the minority, living among a Muslim majority, their churches were spared. Without doubt, the function of this selectivity is to spread distrust between the Croats and Muslims so that the Muslims get the impression that "*krst*" (the word for cross in Serbian) is not at war with "*križ*" (the word for cross in Croatian), but only with the "crescent." In this way, the faulty idea of a religious war is being suggested which then finds rich soil owing to the evident fact that the aggressor does not have even tactical reasons to desist from merciless eradication of all traces of the Oriental-Islamic culture, e.g mosques, graveyards, and cultural monuments.

But it is impossible to properly dispute the thesis that this war is not a religious one without, at the same time, trying to, at least, answer to the question of what really caused it. Only a part of the truth is seen when attention is called to a great number of accumulated contradictions out of a total economic, political, cultural and, above all, moral crisis of society from which it proceeded.

The common denominator among all these factors is, undoubtedly, the absence of democracy. Despite all difficulties, the war would not have been used as the means of "solving" the total confusion reigning in these regions had it not been combined with the following fatal principle. "*All members of one nation must live in one state!*" which was offered as the motive, goal, and means of the war. Those who openly boosted this principle into primacy became the main cause of the cataclysm. The champions of this principle in the order of the hierarchy of causation were 1)The Serbian Academy of Science and Arts; 2) The General-staff of the Yugoslav National Army (JNA) which created a strategical and tactical vision of creating a Great Serbia under the mask of preserving the Yugoslavia of that time; 3) Slobodan Milošević, with his mental dispositions and recognizable personality profile, politically operationalized all this and was, at the beginning, the instrument of implementing this idea. Soon afterwards he instrumentalized the Academy and the General-staff, leaving an indelible trace on the shape and course of these somber events; and 4) The Serbian Orthodox Church initially gave only discrete support, but later it blessed, through her many bishops, every step of the actual Serbian policy.

Thus, no religious motives are in question; rather, this is a question of profane, political interests which are basically reduced to a *war for territories*, which--even when they are mixed--*must become ethnically homogenous* and represent *support for creating a "clean" national state.* Anyone who is even a little bit reasonable, might have suspected, if not exactly foreseen, the tragic results of such policy in which all are losers. All feel its bitter fruits--some directly and others indirectly--or will feel them as early as tomorrow. Because, without the application of biological extermination (genocide, "ethnic cleansing") or, in milder version, survival under the condition of mass migration (so-called "human resettlement"), the idea of all nationals living in a single state is deprived of realizability.

Temptations of Holding Together

In B&H, Catholicism, Orthodoxy, and Islam meet and interact and, to a degree, even oppose each other. They appear as special civilizational aspects of their respective cultures, traditions, conceptions, and spirituality. Their renewal, redefinition, and revalorization become historical imperatives of Bosnia's complete integration into the world and, especially, into Europe.

The relationship between religion and nation is one of the main issues. Religion is, conditionally, a *universal* community in heaven, while nation is a *particular* community on earth. From this it is evident that religion *per se* can not support national differentiation, but doubtless, in given historical circumstances a specific confession, church, religious community can and does. Our sociological examinations offer a basis for the conclusion that religion is deeper, stronger, more lasting and more stable, while national feeling is more divisive, more superficial, more liable to freakish political conduct. Religiosity is predominantly immanent, while the national is more subjected to vacillation and oscillation. This is because religion responds not only to onto-anthropological questions, being the organizer of collective rituals, but is strongly interlaced with social communities. The thesis about *homo religious,* the human "incurably religious" is, in fact, an idea, that has been formulated by the claim that there is only one faith which appears in historically different forms. Yet, religion's "being condemned" to life in specific historical forms does not exhaust itself in this manner.

Max Weber claimed that faith in the common origin, based on the similarity of customs, languages, and culture, regardless to what extent it is historically verified, creates an exceptional "feeling of ethnic honor" by means of which a heterogenous community establishes unity. According to him, the similarity of origin is not sufficient for creating a nation, no more than difference in language and religion present obstacles. Still, this sociologist repeatedly emphasized the element of *political power*, not only as a *source* of national feeling but, what is more, as its *specificity*.[1] Treating nation as an eminent *ethnic-cultural* phenomenon, Weber was inclined to measure the maturity of civilization and the cultural level of society according to the degree of the importance of this cultural factor. It should also be added that each national community, in the process of its own formation, depends on the potentials of spirituality hidden or expressed in the nation concerned; in addition, that destiny favors more those nations which establish themselves against other nations in differences based on *secular* elements.

If the Islamic religion is not only a relation towards the transcendent (God-Allah), but also a way of living the whole of life, then it is not difficult to observe the scope and power of its influence in the domain of establishing national differences. Many experts of Islam find its historical advantage in the fact that--as distinguished from the European Middle Ages--it had a rich and opulent civilization. Originally, Islam was completely directed towards its starting point, persistent searching for transcending time in the process of repeated, continual return to the nation. However, having prevailed once, the idea of Islamic society in certain socio-historical conditions became dominant. But this is exactly the point at which it started to transform itself into the shell of social and state constitution, trying to regenerate from within, and it was on this score that it failed its own historical chances. Although the contemplative, scientific, and artistic creation was of many kinds, religious ethics, which directed the human being towards suprahistory as the *only* reality, contributed to the considerable reduction of the philosophical concept of the world. All this would eventually become particularly prominent in B&H, and it narrowed the historical possibilities of Islam even more, coinciding with the time of their constriction in the primordial country of Islam. Here, and not in the existence

---

[1]Max Weber, *Wirtschaft und Gesellschaft*, Studienausgabe, Hg. V. J. Winckelmann, Kiepenheuer, in Witch, (Köln-Berlin, 1964), 313-316, 674-678.

of a "Muslim island" in the sea of "Christian Europe," are the causes of the historical slow down of the formation of self-consciousness of Bosnian Muslims.

There is no doubt that the influence of Islamic civilization on Christian spirituality and *vice versa* was effective and still continues to be such. However, despite the passing of centuries, the creations of a spiritual culture, in which the manifestations of the religious spirit and religious rites are implicitly present, had a limited influence in B&H. The Islamic literature in Oriental languages did not go beyond the educated and privileged Muslim minority.

The process of Europeanization which later on gripped these regions, strengthened inside Muslim ethnos the original Slavic (above all of the Catholic-Bogumil-Glagolitic) component and thereby contributed to the intensified reverting to their origins, with a spirituality already enriched by the added dimension of Oriental-Islamic articulation with the added ability to broaden the cultural horizon in these territories. This is how a process of obvious interaction started, often with manifold variants and new, unexpected inspirations. Muslims and Catholics were increasingly left to rely upon each other, not only for the purpose of protecting themselves from joint enemies, as is the case in recent history, but also to make the most of mutual civilizational and cultural enrichment.

Catholic spirituality is international in scope and inspiration and has an enviably thoughtful articulation. No other community has so worked out in detail, for example, the socio-political doctrine as is the case with the Catholic Church. It is in the Catholic tradition to gather the intellectual elite, to assimilate temporal changes and not to respond passively to recurrent experiences. The Catholic Church openly both supports and condemns. Nurturing the sense of individual and group dignity, substantial opposition, and discrete political engagement are all aspects of its spirituality.

The spirituality of Serbian Orthodoxy is, first of all, composed of religion, national myth, and folk poetry. The influence of the historical is best seen in this religious community since it is significantly shown in how a nation does not create history, but how history creates the nation.

Every religion has its special system of values and worldviews as well as a peculiar model of culture. The Oriental-Islamic model of culture simply placed Islam as a non-European religion into B&H where it took roots and blossomed in ways that turned out to be a blessing for society. An additional civilization was created. One more color was added which represents an organic, naturally established but different, cultural concept. This pluralism should endure here as an achievement and should not be a reason for tension or desire to eliminate it. Hence, the Bosniac-Muslims, as well as the Serbs and Croats, owe their religion to their national authenticity, although their religion did not establish this authenticity by itself, but it was formed on broader socio-historical assumptions. It is absolutely certain that this national genuineness would never have been established if the cultural and civilizational differences had not existed.

If special Muslim institutions had been founded in the past, it would have been easier to distinguish between the secular (national) and the spiritual (religious). It is characteristic for Muslim believers to easily resign themselves to religious contemplation.[2] They like to meditate regardless of their educational level; they switch to transcendental areas without difficulty and, with roughly equal attention, endeavor to decode, not only the scene in *this world*, but also what is on *the other side*. There was a certain spiritual hunger expressed in the attempt to find out both cultural and ethnic identity by means of this, to cognitively grasp the origin of the Bosniacs-Muslims, their present position and future prospects. The so called *merhamet* (compassion, charity) became transparent. Namely, a Bosniac-Muslim possesses a special kind of humanism which has probably been shaped through centuries, living in a variety of social environments: an ethical and religious mosaic is something that he happens to find by birth. Therefore, the *other* and *the different* is not the object of rejection and contempt, but of respect and esteem to the extent to which it is being reciprocated by the acceptance of its own diversity. This is especially evident in urban environments which are more culturally cultivated and which discretely continue to persist, being deeply aware of contributing a new dimension to the cultural mosaic. Rural Bosniac-Muslims have a mental characteristic to which spirituality is not an ingredient, but to which spirituality can be easily added. I think that the secret of Bosniac-Muslims as the ethnic community in B&H lies in retaining their genuine Muslim identity, yet, simultaneously being Europeans as well. This linking of Islam as a religion, as culture and civilization, with the entire European cultural context can give--without altering theological concepts-- such an innovation that shall be esteemed more and more by Muslims all over the world. Therefore, this culturally and nationally impressive mosaic represents no obstacle, no weight dragging back to the past. Rather, it can be a new animation, a new inspiration so that its characteristic and distinctive features could be displayed in the context of diversities and, consequently, be mutually cross-fertilized with the others.

In the structure of religious conscience of village inhabitants, for example, a more *fatalistic* comprehension and a less *rational-theological* reflection of divinity prevails with the Muslims. It seems as if they are jealously preserving the totality of differences and, thusly, forsaking those cultural values which

---

[2]See Esad Ćimić, *Socijalističko društvo i religija,* (Sarajevo: Svjetlost, 1966); Esad Ćimić, *Drama ateizacije,* (Belgrade: Mladost, 1984), 82-100.

could--because they are different but not opposite to theirs--enrich their own culture without jeopardizing its essence. Paradoxically, their authenticity could become even more pronounced if it were intertwined with other rich cultures. Religion is that which inseparably links the Muslims throughout the whole world, but the Bosniac-Muslims have the advantage to receive--when they open themselves to the influence of other cultures--new nuances in their rich cultural ledger without losing anything essential that makes them special. The starting-points of this process depend on the interaction and reciprocal readiness of others to receive and send out that which lifts them into higher spheres of individual and social creativity.

Perhaps, continuity was preserved in all three religions, but it was manifested in different ways. Of the three, the Catholics have the most intellectual formation. The Catholic Church retained in their sanctuaries rhetoric, music, art, and in rarer instances, a philosophical culture. Its members hold a high degree of self-confidence. Catholics traditionally practice their religion explicitly. Whenever both religion and nation make claims upon the individual, religion tends to take the upper hand, except in crisis situations when the national devotion prevails. When Catholics use religion to protect their national interest, this is a proof of the endangerment of their nation. This process is never a detriment to religion as a speculative factor and an expression of personal sensibility. Few significant arguments escaped the attention of the intellectual elite of priests. Neither should it be underestimated that about 90% of all Croats received the sacrament of baptism.

Orthodox religiosity is more a matter of *customs* and less of a spiritual or speculative nature. Burdened with the historical reality, this religion was too frequently transposed into the secular, often expressing itself entirely in an ethnic dimension. The formal relation of Serbs towards Orthodoxy may be gleaned from the data that the number of baptized Serbs varies between 7% and 20%. If we add to this that a thin layer of authentic Christianity is present in the structure of the religious conscience of the Orthodox Serbs, while everything else is syncretism impregnated with the elements of paganism, then it is not difficult to create a rather pessimistic conclusion regarding the spiritual shape of this religiosity. Pastoral activity is nearly reduced to liturgy which, in turn, has become a typical example of religion being drowned in the national dimension. Here lies probably the source of its vast politicization which becomes a slippery ground for various manipulations as well.

With adherents of Islam, things are more complex. This religion has its secular consequences. At first, Islam incorporates into the family and neighborhood, trying to standardize the entire secular life. Islam is originally much more totalitarian: secularity and spirituality are mixed more than in the other two religions. This circumstance has also become complicated by the fact that Bosniac-Muslims considered the world Islamic community as a surrogate for national community until the recent formal acknowledgment of their national status. Without having developed national institutions, they used to count on settling religion in secular zones while the secular was to be incorporated again into the religious issue. This is one of the reasons why the processes of contemporary secularization have enormously gripped this religious group. Research shows that one half of the Bosniac-Muslims were involved in more or less continuous religious life.[3]

Reflecting on the above insights, one must take into consideration the history during which numerous aggressions and long-lasting occupations took place. These three faiths and the cultures which grew out of them are equally a challenge and a danger. They are a challenge because it is not a little advantage to possess three cultural layers on a single socio-cultural territory. Cultural traditions and current cultures, partly springing from them, enable and stimulate multidimensional spiritualization. This gives rise to a daily critical relation towards one's own culture as well as to other cultures, constantly warning that not only next to you, but also along-side of you, and in better cases even inside you, lives that "other" that can even be more productive than "this one." In Bosnian environments with a higher degree of democratic life, along with the appreciation of each particular cultural individuality, cultural divisions run less between cultures and people and more through people. They are a *danger* because these differences in closed, traditional, rigid socio-cultural environments may be the source of estrangement, rejection, and suspicion. Then the situation arises in which *the allegedly different* is being experienced not only as *other,* but as the source of tension, accusation, and wariness.

Surely a certain Oriental despotism has been established in a disguised form in Bosnia. However, it is wrong to think that it affected only the Bosniac-Muslims' mentality. As soon as one takes off the cultural wrappers, essentially the same human behavior will show up among Bosnian Serbs, Muslims, and Croats. The differences are often reduced to cultural value. As an illustration, one can mention the mentality of the Bosnian Franciscans who have fortunately combined the characteristics of their own faith with that which they had assimilated from Islamic culture. This may well be the reason for their gift of exceptional vitality and for their persistence on the "vanguard" of Christianity, successfully resisting all pressures. It is a sign of spiritual inferiority if one

---

[3]Relevant indicators for all three religions are comprised in the book E. Ćimić, *Socijalističko društvo i religija.*

thinks only about how much influence this or that culture has exerted while neglecting to see how much influence each of them has received.

The Value Awareness of The Three Theistic Religions

A sociological research of mine carried out as far back as 1965 is still significant nowadays in many ways. It seems to me that at least in one segment of the society of that time there were reflections of social structures which anticipated tectonic tremors of multi-layered social relief. Both occupational choices and esteem of socio-spiritual values could be observed differently among the three main confessions. Here is what this scale of values in different confessional communities looks like:

Catholics

1. *The priest as intellectual and moral authority.* Catholics consider that the priest, in distinction from other occupations, is not allowed to forget, not for even one moment, that his vocation is exceptional and sacred. In the intellectual sense, he represents authority both in regard to the educational degree and in terms of actual knowledge; he is able to provide instructions for diverse areas of life; he is very well informed and in practice shows the range and power of his own thoughtfulness. In regard to moral authority, the priest is expected to behave consistently in all situations.

2. *Technical intellectual.* The inclination towards empirical understanding gives advantage to intellectuals doing a certain job and approaching life with practical impact. Although to a limited degree, the rationalism of the Western civilization is present here. The esteem of the technical intellectuals includes implicitly dissatisfaction with the level of institutions educating in the field of humanities.

3. *The humanities intellectual.* He/she is to some degree regarded as an 'unsuccessful' priest since he/she, too, is engaged in the nonmaterial dimension of life, but on this worldly side. This makes it possible for the humanistic intellectual to affect some consequences, but not indefinitely. In a sense, he is always being evaluated in respect to the impact of his work, which usually turns out not to be in his favor.

4. *Political activist.* Undoubtedly, this is a contingent vocation because almost all respondents evaluated this vocation not by itself but in their ability to provide space for undisturbed exercise of other vocations. Judging by the respondents' answers, the understanding of politics in the sense of eliminating its particularity and alienation is far from its ability to master people's

consciousness. Politics is likely to be experienced as a fateful power which can be an efficient servant, but is a bad master.

5. *Benefactor*. According to the respondents' evaluation, this is the one who helps the weak and feeble. Here religious charity becomes prominent: sympathy towards the one who suffers results from the antipathy towards suffering. Compassion appears only when someone else's happiness is being violated. Therefore, one's own happiness is not the goal of morality, but is its basis and assumption. Two moments explain why this value occupies just this place. One is that it seems to be included implicitly in every religion. The second is that, possibly, unconsciously and indirectly, it expresses the longing for a society in which charity will be needed less and less.

Bosniac-Muslims

1. *Political activist*. It should be noticed that the high status of this vocation is exclusively linked with the specific characteristic of being a carrier and protector of the idea of brotherhood/sisterhood and equality. This is partly the heritage of the Islamic *merhamet* (humanism). But it would be an oversimplification to reduce it to one Islamic (religious) truth that is passed down from generation to generation. Undoubtedly, it originates in the recent past when social insecurity and plain biological revival simply required such broad humanistic principle. Accordingly, the politicians are primarily evaluated by their relation toward this idea and its realization and only secondarily by other activities of theirs. Wedged in between "*krst*" [Serb word for the cross] and "*križ*" [Croat word for the cross], the Muslim cultivated social insecurity through history and considered it a privilege to achieve equality with others.

2. *Technical intellectual*. The place occupied by this vocation is not inconsistent with the Oriental-Islamic tradition which is in part defined pragmatically. In other respects, this vocation is perceived as among the Catholics.

3. *The intellectual in the field of humanities*. The reasons are the same as for Catholics.

4. *The priest (hodzha)*. Even for the traditional Muslim awareness, it is not characteristic that this vocation is to be singled out, much less to be given an aureole of sanctity. This is consistent with the theological concepts of Islam. (Hence, it is quite understandable that the vocation of judge *[cadi]*, who administers justice according to religious, civil, and penal laws based on the *Qur'an*, is considerably more esteemed than the *hodzha*). Since recently they started to receive a better education, up to the highest level of university degrees, Islamic priests will, probably, be valuated more highly. They had in the

past, with few exceptions, received no formal education and were only inadequately trained, and this degraded them in the believers' eyes.

5. *Benefactor*. The same valuation as for Catholics.

The Orthodox

1. *The warrior, epic hero*. To the present, the cult of hero has retained its privileged place on the scale of values. He is an idealized defender; he is a guarantee that the tribe will remain protected. He is assigned to the role of conquering new territories in the function of strengthening the tribe. The fanatic aspect of patriotism, releasing new energies in every insurgent movement, is based on it. The idealized hero always watches over his folk and warns them that one never knows at which crossroad death is waiting, and it is never quite sure if the knife is at one's throat or in one's hand. (There is a passage in Dobrica Čosić's novel *Deobe* where the hero says,

> We like the knife most. Children like a knife. The men will perish for a gun. They give a field for a gun. We take an oath on the knife. That's the way we are. . . . When you have gun, you have a field. You save your head. With a knife you can both repay debts and win a law-suit. Every woman must lie down with the one who has gun. Is this our fault? No, we are not to blame . . . . Since the beginning, this is the way of this world.)

2. *The intellectual in the field of humanities*. The reason for the high esteem of this vocation is due to a romantically perceived fighting spirit of this vocation. The absence of a demand for instant efficiency also exalts this vocation. The practitioners of this vocation encourage the hero and animate his campaigns or his courage while his glory is lauded for posterity.

3. *Political activist*. In the view of almost all respondents, he is not the sole source of power. His reputation largely depends on his ability to influence the society and bring about changes. This vocation is viewed as bringing about the epic tradition of heroism and the intellectual in the field of humanities as being engaged in this process.

4. *Technical intellectual*. He holds this position by virtue of dexterity and handicraft skill rather than the ability of spirit. Although it is paradoxical, just because this vocation in the process of its own functioning is being demystified, it does not have a high status. Efficiency is admired because it does not give space for imagination and reflection. Everything is so clear in this vocation that it gives no possibility for hesitation nor can it be related to the epic exaltation of brave men.

5. *The priest*. In this vocation, there is nothing sacred according to the respondents. It is reduced to an occupation. There is even the inclination to evaluate it according to the *popadija* (priest's wife); every failure in choosing his own wife automatically disqualifies the priest as a man whose advice and

instructions for life should be sought, especially in solving the dilemmas of life.[4]

Conclusions

How should these findings be interpreted? It is apparent that the awareness of values by their inner structure conjures up a dramatic focus of social and spiritual fermentation where the vital power of aroused energies is viewed and zealous carriers of certain ideologies, being more or less religiously colored, separate themselves. Almost by the very nature of the matter, the tradition depends not only upon the structure of religious consciousness, but also upon the social impact of the principles on which the religious confession is being established. Therefore, the fate of the tradition is determined by what religion is *eo ipso* and by the social environment and its special effects produced by the religion.

We found out that there is no great distance between Muslims on the one hand and Christians on the other on the level of *popular culture.* Belief in one God who may be accessible by various ways lessens this distance, but specific appeal to historical experience and memory increases the distance between the religious groups. *Learned culture,* paradoxically, enlarges this distance and rigidifies it.

The congeniality and identity of the scale of values of Catholics and Muslims is first of all the result of historical circumstances and also the remoteness from the Orthodox. It is evident at first sight that the Muslims and Catholics have three identical values in terms of position on the scale. The specific predicament of Muslims throughout history and in the current situation has brought about an essential difference with regard to the first value. On the other hand, the first value of the Orthodox is a category which does not appear among Catholics and Muslims at all.

However, it is evident that the scale of values of the Orthodox is by far much more consistent in relation to, cautiously said, "the confusion" of the

---

[4]These findings are based on the research of theists in Herzegovinian villages carried out in 1964. Three decades have passed since then. But, when the subject under discussion is the structure of awareness, especially the awareness of peasants, it is safe to assume that nothing essential has changed. In any case, new research would be instructive. (Partial results of this research have been presented in the article "O vrednotama" (About Values") published in *Radovi* (Department of Social Sciences, Faculty of Arts in Zadar 1978/1979).

In regard to the results obtained in the course of the research, I made efforts not to introduce my own attitudes into the scale of values. Endeavoring to resist projections of my own awareness, I carried out informal conversations out of which I deduced joint values which then appeared most often. The polling comprised a sample of 500 examinees of various ages, school qualifications, occupations, and the like. Additionally, 50 more interviews were carried out relating to the obtained scales of values.

system of values in Catholics and Muslims. This is even more so if we take into consideration the current socio-political context in which the system of values of the Orthodox religion, almost literally, asserts itself: namely, as it has been established, the Orthodox are warriors (heroes) by their mental constitution. They are the nation that needs intelligence in order to be exalted, whose heroism is to be chanted, whose political activists operationalize politically the land that was conquered, whose technical intellectuals organize life in the land that was conquered and, finally, the priest who blesses all these together. "The Log Revolution" in "Krajina" started just in this sequence.

One of the possible interpretations of the given scale of values is their analysis of who is the carrier of *national sovereignty*. The metaphor for sovereignty among the Muslims is the *political activist*; with the Orthodox it is the *hero*; for the Catholics the historical protector is the *priest*.

9

GENOCIDE AGAINST BOSHNIAKS

Sulejman Mašović

From the fourteenth century, the Turks gradually occupied the territory of the Balkans. Medieval Bosnia, which since the ninth century had its statehood, kept its autonomy also in the new Turkish empire. Along with others, Bogumils massively accepted Islam as they had been persecuted as an expanding sect by both the Eastern and Western churches. Because of agricultural needs, the Turks resettled Serb tribes from the area of the Carpathians and other parts of Eastern Europe while western Bosnia was settled by Croats. In the central part, Muslims were the majority. To the end of the eighteenth century, they were all called "*Bosantsi*" [Bosnians or in Turkish *Bosnevi*]. They enjoyed a complete equality of religion, language, and culture and conserved all monuments.

After the French Revolution (1789), nations were being formed in Europe, and national ideas gained strength with the significant assistance of religion. Under the powerful influence of the neighboring countries of Croatia and Serbia which had their traditions for several centuries, Catholics in Bosnia were declared as Croats, the Orthodox as Serbs. Since the nation is less significant in Islam, the Muslims in Bosnia remained "Bošnjak" [*Boshniaks*] and continued with the help of Turkey to develop a great religious and cultural heritage, especially in education, health, social security, and a rich, predominantly Middle Eastern architecture. *Vakufs* (endowments of rich individuals) were the economic basis for maintaining mosques, libraries and hospitals. Frequently, new cities grew around such institutions.

Due to the weakening of Turkish power in the Balkans under the pressure of Eastern and Western Christianity, Bosnia was annexed to Austria-Hungary in 1878, which favored Christians. Therefore, Muslims had to struggle for religious and cultural autonomy and succeeded in retaining Bosnia's autonomy. The new Kingdom of Serbs, Croats, and Slovenes that came into being after World War I (1918) was forced to guarantee this autonomy by the Vidovdan

Constitution (1921), but King Alexander voided it by instituting a dictatorship in 1929. In the new Communist Yugoslavia (since 1945), Bosnia retained its independence and became one of the six socialist republics. Since it was impossible to persuade the Muslims to join either Serbdom or Croatdom, as these were based on the Christian religion, they were constitutionally named "Muslims" (1971). Since this name is the symbol of their faith, yet they are located in Europe, they, by necessity, officially took on the name "Boshniaks" in the new state of Bosnia and Herzegovina which came into exietence with the disintegration of Yugoslavia (1989/1990). This state was internationally recognized and was accepted into the membership of the U.N. and other international organizations.

Naturally, immediately upon the secession of Slovenia, Croatia and Bosnia and Herzegovina also declared their independence. The Serb *chetniks,* who held in both Yugoslavias the government and the army, used their units and armaments, which had been subsidized in the previous half a century by all inhabitants of Yugoslavia, to start a massive genocide (1990), first against Croatia (by destroying cities from Vukovar to Dubrovnik), and then even more devastatingly against Bosnia and Herzegovina since 1991. Ethnic cleansing, as the Serbs called this genocide, had for its avowed goal the destruction or expulsion of all non-Serb people, which they attempted to achieve with the greatest cruelty and bestiality.

Genocide, especially in B&H, has already been studied at hundreds of international and regional meetings, analyzed in thousands of articles, books, and other materials supported by eyewitness testimony. According to the last figures of the U.N., Amnesty International, Helsinki Watch, and others, hundreds of settlements were burned down; over 300,000 were killed, of which 70 per cent were children; 100,000 were tortured in camps; 50,000 women, children and men were raped; and over 1,500,000 were exiled. Serbs occupied at one point 70 per cent of B&H. They established separate Serbian states with capitals in Banja Luka and Pale; they destroyed countless religious objects (1,200 mosques and 300 Catholic churches), as well as educational, cultural, social, and health institutions. Numerous international experts and delegations who came from all over the world confirmed that by the number of crimes and cruelty it is hard to find a match in world history to what has happened here.

Another horrible fact is the inefficiency of the U.N. and its agencies, of NATO, and of the European Community. Of the 150 conflicts which the U.N. recorded as having taken place over the past 50 years since WWII, the genocide in B&H, according to many, is the worst in regard to the total number of victims, torture, and deportation of the population. International agencies passed dozens of resolutions on the conflict in B&H but with little impact. A unique instance of the failure of international organizations was that the governments of Croatia and B&H were forbidden to purchase arms while the Serbs had plundered the armaments of the former Yugoslav Army and could freely purchase arms from Orthodox countries. The embargo punished the victims and rewarded the aggressor.

It is astonishing to small nations that of the 40 resolutions of the U.N. and European Community (E.C.) which directly or indirectly prohibit coercion, genocide, and other forms of torture, not a single one was applied to this case although the aggressor could have been easily punished from the very beginning. During the celebration of the 50th anniversary of the establishment and activity of the U.N. (1995), a cloud of profound disappointment hovered over this organization; demands were made to effect changes in the international security system. This inefficiency was primarily due to the reduction of the influence of the so-called Great Powers, which protect themselves by the vast privileges of the Security Council, and to the introduction of responsibility for U.N. functionaries and statesmen who are engaged for the protection from genocide. If Boutros Boutros Ghali and his co-workers and the numerous politicians who protected the aggressors were taken to the international court for their lack of success, genocide could not be spread.

A great deal of research and evidence prove the special cruelty toward Muslims in B&H and in the rest of the Balkans. This is the tenth genocide in the last two centuries in which a total of about a million people were killed while about four million were deported from B&H to Turkey alone and approximately the same number from Kosovo, Macedonia, and Sandzhak. Many villages were destroyed. Muslims were expelled from territories between Belgrade and Salonika and over a thousand mosques as well as cultural and other Muslim public institutions were destroyed. Similar to the destruction in the summer of 1995 of Srebrnica and Žepa, cities were turned into graveyards. None of this brought about any reaction or support to the victims.

Abundant research and published documents point that the deeper sources of this xenophobia and racism reach back to the collapse of the Serbian state at Kosovo (1389). Milovan Djilas, the renowned Montenegrin ideologue and formerly Tito's closest collaborator, pointed out that the Serbs never accepted a real faith, but were rather Christians only superficially while basing their life on ancient myths. After liberation from Turkish overlordship in the nineteenth century comes the development of the ideology of Garashanin's *Nachertaniye* (1844)[1] which megalomaniacly decided to acquire all regions in which there is

---

[1]Editor's note: Garashanin was the foreign minister of Serbia in the 1840s during the time of its gradual liberation from Turkey. In his writing *Nachertaniye*, he drew up a blue-print of the hoped for liberation of all Serbs and his notion of how far the borders of Serbia

even just one Serb. Later the Serbian Academy of Science and Arts and other cultural institutions augmented in 1986 the theories of a chosen people who, after the retreat of the Turks, ought to rule the Balkans. Upon this premise was developed both the oral and written Serb literature, school texts, and so-called science with which even today politicians manipulate the media and fool their people as well as the international community.

The second profound causation is the influence of Europe which since the establishment of Islam in the seventh century developed ever-growing networks of hatred and struggle. The second phase, by means of the eight crusades between 1096 and 1291 of the united church and state, brought about great bloodshed even in Jerusalem, the holy city of the revealed religions. After their defeat by Salahudin Eyubia, Europe and especially Byzantium with the Orthodox Church gave every possible support to fight the Turks in the Balkans until the rebellions in the 19th century. This crusading spirit still holds sway among a segment of Western politicians and other experts encouraging them to support genocide out of fear from Islam, the Muslim state, and similar feelings.

Attempts are now being made to lessen the effect of these terrible realizations by accepting numerous refugees from B&H in many European countries, the sending of humanitarian aid to B&H and Croatia, and the numerous interventions of humanitarian organizations for peace and for the termination of all types of violence. After five years of destruction, there are now also more effective peace-making activities, as were Dayton and Paris, but not without supporting the aggressor by means of recognizing their territorial gains.

Boshniaks are deeply disappointed by the great passivity of religious and secular intellectual circles upon finding out the great savagery perpetrated upon them. In 1941/42 in Sarajevo and other cities of B&H, there were initiatives and endorsement of about 40 resolutions by citizens and the Islamic Community against the Nazi persecution of Jews, Serbs, Romas, and others due to which a number of the signers perished. Now, with few exceptions, the most important people of the West are silent, including our neighbors. It is true that numerous dialogues took place between believers on all levels, but nowhere did the Orthodox Church acknowledge its role in the genocide nor request repentance and punishment of the perpetrators. Without this, there is no hope that the attitudes will change or morally improve.

The Islamic world, which makes up a fourth of the world population, stressed at numerous international meetings its consternation over the genocidal

---

should eventually go. Serbs have been accused by their enemies of relentlessly pursuing this goal to this day .

crimes in B&H and asked from the U.N. and E. C. more effective defense of the innocent. The *Qur'an* as the last revelation of God to humanity stresses in many passages the deepest humanism and democracy, recalling that God created many and various peoples in order for them to get to know each other and together advance, rejecting every advantage to any nation, race, or political power over others. Muhammad always stressed that the best believer is the one who is helping others without regard to the religion and quality of that person, because all have the same divine soul and because suffering is difficult for every living being. Many of these principles, for instance the love of one's neighbor, are also emphasized in the Bible, which indicates that all world religions jointly need to oppose the growing materialism that is the source of moral and social evil, for instance the ruin of the family, lust, alcoholism, drugs, crime, and the poverty and hunger in less developed areas upon whose riches the North bases its affluence.

We are hoping and expecting that the publication of this book will be a serious contribution to the advancement of the real truth about the sufferings of B&H, which are greater than those of the other ten or so war-torn areas in the world. Divine truth given in all holy books, that the one who does not prevent evil participates in its spread, calls upon all positive forces in the world to much more forcefully stand up in defense of victims and contribute to a real and lasting peace.

Translated from Croatian by Paul Mojzes

10

SERBIAN ORTHODOX CHURCH, THE DISINTEGRATION OF SECOND YUGOSLAVIA, AND THE WAR IN BOSNIA AND HERZEGOVINA[1]

Dragoljub Djordjević

> In the last two years we experienced three great historical changes: the fall of the Communist empire, disintegration of the Yugoslav community, and a horrible war of hatred and coercion. Some were involved in these events, others to a lesser degree, but all of us bear equally the incurable traumas, repressed fears, and broken expectations. This is why it is very difficult to be entirely objective and entirely exclude our deceptive feelings in evaluating these three changes.
>
> Jakov Jukić

The Fundamentals of Orthodoxy and of the Serbian Orthodox Church

About Orthodoxy in general and specifically Serbian Orthodoxy and the Serbian Orthodox Church (hereafter SOC) there are inexcusably few good monographs and books in western literature and journalism. Therefore the German theologian Ernst Benz states correctly

> To the non-Orthodox inhabitants of Western Europe it is fairly hard to understand the Eastern Orthodox Church because the people in the West do not have enough knowledge about the life and teachings of Orthodoxy, but the actual rigid knowledge is covered with prejudices and disagreements, partially confessional and partially political in nature."[2]

---

[1]The text of this chapter was written for a project "Ethnic and Confessional Relationships in the Balkans," that is being carried out by the Institute for Social Research of the Philosophical Faculty in Niš and is financed by the Ministry of Science and Technology of the Republic of Serbia.

[2]Ernst Benz, *Duh i život Istočne Crkve* [Geist und leben der Ostkirche], (Sarajevo: Svjetlost, 1991), p. 9.

If it is like that in Western Europe one can only imagine how many "black holes" exist in the knowledge about Orthodoxy among average people in the United States. I doubt that the situation is much better with the more educated part of the population, except, of course, narrow specialists in religious studies. Hereby I do not wish to blame Western people; the blame lies with us who live or have our origins in the so called Byzantine-Orthodox culture who did not make the effort to inform in a timely and sound manner the rest of the ecumenical world with Orthodoxy, this equal, third wing of Christianity.[3] I am certain that at this unfortunate occasion, namely the war in Bosnia and Herzegovina (B&H), it is necessary to provide a short survey into the fundamentals of Orthodoxy and SOC for American readers.

Over many centuries of internal, spiritual and external, secular rivalry for primacy and leadership between Constantinople and Rome Christianity was divided in a schism in 1054. Gradually significant theological and organizational differences came to exist between Christian denominations. Orthodoxy--the right thinking, the right belief of the Christian religion, respect for the traditions of religion, the gathering of all Christians[4] in which the process of branching out lasted for centuries--at this time consists of autocephalous churches all of which have a common faith and cultic practices.

Serbs are among the oldest Christian Orthodox peoples. Having moved to the Balkans in the 6th century--having rejected initial Christianization because of the tenacious refusal of the still pagan population--they became Christian toward the end of the 9th century. However, only atn the beginning of the 13th Century (1219) did the Orthodox Church become autocephalous, thanks to St. Sava (1174-1236) who achieved the acknowledgement of autonomy from the ecumenical patriarch and became the first Serbian archbishop. During the next

---

[3]In the last few years my writing was directed to this end: "Confessional Mentality as a (Dis)Integration Factor," *Innovation* 3 (1) (1990), 107-116; *Is Atheism Dying Out in Eastern Europe?* 21st International Conference for the Sociology of Religion (Maynoot, Ireland, 1991); *Why Orthodox Serbians Become Adventists?* (Society for the Scientific Study of Religion Annual Meeting, Pittsburgh, PA, 1991); *Orthodoxy Between Heaven and Earth: The Case of the Serbian Orthodox Church* (SSSR Annual Meeting, Washington, DC, 1992); "Secularization and Orthodoxy: The Case of the Serbians" *Orthodox Forum*, 7 (2) 1992, 215-220; "Konfesionalna identifikacija i tolerancija,"[Confessional Identification and Tolerance], *Kultura* 25, 1993, 91-92; *Towards the Sociology of Orthodox Christianity* 22nd ISSR Conference (Budapest, Hungary); *Eastern Christianity, War and Peace* SSSR Annual Meeting, Albuquerque, NM, 1993; "Religious-Ecclesiastical Complex, Disintegration of Second and Future of Third Yugoslavia," *Filozofija i društvo* 10 (6), 1994, 329-340; *Sekularizacija, religija i razvoj jugoslovenskog druš*tva [Secularization, religion and development of the Yugoslav Society], 2nd JUNIR Conference, (Niš, Yugoslavia).

[4]Čeda Drašković, *Rečnik pastirsko-pedagoške teologije* [Dictionary of the pastoral-pedagogical theology] (Belgrade: SUPSJ, 1982), p. 27.

century, during the rule of Emperor Dušan the Mighty (1331-1355), when the Serbian empire reached its apex, being the largest and mightiest in the "Byzantine commonwealth"[5] SOC was elevated to the rank of a patriarchate. The brilliance of the Serbian medieval state, with the central role of the SOC is deeply embedded into the collective memory of the Serbs and it is not surprising that the contemporary generation is also "dreaming about the return to that glorious era."

The tragic fate of Orthodoxy and SOC begins with the invasion of the Balkans by the Osmanli Turks when the Serbs, after a determined defense, fell into Turkish slavery in the 15th century (1459). The Islamic enemy ruled for full five centuries with the Serbs regaining independence only in the second half of the last century (1878). The autocephaly of the SOC was regained even later, in 1920. During this period the inhabitants became impoverished and were brought to the brink of biological annihilation, while the forcible conversions to Islam and with the inescapable uniatization of the Serb ethnic being brought about mass alienation. It is a historical fact that Serbs sacrificed greatly in their resistance to the imposed religious conversion: first to Islam, from which contemporary Bosnian Muslims originate, others into Catholicism, from which large numbers of Croatianized Serbs derived.[6]

Serbs experience Orthodoxy in a national manner and as a synthesis of the national spirit and the teachings of the Church. Their faith grew and is fulfilled in the following characteristics: 1) Orthodoxy Christianized Serbian customs, habits, and pagan cults, so that Serbs are the sole Christians who have a holiday, "*slava,*" which is the celebration of their baptismal name and family saint. 2) SOC is traditionalist, favoring the patriarchal structure and morality, hierarchy and the voluntary submission of the younger to the older, of the female to the male . . . which means that Christ in heaven, the anointed king in the state, and the oldest male member of the family (usually father) in the home rule. 3) Orthodoxy brought about the closeness of the people, the state, and the church--the so called symphony, the harmony between state and church, secular and religious rule. 4) As a result of this symphony, the church and people, in addition to the saintly church rulers, martyred monks and women, canonized also their rulers, especially those of the medieval dynasty of Nemanjić (22 canonizations). 5) SOC has deeply sown into the Serbian soul the cult of

---

[5]D. Obolensky, *Six Byzantine Portraits* (Oxford, Clarendon Press, 1988).

[6]Perhaps in this collective memory one may locate the definite animosity especially toward Islam and everything that is related to it. (Serbs to this day name colloquially Bosnian Muslims as "Turks" although they full well know that this is incorrect and that they are of Slavic blood. Serbs in general, and especially Bosnian Serbs do not wish and will never agree to live in an Islamic country.)

Kosovo, which emerged after the tragic defeat by the Turks in the Kosovo Field. The defeat was transformed into a spiritual Christian victory since the saint prince Lazar and his lords and army took communion prior to the battle and opted for the eternal "kingdom of heaven" instead of the temporary "kingdom of this world." 6) The millennial struggle for survival gave rise among the Serbs to a heroic vision of faith and the meaning of life--it is worthy to fight and die for "the honorable cross and golden freedom," for Orthodoxy, and national independence. 7) Serbian Orthodoxy was always tolerant, never aggressive and exclusive.[7]

All SOC and Serbian Orthodox characteristics can be summed up as follows: "Serbian Orthodoxy is *Svetosavlje*," when the fruitful life and varied activity of Saint Sava became the synonym of Serbian national faith."[8] "*Svetosavlje* is nothing but Orthodoxy, but Orthodoxy of the 'Serbian style and taste.' That means Orthodoxy fulfilled in the history and experience of the concrete Serbian people."[9]

Serbian Orthodox Church and the Disintegration of Second Yugoslavia

The first (1918-1941) and second (1945-1991) Yugoslavia were the example of multiconfessional societies because in them at least three cultural circles interacted: western-European, namely Catholic-Protestant, Byzantine-Orthodox, and Ottoman-Islamic. Rarely could one encounter anywhere else in the world in such a small geographic and demographic area such a great diversity, which was a priceless treasure. But sometimes pluralistic living leads to visible tensions which can slide into disintegration, and even dissolution of a given society. Religions and confessions, by definition can be one of the key factors for integration of the inhabitants in pluriconfessional communities, but they can also work in the opposite direction. My thesis is that the great strengthening of confessional mentality, along with other unwanted circumstances, acted more disruptively than integratively and thereby destroyed the fruits of multiculturalism.

The spread and strengthening of the confessional spirit lead to the insistence on one's own religious form, which stands out sharply and opposes other confessional entities. Interconfessional tension is created when confessional

---

[7]The noted Croatian sociologist of religion Esad Ćimic provides a twisted picture about Serbian Orthodoxy and SOC. [See Ćimic's article in this book under the title "Bosnian Crossroads"-editor's comment].

[8]See Obolensky, *op.cit.*. for a more detailed narrative about St. Sava.

[9]Irinej Bulović, "Pravoslavlje, svetosavlje, duhovnost" [Orthodoxy, *svetosavlje*, spirituality] in *Šta nam nudi pravoslavlje danas?* [What does Orthodoxy Offer to us Today?] (Niš: Gradina, 1993), 12.

mentality and identification--up till then a completely legitimate phenomenon--loses its origination and at once takes on a disintegrating role in a multicultural community.　If we recall that time prior to the destruction and war in Yugoslavia (the second half of the 1980s) one will notice how the growing nationalism among all Yugoslav nations generated the spread of confessional mentality.　In a short time, the opinion was created that if one had not opted for a confession it meant that one would not be loyal to their nation and republic. At once all Serbs had to become religious, active Orthodox, Croats Catholics, while the Muslims (in Serbian the use of a capital letter designates a specific nation) rushed to regard themselves muslim (the small letter "m" designates religious adherence).　The republics started to create monoconfessional states, the sacralization of the ethnic and confessional origin.　Regretfully that became tragic for the multicultural community and contributed to its destruction by means of a horrible hatred and use of force.[10]

Already then I was issuing warnings that because of the deep rootedness of confessions in the ethnos, in the uncritical identification of nation and religion, and the memory of the distant and near past that the Yugoslav religious space is prone to quakes and that the absence of dialogue, tolerance, and ecumenism between religious organizations could be fatal for survival. None of the religious organization in the country were or wanted to be aware of the delicacy of their mission in a multiconfessional region so that they could deal with each other subtly. Churches were contesting each other, peoples argued, the faithful brawled, and all of them knew that "if the churches do not reconcile, nations will neither." Instead of the increase in responsibility for togetherness ties were broken, churches did not reconcile, and the result was disintegration through war.

In a more concrete analysis of the participation of the SOC in the disintegration of Yugoslavia, one should point out that this came so that the old ecclesiastic structure which was completely marginalized during the Communist period suddenly became revitalized and grew into a significant national and political factor.　First, the desecularization of all of Eastern Europe, which is the backdrop of the fall of all socialist systems, had an impact upon Serb society. The strengthening of Catholicism and Islam in the vicinity led to the

---

[10]The renowned Serbian sociologist Milan Tripković openly blames religions and church organizations for the war: "One of the paradoxes of human life is that religion or, more accurately church organizations, all which call upon the one God and preach love of neighbor, most durably and most deeply divide people, causing great bloodshed and causing all kinds of sufferings to mortals.　To prove this thesis one need not go any further than in the area in which we live and from the sincere introspection into one's own soul and heart." Tripković, *Samoniklice* [Self-germinations] (Novi Sad: Futura, 1993), 51.

strengthening of Orthodoxy and SOC. Then, in the 1980s the Yugoslav Federation fell into the most profound moral, political, and economic crisis, when people, as they looked for any kind of solution, turned to a large measure to the church and religion. Serbs, like some other Yugoslav nations, felt they were the greatest casualty in the hopeless social crisis, and SOC explicitly held and nurtured this conviction. Lastly, some major events were taking place simultaneously which directly struck the consciousness and subconsciousness of Serbs and increased the role of SOC. The famous conflicts with the Albanians in the province of Kosovo, "the holy land of the Serbs," are particularly significant in this respect. Thus the radical turmoil in the three concentric circles in the countries of Eastern Europe, in Yugoslavia, and in the Republic of Serbia decisively enlivened Orthodoxy and SOC.

On the other hand, several critical sociologists, to among whom I belong, taking into account the above mentioned reasons as the wider context, nevertheless see as the cause of religious renewal and strengthening of the SOC in a sole cause: the extreme growth of nationalism.[11] And, indeed, in those years in Serbia, and more or less in other Yugoslav republics, an explosion of nationalism and the homogenization of people took place. This process in Serbia, masterfully and shrewdly directed by Serb Communists, now renamed the Serbian Socialist Party, did not take place without the influence of SOC and was also religiously tinted. Because, surely, politicians would not have been able to carry out such a firm and encompassing homogenization of the Serb ethnos if it were not for both the open and concealed, vocal and tacit support of SOC. Even the scenario of the process of homogenization which was carried out at mass meetings and assemblies of citizens was seasoned with proreligious and religious iconography; the display of pictures of political leaders, historical figures, saints, the participation of priests and similar all resembled Orthodox liturgical processions.[12]

It is of little consolation for all of us that this happened simultaneously in other Yugoslav republics, and even lesser comfort for the religious communities (SOC, RCC among Croats and Slovenes, and the Islamic community) all which fell into the trap of "dirty" politics. To put it concisely,

---

[11]See also David Martin, "The Secularization Issue: Prospect and Retrospect," *The British Journal of Sociology* 42 (3), 465-474. This British sociologist evaluates the religious renewal in post-socialist countries as incidentally religious but basically nationalistic, whereby the "passionate pilgrimages of Serbs to the monastic holy places in Kosovo" may be regarded as "nationalistic."

[12]SOC later decisively distanced itself from the then and the present ruling regime in Serbia headed by Slobodan Milošević, but by this time the process was accomplished. See details in the research study of Radmila Radić, "Crkva i 'srpsko pitanje'" [The Church and 'the Serb Questions'] *Republika* 7 (121), 1995, I-XX,

the religio-ecclesial complex, including the SOC, actively participated in the disintegration of Yugoslav society among others, because it a) permitted the inflammation of a confessional mentality, b) openly contributed to the homogenization of nations and was politically instrumentalized, legitimating the just enthroned nationalist leaders, those who recklessly destroyed the country, c) rejected the importance of ecumenism and dialogue as a condition of life in multiconfessional communities.

Serbian Orthodox Church and the War in Bosnia and Herzegovina

In the beginning of the war, in 1991, on the territory of the former Yugoslavia, religious dignitaries did not accept that these conflicts were (also) religious in nature, but everyone cheered on their "own" side. The Catholic press published articles supporting Croats and Muslims; Orthodox churches 'naturally' held the Serbian side. It turned out that confession and self-criticism were not esteemed values among Yugoslav religions, confessions, and faith communities. Always one quickly blamed others. Thus during the unparalleled war destructions in B&H the Roman Catholic Church among Croats blameds the leadership of SOC, which reciprocated fully, while the Islamic Community blamed both churches. Moreover, the indictement will be extended to entire nations, conceived primarily in a confessional manner. Therefore it could happen that Croats do not fight Serbs and those in turn against Muslims and vice versa but Catholics against Orthodox, Orthodox against Islamic believers, Christians against Islamic believers. The civil-ethnic conflict, greatly heated up by the religious dimension, plunged into an unscrupulous religious war. I am not claiming that religions, confessions, and ecclesial organizations are primarily and exclusively accountable, but only that they are accomplices and in certain situations even actively engaged in the conflict, whereby they bear part of the responsibility.

The religious-ecclesial element consisting of SOC, RCC, and the Islamic community could have been a barrier to the brutal partitioning of Yugoslavia, if not actually have prevented it. However, to the contrary, implicitly or explicitly it agreed to the unfolding of the Yugoslav drama, occasionally even emphatically supporting Yugoslavia's demise.

Many will not agree with my definitive assertion that the war in B&H is, among others, also a religious one[13] but has now been admitted even by the leading Yugoslav theologians (the Orthodox Radovan Bigović, the Catholic

---

[13]E.g. Esad Ćimić, "Bosanska raskrižja," [Bosnian Crossroads], *Društvena istraživanja* 3 (6) 1994, 611-628.

France Perko, the Protestant Aleksandar Birviš, the Islamic Hamdija Jusufspahić)[14] The war is religious if not by its inner content then by its external appearance. It suffices to take into account numerous statements, pronouncements, and the concrete behavior of a part of the hierarchy and clergy, read the religious newspapers and journals, count the systematically destroyed religious buildings and structures, and analyze the many religious graphitis, photograph the religious emblems on military uniforms, etc. Add to this another important factor,

> All in all, one has to conclude, that for both Christian churches, speaking doctrinally, this war cannot be characterized as religious according to intentions and even according to the results. On the other hand, for the Islamic community, it is, without doubt, entirely religious. And by that very fact the bloody conflict becomes a confessional struggle.[15]

Still, above all theoretical speculations the absolutely strongest argument for treating the war also as a religious one is reflected in the fact that the majority of the Serb, Croat, and Muslim population in B&H experiences it and participates in it as being religious.

If we focus our attention upon SOC, one must say that it rejects the notion that Serbs are solely culpable for inflaming the war and that they are the sole aggressors. In a civil-ethnic and additionally religious war there can be no black and white division into "only good and only bad." But logic demands that each side in the conflict bears responsibility and ought to confess their sins.[16] Serbian Patriarch Pavle (Stojčević), a monk whom many believers regard as a living saint, always promoted a just peace for all peoples in the former Yugoslavia, and contended that the war crimes were evil deeds perpetrated by all parties in the war.

> War is always a calamity, and civil war is a calamity of calamities. While in a war the enemy attacks from the outside in a civil war neighbors, co-citizens, and relatives become enemies. Therefore it was correctly concluded by a well-meaning and thoughtful man who came to Bosnia and seeing reality said that the Serbs are defenders of their homes as well as assailants, that the Muslims are defenders and assailants, and so are the Croats." [17]

---

[14]E. Štitkovac, *Različiti putevi do Boga* [Different Paths to God] (Belgrade: Belgrade Circle, 1995).

[15]M. Jeftić, "Konfesionalni element medjuetničkih sukoba u Jugoslaviji," [Confessional element in interethnic conflicts in Yugoslavia], *JUNIR Godišnjak* 1(1), 1994, 88.

[16]Here I am paraphrasing my text "Orthodox Christianity and the Serbian Orthodox Church in the Second and Third Yugoslavia" in *Religiones et societa* to be published in 1995.

[17]"Crkva i politika" [Church and Politics] in *NIN*, Nov. 11, 1994, p. 13,

Nevertheless, the SOC is frequently accused of carrying out a nationalistic, war-mongering politic, especially after it stated its solidarity with the Serb people in B&H (*Republika Srpska*). It is well known that the Federal Republic of Yugoslavia imposed a total embargo except for humanitarian aid toward the Serbs in B&H, because they did not sign the peace proposal of the Contact Group. Other than the population of FR Yugoslavia--which now is unable to help their brothers in B&H, only the SOC stood by Bosnian Serbs. The Church cannot and ought not act differently for the simple reason that it is the church of the entire Serb people, no matter where they may live, and because the Church stands for peace, but one that is just ("justice is the condition for peace"). The SOC is not for prolonging the war,[18] but it is openly against an unjust peace coerced by any of the parties. "As pastors of the church and keepers of the soul of our people we cannot--crying out to God--accept injustice as justice, especially because we know that every ultimate solution forced upon the Serb or some other people could become the source of new calamities and bloodshed in this region."[19]

The SOC is aware that its statements and positions will be understood and supported by the sisterly Orthodox Churches and by the entire Serb people, but be doubly misunderstood first by politicians and by some religious leaders in the West[20] and secondly by domestic rulers, especially the Socialist leadership of Serbia.[21] Therefore in the message of the principal session of the Holy Synod of SOC it was stated,

> Once more we are witnessing before God, Orthodoxy, and Christian peoples, before all people of good will that we, as pastors and spiritual leaders, do not consider ourselves identical with the governments on either side of the Drina River but we cannot separate ourselves from our, although sinful, nevertheless still a People of God in the ecumenical family of peoples, but stay with them on the cross upon which they are crucified. We know that in the world there are politicians and even religious leaders who do not understand our pastoral

---

[18]That does not mean that some bishops may not favor protracting the war, but they are in an absolute minority and they belong to the so called "hawkish wing." Which church is not divided between "hawks" and "doves?"

[19]Sveti arhijerejski sabor SPC [Holy Synod of the SOC), *Politika*, November 5, 1994, 12.

[20]For instance there was speculation that international ecumenical organizations asked the suspension of the SOC from membership in WCC and European Council of Churches. It turned out that this was merely the desire of malevolent individuals and not a not at all official and formal requests.

[21]"As a national church, which first of all serves the interests of its people, SOC had over the last years had a consistent position unlike many parties and individuals." See Radić, *op. cit.*,XX.

care, love, and service for human salvation, inspired by Biblical examples of
the prophet Moses and Apostle Paul.[22]

The SOC is for the establishment of peace in B&H but with the respect of the
rights of the Serb people for self-determination, a right to which all the other
people of the former Yugoslavia already availed themselves.

Translated from Serbian by Paul Mojzes

---

[22]SAS SPC, *Politika*, Nov. 5, 1994.

11

SERBIAN ORTHODOX CHURCH AND THE WAR IN BOSNIA AND HERZEGOVINA

Radmila Radić

Between 1980 and 1995, the Serbian Orthodox Church reentered the public and political sphere from the social margin where it was located the previous forty years. The questions which are being raised, are different: the manner of its return, its position in society, the degree of influence which it obtained, the answers which it offered about fundamental problems, its religious and political activity, and related issues.

For the period from 1980 to 1995, one can use only the press sources (primarily state and church publications) with only a minimum of other sources. Therefore, this study can hardly be regarded a historiographic study; rather, it is a type of chronicle.

The Serbian Orthodox Church (hereafter SOC) was during its historical development structurally an autocephalous, independent church, closely connected to the state upon which it was materially dependent and, therefore, vulnerable to every governmental pressure. The political life of Yugoslavia since its founding in 1918 was characterized by two interpretations of the nature of the state. According to one, the Yugoslav state was the expanded Kingdom of Serbia; by the other, it was a community of nations. SOC, which envisioned itself as the religious and national defender of the Serbian people, advocated the first principle. It did not treat the national problem as a separate political issue but only as a form and ingredient of religion. Therefore, it always attempted to appear as a national and not just a religious institution.

Political conditions during WWII (the destruction of the church organization, genocide of the Orthodox population, civil war, etc.) and immediately after the war, were so tragic for the SOC that it could not recover quickly. Disorganized by war, depleted in its membership, and with a destroyed material basis, without international backing, with the legacy of the bearer of

Serb hegemonism, the SOC faced an opponent who possessed power and the ability to take advantage of the Church's weakness. Besides, SOC completely identified itself with Serbia as a state and the Serbs as a nation. The establishment of a federal Yugoslavia SOC was interpreted as a loss of statehood and with it, the loss of the national identity of the Serb people. Powerless to resist the pressures of the Yugoslav state because of its structure, age-old practice, and dependency, SOC increasingly fell into a condition contrary to its own nature.

In the post WWII period, the religious communities were gradually but successfully removed from social and political life to societal marginalization. The picture of general and fundamental rights and freedoms and idyllic social relationships had been advanced steadily and at length, but in the background, many unresolved problems remained, waiting for the suitable moment to powerfully erupt upon the historical scene.

The revitalization of Orthodoxy came in the middle of the 1980s at the time of the breakup of the socialist system, the crisis in society, and the liberalization of social relationships. Changes within SOC became evident at the beginning of the 1980s when the question of the relationships between Serbs and Albanians in Kosovo was raised. A group of younger theologians appeared on the scene who demanded a greater mobilization of the Church and an emergence out of the lethargy into which the Church had fallen. The non-existence of any type of opposition in the previous phase of social development attracted to the Church all those who thought differently because under its wings they could find at least some sort of legal resistance. SOC, thus, became a haven for the political and national alternative and offered legitimacy to a segment of the nationally-oriented intelligentsia. Under its wings, the nurture of national continuity, the cult of national and religious heroes and, in general, of national history, Cyrillic script and traditional customs and values took place. With the deepening of the general crisis and the breakup of the Communist system, the credibility of the traditional resolution of existential problems was restored. Thereby, Orthodoxy gained in significance for the cultural and national uniqueness of the Serb people and for its homogenization and identification in contrast to other national and confessional loyalties. However, the conditions that contributed to the revitalization of religion simultaneously contributed to the nationalistic and every other type of misuse of the Church.

SOC steadfastly held that it alone in history was the defender of the Serb people and that it never abandoned them, that it is above the state, and that it represents the supreme moral arbiter; hence, its intention and views cannot be questioned. Any suggestion about the politicization of the church was rejected, but a part of the clergy and the episcopate together with a part of the intelligentsia raised issues and offered solutions at a very early stage regarding the Serb national question, the organization of the state, the role of the church in society, the relationship with the West and the East, and similar points. In this manner, an ideology was formed which increased the crisis and opened new fronts. The desire to return to former positions in society became more open, and the ruling regime and opposition parties and leaders were being supported by the Church as long as they offered the hope that they would fulfill expectations. The political decision-makers could not have succeeded in carrying out such a successful homogenization of the Serb ethnos if it were not for the support of the Church. But it is likewise true that when paths began to diverge, a segment of the church representatives acted militantly and exclusivisticly, not only toward Communists, atheists, and religious sects, but even toward some of the originators of this nationalist ideology.

Since the beginning of the new round of wars on Yugoslav territories, SOC offered great moral and material support to the Serb population in places where the war raged. Especially meaningful in this regard were the visits and contacts with other Orthodox Churches, whose representatives carried messages of support. The top leadership of SOC in its declarations always started with the assertion that the Serb people were not the aggressors but the imperiled side which now for the second time in its history was experiencing genocide. Thus, they justified the war, declaring it as defensive. The SOC believed that as the only and final solution of the national question was the unification of the entire Serb people; one must not lose sight that any other solution would mean the breakup of the Church administration.[1] War crimes were sharply denounced, but those that were perpetrated by Serbs were most frequently interpreted as excesses. The episcopate was not entirely unified on many issues, but its larger segment consisted of prelates who originated from war zones. Appeals for peace, negotiations, and the discovery of just solutions were the constant theme of all

---

[1]After WWI, SOC was formed as a single organism. Its breakup began already in 1945 with the creation of autonomous federal units which demanded ecclesial autonomy (Macedonia, Montenegro and even Vojvodina and Slovenia), but also with difficulties in establishing authority in certain dioceses in the diaspora. SOC never accepted the decisions of AVNOJ (Antifascist Council of People's Liberation of Yugoslavia), regarding it as a "coercive act" that invalidated all previous wars of Serbia without taking into consideration the will of the Serb people. Creating independent states on the territory of the former Yugoslavia and their recognition by the Federal Republic of Yugoslavia and the international community, the dioceses of SOC came into a situation analogous to the diocese abroad. Taking into consideration the tendency of the Ecumenical Patriarchate (in Constantinople) to place under its control the diaspora Orthodox communities, the existing problem with the Church in Macedonia, the events surrounding the establishment of the Orthodox Church in America, and other issues, it is questionable how SOC would establish its jurisdiction over these dioceses.

church leaders, but the "just solution" they almost always considered was that which was in the interest of the nation they represented. As a national church, whose priority it is to represent the interests of its own nation, SOC had a consistent stance over the past years in contrast to many political parties, groups, or individuals. It is still undecided whether SOC ought to first of all respond to its calling as a Christian Church or as a national one, and whether the consistent support of nationalistic options did not lead SOC into a heresy called *philetism*.[2]

Return to the Political Stage

The exploration of sociologists during the sixties and seventies and the beginning of the eighties in various regions of the former Yugoslavia showed that the process of secularization was most effective exactly in regions where the Orthodox population was in the majority.[3] The official census of 1953 which contained also a question of religious affiliation--questions which where thereupon left out from all subsequent censuses until 1991--showed that only 12.6 per cent were atheists. At the end of the 1960s and beginning of 1970s, this percentage gradually rose. For instance in Serbia in 1975, it rose to 25 percent. At the beginning of the 1980s, the percent of those who identified themselves as believers became more pronounced. This is the period of the beginning of the manifestation of the social crisis, especially its political form, which was to culminate in the subsequent years. The 1991 Census showed that of the 8,733,952 people of the Federal Republic of Yugoslavia (Serbia and Montenegro) almost 80% claimed to be Orthodox.[4]

---

[2]Philetism derives from a Greek word "Phile" which means tribe. At a Local Council in Constantinopolis in 1872 which considered the question of people-nation-nationalism in the nineteenth century, the decisions of which continue to be canonically valid for the entire area of the canonical jurisdiction of Orthodoxy, philetism was condemned as "a heresy which places the national idea over the unity of faith." (Rev. C. Fotiev, *The Living God* (London: Overseas Publications Interchange, 1989) 343.)

[3]In the opinion of Dragoljub Djordjević, there are three key factors which influenced secularization on the territory of SOC: suffering in WWII, the Bolshevik regime, and the internal weaknesses of the Church as an institution. (Dragoljub Djordjević and Bogdan Djurović, "Sekularizacija i pravoslavlje: Slučaj Srba" [Secularization and Orthodoxy: The Case of Serbs] in *Gradina* 10-12, Niš, 1993, 219-224.)

[4]*Census '91, Population*, II, Belgrade, 1993. Sociologists of religion show that one needs to distinguish the confessional belonging of a population for its religiosity. Confessional adherence may mean "actual linkage to a concrete confession, traditional linkage, and recognition of confessional heritage." (Dragoljub Djordjević, "Opšta socioreligijska i konfesionalna panorama stanovništva u SFRJ [General socioreligious and confessional panorama of the population of the SFRY in *Religija i društvo* [Religion and Society], Belgrade, 1988.)

The expulsion of Serbs and Montenegrins from Kosovo, the increase in temperature in the discussions of the relationship between Serbia and its regions, the movement of the population toward their national nucleus, the general increase in nationalism, anti-Serbian slogans in some cities, economic distress, and many other reasons started to fill the churches during major holidays, especially in urban centers. This created, in the opinion of some theologians and others, the possibility of a shift from the worry whether Orthodoxy would survive the crisis in a secularized world to an intensified religious renewal. In due time they started thinking about the restoration of the position which SOC once upon a time enjoyed politically.

The Problem of Kosovo

In April 1982, twenty-one priests signed the "Appeal" directed to the highest authorities of Serbia and the Federation, the Holy Council of Bishops and the Synod of Bishops.[5] Among the signatories were three most eminent theologians-monks Atanasije Jeftić, Irinej Bulović, and Amfilohije Radović. The text of the "Appeal" epitomized the "raising of the voice to protect the spiritual and biological existence of the Serb people in Kosovo and Metohija." It was the beginning of a new phenomenon in the Church--sending petitions within and outside the church, but also with an emphasis on comprehending the role and significance of public opinion. The latter brought about a visit of a group of bishops to the USA, where they visited the Congress and State Department and requested "an intervention because of Kosovo." In June of the same year, *Pravoslavlje* [Orthodoxy] published the text of Atanasije Jeftić "From Kosovo and Around Kosovo" in which he stated,

> Today one, tomorrow seven, and day after tomorrow to the last!--this is the haughty slogan and message of Albanian irredentists to Serbs in Kosovo, published these days in the press, which most clearly reveals their real and ultimate goal. The extermination of the Serb people in Kosovo and Metohija is the message of Albanian Nazis which lasts several decades. In the past this genocidal intention was whispered--sometimes loudly, but during the last decade it often became a drastic act of psychological and physical terror, and even public crime.[6]

Toward the end of 1983, Atanasije Jeftić began in *Pravoslavlje* an essay entitled "From Kosovo to Jadovno" in which he makes the parallel of the victimization of the Serb people in various parts of Yugoslavia. He provided

---

[5]The Holy Council of Bishops is a meeting of all bishops, the regular session of which is usually in May of each year. They sometimes meet in special sessions in times of crises. A Synod of Bishops consists of four bishops elected annually and the Patriarch. The Synod acts as an executive committee, meeting weekly or bi-weekly.

[6]*Pravoslavlje*, no. 366, 1982.

details of attempted rapes, attacks on Serbs and Serbdom, data on the mistreatment of monks and nuns, murders, etc. Additionally, he wrote in detail about pits [in which the massacred were hurled] and concentration camps in Croatia where Serbs were massacred during World War II.[7] Further, he gave an interview to the paper *Student*, in which he replied to the question how he perceives the situation in Kosovo, considering that the leaders of the Central Committee of the Communist Party of Serbia spoke out sharply. He said, "It was high time that the rulers of Serbia say something more concrete about the situation in Kosovo. Because [previously] what they used to say was only general--in principle, which did not reflect the actual situation in Kosovo . . . ."

What Kosovo means to Serbs was described by Archpriest Božidar Mijač in the text "Light from Kosovo," in which he stated,

> Kosovo is not only a physical domicile but also a metaphysical creation. . . . This Serbian habitat includes heaven and earth. It is the *nomen* of the spirit in the phenomenon of time and space. It is the best proof that to belong to a land is not essentially a numerical majority of the population but something much more: it is a spiritual creation which was established and which exists in a higher existential manner. Idiogenesis in this case is more weighty than ethnogenesis."[8]

The publication of the Serbian Patriarchate, *Pravoslavlje*, continually published archival documents with suitable photographs about the crimes carried out on the Serb populace in Kosovo during the last century. It was symptomatic that these were mainly petitions and complaints of Serbs directed to Russian tsars. As a direct result of the nurture of the myth about a "'universal defender of the Orthodox," the Russian Patriarch Pimen was exaltedly greeted in Kosovo in 1984 *en masse*. Ovations directed at him and the number of gathered Serbs in front of the monastery Gračanica is material useful for a serious analysis.[9]

Ideological Basis

Using Kosovo as an unresolved problem within Serbia and Yugoslavia, SOC offered itself as the underpinning of traditional national security and the center of national life, affirmed by century-old experience, because it is the only institution "which never in its history betrayed the Serbs." The ideological foundation of such activity was the synthesis of the teachings of Bishop Nikolai Velimirović and Justin Popović. There is no church publication from the middle of the 1980s that did not in each issue publish some text of one of these two "permanent prototypes and models of newer Serbian spirituality" or an essay about them. Especially persistent was *Glas Crkve*. In it the authors were settling

---

[7]*Pravoslavlje*, nos. 400, 404, 405, 1983 and 1984.

[8]*Pravoslavlje*, no. 388, 1983.

[9]*Pravoslavlje*, no. 422, 1984 and *Glas Crkve* [The Voice of the Church], No. 11, 1984.

all accounts with the opponents of Bishop Nikolaj, and an action to return his remains from America was initiated; he is celebrated as a saint and example of a real Serbian bishop.

Justin Popović is regarded as a great teacher of Orthodoxy, and these authors follow his typology of separating the European man from *Svetosavski* god-man.[10] He wrote that European culture rests upon the human being as the foundation and that humanism is its main architect. Hence, the European man regards himself as god.[11] Therefore, nihilism and anarchism are the logical conclusion of European culture--the inevitable end phase of European humanism and relativism. Humanism, according to Popović, inevitably leads to atheism, goes through anarchism, and ends in nihilism.[12] The Serb people, based on "Christ's immortal people," are stronger than any death because its historical emergence is not a meaningless accident but "has its mission in this world, a task in eternity, which is accomplished by the belief in the eternity of the spiritual world and in a higher meaning of human history--believing in God."[13] The decadence of the people begins when they opt for material goods because "atheism and nihilism are the flip sides of the same de-divinization and de-spiritualization of the human being."[14]

The model of returning to one's roots made it possible to use only two authors out of the entire European heritage--Gogol and Dostoevsky. From the middle of the 1980s, the Church press with increasing frequency published texts which explained that the position of the Serbian people is a result of mistakes of the past. The solutions for terminating the crisis are given in texts like the one that appeared in 1984 in *Glas Crkve* entitled, "What is Serbian Nationalism?" The anonymous author replies that it is

---

[10]Saint Sava was the son of a great Serb king who became the first Serb archbishop and who became the paradigmatic figure of all that is authentically Serbian Orthodox [translators comment]. "The wholeness and perfection of one's personality man achieves through union with the God-man. God-manlyhood is the only category through which appears the entire manyfold activity of the Orthodox culture. . . . The conscience of the Serbian people are saints headed by St. Sava." (Justin Popović, "*Svetosavlje*--pravoslavno hrišćanstvo srpskog stila i iskustva," [*Svetosavlje*--Orthodox Christianity According to Serbian Style and Experience], *Pravoslavni misionar* [Orthodox Missionary], 4, 1985.)

[11]Justin Popović, "Svetosavska filozofija prosvete," [Svetosavska Philosophy of Enlightenment], *Glas Crkve*, No. 3, 1986.

[12]*Ibid.*

[13]Lazar Milin, "Razgovori o veri," [Conversation about Belief], *Apologetska čitanka* (Belgrade, 1965); L. Milin "Vidovdan," [St. Vitus Day], *Pravoslavni misionar*, No. 3, 1982.

[14]J. Popović, "Na bogočovečanskom putu," [On the Path to God-Manhood], (Belgrade, 1960) 259; N. Velimirović, *Rat i Biblija* [War and the Bible] (Kragujevac, 1931) 130-132; J. Popović, *Dogmatika pravoslavne crkve* [Dogmatics of the Orthodox Church], Vol. 3, (Belgrade, 1978) 832.

a state in which Christ is the tsar, art in which Christ is the magic; the school where Christ is the teacher; slavery, which can be endured only with Christ; the fabric of the history of the Serbian people is based on Christ while the thread are "saints [male and female], heroes, and martyrs of Christ . . . ."

In the same issue, one can find another essay entitled "Is it Sufficient to be a Good Serb While Faith is Peripheral?" in which it is revealed that a Serb without faith is not a real Serb and "hence a man without a mind would not be our leader, neither would a Serb without faith be our partner!" The elaboration of this maxim one may find in *Pravoslavlje* under the title "When will the Orthodox Serb Have it Better." The author signed the article as "Your Priest"; he presented in ten theses his long-range program of national stabilization. According to him, the situation will improve when Serbs everywhere acknowledge without embarrassment and without repercussions that they are Orthodox Christian and offsprings of St. Sava and when they start to attend church, baptize their children, write in the Cyrillic script, have church weddings, etc.[15]

Heavenly Serbia

During the year 1987, SOC started to prepare for the celebration of the 600th anniversary of the Battle of Kosovo. For that purpose, the monk Atanasije Jeftić published "The Kosovo Pledge" in several installments. He cited Bishop Nikolaj Velimirović, according to whom Prince Lazar opted for the

Heavenly Kingdom in the name of the entire Serbian people (akin to Moses' People of Israel) and it became the strongest expression of the meaning of our history and its governing idea . . . .Kosovo (i.e., Lazar's choice and option at Kosovo) showed that our history played itself out on the highest level, on the tragic and exalted border between heaven and earth, divine and human. Kosovo is also a testimony that as a people we never struggled for insignificant issues and we were never able to be sincerely excited about trivialities and transiency.[16]

In 1988 the reliques of Prince Lazar were carried from the monastery Ravanica by way of the diocese of Zvornik-Tuzla, Šabac-Valjevo, Šumadija, and Žiča to Gračanica in Kosovo so that there they would await the commemoration of the 600th anniversary of the Battle of Kosovo. Everywhere they were received very reverently and with the massive turn-out of the population. In the epistle issued by Bishop Jovan of Šabac-Valjevo at that occasion, he mentioned the term "Heavenly Serbia" which will subsequently be used frequently.

Prince Lazar and Kosovo Serbs primarily created a heavenly Serbia which by today surely grew into the greatest heavenly state. If only we count the victims of the last war, millions upon millions of Serb men and women,

---

[15]*Pravoslavlje*, no. 419, 1984.

[16]*Glas Crkve*, no. 2, 1987.

children, and the infirm were killed and tortured in greatest torment or hurled
into the pits and caves by *ustaša*[17] criminals, then we can imagine how large
the Serb kingdom is in heaven.[18]

The polemics with *Glas Koncila*[19] which began toward the end of the
1980s continued. Especially barbed were articles from 1990 about the number
of Serb victims in the Jasenovac concentration camp, the massacre of Livanj,
etc.[20] Archival documents about Serb genocides in the Independent State of
Croatia during WWII were regularly appearing in *Pravoslavlje*.

Rev. Dragomir Ubiparipović from Sarajevo wrote toward the end of 1988
an article for *Glas Crkve* under the title "Cultural and Religious Genocide of
Orthodox Serbs in Sarajevo." According to him, cultural genocide was reflected
in the protection of cultural monuments of "our centuries-long enslavers, the
Turks, which for five full centuries retarded the high achievements of Christian
culture of the Balkans," in the neglect of Serbian churches, cemeteries, and
museums of Serbian history, and the disregard of monuments of Serb history for
tourist purposes at the advantage of monuments from Turkish times.   The
Sarajevo newspaper, *Oslobodjenje* [Liberation], impeded the rights of the
Orthodox by its unwillingness to publish obituaries in the Cyrillic script and by
deletion of the words *parastos* and *opelo* [Orthodox religious funerary rituals]
from the obituaries.[21]

The Holy Council of Bishops of SOC at its meeting in May 1990 sent a
request to state authorities to permit the excavation of victims from WWII and
their dignified burial. Then during the entire year, there were reports from B&H
(Bileće, Kupres, Fahovići, Vlasenica, etc.) and Croatia about funeral rites for the

---

[17]*Ustaša* is the name of the Croat Nazi extremists troops that operated during WWII akin
to the German SS units.

[18]Bishop Danilo Krstić and monk Amfilohije Radović published in 1982 a catechesis
under the title "There is no More Beautiful Faith than the Christian" in which they wrote that
Prince Lazar, together with his army and the people opted for the "Heavenly kingdom," i.e.,
Christ's eternity instead of the transient earthly kingdom. According to the authors this is the
Kosovo option and pledge. The priest, Božidar Mijač, in *Teološki pogledi* [Theological
Views] in a study entitled "Eschatology" also wrote "At Kosovo the Serbian people voted
with their soul for the Eternal Kingdom and that was and remains its real choice. From then
on all Serbs, being loyal to that pledge, become the People of God. Christ's New testament
people, the Heavenly Serbia, is a part of the new Chosen People of God. . . . In the light of
their choice for the Heavenly Kingdom one should understand all the tragic events in Serb
history, and especially the present one's . . . ." (*Teološki pogledi*, Nos. 1-2, (1988) 8.

[19]*Glas Koncila* [The Voice of the Council] is a Roman Catholic weekly published in
Zagreb.

[20]Pravoslavlje, nos. 559, 564, 568 all in 1990 and *Glas Crkve*, nos. 1,2,3 in 1990.
[Translator's Note: The concentration camp in Jasenovac, Croatia, during WWII played a
similar role to Serb memory as Auschwitz plays to Jewish.]

[21]*Glas Crkve*, no. 4, 1988.

victims of genocide, excavation of their bones, and their reburial. These reports were usually accompanied by numerous details of how the victims were killed. Simultaneously, the clergy of SOC was spreading alarm from B&H that again the atmosphere of the "resurrected *ustaša*" movement was manifest and that the Serbs must remain united and vote at the impending elections for those who will, in addition to other important factors, guarantee the protection of religious and national values.[22]

In December of 1990 at the special session of the Holy Council of Bishops of SOC, due to the prolonged illness of Patriarch German Djorić, a new patriarch was elected, Pavle I, previously the bishop of Raška-Prizren. Amfilohije Radović[23] was elected as the Metropolitan of Montenegro (at a time of agitated discussion about the possible autocephaly of the Church in Montenegro) while Irinej Bulović[24] became the Bishop of Bačka. The Holy Council of Bishops decided that the year 1991 be dedicated as the liturgical-

---

[22]*Pravoslavlje*, no. 567, 1990 and *Glas Crkve*, nos. 1,2,3, 1990.

[23]The ceremony of enthronement of Bishop Amfilohije as the metropolitan of the Montenegro-Coastal Area was attended by the President of the Presidency of Montenegro, Momir Bulatović, President of the Serbian Democratic Party of B&H, Radovan Karadžić, the member of the Presidency of B&H Nikola Koljević, and others. *Glasnik* the official bulletin of SOC in January 1991 wrote that the guests at the ordination were "gladly received by Serbs from Montenegro . . . in Serb Montenegro. . . ."

[24]In the speech during his installation--which provided the opportunity of presenting the program of the newly installed prelate--Bulović avoided any reference to concrete political circumstances. He supported the renewal of monasticism, dissemination of ecclesiastical education and service to "all-Orthodox unity" and "dialogue of love and understanding between Christian brothers." His view of the political engagement of a clergyman and of believers in general, he expressed in an article "The Church and Politics" that was published half a year earlier in *Pravoslavlje*. About the relationships between state and the church he said, "The only natural and healthy relationship would be mutual support and cooperation, with the full respect for the differences and a full awareness about the limits of cooperation. A Christian state, a state church, a state without a church or a state instead of the church--all of these it seems, are various forms of the same utopia. A free church in a free society is the only formula which can meet the demands this worldly state politics and heaven-earthly church policy. . . ." About the political engagement of clergy, Irinej said, "Truly a clergy person as an agitator or representative of any political party, even the most humane, even the one inspired by Christianity, would be a caricature. Such a clergyman would be a man who leaves the primary for the marginal--he would be simply a man doing someone else's job." (*Gradac* 110,Čačak, 1993, 6-7). Justin Popović somewhat earlier wrote the following "Political parties, tacitly or openly, in principle advocate the use of force or coercion, especially when they are in power. *Svetosavski* clergyman because of the inspiration of the gospels should not belong to any political party because a clergyman who aspires to be a *svetosavski* clergyman must rule the people with love, serving them and sacrificing for them. . . . It is *Svetosavski*, it is Orthodox for the clergyman to be first of all a priest who is the spiritual leader of his people, and as such he belongs to the entire nation." (*Hrišćanska Misao* [Christian Thought], nos. 6-8, 1993.)

prayerful commemoration of the 50th anniversary of the affliction of SOC and the genocide and that the clergy and people continue to work on the unearthing of the remains of innocent victims and their dignified reinternment. The Holy Council of Bishops sent a message to the people to vote for those "who are truly faithful to God and Serbdom"[25] and not to those who make big promises.[26]

One of the first messages of the new Patriarch announced at Easter 1991 had to do with "the disclosure of location of extermination and graves of neomartyrs and neosaints." The Patriarch repeated the words of his predecessor that one must forgive, but one mustn't forget, and emphasized that one must not forget the fact that the sin of "unparalleled crime" was unrepented, which is being affirmed by contemporary events. The Patriarch requested that everything should be done to bring to life "the community of spirit and prayer with the holy victims innocently exterminated and to do everything to never forget or diminish their sacrifice.[27]

The burial of the victims of *ustaša* terrors in B&H commenced already in January and continued throughout the year 1991 (in Žitomislić, Prebilovci, Ljubinje, Trebinje, Majevica, Banja Luka, etc). Among those who personally descended into the slaughter-pit in Golubinka were the President of the Serbian Democratic Party (SDP), Radovan Karadžić, the member of the presidency B&H representing SDP, Nikola Koljević, and the artist Milič of Mačva.

Attitude Toward the War

Patriarch Pavle sent a letter in October 1991 to Lord Carrington, the president of the International Conference on Yugoslavia, in which he stated that because of the genocide in the past that took place on these territories, Serbs cannot be a part of any type of independent Croatia but have to be under the same roof with Serbia and all Serb Krajinas [border regions]. "It is time to comprehend that the victims of genocide cannot live together with their former but perhaps also their future executioners." A similar letter was mailed on November 4, 1991, to the president and all participants of the Peace Conference in The Hague. The delegation from the Special Session of the Holy Council of Bishops of SOC met with the vice president of Yugoslavia, Branko Kostić, and the President of Serbia, Slobodan Milošević, and transmitted the request that neither the President of Yugoslavia nor the representatives of Serbia and Montenegro should permit during negotiations in The Hague or elsewhere the

---

[25]The term used is *rod*, which indicates close blood relationship like in a clan or extended family, but the connotation is "all Serbs."

[26]*Pravoslavlje*, no. 576, 1991.

[27]*Pravoslavlje*, no. 576, 1991.

imposition upon the Serb people "the most tragic solution of its questions." Dr. Kostić expressed during this meeting a special recognition to SOC for its previous efforts to defend the Serbs and added that it has an inestimable role.[28] The Holy Council of Bishops's working group also met the representatives of opposition political parties in Serbia and expressed its views about the need to establish a government of national salvation. In an official declaration of the Sabor, all Serbs are given notice that SOC permits only a defensive and liberation war when it is imposed upon them and rejects every war of aggression. "The Serb soldier must be characterized with humaneness and courage; he must fight with chivalry and not besmirch himself and his people with crimes and injustice."

Several months prior to the outbreak of the war in B&H, a delegation of the Islamic Community headed by Haji Hamdia efendi Jusufspahić, the Mufti of Belgrade, met with Patriarch Pavle and on that occasion an appeal was issued for peace and against the misuse of religious faith for national-political purposes. A month later, at the beginning of September 1991, Patriarch Pavle also received Alija Izetbegović, the president of the B&H presidency, who said to the patriarch, "Muslims will never raise their arm against Serbs" and that problems can be solved only peaceably.[29] In October, however, the Memorandum about the sovereignty and independence of Bosnia was declared, and during the same months Serbs declared in a plebiscite their intention to remain part of Yugoslavia, and in December they decided to form the Serbian Republic of B&H.

In January of 1992 at the extraordinary session of the Holy Council of Bishops of SOC, a declaration was made in which the hierarchs supported the liberty and rights of the Serb people of B&H and the Serbian Krajinas saying, "No one's deals with the governing rulers of Serbia, which has no mandate to represent entire Serbdom, or with the representative of the Yugoslav Federation or with the commanding structures of the Yugoslav military, are binding for the whole Serbian people, without their consent and without the blessing of their spiritual Mother, the Serbian Orthodox Church." The declaration continues by supporting the "demand of the people of B&H for a life in freedom and their process of self-determined political organizing."[30]

Toward the end of February and beginning of March 1992, Serbs in B&H proclaimed their statehood and boycotted the referendum of independence of B&H. On the streets of Sarajevo, they set up barricades. In the middle of

---

[28]*Pravoslavlje*, nos. 591 and 592, 1991.

[29]*Pravoslavlje*, nos. 585-586, 587, 1991.

[30]*Pravoslavlje*, no. 598, 1992.

March, the UN set up an office in Sarajevo, and on April 6th the European Community recognized the independence of B&H. Two days later Alija Izetbegović proclaimed a state of emergency.

The *Reis-ul-Ulema*, Haji Jakub Selimovski, sent to the Patriarch Pavle a letter on April 9th, in which he informed him that on April 8, 1992, Zvornik was attacked and that the attackers were the units of Željko Ražnjatović-Arkan[31] and Serb members of the Serbian Democratic Party. Selimovski wrote that Muslims are being killed only because they are of a different faith and that many of the attackers are saying that they are doing this to defend Serbdom and Orthodoxy. Selimovski expected an earlier condemnation of aggression by the Patriarch because Serbs and Croats were also perishing in B&H, but Arkan's units were carrying out a massacre in Bijeljina. The Patriarch replied that SOC did everything to prevent the break-out of enmity, but that he sees that the Serbs are not the instigators of the conflict in B&H although there are some who "in self-defense acted violently" and their crimes are to be condemned.[32] In the editorial commentary of *Pravoslavlje*, Dragan Terzić wrote at this time that Serbs in Bosnia do not want to live in a *jamharia* similar to Libya, and that under the rule of *mujahedins*, they would have the same status that Christians have in Muslim countries, namely they would be slaves--a condition which they already experienced during the five hundred years of Islamic occupation.[33]

"Western Serbs" as an Example

At the beginning of the 1990's, ever more frequently it is being suggested that the

> Church is the most appropriate and most responsible institution for the preservation of the Serb national Orthodox identity. . . . The church has the obligation to say what it thinks about state policies, to warn, correct, direct, or

---

[31]Ž. Ražnjatović-Arkan claimed that he was the greatest darling of the patriarchate and stated that his commander-in-chief is Patriarch Pavle. He had his army baptized by Bishop Lukijan in Dalj and he carried on him the picture of St. Nicholas signed by the Patriarch. (*Duga*, Nov. 8-23, 1992). Ž. Ražnjatović Arkan showed up in front of the Patriarchal palace with the intention of becoming the personal bodyguard of Patriarch Pavle. At that time Bishop Atanasije reacted and asked Arkan to leave, saying that he "cannot be some sort of *emblem* under which the Patriarch will go to the church of St. Sava." Later this bishop commented, "My position was clear. Arkan cannot be a patron to the Patriarch and his *emblem*, but I never denied that Arkan is defending the Serbs, but he is not the only one. Arkan is a fighter where he is needed, but Stanoje Glavaš was also a hero and when they wanted to elect him as the leader of the rebellion [First Serb Rebellion against the Ottomans in 1804] he said, "People, don't [choose] me. I am a *hajduk* [a freedom-fighter-brigand]. And they selected Karadjordje." (*Duga*, Jan. 31-Feb. 12, 1993).

[32]Pravoslavlje, no. 603, 1992.

[33]*Pravoslavlje*, no. 598, 1992.

condemn if this policy is hurtful to citizens, namely church members. Whether one likes it or not, the Church is the sole moral arbiter in state-political matters, because they have a direct impact upon the people for which the Church is responsible before God and history. The Church has no pretensions to replace the state government but only that it has the right to control the government from the outside and to express its judgment--all for the well-being of the people.[34]

In line with this, the poet Slobodan Rakitić stated that the time has come for SOC to get the determinative role in the fate of the Serb people[35] while the priest D. Ubiparipović called the Church to show the way even at the expense of conflict with the government.[36]

The open attacks upon the regime by representatives of SOC continued, as exemplified by the presence of the Patriarch at the St. Vitus assembly of the democratic opposition in Serbia, the editorial commentaries of *Pravoslavlje*, the June letter of Bishop Artemije of Raška-Prizren, the support to student demands, etc. The basis for these attacks--combined with the forementioned unfulfilled demands of SOC, with the Communism as an evil imposed upon Serbs, with Yugoslavia as the greatest Serb mistake and wound, etc.--is the dissatisfaction of SOC by the degree of attention the governments of Serbia and Montenegro gave to the Serb people of B&H. Gradually, these criticisms revealed a projection of the ideal Serb state. Thus, for instance, they stated that "it is the centuries-old Serb aspiration toward unity" which always collapsed when Serbs abandoned the St. Sava form of Orthodoxy as the sole spiritual and moral force for the liberation and unification, because Serbs rise to rebellions only in the name of the Orthodox faith and the testament of St. Sava.

> At this time many politicians speak about the need of national unity, which in itself is positive. In this regard the ruling Socialist (Communist) Party is conspicuous. But the mistake is that they do not offer the basis of this unity, they do not point to the unifying factor without which national unity cannot be accomplished. Serbdom without Orthodoxy, as previously stated, is impossible; it is a mere abstraction."[37]

Therefore,

> [f]or Serbs to live again in the new Serb state several conditions are necessary. If the government of the state and its highest leadership are not Orthodox, i.e. they do not have a spiritual relationship with the Serbian Orthodox Church, do not attend worship, do not partake of the eucharist, do not celebrate their *krsna slava*,[38] do not invite priests for the sprinkling of holy water, and if they don't cross themselves, then they cannot be legitimate Serb representatives. Although

---

[34]*Pravoslavlje*, no. 613, 1992.

[35]*Pravoslavlje*, no. 605, 1992.

[36]*Glas crkve*, no. 2, 1992.

[37]*Pravoslavlje*, no. 608, 1992.

[38]A special Serb holy day of celebrating the saint's day on which allegedly the family's ancestors converted to Christianity.

such people rule Serbia, Serbs cannot regard them as their own, for Serbia was long ruled by the Osmanlies, yet that did not mean that they were Serb statesmen. . . . Fortunately, there are Serb lands that have all the features of a Serb state. Those are the Serbian Republic of Krajina and the Serbian Republic of B&H. In these lands the emblem and hymn are Serbian Orthodox. Their highest leaders attend worship, celebrate their *krsna slava*, they introduced catechism in their schools, use the Cyrillic alphabet in their business, accept clergy as spiritual leaders and not as enemies. Whether some day Serbia and Montenegro will become Serbian states only time will show.[39]

The leadership of SOC developed in the course of the year 1992 a very lively political activity. Patriarch Pavle sent to the General Secretary of the U.N. Boutros Boutros-Ghali, the *Reis-ul-Ulema* Haji Jakub Selimovski, and Cardinal Franjo Kuharić a letter regarding "the criminal aggression of the Croatian army on the Serbs of Eastern Herzegovina." The Patriarch proposed a meeting of religious leaders with the purpose of issuing a joint statement and appeal for peace. Then toward the end of June, he sent a letter to Boutros-Ghali, Douglas Herd, Lord Carrington, and others regarding the tragic situation of Sarajevo Serbs, but also about the travail of the population of other faiths with the petition to assure the delivery of humanitarian aid to all three sides, to prevent outrages, and to end the animosities. In November, a meeting took place between Patriarch Pavle and Cardinal Kuharić in Geneva after which an appeal for peace was issued. In October, Patriarch Pavle visited America while in December there was a meeting between representatives of SOC, the Roman Catholic Church, and the Islamic Religious Community in Bern. Simultaneously, the church press wrote about "Serbia being threatened by the entire West," about how Serbs cannot expect aid from non-Orthodox countries, about the leading role of "papal servants Italy, Austria, and Germany," and about their attack upon Serbs and Serb hearths. In December 1992 in a Statement of the Special Session of the Holy Council of Bishops of SOC, they rejected the accusations against Serbs from B&H about the rapes of Muslim women, and they stated that they had evidence of witnesses about outrages against Serb women and children.[40]

The constant feature of these statements of SOC was to stress the self-determination of peoples as a natural right and the rejection of "illegitimate AVNOJ borders."[41] This was specially manifested during some key moments when the church leadership was in disagreement with the position of Serbia's government. The referendum of Serbs in Bosnia prior to their rejection of the

---

[39]*Pravoslavlje*, no. 614, 1992.

[40]*Pravoslavlje*, no. 618, Dec. 15, 1992 and *Glasnik*, no. 12, Dec. 1992.

[41]Reference is to the establishment of internal borders between the republics of Yugoslavia and a session of the Antifascist Council of the People's Liberation of Yugoslavia which convened during World War II under Tito's leadership.

Vance-Owen plan was expressly supported by a special Holy Council of Bishops statement. Delegations of the Patriarchate ever more frequently visited "Serb lands." Thus, the patriarch visited both Pale and Knin, and somewhat later Goražde, just prior to the NATO bombardment of Serb positions.

During the three war years--which were simultaneously also years of multi-party politics--the relationship of SOC toward the Serb opposition political movements had an easily perceivable evolution. The opposition, to which the SOC was erstwhile positively inclined, lost the Church's support because they were allegedly "insufficiently national and undeveloped for the times and the regime." The conflict first broke out between Bishop Atanasije Jeftić and the academician Dobrica Ćosić; somewhat later the same bishop entered into a sharp polemic with Vuk Drašković. When the news came from Trebinje about the persecution of Muslims and the destruction of the mosque, the Belgrade government asked for an explanation from Bishop Atanasije whose diocese this was. In his reply, the bishop answered that this was not the only insult against the Serb people by its government of which President Ćosić is a part. Bishop Jeftić then proceeded to fault Ćosić for not showing interest when in Herzegovina Serb churches and villages were being burnt down and destroyed and when a considerable segment of Herzegovina was abandoned to the Croats. Dobrica Ćosić replied to Jeftić on February 16, 1993, that Serb people are not being disgraced only by the political government of Belgrade, Pale, and Trebinje but also by the bishops governing from their palaces and that the bishop should ask himself whether he personally might not be such a sinner.[42]

In the communique related to the meeting of the Holy Council of Bishops of 1993, again the regime of the country was sharply attacked and was urged to make place for a better government.[43] In commentaries above the communique, it was apparent that the church leadership was dissatisfied with the alleged conciliatory posture of the regime to the international community in regard to events on the other side of the Drina River. Such commentaries were confirmed in the "Appeal" of Bishop Atanasije Jeftić on St. Vitus Day 1993 due to the

---

[42]Atanasije Jeftić replied that thanks to Ćosić and his 'patron' "Serb Svetosavska Herzegovina" has been reduced to a nearly untenable situation and that Communism will push the Serb people into an "AVNOJ graveyard from which there is no resurrection" *NIN*, February 12, 1993 and March 12, 1993.

[43]"The government which is most responsible for the situation in which we all find ourselves do not have the power nor sincere trust nor leverage to lead the people to the right path. They should yield their place to others, quietly, cooperatively, patiently. Thoughtful and moral elements of our people ought to be summoned who would unselfishly and in a nonpartisan manner accept to participate in the common responsibility for the fate of Serbia, Montenegro, Republika Srpska, and Serb Krajina and our entire people." *Pravoslavlje*, nos. 629-630, June 1-15, 1993.

"sacrifice of Eastern Herzegovina" in negotiations with the Croats and variants of the Vance-Owen plan.[44]

The church press with evident sympathy wrote increasingly about the attitude of the government on the other side of the Drina River toward the Church. Toward the end of April 1993, Metropolitan Nikolaj Mrdja, who replaced Metropolitan Jovan of Zagreb, gave an interview in which he stated that the military in Bosnia became Orthodox and that general Mladić accepts all the suggestions of the Metropolitan.[45] *Pravoslavlje* wrote that the Serb army battles under its Serb national tricolor, acts in accord with the Orthodox tradition, and models itself according to national heroes.[46] The pupils of the Bosnian Krajina suddenly loved their new subject, "catechism," and the army, their chaplains.

> The new merger with the faith of their ancestors strengthens the proud Krajina Serbs in their awareness that above the supersonic airplanes of the NATO pact which break the sound barrier flying above the villages of the Krajina, there is the dear almighty God and his righteousness and along with him are Serb saints along with St. Sava and they are mightier than all that earthly power that threatens them.[47]

In May of 1993, during the festivities of the *krsna slava* of the Church in Foča, Metropolitan Jovan in his promise to the faithful stressed the meaning of the support that the Serbian Orthodox Council gave to the Republika Srpska and especially the efforts of the Serb people to finally obtain their state.[48] These efforts are illustrated in the writings of Fr. Dragomir Ubiparipović, a priest from Sarajevo, who in his daily column, "At the Dusk of War in Bosnia & Herzegovina," wrote that the Church was too engaged in politics.

> "Enlightenment" revived only due to the full support of the Church. Church space and festivals were used for the promotion of leaders of the Serb Democratic Party and they were recommended to the people. In the limitless support our tendency toward excess was clearly expressed. It went so far that even party leaders were confused by the support and the too flattering evaluations of these leaders--about their alleged God-given messianic roles. And why not when clerics issue unprecedented songs of praise in which they reminded them in front of the people "that God himself sent them to save the Serb clan".... Such

---

[44]*NIN*, June 4 and July 9, 1993.

[45]*Duga*, April 24-May 7, 1993.

[46]The Yugoslav People's Army was criticized in the church press because it retained the same ideology and the same relationship toward the clergy as it had prior to the Transformation. They requested the creation of a new Serb officers corps and the return to "the Serb tradition." *Pravoslavlje*, no. 628, May 15, 1993, and no. 640, November 15, 1993.

[47]*Pravoslavlje*, nos. 631-632, 1993.

[48]*Pravoslavlje*, nos. 633-634, August 1-15, 1993. At the session of the Assembly in 1994, satisfaction was expressed in regard to catechism in the Republika Srpska and Krajina and it was requested that the same ought to take place in Serbia and Montenegro. *Politika*, June 3, 1994.

unrestrained service of the Church to politics and the Church's help that such policy might obtain the trust of the people, this too obvious symbiosis and common work in the same field, absolutely expected, after all these events the common division of successes and failures. Therefore one is to expect that the Church will be richly rewarded by the new government. But if one raises the question of responsibility for the outcome of the war (destruction and victims) in addition to the political and military leaders one should expect that the Church will also be mentioned.[49]

Comparing the situation of SOC in the first, second, and third Yugoslavia with the situation in the newly-formed Serb states, metropolitan Amfilohije Radović stated that SOC felt like a victim in all three Yugoslavias, but that momentarily it is in danger of being manipulated and that situation will be worse than its previous troubles.

> The apparent freedom of the Church's activity but without its real return to its place in society and creating conditions for its operation are the dangers of deceiving both the Church and the people. There is hope only in the mutuality between the Church and the state that is being born and is being revealed after the great tragedy on the territory of the newly-formed Serb states of Bosnia & Herzegovina and Serb Krajina as well as signs of renewal there through the blood of suffering.[50]

The leader of the Bosnian Serbs, Dr. Karadžić, evaluated the relationship between the Church and state as excellent at the beginning of 1994. "Our clergy is present in all of our deliberations and decisions, and the voice of the Church is heard as the voice of the highest authority." Karadžić added that everything he received in his life he owes to his faith and the Church and that all he does he "does with thinking of God."[51]

However, that even these relationships were not idyllic and without shadows can be seen from a letter of Bishop Atanasije sent to the President of the Trebinje county in which he sharply attacks him because he tolerated the activities of the Adventist Church on the territory of the Zahum-Herzegovina diocese and because of the activities of the ADRA humanitarian organization. Bishop Atanasije states,

> We are talking of a well known Western aggressive, extremely Protestant, fanaticized and anti-Orthodox and anti-Christian sect, which began in America during the last century and has financed from that time till now (from where, as

---

[49]*Svečanik*, no. 1-2, 1993; *Hriščanska misao*, no. 6-8, 1993.

[50]*Hriščanska misao*, no. 6-8, 1993. Nebojša Krstić, commenting in *Svetigora*, no. 28 of June 1994, the statement of Amfilohije Radović about the Church being the victim of all three Yugoslavias said that "the definition of Yugoslavianness" of Bishop Nikolaj Vclimirović, according to whom Yugoslavia is "a state without God's blessing, a school without faith, politics without honor, army without patriotism," because Yugoslavia is a spite to Christ, a spite to St. Sava, a spite to the people's past, a spite to every people's sacredness--a spite and only spite." Krstić concluded that Yugoslavianness represented one of the great "Serb calamities" in their entire history.

[51]*Srpski Slon*, Sremska Mitrovica, 1/1994.

you see, all evils come to us, especially to Republika Srpska, which is simultaneously in its birth pangs and in a deathly gasp on the cross upon which we are crucified by their America).

At the same time when theses are being developed about the absolute innocence of the Serb people, the intention of nearly the entire world, especially the West and America is "to obliterate, devastate, and smash the Serb lineage."[52] Serbs are being summoned to return to their spiritual foundations and roots, history, church, and tradition and to develop a "positive nationalism."[53]Žarko Gavrilović wrote,

> AVNOJ Yugoslavia is a terrible grave of the Serb people, a masked curtain of the slaughter of Serbs, the torture and rape of Serb history, Serb ethnological being. Now it is clear to all of us that this AVNOJ creation was only a "Trojan horse" for the penetration of the Vatican, Germany, Austria to the South, and East and *jihad* to the North and West . . ."[54]

Patriarch Pavle

Between April and July, 1994, Patriarch Pavle twice visited the Republika Srpska and then the Slavonian diocese, Canada, and the USA. Each time he called for peace and humanity and distanced himself from war crimes[55] although he stressed the duty of active struggle against evil and blessed "the defensive struggle during an imposed war." At the beginning of May, he personally visited the Jewish community on the occasion of the publication of "The Protocol of the Elders of Zion," and he stated that it was a non-Christian book. His policy of cooperation and "pacifism" were expressed during the visit of the Patriarch of Moscow and All of Russia, Alexy II in the middle of May. During the visit of the Moscow Patriarch, Cardinal Kuharić and Patriarch Pavle met at the Sarajevo airport (at which Mustafa Cerić, the *Reis-ul-Ulema* was also supposed to participate but did not with the explanation that SOC did not raise its voice against the crimes which the military units of Republika Srpska carried out over Muslims), on May 17th, and a declaration for peace was signed.[56] This position of the Patriarch was resisted and criticized within SOC. During the meeting of the Holy Council of Bishops, there were writings about the disagreements between the Patriarch and Artemije, the bishop of Raška-Prizren. The problem was the question, "Is God the Father of all or only of believers?" The Patriarch answered

---

[52]*Pravoslavlje,* no. 622, 1993.

[53]*Glas crkve*, no. 1, 1993.

[54]*Svečanik*, nos. 1-2, 1993.

[55]*Pravoslavlje,* no. 651, May 1 and no. 652, May 15, 1994; *Politika*, June 22 and July 17, 1994; *Svetigora*, no. 29, 1994.

[56]*Politika*, May 18, 1994; *Svetigora* entitled the report of the visit "One faith, one church, one power," no. 28, June 1994; and *Svetigora*, no. 29, 1994.

in *St. Prince Lazar*, saying that about his statements and convictions the Lord will give the final answer. But another attack followed in *Duga* in which Željko Poznanović wrote,

> . . . "The double tongue" politics is not unsuitable to church people and because people do not know what diplomacy is and what is truth and because the constant support of peace may make an erroneous impression among people that our faith discredits the righteous struggle of our people, that the Church does not support this struggle or even that this war for the creation of the Serb state is meaningless (which we could hear) . . . . As for the peace of Christ and world peace (which will be brought about only by Anti-Christ providing we bow to him) ever Serb, provided he looks at the past of his people will see clearly that on Earth and in history the peace of Christ can be received only through struggle and triumph, but never by proportionality, "pacifism," and ecumenism.[57]

Between Pale and Belgrade

In regard to the situation in B&H in the middle of 1994, SOC again evoked the media interest because of its position. "The appeal to the Serb People and World Public" from the episcopal conference of SOC of July 5th provided a clear expression of the position of SOC about the negotiations over B&H. "With full responsibility before God and our people and human history we are calling the entire Serb people to defend the age-old rights and liberties of their own vital interests, necessary for the physical and spiritual survival and endurance on land of the fathers and grandfathers." The bishops rejected the suggested maps and stated that people should determine their future in a referendum. *Svetigora* of June 1994 published three speeches of Bishop Nikolaj Velimirović sent to Serbs in B&H. The first was from 1912 where he called Serbs to organize, work, and endure. In the second, he tells them that without God there is no valor, and in the third from 1940, he writes to Sarajevo that they should be glad for Belgrade and the unity of the fatherland. The next issue provided commentaries about the maps suggested in Geneva and concluded, "Once again it has been confirmed that only the Church never abandons its people, that only she stays to the end, that only she preserved it through history, and that she will maintain it through the ages."

Dr. Žarko Gavrilović stated that there is no alternative to the church in its position that one must stand with the Serbs in Bosnia while another theologian, Nebojša Krstić, wrote, "Let's not forget that our co-nationals in Republika Srpska and Republika Srpska Krajina are in a bloody war for the Serb honor and fatherland, but also that we in the FR Yugoslavia are prisoners of a Godless leftist order installed and supported by world masonic power centers."[58]

---

[57]*Duga*, June 24, 1994; *NIN*, June 10, 1994.

[58]*Svetigora*, no. 29, 1994.

At the Assembly of the Republika Srpska at Pale, deliberation occurred about the acceptance of the Bosnian peace plan proposed by The Contact Group; at these talks, Metropolitan Nikolaj and bishops Vasilije and Atanasije were present. Bishop Atanasije relayed the message of SOC that one cannot again accept the partitioning of the Serb people. The Montenegro-Coastal Zone Metropolitan Amfilohije sent a telegram on July 5, 1994, supporting the Assembly of the Republika Srpska stating,

> Having revived in yourself the faith in God's justice, you renewed St. Lazar's loyalty to the people and raised the dignity of the Serb people. Your decision will unmask all the deceptions of the democracy of the so-called New Order but also reveal who really hides his love of power behind the alleged concern for the people and appeal to the people. May God help you.[59]

After the decision of the government of FR Yugoslavia to break political and economic relations with Republika Srpska, an urgent emergency meeting of the Holy Council of Bishops of SOC was convened, and a few days earlier the Montenegro archdiocese requested that the representatives of the Montenegrin Assembly reject that decision. This request to the parliamentarians sounded very militant and was much sharper from the official statement of the Patriarchate issued after the special session of the Holy Council of Bishops.[60] This statement was understood as siding with the Bosnian Serbs. That provided numerous commentaries in the domestic and foreign community as well as censure of SOC for public display of nationalism (e.g. by the World Council of Churches). The Bačka Bishop Irinej Bulović proclaimed that the Church did not side with one side against the other.[61] He repeated this at a press conference in Moscow during the visit by a SOC delegation in October, adding that the responsible decision-makers ought to take into consideration the interest of all three groups in B&H. Several days prior to the meeting, the Patriarch was in Pale and then requested an appointment with President Milošević. He tried to intercede in the reconciliation but was unsuccessful. The essence of the Patriarch's and SOC's position was clearly expressed during the visit to the Russian Orthodox Church. In conversations in Moscow, Patriarch Paul stated that the Church believes that hostilities must be immediately ended and peace negotiations must begin which will provide equal rights to all sides for state self-determination, i.e. that Serbs in Bosnia will sign a peace plan "if they are guaranteed the right of self-determination, namely a confederation with Yugoslavia."[62]

---

[59]*Svetigora*, no. 30-31, 1994

[60]*Politika*, August 11, 1994; *NIN*, August 12, 1994.

[61]*Politika*, August 28, 1994.

[62]*Politika*, October 11, 1994.

Further events, however, did not develop in the direction desired by SOC. Instead of peace negotiations, bloody war conflicts continued even outside of B&H. The Holy Synod on May 18th, stated (during the Council session) "the final destruction of the Slavonian diocese." At the end of the same communique it is stated, "After all this and as a consequence of these events came the retaliation by the Serb side, first the irrational bombardment of Zagreb, and then also to senseless revenge by desperate and distraught refugees over Roman Catholics in Bosnian Krajina."

The key segment of the SOC Council message was the next passage:

In the most profound conviction that the conciliarly expressed consensus of the Church supports the vital need and long-range interest of the Serb people, the Council appeals to all who are responsible in this fateful moment, that despite the unprecedented pressure of world powers, refuse to recognize the state of Croatia and Bosnia and Herzegovina in their artificial ("AVNOJ-created") borders, as long as one hopes to find by negotiations a final solution of this tragic civil conflict. The Council believes that the recognition of Croatia and Bosnia and Herzegovina would mean the final legalization of an act of coercion--secession at the expense of Serb people. Thereby, one would officially recognize the subservient status of the Serb people in relation to other south Slavic people, including also those newly-founded on ideological grounds, while the Serb people and their states--first of all Serbia and Montenegro--ought to take all responsibility for the outbreak of the war and for all its horrible consequences. A just and self-defensive war of the Serb people would automatically be considered an aggression.[63]

The events of the next few months were exactly what the Church was afraid of. At the end of August in Belgrade, an agreement was signed between the Pale and Belgrade leadership about their joint participation in negotiations in Dayton. At that occasion, the president of Serbia, Slobodan Milošević, was designated to represent the interests of Serbs on both sides of the Drina River. That agreement was signed also by Patriarch Pavle.

The negotiation in Dayton and Paris agitated the church circles. Bishops, particularly those outside Serbia regarded that the President of Serbia betrayed the agreement about minimal Serb national interests which was guaranteed by the Patriarchal signature. SOC became, after all that happened during four years of war, the great loser. Four dioceses, Dalmatia, Gornji Karlovac, Slavonia, and Bihać-Petrovac remained without priests or believers. In the hub, remained thirteen dioceses while all the others were in the diaspora. The press relayed information about the views of certain bishops who were disappointed with the results of the peace accords and with the withdrawal, and then the disagreements in the episcopate, and the demand of some bishops that the Patriarch should resign because he signed the Belgrade agreement, and so on. In the Patriarchate, such

---

[63]*SV*, nos. 38-39, 1995.

news was disclaimed, but not convincingly. Even the Belgrade Catholic archbishop, France Perko, in his Christmas address wished "the leadership of the Serbian Orthodox Church strength to lead their believers toward the future love of the year 1996," and in a pre-Christmas meeting with journalists he gave a few suggestions to the Serbian bishops about the need for unity and affirmed the stories about the dissatisfaction toward Patriarch Pavle.

Finally, on December 21, 1995, the third session of the Council of SOC of that year took place behind closed doors. The main theme was the future of Serbs in Republika Srpska and the possibility of the return of bishops of the SOC to the dioceses from which they were expelled during the war. After the session, in a text, the final version of which was composed by Metropolitan Amfilohije, the banished priests and bishops are called to return to their dioceses, and the patriarch's signature on the agreement of August 29th was declared invalid. The session ended, in the opinion of many, in a compromise because the peace was backed although it was declared unjust. In the Christmas message, SOC proclaimed that it is for peace but not for imposed peace.[64]

One of the most tragic periods in the history of SOC seemingly is coming to an end but the Church is facing open and new questions that it will have to solve as soon as possible. One of these questions was formulated recently by Radovan Bigović, a theologian of the younger generation as follows:

> How will the Orthodox Church in the twenty-first century again be a "city which stands on a hill" and "the mirror" of the world? . . . . A fundamental turnaround is needed, a new direction and a rechanneling of energy. It is more than necessary without delay to put on the agenda the question about itself and its self-identity, because many social anomalies during the past few centuries profoundly jolted its identity. . . . Much points to the need for the local autocephalous Orthodox Churches to voluntarily permanently repudiate their 'national' and 'state-establishment' roles which were imposed upon them by centuries of slavery of Orthodox people, on which it expended enormous energy. God conceived of the world as all-encompassing brotherhood, as a living divine-human community, i.e. as a Church and not as a state or nation. No type of state can be based on the gospel of Christ. Only the Church of God can be built on it. All attempts to create a 'Christian' or 'Orthodox' state were tragic and became the greatest blasphemy by Christians to the world . . . .[65]

Translated from Serbian by Paul Mojzes

---

[64]*NIN*, no. 2348, December 29, 1995; *Politika*, January 6, 1996.

[65]*Politika*, January 6, 1996.

12

THE SERBIAN ORTHODOX CHURCH'S VIEW OF THE ROLE OF RELIGION IN THE WAR IN BOSNIA & HERZEGOVINA

Dimitrije M. Kalezić

Since this text is offered to readers who are geographically, culturally, and otherwise holding viewpoints very remote from the battleground of Bosnia and Herzegovina, several preceding remarks will be furnished for the sake of clarification.

I.

1. Religion is the most comprehensive of all human activities. It manifests not only the all-encompassing fullness of people, taken as a natural phenomenon, but also something greater and more intriguing, namely, the real connection between God and people—their corelationship. That is why the Kingdom of God, which is neither human nor of this world (John 18:38), represents a reality of a higher order, and its seeds are already germinating here on Earth. This, of course, is dependent on the intimate appropriation of God's grace by humans, together with the science of supernatural Revelation. The peace of this Kingdom is the peace of God which is seriously needed and necessary for people in general, particularly for people of faith.

2. The Christian faith is primarily oriented towards the inner human essence as a subject. Within the human self, we see the openings of bottomless depths and limitless widths which no natural religion can secure, let alone fulfill with the grace of God. For this reason, every gesture and act accomplished by each person, his/her every thought and feeling, represent an effluence of this inner content. The Church, being the real mystical community and communion between God and people, represents a tangible continuation of the Godman Jesus Christ through the centuries. Within Him, in the fullest sense of the term, we

experience the grace-mediated union of God and the human being, so that God is--God, and humanified, and man is--man, but deified. In the Person of Jesus Christ, we behold the full identity of God as Original and the human as His material image. This identity exists in His church, naturally, for those who see Him through eyes of faith, investing the totality of their being--primarily their heart or person.

The Church of the East is orthodox, and this means ortho-thinking in relation to God, and ortho-worshipping in relation to God. Its identity, therefore, lies within its orthodoxy, deeply immanent to it. This identity, primarily, implies its self-identity, that is, its authenticity. As offshoots of this key identity, we discover two other levels of identity: identity with God and identity with man. The life of the Church is conditioned by this identity; to abandon or lose it would entail self-denial and self-dismissal. The action of the Church and Church-ingrown man is, thus, correct ("orthic"). Between orthodoxy and orthopraxy, there is an identity although orthodoxy, in distinction to orthopraxy, does not abide in the sphere of strict, historical reality. These two elements mutually affirm each other: orthopraxy is rooted in orthodoxy not in the world where it manifests itself, and orthodoxy, on the other hand, reveals itself in orthopraxy. Orthopraxy is not reducible to formal "rightness" or "validity." This is why orthopraxy is defective if orthodoxy is missing as its guarantee, in which case it is simply non-existent, despite a formal accuracy of execution or realization.

3. As was the case with other Slavic people, the Serbs were a pagan people (Slavic: *narod*) before migrating to the Balkans. In other words, they possessed a natural and elementary religiousness, coupled with a moral code which, also, remained on the level of the natural. The spheres of the supernatural as well as the dimensions of divine moral laws were, simply, non-existent or non-accessible. These categories, perhaps, were only intuited, but they were devoid of any clear belief, for there was no immediate experience of something higher and overreaching in relation to neutral, earthly existence.

The loftiest achievement, in such a framework of conditions, was the promotion of natural law which, in final consequence, is not of the order of nature or exclusively natural, but is of the order of divine reality, God-given, and introjected into nature. It is explicitly referred to by St. Paul, the "Apostle of the heathen," in the Epistle to the Romans (Rom 11:13; 2:13-15). This law is not disavowed or erased by the God-given supernatural law, manifest through Revelation which received its fullest form and content in the Person of the Godman Jesus Christ (Heb 1:1-2)--the one and true mediator between God and man. Natural law, thus, becomes more profound; new, hereto unknown domains are uncovered. It becomes more meaningful, enriched by immaterial meaning.

It becomes more concrete; in Christ, God and man live in symbiosis--Christ is the real Man in whom all the fullness of the Godhead dwells bodily (Col 2:9).

Having reached the Balkans, the Serbian people encountered Christianity. At first via the southern, Hellenic route; later via the Moravian mission (863 A.D.) the same form of Christianity arrived from the north. In the eleventh century, the Church was divided by the Great Schism (1054), and the Serbian lands, Bosnia included, were allocated to the realm of the Eastern Christian Church, namely, Orthodoxy. The relatively minute indigenous Balkan populace was gradually assimilated. Those states lining the peripheral ring towards the West came under strong influence from Rome, via the Adriatic coastline, inhabited by Romans, confessing the western rite of Christianity from the early Christian times.

In 1219, the Orthodox Church in Serbian lands became organized in the form of a local autocephalous archdiocese. Furthermore, in 1346, it received the dignity of becoming a patriarchate. Before the end of the fifteenth century, all Serbian lands, successively, became suppressed under the yoke of Turkish occupation which, eventually, resulted in Islamization. Roman Catholic missions, on the other hand, were quite successful in converting a considerable number of the Orthodox-faithful, and this commenced only after 1291, when the Serbian king Dragutin invited the Franciscans into Bosnia. The other portion of the remaining Orthodox populace received the religion of the Turkish occupier, that is, Islam, by persuasion or by force, through greed or through fear. Be as it may, the process of conversion was under way. Two religions, Christianity and Islam, thus came into existence in Bosnia. Furthermore, Christianity bifurcated into two confessions, namely, Orthodoxy and Roman Catholicism. This was to last for centuries. Three dogmatic worldviews and three philosophies of life, three systems of ethics and three types of ethos, three mentalities and three psychologies, thus appeared. Nevertheless, one common language did remain although in three modalities. This triple enticement of common ground and roots, stemming out of a unique family tree, represents the inexhaustible theme of the literary masterwork of Ivo Andrić, beginning with his doctoral thesis,[1] followed by shorter and lengthier stories and monumental novels, culminating in brilliant and diverse essays. Therefore, we are grappling with the fact of a formerly unified people lacerated in a threefold schism, drifting through multicentennial fusion and fission. That is why its ethnic life was and is so densely interwoven with various influences to which many individuals, even vast groups, finally yielded. Still, the wholeness of its natural

---

[1]Die Entwicklung des geistigen Lebens in Bosnia unter der Einwirkung der türkischen Herrschaft, Graz, 1924.

unity does project through the layers of language, history, literature, custom, music, melos, and through the oneness of its natural tree, although the acceptance of the divine supernatural Revelation did develop into two branches, that is, two interpretations of Tradition: Orthodoxy and Roman Catholicism. Yet another branch was later to embrace the new monotheistic religion, Islam.

In other words, the fact of their disunity is an ascertained historical phenomenon. Regrettably, the ethnic being of this people is so deeply and ever so seriously undermined by the element of disunity that this, retroactively, represents a more fundamental determination than those particular aspects of unity. The corpus of the Bosnian ethnobeing, thus became fissured and enlarged into a ravine.

The Serbian Church works among its flock and directs it toward inward renewal and healing of the internal brokenness. Time has seen the gradual increase and intensification of the aforementioned disunity. The element of unity, on the other hand, is now severely shaken, dispersed, and entered into a stage of decomposition. Since it is a community of supernatural origin, already being realized within history, the Church represents a spiritually cohesive force, acting from within and not by means of external mechanical and forceful action. In relation to those people who do not stand in her fold, the Church values their God-given inner freedom of will, freedom but not the misuse of freedom. The issue is a healthy personhood and its original qualities.

II

If the foreign reader takes into account the aforementioned arguments, it may become clear that the Serb people of the Orthodox confession live in Bosnia and Herzegovina as the oldest of the three ethnic communities which are now its inhabitants or, more precisely, of the three proclaimed confessions. In other words, out of separation from the Serbian populace emerged two almost entirely different ethnic and confessional bodies. The Serbian people, including its Church, were at the beginning almost the only, and later on, our times included, the most numerous community in Bosnia and Herzegovina. As recently as the middle of the nineteenth century, Vuk Stefanović Karadžić spoke of one people, namely the Serbian one, separated into three "laws" (and here "law" signifies Faith, confessional law, i.e. Orthodoxy, Roman-Catholicism, and Islam).

Since it is her obligation to implement maternal care for her people, her faithful, and those potentially faithful, the SOC, despite the suffocating climate of the current war in Bosnia and Herzegovina, still managed to care for the spiritual needs and biological survival of the people of God, conferred on our

Church as its essential duty, and proved itself to be active and objective. The Church incessantly voiced the word of the just peace of God, advising its flock to abstain from inhuman behavior. The Orthodox faithful of the SOC have for more than one millennium been the custodians of their homes, preserved despite the trials of many centuries, regimes, and states. The historical monuments of Orthodoxy are by far the oldest amongst those to be found on Bosnian grounds, whereas the historical signs of the two other confessional entities are of an incomparably younger chronological age. Holding to the roots of eternal depth and width of ecumenical Orthodoxy, the SOC, as always, expressed a lively and indefatigable activity which represents its vital task. The question of divine rather than human justice--even if human justice turns out to be that of the powers of this world--is its constant preoccupation. The Church obeys both laws, the natural-moral as universally obligatory, and the supernatural as particular and higher.

1. Having deep and steadfast belief as to the moral and psychological power of prayer as communication with God, the Church has appealed to its clergy to support its daily worship with a supplication in favor of those who are suffering due to the destruction of war. This has been Church practice since ancient times. If present-day suffering is allowed by the Will and Providence of God, then it is to be endured in patience and purity as becomes the people of God, strengthened by the refusal to behave as those filled with the psychology of spite and hatred, destruction, and killing. In this manner, God is petitioned through prayer to steer us and our enemies towards the light of intelligence and cognizance of truth through "change of mind" (Greek: *metanoia*), that is, repentance. The faithful can reap neither honor nor success if their victory is achieved at the expense of harmony with the will of God. Perhaps this might be consistent with human justice, but in relation to divine standards, it is worthless in the ontological sense. Furthermore, in the moral sense, such a victory would equal defeat and shame.

In addition, we can point to another prayer of supplication to aid the afflicted. In the text of this service (the *akathistos*), the moral motives are dominant. The problem of suffering in the light of divine Providence is aptly stressed, but human self-control and adherence to moral considerations is also emphasized. All of this, naturally, flows out of the Bible, that book of timeless wisdom and eternal life: "Repent therefore of this thy wickedness, and pray to God" (Acts 8:22), and "do not cease to pray" (I Col 1:9). All of this is directed towards the goal of securing abundant love between people, particularly amongst the faithful (Phil 1:9), that is, towards the objective of love and its warmth, as opposed to luke-warm indolence, especially against ice-cold hatred, i.e. poisonous anti-love.

2. In addition to the prayers, we have their application to life. The words of Christ challenge all the readers of the Bible whether we have done anything for the least amongst His brethren (Mat 25:45; Prov 14:31; Zech 2:8). Essential and diversified humanitarian aid was collected and sent to the most acutely endangered destinations where it was distributed to all who were in need. Furthermore, this noble service was begotten and developed within the armfold of SOC. Other Orthodox and non-Orthodox Churches, humanitarian organizations, and associations were urged to follow the same exemplary effort. For when one member or organ suffers within a great ecclesiastical organism, then ill consequences are felt throughout the whole organism (I Cor 12:26-27). All the faithful were beckoned not to grow weary of well doing (Galatians, 6:9). The charity-fund, *Čovekoljublje*, ["Philanthropy"] of the SOC represents the crown-result of these efforts.

For the purpose of telling the real truth concerning the Serbs, the SOC has "knocked" on the doors of its sister Orthodox Churches as well as other Christian churches, charitable and peace-making societies, and associations, appealing before them for the sake of divine justice to approach the Serbian question responsibly with adequate attention and discernment. This is for the benefit of Serbs as well as others with whom they are in conflict, but also particularly for those parties who have succumbed to media disinformation. It is neither good nor honest, particularly for keen foreign analysts, to condemn any of the three conflicting sides if this position is based on irresponsibly disseminated half-truths and disinformation by the media. Judgement-Day entails answering for each and every word (Hebrews, 9:27), and on that terrible Day, no possibility for concealment or excuse will be provided. As Christians, we are obliged to give truthful information. This applies also to those who do not consider themselves Christians or religious in any particular sense.

In carrying out its high and responsible mission, the SOC never issued condemnations of anyone, thus promoting the words of our Savior: "Judge not, that ye be not judged" (Mat 7:1; Lk 9:37). Only the Lord has the right for "revenge" (Deut 32:35; Heb 10:30; Rom 12:19). More importantly, the Church gave no encouragement in word, let alone a blessing to anyone's wrong-doing or to any form of evil, neither Serbian or others'. The just peace of God was upheld as the basis for action as well as its ideal. No misdeeds were justified. Rather, they were the cause for indignation. Two significant achievements are, thus, accomplished: the faithful are encouraged to practice dignified self-control while enemies are not condemned, but rather, prayers are said for God to guide them to wisdom and the understanding of truth--through such repentance which ought to entail moral renewal and comprehensive restoration. Finally, we do not believe that there is a religious community in the world, provided it is healthy and loyal to its convictions, which would refuse to embrace the aforementioned tenets into its programs, that is, its vocation.

Even more immediately obvious or, inversely, obviously immediate, was the invitation extended to foreign delegates and observers to see for themselves the concrete state of affairs where the conflict was taking place. It was and is up to them, according to their conscience and without pressure to gain sight and insight in relation to the question of historical primacy: which community was there from antiquity, who came later and/or left, and for which reasons; who instigated strife; who is attacking and who defending oneself, one's life, and ancient sacred values, homes and hearths, churches and monasteries, cemeteries, and so forth. We are dealing with old and new proofs of a historical and spiritual nature. Besides other visitors to the turbulent battle-grounds of Bosnia and Herzegovina, we would especially wish to stress and select the visits of two Orthodox patriarchs: Alexis II, the spiritual head of the most numerous Orthodox Church, i.e. the Moscow See (1994), and Theoktistos, Patriarch of the neighboring Romanian Orthodox Church (1995). Particularly indicative is the feat of the Russian patriarch who, following a set agreement, arrived at Sarajevo airport, only to learn that his dialogue-partners, i.e. the Archbishop of Zagreb, Cardinal Kuharić from Zagreb and Mr. Cerić, head of the Muslim religious community, never appeared. The former did not arrive on time, and the latter withheld even an apology. Is it inappropriate to wonder whether they were interested at all to discuss the possibility for peace?

Numerous are the bishops and other clergy, Orthodox and non-Orthodox, who, providing humanitarian and other aid, arrived on the spot to directly examine the real situation. To this end were geared many observer missions. Some of them wrote or spoke about it, but some remained reserved, be it because of lack of incriminating material against the Serbs, or be it to suppress supportive evidence for the Serbs, we cannot know. Be as it may, it is certainly a matter for their conscience and personal courage to openly witness the truth. The SOC, on the other hand, fulfilled its duty (Romans, 12:18). As Church, she refrains from pressuring the freedom of the observers with inducement of positive statements. Those who had cause for critical remarks voiced them. But those, who found no essential reason for condemnation yet, nevertheless, remained silent, will have to answer for this within the deep recesses of their will. The reason for their not communicating vital information lies in the innermost of their decision making for which they are responsible before people, but in front of God nothing can or will be concealed.

3. The war in Bosnia and Herzegovina for more than four years manifested behavior which has frequently broken even the most elementary military code of honor or, for that matter, any civilized values. It has absolutely

nothing in common with Christian morals. The predicament of war, no matter how difficult it is, still does not oblige the participants to conduct themselves as sub-humans, and certainly not as non-Christians, nor does it justify them in any acceptable sense. Apart from pragmatic evil acts, we can notice the other level, the methods of disinformation launched by global mass-media, incessantly emitting partial and non-objective information without the slightest of efforts to determine its accuracy. The clashing parties in the midst of this conflict, it seems, lamentably can not help behaving deplorably. In other ex-Yugoslav lands and even more so in the Diaspora, this is not the rule. Although not very fond of each other, those people, nevertheless, in a civilized manner do not shed blood. Their mutual relationships have often been strained and poisoned because of the paternalistic and selfish actions of a third party who are neither spiritual nor cultured, neither moral nor humane. Thus, such people are not contributing positively to the authentic interests of all three communities that are in conflict.

Several vivid examples may suffice in illustrating the deceit and tragedy that such influence has instigated. The deaths of a large group of people queuing for bread in the Muslim-controlled Sarajevo market place, and later (August 28, 1995) an even greater number of people were seriously injured there, close to the scene of the previous massacre. In July 1995, when Serbian armed forces entered Srebrenica, there were more Muslim casualties. For all, especially the dramatic and real suffering of the Muslim population, the Serbs were immediately blamed. These reports about the tragedies which seem to have been written before the occurrence of these events were allegedly "comments" about the events. Only the Serbs were accused. To many, at first sight, this seemed logical. These reports were, sadly, welcomed by certain centers of power, and the further satanization of Serbs, repercussions, and similar results took place. But what is logical is not necessarily factual. When balanced and nonbiased reports, based on examination of experienced experts, demonstrated some time later, that these were montage and deceit, only a handful of the international media released these findings into the global ether. Not a single word of apology was heard. No pleas could be heard for payment of a just recompense to the victims and for material loss. It seemed that the bombing retaliation was the "normal" thing to do, although it was not. Furthermore, towards the end of September (September 17, 1995) tentative admission from some responsible persons of the international community appeared to acknowledge that the international community, in fact, implemented a series of wrong and harmful decisions in regard to Bosnia. But this is of no avail when a forcible political settlement was flogged-out from under the rubble of the underbelly of the Balkans. This regrettable and cynical situation cannot be but rejected by a healthy, deified, and noble intelligence. However, not everything has collapsed into the abyss of evil: no matter how greatly enticed by political, historical, and spiritual "falleness," the fate of Bosnia has not altogether fallen away from God's embrace; it can not escape His omniscient eye nor can it detach itself from His justice. Omnipresent and Allseeing God is the immediate knower of intent and thought, deed and action of those in strife and those who "observe."

All those who oppose evil deeds, regardless of their source, consider those who spread disinformation and the mighty ones who condition such "news" as the people who have severed their ties from the Christian model of conduct and who do not adhere to universal human principles of ethics. Of course, to what extent attackers and the attacked, observers and reconcilers, answer the voice of their conscience, remains a secret, known only to the individual and God. The unconditional justice of God awaits us all: partakers of this tragedy, the various mediators, the writer of these lines and, of course, those who will read them. We are confronted with a morally-rooted proposition and the psychological openness for sharing in the suffering of our fellow human beings: is it compassionate participation in the misfortunes of other people's trials or a calculated delay and acceptance of misconstrued explanations? With what can one fill the abbysmal emptiness between the real and the fictional? With a tranquil conscience or with nervousness and a disturbed conscience? We cannot unravel this problem, and we wish to abstain from suspicious and incompetent guessing. Ultimately, nothing shall escape the knower whose knowledge rests within the unsearchable treasury where nothing decays or returns into nothingness.

4. The SOC refrained from condemning by name those perpetrators whose deeds had visible consequences; this was left to the judgement of God. Moreover, if condemnation were the results of false reports, it would be worthless and shameful. The SOC never trusted first reports; all of them were first, as a rule, subjected to serious and conscientious examination.

5. Many analysts regard this war as religious; others, as ethnic. At the core, this war, in fact, is not religious if viewed from the perspective of the SOC for, strictly speaking, there is no religious motive. Nor is this an ethnic war; Bosnia does not totally encapsulate the three ethnic communities. This is even more so because on *both* sides there are members of each group who have animosity towards one or the other group. This is mostly so because, in essence, these groups represent three offshoots of the same family tree. Various external historical storms have detached one group from the other, only later managing to internally divide them against each other. In the first centuries, they comprised an organic whole, and all was well.

Such as it is, this war, primarily, is a civil conflict. It is the ill-conceived product of moral ruthlessness, spreading from the futile atheistic desert, and only in secondary consequence does it include confessional, ethnic, or other components. But when viewed from the Muslim perspective, it is clearly religious: the interpretations of their spiritual and intellectual authorities lead to the conclusion that Islam does not tolerate any other state model except the Islamic model. If this were a religious war it would have been different. One religion would fight another: Islam against Christianity. But this is not the case. The situation is that Muslims and Roman Catholics with the help of other Christians from the west go against Orthodox Serbs.

In times past, although Bosnia did share in misunderstandings between these confessional entities and allegedly ethnic opposites, it still enjoyed the minimum of universal human mutual respect; closeness was, thus, preserved and related to the depths of human spirit. Responsibility was never totally neglected. However, modern time has produced something altogether novel: two generations have grown up while atheistic ideology prevailed. The generation which embraced atheism as the ideology replacing religion counted amongst its rank and file not a small number of those who projected their narrow interests and malicious spite above and before universal human values, thus commencing the process which has been culminating before us for nearly fifty years. Ideological blindness was the ideal atmosphere for the birth of totalitarian theism which coercively communifies on the one hand, and, on the other, for pragmatical materialism which suspends moral norms. Then external interests clashed, but the authentic expressions of spiritual needs of those people immediately concerned was least responsible for the clash.

The discouraging lack of sound psychological and moral sentiments on the part of these "external factors" as well as for their instrumentalistic behavior, brimming with intolerance and overreaching the limits of humanistic concerns, seriously repressing even the loosest civil norms, indicate that this war, at its kernel, falls far away from the subtlety of the spiritual or from possible premeditated motives of the confessional. The horrifying spiritual poverty of those who instigated this war provoked reaction from those who felt endangered. The challenge had to be accepted: mindlessness from one side, alas, provoked its equal response from the other. Pressed for life, those who were attacked had no other option but to defend their elementary right and obligation--not having, as the case proved, many other realistic alternatives, i.e. choice of methods.

If we are to judge this war on grounds of its soulless dynamic and total absence of the ethical, it is then, at best, ideological. But it is not a moral one, and still less is it religious. To label it accurately, we could say that this war is not only non-religious but, furthermore, directly anti-religious, anti-confessional, and anti-moral. As such, it has contaminated the soul with hatred, causing devastating spiritual sickness. The vital element of the conscience, however, we firmly believe, was not affected in its innermost recesses. But the inferno of war has in many instances neutralized, isolated, and almost annihilated this essential capacity, so that many individuals, although biologically alive, are nevertheless spiritually dead. This gave rise to obsessive reflexology. Those individuals and groups who have not managed to root their theory and practice in universally human, purely natural or, luckily, in Christian ethics, found themselves prey to a pattern of behavior seriously reduced by the lack of the spiritual dimension. Only from the pneumatological depth, opened to supernatural God and in communion with Him, does humble peace and renewal of personhood come forth.

In this war, the Church has found its share of involvement inasmuch as it has affected people, and war has done this ever so powerfully, surrounding them with the circle of death, and providing not only biological destruction. The horrific modes of killing have proved to be so thoroughly degrading that even lower life-forms, animals, cannot match it.

Despite this state of affairs, the Church still finds operative space for urgent appeal, warning, and advice in hope of the possibility of accepting divine and enlightened human justice in distinction to the life within the rifts and beguilements of unhealthy "humanized" justice. The moral law of Christian behavior is obligatory for Christians, no matter whether they are soldiers or not, for soldiers are human beings too. But people of a different religion, or those of non-religious conviction, or even those atheists who fanatically idolize their ideology, can not escape, as the ideal obligation, what is universally human and healthy in behavior. When unable to influence people in a corporate sense because of their subhuman values, one must qualify men as beings belonging and participating in the intellectual and moral order. People who are devoid of any affinity for perceiving and experiencing such values are bound to lose their essential human attributes--they become de-humanized, which is connotative of the biblical parable of "salt that hath lost its savor" (Mt 5:13; Lk 14:34).

Even the most rudimentary thought is able to register the fact that these unhappy people have succumbed to a state of sickness. In such a state of affairs, they are preoccupied by a neurotic loss of concentration which, subsequently, prevents any possibility for discernment. We envisage two departure points for a saving approach: firstly, the humanitarian basis, obligatory for anyone who might have heard of the Bosnian catastrophe; secondly, the higher and special basis of grace which is obligatory for all of the believing people of the Church. The SOC, as a particular member of the mystical Body of the ecumenical Church of Christ, participates on both levels, acting as diligently as possible. Everyone is clearly aware that there is no healing without objective diagnosis and adequate therapy. But whether we shall assess the former and implement the later depends not on our know-how, but on the *will* and on the personal honesty of each individual. The question is will they or will they not proceed according to their knowledge? Anyone who is capable of "hearing" the voice of his/her conscience--approving or disapproving a particular thought, intention, or act--must responsibly answer its appeal. By doing so, all of us individually are put to trial and test, securing insight as to whether we are fit to bear the critique of our conscience under the condition that it is healthy and alert. It is at this point that we draw into a direct encounter with God--alone and with no mediators. The regenerative effects of such an action of grace, if voluntarily accepted, will also reflect onto our neighbors--the "least" amongst us, as our Lord Jesus Christ names them (Mt 25:45). This is and will be of double significance for both parties: for welldoers it indicates that they represent an authentic function of the church, and for the "least" amongst us it proves that they are members of the same organism, not being expelled into oblivion or even annihilated.

Ever since it was established in A.D. 1219, the Orthodox Church in Serbia has been in accord with the aforementioned fact. It tried to reassert the achievement of its first archbishop, Saint Sava, who has always managed to ground his projects within the life-giving example of the divine Founder and Head of the Church itself--Lord Jesus Christ, ever remained the Way, Truth and Life (Jn 14:6), never changing and ever identical to His own eternal Self (Heb 13:8). Care for its own people, for their soul and body, and for every and each individual as well as for humanity as a whole is the deepest foundation and highest achievement of its eternal and unperishable mission. The more diligent the Church is in realizing this goal, the stronger is the appearance of its witness as the Church of the people of God, particularly in the present-day murky currents of history, comprising the condensed evil that serves even the strongest of inter-human relationships.

Three factors are involved in the present war in Bosnia, three people. They are now divided into two opposite blocks, but formerly they were three and separate. Obviously, this further indicates the confusion arrived of their relationships. Peace-keeping forces are the armed troops devised for protecting peace and order. Although they have no mandate for direct engagement on behalf of one of the three sides in conflict, often they have abandoned their impartiality and main objective, thus joining the Muslim-Croat coalition--even providing military support. Even as we write, they are engaged in the destruction of Serbian military equipment, and the consequence of this is the frightful destruction of civilian life and property (cynically described as "collateral damage"). From the moral point of view, they are supporting the wrong option, i.e. more killing and fighting, and further discrediting their proteges. This, naturally, serves as no positive attribute to themselves either. These interventions are causing further shock and disruption of the already turbulent Bosnian soil. The inner peace of those people is now seriously endangered; this is invoking reactions from individuals and collectives--peace groups, humanitarian organizations, cultural and spiritual associations. Even diplomatic outcry has been noted. Luckily, the human element, at times anaesthetized, has not vanished altogether, but is growing in awareness.

Is it to be expected that these events should and can leave one major religion silent and indifferent?

Is it likely that the SOC will cover up the tremendous unrest, contradictions, and moral abysses? And this obviously concerns a member of her own Body.

Find the answer yourself, dear reader, either according to human or divine light. Consult your conscience beforehand--in seclusion and peace. Listen to the voiceless word; penetrate the meaningless void and seek the deeper indestructible Meaning. We are convinced that Meaning is more profound, valuable, and deep than the lack of it which, generally, fails to succeed in negating the Light of true Meaning in its attempt of definitely eradicating it.

Translated into English by Bogdan M. Lubardić,
Theological Faculty, SOC, Belgrade

13

SERBIAN RELIGIOUS NATIONALISM, CHRISTOSLAVISM, AND THE GENOCIDE IN BOSNIA, 1992-1995

Michael A. Sells

There is little doubt that after 500 years of Ottoman slavery, the Serbian people have a right to despise the Muslim Serbs who betrayed their faith and enslaved their own brothers. The almost casual dehumanization of Slavic Muslims (never explained or argued) is combined with graphic accounts of the Ustashe atrocities against Serbs in World War II and a defense of attacks on Jews as Christ-Killers by the Serbian Bishop Nikolaj Velimirović.[1]

The claim that the Serbian people have a right to despise the Muslims Serbs [sic] is both common and extraordinary. It is common among Serbian ethnoreligious militants and can be heard in their attempts to justify assaults on the Bosnian Muslim civilians from 1992-1995 that were documented by the world's major human rights organizations and labeled genocide by the International Tribunal on War Crimes in The Hague and by the major human-rights groups.[2]

---

[1]V. Todorović, "A Little More Truth," *Public Affairs,* SAVA, August, 12, 1996, posted on New York Times Bosnia forums, *The Religion and War* forum, August 22, 1996.

[2]While all sides suffered in the tragic conflict, there is no moral equality in the actions of the various parties; different sides engaged in violence against civilians to different degrees, with different intent, and with differing degrees of planning and organization. The International Tribunal on War Crimes in the Former Yugoslavia has issued scores of indictments, against Muslims, Serbs, and Croats. Seven of those indicted, officials of the Republika Srpska, have been charged with genocide: Radovan Karadžić, General Ratko Mladić, and the commanders of the Sušica, Brčko-Luka, Prijedor-Keraterm, and Omarska concentration camps. All those charged with genocide were part of an organized campaign taken out primarily against unarmed Bosnian civilians, and the crimes they are charged with involve attacks on civilians not part of any military necessity.

The complete texts of the genocide indictments and other documentation by human rights groups and war-crimes investigators can be found under "Bearing Witness" at the Community of Bosnia Web Page: http://www/haverford.students.edu/vfilipov/. This site is

Yet the statement is extraordinary in another way. In other formerly colonized nations (which include many nations in the world), we might find a few making the argument that "the people are right to despise" those who share the religion of their colonizer, and using such an argument to justify genocidal actions against the people of the other religion. In most nations, such an argument of undying religion-based hatred would not be taken seriously. We might find voices in Africa, Asia, or the Americas condemning Christianity for complicity with the colonization of large parts of those continents and the attendant atrocities. But we would find few voices stating that present day Christians in those areas should be despised for what was done centuries ago, particularly when the implications of what has been or will be done to the "despised" group are as clear as they are in Bosnia.

How can we explain this radical position among Serbian nationalists, and how can we explain the acceptance of it--or the refusal to condemn it--by a large segment of the Serbian church and population? The intractable stubbornness of this hatred has made it easy for Western policy makers to dehumanize all the people in the Balkans as some kind of special species of "age old" haters. But there are two problems with the "age-old" hater stereotype. First, it is not reciprocal. There are those among the Bosnian Muslims who despise Serbs because of their religion, but there is no equivalent public Bosnian Muslim ideology according to which all members of the Serbian Orthodox Church should be despised because of their religion, nor has the Bosnian government engaged in the kind of systematic attack on Serb civilians and religious monuments that was carried out by the Serb leadership in Pale and Belgrade.[3] Second, the ideology that has constructed the notion of eternal hatred is not itself eternal. That ideology was developed in the revolutionary period of Serbian nationalism in the nineteenth century and reconstructed in a particularly uncompromising new form by Serbian clergy and intellectuals in the late 1980s.

The basis of the ideology is the analogy between the death of Prince Lazar in 1389 to the crucifixion of Jesus and the related view that any conversion by a Slav from Christianity to Islam constitutes a race-betrayal. Let me emphasize from the beginning that the Kosovo story does not necessarily

---

connected to a number of other major sites of human rights and war crimes documentation on Bosnia.

[3]There were individual crimes against Serbs, but many of the perpetrators, both in Sarajevo (the gang leaders Juka, Caco, and Čelo) and at the Čelebić camp near Konjic have been arrested. Large Serb populations remain in Tuzla and Sarajevo and have not been subjected to the ruthless persecution leveled against Muslims throughout the Republika Srpska although there has been discrimination by militant members of the SDA ruling party in Bosnia against Serb, Croats, and others not identified with the party.

imply Christoslavism. Indeed, throughout much of Serbian history it did not imply Christoslavism. Christoslavism is one particular way of interpreting the Kosovo story, one that has dominated Serbian culture since the late 1980s. Christoslavism is the belief that Slavs are inherently Christian and that any conversion of a Slav to another religion is a conversion of race or ethnicity: from Slav to Turk. This ideology of conversion as racio-religious transformation is bound up with a particular way of presenting Kosovo: the presentation of the Serbian Prince Lazar, killed in the battle of Kosovo in 1389, as an explicit Christ figure, surrounded by disciples, betrayed by a Judas (Vuk Branković), killed by Christ-killers (Turks), and avenged by a hero, Miloš Obilić, held up as a model for all Serbs.

In this chapter, I outline the major components of Christoslavism and the role of Serbian Orthodox religious leaders in promoting it. Elsewhere I have discussed in detail the various historical phases of Christoslavism. Here I can only outline them and must refer the reader to the longer treatment for detailed documentation, sources, and further argumentation.[4] The major phases of Christoslavism are:

The Period of "The Mountain Wreath," Written by Prince-Bishop (Vladika) Petar II Petrović, Njegoš

The "Mountain Wreath" was published in 1847. "The Mountain Wreath," a historical drama in verse, portrays and glorifies the Christmas-eve extermination of Slavic Muslims at the hands of Serb warriors. It is based upon a famous campaign said to have been carried out against Slavic Muslims in late-eighteenth-century Montenegro known as the *Istraga Poturica* (extermination of the Turkifiers).[5]

The drama opens with Bishop Danilo, the play's protagonist, brooding on the evil of Islam, the tragedy of Kosovo, and the treason of Vuk Branković. Danilo's warriors suggest celebrating the holy day (Pentecost) by "cleansing" *(čistiti)* the land of non-Christians. The chorus chants: "The high mountains reek with the stench of non-Christians." One of Danilo's men proclaims that struggle

---

[4]Michael A. Sells, *The Bridge Betrayed: Religion and Genocide in Bosnia* (Berkeley: University of California Press, 1996). For the Kosovo tradition, see Thomas Emmert, *Serbian Golgotha: Kosovo, 1389* (New York: East European Monographs, 1990) and Wayne Vucinich and Thomas Emmert, *Kosovo: Legacy of a Medieval Battle* (Minneapolis: University of Minnesota, 1991). See also the important study of Alexander Greenawalt, "The Nationalization of Memory: Identity and Ideology in Nineteenth Century Serbia" (Princeton University Bachelor's Thesis, April 15, 1994).

[5]See Milovan Djilas, *Njegoš: Poet, Prince, Bishop* (New York: Harcourt, Brace & World, Inc), 310-396.

will not end until "we or the Turks [Slavic Muslims] are exterminated."[6] The references to the Slavic Muslims as "Turkifiers" (Poturice) or as "Turks" crystallizes the view that by converting to Islam, Slavic Muslims have changed their race or ethnicity and have become Turk. When the Muslims propose a *kum* ceremony of reconciliation, they are told they will have to be baptized. When they suggest an interreligious *kum* ceremony with Serbs infants being baptized and Muslim infants having a ritual haircutting (*tonsure*), they are rejected with vilification of Islam and its prophet, and vilification of Muslims as "spitters on the cross."

After some hesitation on the part of Danilo, Abbot Stefan persuades the Serbian nobles and clerics that they must follow the example of Miloš Obilić and avenge themselves against "the Turks." The drama concludes with the triumphant extermination of the Slavic Muslims--man, woman, and child--and the razing of their buildings and towers. After carrying out the extermination, the Serb warriors return to take communion without going to confession. The taking of communion without confession shows that exterminating Muslims was considered a sacred act, purifying in itself, since normal acts of blood vengeance always required confession.

As "The Mountain Wreath" appeared, the correlation of Prince Lazar's death to the crucifixion of Jesus was being fully elaborated in Serbian culture. Although in earlier periods of Serbian literature, there were analogies between Kosovo and Golgotha, it was the mid-nineteenth century that saw the full iconography of Lazar, surrounded by his knight-apostles, at a last supper portrayed in explicitly Christological terms. Thus, when "The Mountain Wreath" celebrates the extermination of Slavic Muslims as a revenge for the guilt they are supposed to share for the death of Lazar five hundred years previously, the Slavic Muslims are put into a perfect parallel with Jews at Good Friday services when Christian anti-Semites would direct crowds to persecute Jews as killers of Jesus.

The Novels and Writings of Yugoslav Nobel Laureate Ivo Andrić

In the works of Andrić, the themes of "The Mountain Wreath" were adapted to a more explicit ideology of race and conversion. In his dissertation, Andrić cites the verses of "The Mountain Wreath" according to which only the greedy or cowardly converted to Islam.[7] This dictum of Njegoš is then not only accepted

---

[6]Bishop Petar II Petrović (Njegoš), *The Mountain Wreath (Gorski vijenac)*, translated and edited by Vasa Mihailovich (Irvine, Ca: 1986), v. 95, v. 284.

[7]Ivo Andrić, *The Development of Spiritual Life in Bosnia under the Influence of Turkish Rule*, edited and translated by Želimir B. Juričić and John F. Loud (Durham: Duke University Press, 1990), 20. The dissertation was composed in German and presented to the Dean of

with enthusiasm by Andrić, but stated by Andrić to be the voice of "the people." Clearly, in Andrić's view, the Slavic Muslim is always a non-person; how could it be otherwise if "the people's" judgment is that such a Slavic Muslim represents the greedy and cowardly. Andrić fully adopts the language of racial transformation in treating the Slavic Muslim; they have become Turk and their descendants are--in the mind of "the people" no doubt always Turks. Andrić's notion of conversion--now a commonplace in Serbian and Croat nationalism--is based upon a special set of convictions. Presumably, the ancient Slavs who converted to Christianity did so only out of pure motives, never influenced by politics or economics, while the Slavs who converted to Islam did so only out of political and economic reasons, never out of personal reasons of faith. Such an ideology ignores completely the complexity of the conversion process while the continued emphasis on conversion as racial transformation confuses religious identity with racial or ethnic identity.[8]

For Andrić and other Serbian nationalists, the Devsirme system of the Ottomans, whereby children would be taken to Istanbul, raised as Muslim, and made part of the Ottoman Janissaries, was the symbol of such transformation. It was a "blood tribute," whereby the essentially Slavic souls would be made captive of a racially alien religion. Although such a system was applied to both Christians and Muslims, and although many, such as the famous Bosnian Mehmed Pasha Sokolović, rose to high positions through it (Mehmed Pasha became a grand Vizier and married Princess Esmehan), Andrić and other Serb nationalists portray it as a uniformly brutal process directed against Christians.

In his most famous novel, *The Bridge on the Drina*, Andrić offers two powerful metaphors of his ideology. In the first, construction on sixteenth-century bridge that was commissioned by Mehmed Pasha Sokolović in Višegrad

---

the Faculty of Philosophy at Karl Franz University in Graz, Austria on May 14, 1924 under the title "*Die Entwicklung des geistigen Lebens in Bosnien unter der Einwirkung der türkischen Herrschaft.*"

[8]The premise of Andrić, that those who converted to Islam were immature Bogomil Slavs still not separated from their "heathen" past, and the premise of V. Todorović that they were Serbs, are both based upon a crude and discredited ideology of conversion. Modern scholars have shown that conversion in Bosnia was a multifaceted process with differing groups converting in differing directions. Thus, it would be impossible to identify any present group of Catholic Croats, Orthodox Serbs, or Slavic Muslims as "pure" descendants of any particular group in the medieval period. See John Fine, *The Bosnian Church* (Boudler: East European Monographs, 1975); and "The Medieval and Ottoman Roots of Modern Bosnian Society," in *The Muslims of Bosnia-Herzegovina: Their Historic Development from the Middle Ages to the Dissolution of Yugoslavia*, Ed. M. Pinson (Cambridge: Harvard University Press, 1993), 1-21. Both Fine and Malcolm, *Bosnia: A Short History* (New York: New York University Press, 1994) show that the Orthodox Christians in Bosnia only in the post-medieval period came to identify themselves explicitly as Serbs.

is being held back by fairies (*vila*) who decree that the bridge cannot be completed until two Christian children are walled up within the bridge. Two holes in the bridge are interpreted by the local people as places where the infants' mothers would suckle them. The implication is clear, even without explicit statements in Andrić's dissertation: the metaphor is of an essential Christian soul buried alive within the alien encrustation of the Turk. The novel's protagonist is viewed by Andrić's omniscient narrator as a Christian soul similarly walled up within the alien religion.[9]

The second metaphor is the graphically described impaling of a Serb dissident by the Turkish overseer and his Gypsy helpers. The metaphor is an explicitly Christological passion scene, and like the meditation on the Stations of the Cross, it dwells on the physical aspects of the torment, lingering over each with literary power. Many readers cite this passage as unforgettable. For Andrić and other Serb nationalists, the practice of impaling is the symbol of Turks (both Anatolian colonizers and Slavic Turkifiers), despite the fact that impalement was practiced by Christian rulers in Eastern Europe as well, and that the most famous impaler in history was the Christian Orthodox Count Vlad, A Vlach prince, whose victims were dissidents and Turks.

The Conflict over Kosovo, the "Serb Jerusalem" and Site of Serbia's Most Sacred Venue and Most Brilliant Religious Art and Architecture, and the Resurrection of the Ustashe

The tension in the Serbian province of Kosovo between the majority population of ethnic Albanians and the Serbian minority grew steadily after World War II. By 1969, Serbian clerics were complaining that they encountered hostility and even vandalism at their shrines. They wrote a reasoned complaint to the government, with specific incidents of harassment and vandalism, and asked for better protection.[10] By 1981, the situation had become even more volatile, with riots by Albanian students, repression by Yugoslav authorities, and increased demands by the local Serb populace for better protection. More incidents of harassment and vandalism occurred. Neither the Albanians nor the Serbs felt safe.

Into this volatile mix, the Serbian clergy threw a match. In a series of highly inflammatory documents, the Serbian clergy charged that "It is no exaggeration to say that planned GENOCIDE [emphasis original] is being

---

[9]Ivo Andrić, *The Bridge on the Drina,* translated from the Serbo-Croat by Lovett F. Edwards (New York: Macmillan, 1959; Chicago: University of Chicago Press, 1977), a translation of *Na Drini ćuprija,* originally written in 1942.

[10]Holy Council of Bishops, 1969 in Gordana Filipović, *Kosovo: Past and Present* (Belgrade, Review of International Affairs, 1989), 354-55.

perpetrated against the Serbian people in Kosovo![11] The charge of genocide against Serbs in Kosovo began to be repeated with increasing intensity by Serbian church leaders and intellectuals.[12] The charge of genocide was unfounded and never backed up with any evidence or argumentation, or with any attempt to align it with the internationally accepted definition of genocide. Even so, the charge soon found its way into the influential "Memorandum" of the Serbian Academy of Sciences and Arts (hereafter "Memorandum") composed by a number of Serbian intellectuals and academicians. Four times, the allegedly ongoing "genocide" against Serbs was mentioned, without any evidence, as if it were an established fact.[13]

There is no more serious a charge than the charge of genocide. To raise a charge of genocide without evidence or argument is an act of supreme irresponsibility in any context, but the charge of genocide was particularly grave given the fact that most Serbs had experienced an actual genocide in World War II at the hands of the Nazis and their Ustashe clients. Throughout the "Memorandum" and the writings of the Serb Bishops, the World War II genocide was recalled. As preparations were made for the 1989 celebration of the 600th anniversary of the death of Lazar at Kosovo, the Serb clergy began supervising the disinterring of the remains of Serb victims of Ustashe genocide. These rites, of an almost infinite emotive and symbolic power, were taken over by radical Serb nationalists who used them to portray Croats and Bosnian Muslims as inherently genocidal people plotting a new genocide against Serbs. There was no evidence of such a new genocide, but the disinterred relics of the very real and very recent genocide of World War II gave a symbolic power to the constantly repeated refrain that genocide was indeed occurring at that very time in Kosovo.

Vidovdan, 1989

A passion play collapses time. At the Good Friday passion play commemorating the death of Jesus or the Shi`ite passion play commemorating

---

[11]Appeal by the Clergy in Gordana Filipović, *op.cit.*, 355-60. The capitalization of GENOCIDE is in the original.

[12]In 1987, 60,000 Serbs signed a petition protesting the "fascist genocide" in Kosovo. In 1988, Serb Orthodox bishops in New Zealand, Europe, and the Americas published a petition entitled "Declaration of the Bishops of the Serbian Orthodox Church Against the Genocide Inflicted by the Albanians on the Indigenous Serbian Population, Together with the Sacrilege of their Cultural Monuments in their Own Country."

[13]The "Memorandum" was not officially published at the time, but leaked in various versions in a highly politicized way. The full text, with a long defense, has now been published on the Internet. For the section alleging genocide against Serbs by Albanians in Kosovo, see http://suc.suc.org/~kosta/tar/memorandum/memorandum.html#status.

the death of Husayn, the boundaries between the actors and the audience also collapse. Rather than viewing a representation of a historical event, the audience *participates* in an event that is eternal and reoccurs in each remembrance in some real fashion. Actors know this, and those playing Judas or Shemr (the assassin of Husayn) know they must exit the stage quickly to avoid being beaten by members of the audience who no longer view them as actors but as the real characters.

Before the great passion play of Vidovdan, 1989, the emotions had been readied. The relics of Lazar had been ceremonially transferred around various areas in and throughout Kosovo as a claim to territory and as a sacred, spatial reminder. The relics of the World War II victims of Ustashe genocide were being ritually uncovered in the same period. The real genocide that occurred in the lifetime of many Serbs and the founding event of Serbian religious consciousness in its analogy with the crucifixion were brought together. All these rivers of time, space, symbol, and memory came together into a roaring cascade at the battle plain of Gazimestan in Kosovo.

There, Serbian President Milošević stood in front of a large backdrop dominated by the Serbian nationalist symbol, a Greek Cross formed of four C's (Cyrillic S's standing for Only Unity Saves the Serb, *Samo sloga Srbina spašava*), and addressed a huge throng estimated at over a million people. Rather than speaking of peace and reconciliation, justice and progress, Milošević talked of "battles and battles to come." The various strands of symbolism brought together at this time and place were powerful: Lazar as Christ, Slavic Muslims as Christ Killers and race-betrayers, the alleged genocide in Kosovo itself, the sacred shrine of Serbdom, the alleged imminent renewal of Ustashe genocide, the disinterring of the bones of victims of Ustashe genocide in a militant context, the ceremonial transfer of Lazar's relics, the collapse of time, and sacredness of space. Yet this nexus needs to be activated. It is as explosive as gunpowder, but it needs to be lit. The story of how Milošević and Croat nationalists such as Franjo Tudjman set about lighting the fuse--provoking conflicts, arming paramilitary groups, and organizing the bloodshed--has been told elsewhere, by its proud participants, in detail, and goes outside the boundary of this chapter.[14]

---

[14]The organized destruction of both Serb and Muslim communities by Croat nationalist forces is another major topic that I cannot treat in this particular essay. See M. Sells, *The Bridge Betrayed*, chapter 5. To my knowledge, after three years of intense investigation, there was no Bosnian Muslim governmental policy of destroying Serb or Croat communities; many of those individuals who attacked civilian communities have been arrested and punished. For an account by Serb and Croat leaders of how Yugoslavia was destroyed, often by principal parties proud of their role in the destruction, see "Yugoslavia: Death of a Nation," four-part video. BBC, 1995; and Laura Silber and Allan Little, eds., *Yugoslavia:*

Yet these symbolic elements, often obscured by the more overt steps toward violence, are crucial to the motivation and justification of the genocide that was to occur in Bosnia-Herzegovina from 1992-1995. The various strands above, particularly the collapse of time and the casting of contemporary Muslims as the evil Turks who killed Lazar and other Serb martyrs, are encapsulated in the famous claim by Belgrade academician Miroljub Jevtić that "the hands of the Muslims who are with us are stained and polluted with the blood of their ancestors from among the inhabitants of Bosnia at that time, namely those who did not embrace Islam." Jevtić brands with the stain of blood contemporary Slavic Muslims for the conversion of their ancestors, centuries ago, to Islam.[15] Once a combination of historical circumstance and political maneuver (the likely pact between Croatian President Tudjman and Serbian President Milošević to carve up Bosnia between them), the rage of Kosovo was directed against the civilian population of Bosnian Muslims.

The Statements and Actions of the Serbian Synod or Assembly of Bishops
In May of 1996, the Serbian Bishops Assembly or Synod made the following claim about the International Tribunal on War Crimes in the Hague:

> The Assembly again expresses its deep misgivings at the unjust and unequal conduct of the representatives of the international community toward the participating parties to the tragic civil war on the territory of former Yugoslavia. For the first time in history, the Hague Tribunal is prosecuting war crimes of the leaders and representatives of virtually only one of the parties to the civil war, the Serbian side, thereby in fact indicting an entire nation. The abuse of justice and international law in The Hague as an instrument of politics, if carried out to completion, will remain as a dark blot on the face of the contemporary world.[16]

The official position of Serbian Bishops, thus, undermined the major hope for identifying the individuals guilty of genocide and crimes against humanity and holding them accountable. In the absence of such accountability, the Serbian people as a whole will be blamed by many, just as many Serbian nationalists have blamed Croats as a whole for the genocide of World War II. By undermining the credibility of the Tribunal, which the Serbian government had sworn at Dayton to uphold, the bishops undermine the major institution that

---

Death of a Nation, book accompaniment. Penguin: Current Events/BBC Books, 1995.

[15]See the translations in H.T. Norris, *Islam in the Balkans* (University of South Carolina Press, 1993), 295-96; and Norman Cigar, *Genocide in Bosnia* (Texas A&M Press, 1995), 29. Cigar recounts a series of attacks against the religion of Islam and Muslims in general by Jevtić in *ibid*, 27-29.

[16]The statement was posted by Father Rastko Trbuhović on the "New York Times Bosnia forums, Religion and War," June 24, 1996.

would prevent their people as a whole from being tarred with the horrendous crimes of certain of their leaders.

The statement by the bishops is itself in error. In addition to indictments against Serb leaders, the Tribunal has indicted a number of major Croat leaders. At the time the statement was made, the Tribunal had attempted on numerous occasions to investigate crimes against Serbs, but had found that it was being frustrated by Serbian officials who refused Tribunal investigators access to Serbian refugees in Serb areas and refused to allow a free investigation. Nevertheless, four indictments for crimes against Serbs by Croat and Muslim officers at the Ćelebić camp near Konjic have now been issued. All four indicted men are in custody at The Hague. Two Muslims were immediately arrested by the Bosnian government upon their indictment and, in clear contrast to Croat and Serb authorities who have refused to cooperate with the Tribunal, the two Muslims were extradited to The Hague. What justice do the Serb bishops expect if they attack the credibility of the Tribunal? The implication of their statement is that they support the position of the Republika Srpska that Serbian authorities should prosecute Serbian wrongdoers.

On July 11, 1996, The Republika Srpska held a major celebration for its "liberation" of the town of Srebrenica on July 11, 1995. According to major human rights organizations and the Tribunal, 8,000 Bosnian Muslims, mostly unarmed civilians, disappeared after the "Safe Haven" of Srebrenica was handed over to General Ratko Mladić by the UN troops who had sworn to protect it. Mladić has been photographed passing out candy to children and assuring them that he would guarantee their safety. The men standing next to those children have not been seen alive. The Tribunal investigators are in the process of unearthing mass graves throughout the Srebrenica area. Serbian authorities have made the following contradictory claims about the missing men: 1) they are not really missing but are being hidden by the Bosnian government; 2) they killed one another; 3) they were killed in armed combat against the Serb army. The corpses unearthed at Cerska show that the hands of the victims were tied behind their back with wire and that they were executed in mass, contradicting all of the above mutually contradictory stories. Do the Serbian bishops expect the Republika Srpska to investigate and prosecute crimes that the Republika Srpska leadership, including President Biljana Plavšić, have officially celebrated as a heroic "liberation"?

In 1992, as news of the Serbian run concentration camps at Omarska, Brčko Luka, Foča, Keraterm, Manjača, Trnopolje, Kotor Varoš, and Batković were revealed, the Serbian Bishops issued the following statement "In the name of God's truth and on the testimony from our brother bishops from Bosnia-Herzegovina and from other trustworthy witnesses, we declare, taking full moral responsibility, that such camps neither have existed nor exist in the Serbian Republic of Bosnia-Herzegovina."[17]   Some have attempted to justify this statement, saying it referred explicitly to the existence of rape camps, yet there the statement itself makes no distinction among camps, and never acknowledges the abuses now known to have occurred at these camps, including organized rape. The attack on the credibility of the Tribunal in 1996 is in harmony with the Serb synod's denials in 1992, at a time when the Serbian Orthodox religious leaders must have known about the camps and about what was occurring in those camps.[18] From 1992-1996, Serbian Bishops have continued to maintain war relations with those accused of instigating the genocide, including the Serbian paramilitary leader Arkan, General Ratko Mladić, and Radovan Karadžić.[19]

Whether what occurred in those camps and what occurred later at places like Srebrenica is associated with Serbian religion and the Serbian Church will depend upon whether Serbian religious leaders will begin a new initiative: to acknowledge openly the crimes that were committed, to support the one institution, the International Tribunal, that has any hope of offering an objective and dispassionate trial of those accused of such crimes, and to offer an interpretation of the Kosovo religious symbolism that emphasizes interreligious tolerance and the shared suffering of humanity, rather than focusing upon the victimization of Serbs and present need to exact the revenge of Miloš on the perceived descendants of those who killed Lazar.

---

[17]See "The Extraordinary Session of the Holy Episcopal Synod of the Serbian Orthodox Church in Response to the False Accusations against the Serbian People in Bosnia-Herzegovina," *Pravoslavni misionar*; June, 1992, 250-51, cited by Norman Cigar, *Genocide in Bosnia*, 89; and "Memorandum of the Holy Episcopal Synod's session of May 14-20, 1992," *Pravoslavlje*, June 1, 1992, 2, in Cigar, *op.cit.*, 78.

[18]At the time of the Dayton accords, Patriarch Pavle broke ranks with the other, more militant clergy, such as Bishop Atanasije. Pavle supported the peace accords, for which he was bitterly attacked by other bishops led by Atanasije. The attack on Pavle, who had been in every other way completely identified with the cause of the Republika Srpska, was clear evidence of the militant, some would say, fundamentalist, stance of the Serbian bishops today. That Pavle would support the bishop's statement undermining the Tribunal and taking the position of the Republika Sprska leadership on the tribunal, shows that he had been brought back into the fold of militant religious nationalism.

[19]Bishop Atanasije distinguished himself for his attack on the Serbian nationalist Vuk Drašković for criticizing Serb militia atrocities in Trebinje. Atanasije went on to criticize the Serb leadership in Trebinje--not for the annihilation of the Muslim community there, but for their failure to persecute the Adventist Protestants as well. Bishop Vasilije of Tuzla-Zvornik, a center of Serbian paramilitary attacks against Bosnian Muslims, traveled to Belgrade to participate in Arkan's wedding. For a fuller account of these incidents and the close relationship of the Serb bishops to the militant Serb nationalists, see Cigar, *op.cit.*,passim, and Sells, *The Bridge Betrayed*, chapter 4.

14

WAR WOUNDS IN CROATIAN CATHOLIC POPULATION OF BOSNIA-HERZEGOVINA

Mato Zovkić

My view of religion and ethnicity in my country is, indeed, influenced by my religious and ethnic identity: I am an ethnic Croat born in Bosnia, educated in Croatia and Italy, a Catholic priest of the Sarajevo archdiocese who has been assigned to priestly office in Sarajevo for the last 27 years, vicar general of Sarajevo Archdiocese since 1987, and professor in Sarajevo Theological Seminary since 1972. I was born in a Croatian Catholic village in Northern Bosnia, and I have experienced since my grammar school my country as a multiethnic and multireligious state because there were several Bosnian-Muslim boys in my grammar school, and because the houses of my maternal uncles were next to the first Serbian houses in the neighboring Serbian Orthodox village (that village was taken over by Serbian forces in August 1992, and according to the Dayton peace treaty included into the Republic of Bosnian Serbs). This essay is going to be more a personal witness than a cool, theological analysis of causes and consequences of the close links between ethnicity and religion in my country.

Bosnia is a small European country of only 51.564 sq. km. with 4,377,033 inhabitants, according to the census of April 1991. Ethnic self-identification at that census was the following: Bosnians-Muslims 1,630,033 (43.5%), Serbs 1,320,738 (31.2%), Croats 760,852 (17.4%), and Yugoslavs 242,683 (5.5%). During the census of 1981, 326,316 (7.9%) declared Yugoslavs. In November 1990, ethnic parties of Bosnians-Muslims (SDA), Serbs (SDS), and Croats (HDZ) won the first democratic elections. This happened primarily because of unsolved ethnic relations during seventy-four years of Yugoslavia as one federal state of six national communities (Bosnians-Muslims, Croats, Macedonians, Montenegrins, Serbs, Slovenians) and two large minorities (Hungarians and Albanians). Persons who declared themselves as ethnic Yugoslavs were mostly living in mixed marriages; they gave up their religious and ethnic differences for the sake of peace and harmony in their families. They also were praised by the pre-war royal regime and post-war communist party as ideal citizens, mostly predestined for better government jobs.

The new government of B&H took office in late December 1990. In mid-1991, Slovenia and Croatia, by virtue of legally organized referenda, declared their independence from Belgrade, and they were soon attacked by the Yugoslav army.

Destructions, Expulsions, and "Humane Resettling"

In October 1991, Serbian local militia, substantially helped by the Yugoslav army, invaded Eastern Herzegovina and destroyed seven Catholic parishes. President Alija Izetbegović, probably wishing to avoid a possible army assault on the defenseless Muslim population, made several statements pretending that he did not know who was burning down Croatian villages in Herzegovina and expressed his conviction that the army would not attack its own people. His hesitant attitude produced major mistrust on the side of Croats in Herzegovina and Bosnia who started buying weapons and organizing their own armed units called HVO.

When Croatia and Slovenia were recognized by EC and other countries in January 1992, citizens of Bosnia-Herzegovina were faced with the dilemma of remaining within a reduced Yugoslavia or looking for full sovereignty of their country. Serbian political and religious leaders in Bosnia expressed their concern by stating that Serbs would feel endangered outside of Yugoslavia as one country for all Serbs. Therefore, they forbade their fellow-ethnics, through their ethnic militia, to take part in the referendum on independence organized by the legally elected and functioning government on March 1st, 1992. On the eve of elections in November 1990, two Catholic bishops of B&H issued pastoral letters to be read in all Catholic parishes. In them, they encouraged their congregations to vote on election day and not to give their votes to members of parties which practiced in the recent past religious or ethnic discrimination of citizens. They did not mention the names of respective parties, but it was obvious that Catholics should vote for HDZ, the only party which promised to protect ethnic and religious interests of Croats in B&H. When in April 1991 the new census was about to take place, Catholic bishops wrote a new letter to their believers, asking them to register as ethnic Croats and Roman Catholics confident that there would be no more civil discrimination on the basis of ethnicity or religious denomination. In February 1992, the bishops asked again their believers to vote for an independent B&H, having in mind the bad experience of the Croatian Catholic population in Yugoslavia which was dominated by Orthodox Serbs as the majority people. On March 1, 1992, only 63.04% of our citizens were able to take part in the referendum, and 62.63% of these gave their votes for their country's sovereignty.

In April 1992, the Serbs started an open war for their ethnically "clean" territory in B&H. In six months time, they took control of Eastern Herzegovina as well as of Eastern, Northern, and Western Bosnia. They expelled hundreds of thousands of Bosnians-Muslims and Croats from their homes, and they destroyed about 600 mosques and about 300 churches. Muslim civil and religious authorities estimate the number of their killed or missing civilians to about 200,000 and of their raped women to about 20,000.

The Muslim population driven out from Eastern and Western Bosnia moved in large extension into Central Bosnia where Croats and Muslims have been living in mixed or separate localities for centuries. In March 1993, armed conflicts broke out between Croats and Muslims in Mostar and in Central Bosnia. They finished only in March 1994, thanks to a federation agreement mediated by the US government. Before these conflicts, Croatian authorities in Mostar "cleansed" about 50,000 Muslims from Herzegovina, and during these conflicts, Muslim authorities "cleansed" about 100,000 Croats from Central Bosnia. Archbishop Puljić made several pastoral visits, trying to trace and to calm down ethnic tensions before and during the confrontation period. In several localities, which were partially or predominantly inhabited by the Croats, he found confidential instructions of Croatian leaders to their fellow-ethnics to leave their settlements even before the arrival of the Muslim army. Probably those authorities supposed at that stage of the war that Bosnia would be partitioned into three ethnic states, and, therefore, the Croats should move from ethnically mixed localities into safe Croatian zones.

As I now know, Croats have prepared and partially caused the armed conflicts with Muslims by "cleansing" Muslims from Stolac, Čapljina, Mostar, and other localities under Croatian control in Herzegovina. I was in Sarajevo in July 1993 when a Jewish leader of the humanitarian organization "Benevolencia" asked me to call via amateur radio operators (the phones of private citizens in Sarajevo were cut off in early April 1992) any high ranking priest in Mostar who could mediate the freeing of a sick Muslim imprisoned by Croats in a concentration camp in Mostar with thousands of other Muslim men. Up to that day, I did not know that such camps existed in Herzegovina. Later on some young priests, my former students, "explained" to me that bringing Muslim men between the ages of sixteen to sixty into concentration camps was necessary because Muslims were an "unreliable element" in Croatian places of amateurs on that day, but I sent my message through another channel.

In the first year of the war, Croats and Bosnian-Muslims used to criticize Serbs for having committed terrible atrocities on the civil population and sacral buildings. Ethnic media in Muslim-controlled Sarajevo unveiled only the crimes of Serbs and Croats and vice versa; Serbian and Croatian media at Pale and Mostar spoke only of criminal activities of Muslims. From personal reports of priests and lay people in the Mostar and Sarajevo diocese, I now know that my fellow-ethnics did commit criminal acts on innocent Muslim civilians and monuments. For a long time, the Muslims boasted that they were the most humane defenders of their settlements, but I know that their fighters have also killed some innocent civilians and two priests, destroyed three churches of my diocese, devastated a certain number of sacral buildings, and destroyed several villages. I saw on the exterior church wall in Travnik the Muslim creed written in Latin characters: "*Allahu ekber* - Allah is great!"

I do not distribute the guilt of war crimes equally to three ethnic communities nor do I look at any of our ethnic communities as "criminal people." It is up to the impartial international tribunal to prosecute and to convict individuals from each ethnic community for their personal criminal actions during this war for the creation of ethnic territories. Despite the presence of some elements of religion, this war in Bosnia was not a war of religions, but a war for ethnic territories within our multiethnic and multireligious country. I do hope that the present cease fire brought about by the Dayton agreement will grow into permanent peace. Serbian forces took about 70% of national territory in B&H in 1992. In October and November of 1995, the Bosnian army and Croatian forces took back about 20% of that territory from Serbian forces.

Discordant Evaluations of War Activities and of the Dayton Peace Treaty
According to church statistics, the Catholic population in the four dioceses of B&H in 1991 was about 832,000, distributed as follows: the Trebinje-Mrkan diocese in Eastern Herzegovina about 16,000 in fifteen parishes, the diocese of Mostar-Duvno in Western Herzegovina about 178,000 in sixty-six parishes, the archdiocese of Vrhbosna-Sarajevo in Central and Northern Bosnia about 528,000 in 144 parishes, and the diocese of Banja Luka in Western Bosnia about 110,000 in forty-seven parishes. Eastern Herzegovina is inhabited by a predominantly Serbian-Orthodox population, Western Herzegovina by predominantly Croatian-Catholics while the territory of Sarajevo and Banja Luka dioceses has been populated for centuries by a mixed population of three respective ethnic and religious communities. During and because of the war, the Catholic population of B&H was reduced to about 400,000 as follows: the archdiocese of Sarajevo from 528,000 to about 200,000, the diocese of Banja Luka from 110,000 to about 5,000, in the Trebinje and Mostar diocese about 20,000 Catholics were

displaced, but they were sheltered by Croatian civil authorities on the territory of Western Herzegovina.

Mons. Franjo Komarica, the Bishop of Banja Luka and Mons. Vinko Puljić, the Archbishop of Sarajevo, opened in Zagreb in the summer of 1992 an ecclesiastical vicariate for Catholic refugees from their dioceses. These vicariates had to take care of priests and their parishioners who were driven out by Bosnian Serbs or who left their homes before the arrival of Serbian forces. Most of them took refuge in Croatia with their relatives or were housed by the Croatian government in vacant hotels and refugee centers. Very soon Caritas directors of the Banja Luka and Sarajevo dioceses had to open their headquarters in Croatia in order to coordinate more effectively the humanitarian aid coming into B&H or to refugee camps in Croatia. Since mail and telephone lines were cut off in April 1992, Caritas people had to bring in and out thousands of personal letters together with basic humanitarian goods.

Due to shortages of food, water, electricity, and fuel, ecclesiastical educational institutions in Bosnia had to be closed down in April 1992. It took ecclesiastical authorities about six months to reopen these centers outside of B&H: the Novitiate of Bosnian Franciscans in Italy, the Franciscan Theological Seminary in Samobor near Zagreb, the Sarajevo Metropolitan Theological Seminary in Bol on the island of Brač, near Split in Croatia.

Bishop Komarica of Banja Luka had to face Serbian rule in his diocesan territory. He asked his fellow Catholics not to take weapons because such action would only give an excuse to the Serbian militia and private armed groups for more violent discrimination against the non-Serbian population. He also asked them not to move out voluntarily because this would contribute towards ethnic self-cleansing. When two of his priests were killed and numerous Catholics were taken into custody by Serbian armed groups, or when Croatian men were brought by force to dig trenches on front lines, Bishop Komarica kept writing letters to Serbian civil and military authorities, asking for the protection of basic rights for non-Serbs in the Republika Srpska. In these letters, he was calling Radovan Karadžić "Mister President." I know some Catholics in other parts of Bosnia and in Croatia who consider Bishop Komarica indirectly responsible for the torture or even killing of some Croats, because he advised them not to leave their homes despite growing Serbian oppression of the non-Serbian population.

Privately, it was recommended to Archbishop Puljić of Sarajevo by some Croatian civil and military leaders in Bosnia to leave Sarajevo and to transfer his episcopal seat to a town with a majority of Croatian Catholics in Central Bosnia. The reason presumably was that Sarajevo had a Muslim majority which, therefore, cannot have any permanent meaning for ethnic Croat citizens of Bosnia. In his pastoral letters, homilies, and public statements, Archbishop Puljić repeated his conviction that Bosnia-Herzegovina should be the single state of all three ethnic communities with a high degree of provincial and local autonomy and with *really equal rights for all citizens and ethnic communities*. In his pleading for human, ethnic, and religious rights of all inhabitants of B&H, he shares his deep personal views and the guidelines of the Holy See. His book, *Suffering with Hope: Appeals, Addresses, Interviews* is now available in English. It contains some of his speeches and documents published between August 18, 1991, and December 23, 1993. From them, the reader can get an insight into endeavors and reflections of a religious leader who shares the suffering of his own congregation and of his fellow-citizens in the besieged capital of B&H. This book also reflects the efforts of this Catholic prelate who drew the attention of the international political community and of the universal Church to the war atrocities and destruction in B&H. From his published and translated documents, foreign readers can discern the way in which Archbishop Puljić strongly supports B&H as a multiethnic and multireligious country.

During the armed conflicts between Croats and Muslims in Central Bosnia, the Muslim-controlled media in Sarajevo incited anti-Croatian feelings in their listeners and their readers in a city with only 30,000 of Croat Catholics out of 380,000 of the predominantly Muslim population. In such a situation, Archbishop Puljić wrote on June 4, 1993, a letter to the Presidency of the Republic of Bosnia-Herzegovina in which he said:

> We have already lived together and survived this siege of the city of Sarajevo for fourteen months. However, relations are becoming increasingly strained, chiefly under the influence of the media. For many people all of us Croats in the city have suddenly become *ustashas*. I therefore want to caution that responsibility can be only personal, never collective. Let us, citizens of Sarajevo who are all enduring this torment together, at least not poison our mutual good relations because they should be a model of common living for the whole of Bosnia and Herzegovina. I would add that the world will see Muslims as a partner worthy of respect to the measure in which they manage to solve the question of Catholics and members of other religions in the area under their control.[1]

Mons. Ratko Perić, the Bishop of Mostar-Duvno who is also the apostolic administrator of the small diaspora diocese Trebinje-Mrkan, is the Catholic religious leader of Herzegovina which is predominantly inhabited by Croat Catholics. Most of the Croatian population in this area, Catholic priests included, hoped in 1992-1993 that B&H would somehow disintegrate and the Western Herzegovina would be included into the Republic of Croatia. This is why they aimed at creating a Croatian ethnic territory in B&H with Mostar as its capital despite the fact that about 600,000 of the Croats of B&H who lived outside of

---

[1]Vinko Puljić, *Suffering with Hope: Appeals, Addresses, Interviews* , p. 177.

this territory in Central, Northern, and Western Bosnia, mixed with Serbs and Bosnian-Muslims. The bishops of Sarajevo and Banja Luka together with the majority of their priests and lay persons asked Croatian political leaders in Zagreb and Mostar to create a political program for all B&H so that every family, regardless of its ethnic and religious identity, can safely live on its property. Most prominent political leaders in Croatia and Herzegovina ignored such suggestions in favor of a "safe" Croatian territory with a possible "humane relocation" of those Croats who now live outside of such an envisaged future, ethnic territory. I know of some local political and military leaders who tried to destroy the mutual trust of Muslims and Croats in some localities of Bosnia and sought to produce conflicts which would result in the relocation of the Croat population or the expulsion of the Muslim population. These same leaders maintained that Croats cannot have a safe future with Serbs or Muslims in B&H and, therefore, a fight for Croatian ethnic and political territory should be a primary "patriotic" duty of every good Croat.

Foreign media, after having discovered in 1993 concentration camps in Herzegovina arranged by Croats for Bosnian-Muslim men in the territory under their control, criticized sharply the Catholic bishops in B&H and Croatia for not condemning more explicitly violations of human rights in such camps. Muslim media in Sarajevo, and especially the present religious leader of Bosnian Muslims, Dr Mustafa Cerić, with his immediate collaborators, rebuked strongly the Catholic religious leaders for the crimes of HVO on the Muslim civil population in Herzegovina and Central Bosnia. I was personally present at such a conference in Sarajevo on October 3, 1993. Having in mind that Serbian-Orthodox bishops and Muslim religious leaders remained at a general level of condemning crimes without mentioning concrete violations of human rights by their own fellow-ethnics, Catholic bishops in B&H and in Croatia followed the same style of declarations and appeals. In their Declaration of November 29, 1993, the Catholic bishops of B&H said,

> Innocent imprisoned civilians are still living in inhuman conditions in spite of daily talks and promises that they will be exchanged. We do not know whether local political authorities have enabled any refugee or displaced person to return home. Every day we follow with pain the increase of inhumanity that makes it impossible to transport greatly needed humanitarian aid to the civilian population. We repudiate all the unjust and inhuman acts committed in this war, and in the name of God's law and human dignity we condemn every method and practice of depriving people and nations of their rights, persecuting the population, 'ethnic cleansing,' genocide and destruction of religious buildings--whatever group or ethnic political community are the perpetrators.

In late November 1993, a meeting of Catholic bishops of B&H with the civil authorities of Croats in B&H took place in Split. I know from personal information by some participants that the civil authorities took that occasion to reproach the bishops for insufficiently supporting the Croatian ethnic cause and for criticizing too much some criminal incidents of individual HVO soldiers or local civil leaders.

At an ecumenical conference in Pécs, Hungary, convened in December 1993 upon the invitation of Dr. John Taylor, a consultant of the Conference of European Churches for the countries of former Yugoslavia, we non-Serb participants from Bosnia and Croatia used the expression "Serbian aggression" until a present Serbian Orthodox bishop rebuked us for using such an impolite word at an ecumenical meeting. Serbs, he said, did not commit any aggression in Bosnia and Croatia; they only were defending their families and their property. He was serious, and he literally meant what he was saying. This incident helped me to realize how crucial it is for religious ministers and leaders to be prophetically critical of their own people in the countries and regions where ethnic and religious identities coincide.

Now that the Dayton peace treaty has been signed, it is welcomed by the Croatian population and religious leaders as a necessary means which stopped the bloodshed. At the same time, it is being looked upon as an unjust peace which has legitimized most of the results of Serbian aggression and which only formally guarantees a safe return of exiles and refugees to their former settlements. Large numbers of houses have been destroyed while those that are in relatively good shape are now settled by Serbian or Bosnian-Muslim families driven out from their residences. Those Croats who have experienced violence and injustice from Serbs or Bosnian-Muslims during this war in their own family and on their own property are disappointed by the Dayton peace agreement because B&H remains in some way one state, despite the high degree of autonomy in ethnic "entities." On the other hand, those who have been driven out from their places which are now controlled by Serbs or Muslims and would like to return one day ask themselves what kind of future can their children have in such places. I am sure our Serb and Muslim fellow citizens who are in an identical position must have similar bitter feelings and dark expectations.

The Challenge of Religious Education for Civil Tolerance in One State of Three Ethnic Communities

Ethnogenesis of ethnic communities in B&H is a sharply disputed question in Bosnia, Croatia, and Serbia. In November 1995, I attended an inter-religious conference and prayer for peace at Florence, Italy. I was asked to take an active part in a round-table on religion and ethnicity, and I was expected to say something about my country and my identity. I told the audience that during my high school and theological studies in Croatia I was taught that the medieval kingdom of Bosnia was largely populated by Catholics, that the Bosnian civil leader was called "ban" like in middle age Croatia, and that, therefore, all inhabitants of Bosnia were in their past somehow Croats. When I was assigned to be a chaplain in Travnik in 1965, I came in touch with local Muslim people. I discovered that they do not feel they are Croats or Serbs but a different ethnic community. I had to respect their sense of ethnic identity, and I still do so as an ethnic Croat citizen of Bosnia. At the same conference in Florence, a Serbian Orthodox bishop was present who told the audience that for Serbian historians all inhabitants of Bosnia in the Middle Ages were Serbs and that only during the Turkish rule in Bosnia (1463-1878) some converted to Islam and others to Catholicism, but they all have Serbian roots. During this war in Sarajevo, Zenica, and other towns controlled by Bosnian-Muslims, new text-books for history and literature were prepared and prescribed by the Ministry of Education. In these books, the official name of the language has been changed to "Bosnian" and all inhabitants of Medieval Bosnia are depicted as ethnic Bosnians, thus making the contemporary Muslims of B&H the most authentic Bosnians.

The Dayton peace treaty foresees the after-the-war reality consisting of two "entities" of B&H with a decentralized and autonomous educational program. Nevertheless, the Ministry of Education and writers of text-books for all levels of education should find an essential consensus in important questions of history, language, literature, and other subjects of general significance. Educational programs and teaching staff can contribute towards digesting the bitter conflicts from the distant and near past and work towards dismantling the revengeful feelings in the hearts of the young generation of Bosnians, Serbs, and Croats. The multiethnic and multireligious character of B&H has been heavily shaken by the war activities 1991-1995, but I firmly believe not destroyed forever.

I know some Croatian Catholic priests in B&H who were tortured in Serbian concentration camps or in Muslim house-prisons. They feel so embittered and disappointed that they would not accept--at least for the time being--any priestly office on the territory under Serbian or Muslim control. They even disagree with the rest of us who are ready to serve our fellow Catholics wherever they decide to settle down and who believe that a tolerant life in multiethnic and multireligious B&H is still possible. I am sure the bishops would not put any juridical pressure on such priests and send them to take care of parishes in the territory under Serbian or Muslim control. These servants of God's people need some time to heal in order to become again spiritual healers, not only of their own congregations, but also of other fellow citizens.

During the 1991-1995 war, religious leaders had to side with their respective ethnic communities because of unsolved ethnic and religious problems which accumulated during the existence of royal and communist Yugoslavia (1918-1991). Most of them wrote declarations, appeals, and protests on occasion of crimes committed by armed men of other ethnic identity upon members of their own communities. They may be blamed for lacking prophetic courage to stop or at least to denounce more explicitly concrete misdeeds of their fellow ethnics.

After this war, the material and spiritual renewal of religious ministers and leaders of B&H face the challenge of educating their own congregations for civil tolerance in their multiethnic and multireligious country. The time of self-justification or of only blaming "others" should be over. Our mutual relations have been poisoned, and we who share our people's every day sorrows are more aware than our political representatives that the process of healing and reconciliation will be painful but possible with God's grace and the good will of involved people. We should comprehend that a new kind of Bosnia-Herzegovina is needed and possible after the disintegration of Yugoslavia and after the cruel atrocities which have taken place in this war which implanted in many hearts the fatal seeds of personal, family, and ethnic revenge. At least those of us who believe that such a Bosnia is possible should act accordingly--precisely as believing persons and as religious ministers.

Our homilies in liturgical celebrations and worship services as well as our religious instruction of school children are unique opportunities to help our adult believers and their adolescent youngsters to put into practice the moral values we proclaim and believe in. We should also take an active part in inter-religious, non-government peace movements. We can and we should encourage our believers to get involved in such movements. During this war, I had a chance to attend several conferences on regions in conflict organized by Moral Rearmament, an inter-religious peace movement founded by the American social worker, Frank Buchman (1878-1961), now centered at Caux in Switzerland. I also attended in 1993 the European Assembly of the World Conference on Religion and Peace (WCRP) in Sweden and the 1994 World Assembly in Italy. At these meetings, I learned to speak "the secondary religious language" as Dr. William Vendley, general secretary of WCRP, proposed for us all to learn when we religious persons coming from different traditions try to make our world a better place to live.

The Croatian Catholic population of B&H is proportionately the greatest loser in this war. Because of the war, half of the Catholics have left or have been driven out from their parishes in Banja Luka, Sarajevo, and Trebinje dioceses. They found a temporary shelter in Croatia, Slovenia, Austria, Germany, and other countries. Most of them will never return to the places of their birth. Those who have remained in their parishes or are about to return to their burned-out homes will become an absolute minority and even greater losers if their spiritual leaders do not help them to cherish their own ethnic and religious identity while respecting the identity of their Bosnian-Muslim and Serb-Orthodox fellow citizens. The future of the Catholic population in B&H will to a great extent also depend on the really humane and equal treatment of Croat Catholics in territories controlled by Serbs and by Bosnian-Muslims.

Selected Bibliography

Aničić, M., et al., (eds.). *Bosna i Hercegovina--Sjeverozapadna Bosna. Genocidom do istrebljenja. Srpski zločini,* [North-Eastern Bosnia. Extermination through Genocide. Crimes of Serbs]. Zagreb, 1995.

Blažević, V., (ed.). *Služenje miru. Ivan Pavao II i Sveta Stolica za mir u Hrvatskoj i Bosni i Hercegovini (1991-1995),* [Serving the Peace. John Paul II and the Holy See for Peace in Croatia and Bosnia-Herzegovina 1991-1995]. Zagreb, 1995.

Gebhardt, G., *Zum Frieden bewegen. Friedenserziehung in religiösen Friedensbewegungen. Die Friedenserziehrische Tätigkeit religöser Friedensbewegungen. Historisch-pädagogische Analyse in religionsvergleichender Typik.* E. B.-Verlag Rissen, 1994.

Goluža,B. *Katolička Crkva u Bosni i Hercegovini 1918.-1941. Bosna i Hercegovina - zemlja katolika, pravoslavaca i muslimana,* [Catholic Church in Bosnia and Herzegovina 1918-1941. Bosnia and Herzegovina--a Country of Catholics, Orthodox and Muslims]. Mostar, 1995.

Johnston, D. and Sampson, C., (eds.). *Religion, The Missing Dimension of Statecraft.* (New York: Oxford University Press, 1994).

Karamatić , M. (ed). *Rat u Bosni i Hercegovini. Uzroci, posljedice, perspektive: Zbornik radova.* [The War in Bosnia and Herzegovina: Causes, Consequences, Prospects: Collected Essays]. Samobor, 1994.

Küng, H. *Ja zum Weltethos.* (München: Piper, 1995).

Luburić, A. (ed.). *Za pravedan mir. Biskupski ordinarijat Mostar u ratnoj drami 1990-1994,* [For a Just Peace: Mostar diocese in war drama 1990-1994]. Mostar, 1995.

Malcolm, N. *Bosnia. A Short History.* (London: Macmillan, 1994).

Puljić, V. *Suffering with Hope: Appeals/Addresses/Interviews,* (Zagreb: HKD Napredak, 1995).

Vukšić, T. *I rapporti tra i cattolici e gli ortodossi nella Bosnia ed Erzegovina dal 1878 al 1903. Uno studio storico-teologico,* Roma, 1991.

Vrhbosna 1990-1995 [Official Bulletin of Catholic dioceses in Bosnia-Herzegovina].

15

RELIGION, CONFLICT AND PROSPECTS FOR PEACE IN BOSNIA, CROATIA, AND YUGOSLAVIA[1]

Gerard F. Powers

Introduction

A history textbook used by high school seniors throughout Serbia blames the outbreak of the current conflict in the former Yugoslavia on the Vatican, which "launched a battle against Orthodoxy and Serbs through the Catholic Church and its allies." The Serbs fought back, it goes on, "to prevent a repeat of the genocide they suffered in World War II." [2]

Josip Beljan, writing in the Catholic journal, *Veritas*, declared:

> The cross of Christ stands next to the Croatian flag, the Croatian bishop next to the Croatian minister of state.... This was truly again a real war for the "honoured cross and golden liberty," for the return of Christ and liberty to Croatia. The church is glad for the return of its people from the twofold slavery -- Serbian and communist."[3]

In November 1992, the leaders of the Islamic, Roman Catholic, and Serbian Orthodox communities in Bosnia stated "emphatically" that "[t]his is not a religious war, and that the characterization of this tragic conflict as a religious

---

[1]This chapter was originally appeared in the *Journal of International Affairs*. Vol. 50, no. 1 (Summer 1996) and is being reprinted here with the permission of the author.

[2]"War-Weary People of Former Yugoslavia Face Uncertain Future," *The Washington Post*, December 17, 1995, A 34, col 6.

[3]Josip Beljan, "Priznata vjernost" (Recognition of Faithfulness), *Veritas*, Nos. 9-10 (Zagreb, Sept.-Oct. 1992), pp. 24-25 (translated by Paul Mojzes), quoted in P. Mojzes, *Yugoslavian Inferno: Ethnoreligious Warfare in the Balkans* (New York: Continuum Publishing Co., 1994), p. 130.

war and the misuse of all religious symbols used with the aim to further hatred, must be proscribed and is condemned."[4]

These three quotes reflect three differing perspectives on the role of religion in the brutal war in the former Yugoslavia. The *religious war* account, exemplified by the Serbian textbook, contends that specifically religious divisions give the conflict in the former Yugoslavia a dimension not unlike the religious wars Europe has known all too well over the centuries. The *Veritas* article provides evidence to support the *ethnoreligious war* account of the conflict. According to this view, the conflict is about nationalism, not religion *per se*, but religion has contributed to the rise of nationalist conflicts. The statement of the religious leaders reflects the *manipulation of religion* account of the war. This explanation acknowledges that religious fears and symbols have been manipulated and abused by cynical ultranationalists for their own ends, but downplays the role of religious differences or religious nationalism in fomenting conflict.

Clearly, there is a religious dimension to the conflict in the former Yugoslavia. National and ethnic divisions correspond closely to differences in religious identity. Serbians have traditionally been Orthodox, Croatians Catholic, and, in Bosnia, Muslim is both a religious and national identity. The hundreds of churches and mosques that have been intentionally destroyed, the ubiquitous appeals to religion in official propaganda, and the use of religious symbols in torture are just some of the ways the conflict has been defined according to a complex relationship between national and religious identity.

Nevertheless, the religious leaders are essentially correct in downplaying the religious dimension of this war. "It cannot be overemphasized," concludes Reverend Peter Kuzmič, president of the Protestant-Evangelical Council of Croatia and Bosnia, "that the genesis of the war was ideological and territorial, not ethnic and religious."[5] The conflict erupted out of the failure of the Yugoslav idea, a failure in which cultural, political, economic, and other factors were far more prominent than religious ones. Yugoslavia dissolved in 1991 into a war over competing and mostly incompatible claims of self-determination. None of the six nationalities of the federation was satisfied with the seventy years of the Yugoslav experiment.[6] The Serbs felt that a more united Yugoslavia

---

[4]Serbian Orthodox Patriarch Pavle, Vinko Puljić, Roman Catholic Archbishop of Sarajevo, Jakub Sclimovski, *Reis ul-Ulema* of Bosnia, Rabbi Arthur Schneier, Appeal of Conscience president, "Appeal for Peace in Bosnia and Herzegovina," Zurich, November 26, 1992.

[5]Peter Kuzmič, "On the Way to Peace in the Balkans," *The Christian Century*, vol. 113, no. 6 (February 21, 1996), p. 201.

[6]Christopher Cviic, *Remaking the Balkans* (New York: Council on Foreign Relations Press, 1991), p. 63.

would end years of discriminatory treatment and give them the power and economic well-being commensurate with their numbers; fearing Serb domination, most of the other nationalities wanted a more decentralized Yugoslavia. After Tito's death, his fragile efforts to balance these competing views of Yugoslavia gave way to a process of economic and political decentralization and disintegration. Serious economic decline coincided with a growing political incompatibility after 1989 between the nascent democratic and nationalist movements in Croatia, Slovenia, Bosnia, and Macedonia and hard-line communist-turned-nationalist regimes in Serbia and Montenegro.

Unable to maintain a Serb-dominated, centralized Yugoslavia, Serb nationalists, backed by a Yugoslav army intent on maintaining its power, have fought for a more ethnically pure Greater Serbia that would incorporate (and, in their view, protect) most of the 30% of Serbs who live outside of Serbia. Slovenia, Croatia, Bosnia-Herzegovina, and Macedonia have sought independence, retaining the internal borders of the Yugoslav republics. Like their Serbian counterparts, some Croat nationalists in Croatia and Herzegovina have sought to unite the Croat-majority areas of Bosnia into a Greater Croatia.

These conflicting claims of self-determination would be difficult to resolve in any situation. The genocidal character of the Yugoslav conflict has been due to the rise of aggressive and chauvinistic nationalisms in the late 1980s, first in Serbia and then in Croatia and Bosnia. Ultranationalists, especially Serbian leaders, have used all manner of violence, intimidation, and propaganda to generate fear of other ethnic, national and religious groups and to destroy any prospects for resolving self-determination claims in non-violent ways that respect the multi-ethnic, multi-national, multi-religious realities of the region.

Of the three accounts of the religious dimension to this conflict, the religious war thesis is the least tenable because it exaggerates the role of religion at least as much as it underestimates the role of other factors, particularly extreme nationalism. The role of religion in the spiral of nationalist violence has been less direct than the ethnoreligious account suggests, yet less a victim of external forces than the manipulation of religion account describes. Religious nationalism has been a factor in this war, especially, though by no means exclusively, on the Serbian Orthodox side. Religious leaders have been mostly well-intentioned and justified in nourishing the historic links between religious and national identity and in defending their community's rights in the face of grave threats. In doing so, they have unwittingly reinforced, or at least undermined their ability to counter, the ultranationalists' project of religious and national chauvinism.

I will develop this argument, first, by examining the claim that this is a cultural-religious conflict. Next, I will consider to what extent religion has legitimized extreme nationalism and violence. Finally, I will look at the prospects for the religious bodies to play a reconciling role after the Dayton Accords.

Religion, Culture Wars, and "Ancient Hatreds"

The religious conflict account of the war in the former Yugoslavia implicates religion in fomenting "ancient hatreds." According to this view, the Yugoslav conflict is merely the most recent in a long history of conflict between three major cultures, which are distinguished primarily by religion. "The conflict is about religion, not ethnicity," Henry Kissinger argues, "since all the groups are of the same ethnic stock [Slavs]."[7] Samuel Huntington also sees religion as a central factor in a clash of cultures in the Balkans.[8] He contends that the Eastern boundary of Western Christianity in 1500 today represents "the Velvet Curtain of culture" that has replaced "the Iron Curtain of ideology" as the most significant dividing line in Europe, a line which has erupted into conflict in Yugoslavia.[9] In Yugoslavia, differences in religion and culture have led to violent conflicts over policy, territory and populations, conflicts which are exacerbated by what he calls, "civilizational rallying."[10] Western Europe, particularly Germany and the Vatican, rallied around their co-religionists, pushing for recognition of Croatia and Slovenia as independent states, muting criticism of Croat efforts to partition Bosnia, and arming Croatia. Russian politicians and the Russian Orthodox Church supported Serbia. And Bosnia became a *cause celebre* for Islamic governments and groups, especially fundamentalists.

Srdjan Vrcan, a sociologist of religion from Croatia, blames the dominant religions in the former Yugoslavia for presenting political, social and national conflicts "as centuries-long conflicts between essentially opposed human types, types of cultures and civilizations" which are virtually beyond mediation and compromise. Moreover, he argues, they have presented "the one side as quasi-immaculate and as the side of the Good as such, and [have] depict[ed] the other in demonical or satanic terms as the incarnation of Evil as such."[11] The result

---

[7]Henry Kissinger, "Bosnia: Reasons for Care," *Washington Post*, December 10, 1995, p. C9.

[8]Samuel Huntington, "If Not Civilization, What?" *Foreign Affairs* 72:5 (November/December 1993), p. 192; Samuel P. Huntington, "The Clash of Civilizations?" *Foreign Affairs* 72:3 (Summer 1993), p. 29.

[9]"The Clash of Civilizations?" pp. 30-31.

[10]Huntington, "The Clash of Civilizations?" p. 29.

[11]Srdjan Vrcan, "Religion and Churches and the Post-Yugoslav War," in J. Coleman and M. Tomka, eds, *Religion and Nationalism* (Maryknoll, N.Y.: Orbis Books, 1995), pp. 63 64.

is an identification of the state not only with a particular nation but also with a particular culture, a politicization of culture that breeds conflict and war.

The contention of Huntington and Vrcan and others that cultural-religious factors define and exacerbate the conflict mixes partial truths with questionable analysis. It is true that Yugoslavia's rise and fall is the story of an attempt, ultimately unsuccessful, to bridge the religious-cultural fault lines which run through the Balkans: between Eastern and Western Christianity; between Latin and Byzantine cultures; between the remnants of the Hapsburg and Ottoman empires; and between Christian Europe and Islamic Asia.

The religious leaders in the region are keenly aware of this cultural-religious chasm. Each, in their own way, feels they are at the frontier, protecting their respective religious and cultural traditions from threats from their two cultural neighbors.[12] The Catholic Bishops, for example, argued in early 1991 that the democratic changes in Croatia and Slovenia were threatened by an alliance between communists and Great Serbia nationalists (including "several of the leading personalities of the Serbian Orthodox Church"), both of whom "are strongly opposed to western cultural tradition [and] democratic aspirations."[13] In 1996 in Bosnia-Herzegovina, Catholic leaders have become increasingly concerned about the Islamicization of the Bosnian government during the course of the war.[14] While church leaders have rejected propaganda about the need to defend Christian Europe from Islam and have supported a united, multi-ethnic Bosnia, Reverend Ante Marić, a Catholic priest in a village near Mostar, is not alone among Croatian Catholics in saying: "The Muslims have a holy war with us. We cannot accept the Dayton agreement."[15]

Bosnian Muslims, though highly-secularized, have also focused on the cultural divide, claiming that the failure of the international community to intervene on their behalf or lift the arms embargo against them is due to Christian Europe's ancient antipathy toward Islam and fear of a politically-significant Muslim community in the heart of Europe. This fear of Islam has been exploited by Croat and Serb nationalists to justify aggressive campaigns of "ethnic cleansing."

---

[12]Vrcan, "Religion and Churches and the Post-Yugoslav War," p. 65.

[13]Letter from the Croatian Bishops to their Brother Bishops throughout the World, "Our Church and Our Nation," reprinted in *Catholic International* 2:16 (Sept. 1-30, 1991), p. 762.

[14]Cardinal Vinko Puljić, "Thoughts for the Assembly of the Representatives of the Council of Europe," Strasbourg, February 13, 1996. Available at the U.S. Catholic Conference, Washington, D.C.

[15]Mike O'Connor, "Bosnian Croats Resist Peace Accord," *New York Times*, February 13, 1996, p. A8.

The link between religious-cultural differences and conflict is most evident among Serbian Orthodox leaders, who are acutely aware of the historic division between Eastern and Western Christianity. Vatican support for Croatian independence and for international sanctions against Serbia, alleged forced conversions of Serbian Orthodox during the war, and alleged support by the Catholic Church for the *Ustashe* during World War II are perceived as recent manifestations of a centuries-long effort by the Vatican to reconvert the Orthodox. The ancient confrontation with Islam also looms large in Serbian Orthodoxy. The Serbian Orthodox Church gave strong support for Serbian President Slobodan Milošević's harsh policies toward mostly Muslim Kosovo in order to reclaim this region, long-considered Serbian Orthodoxy's Jerusalem. Orthodox leaders have also joined Serb political leaders in arguing that war was necessary to prevent the establishment of an Islamic state in Bosnia.

Religious and cultural factors clearly are present in the war. But the explanatory value of these factors is limited. First, the religious dimension of these cultural conflicts is often exaggerated. Despite deep differences, religious leaders themselves do not define the conflict in religious terms. Not only are most of the main political and military leaders not motivated by religion, but the general population exhibits a relatively low level of religious affiliation, especially in the case of Bosnian Muslims and Serbs.[16] Religious practice has increased in recent years with the end of communism and the use of religion as part of the ethnomobilization strategy of Slobodan Milošević, Franjo Tudjman, Alija Izetbegović and other politicians.[17] But many people identify themselves as Muslim, Orthodox, and Catholic even though they do not profess or practice any religion. Yet, given the insane logic of ethnic cleansing, their life might depend on whether they are Muslim atheists, Orthodox atheists, or Catholic atheists. At this point, religious identity has lost its religious meaning; religion has been reduced to little more than an artifact, another way of describing cultural, ethnic or national differences. As Mojzes rightly concludes, "insofar as this is a 'religious' war, it is being fought largely by irreligious people who wear religion as a distinguishing badge but do not know what the badge stands for."[18]

A second problem with the religious-cultural roots of war thesis is that religious leaders have not uniformly or unequivocally supported notions of the

---

[16]In Bosnia, for example, 53% of Croats were religious, 34% of Muslims, and only 21% of Serbs. In Serbia, only 26% of Serbs were religious. In Yugoslavia as a whole, 57% of young people declared themselves irreligious. Lenard Cohen, "Bosnia's 'Tribal Gods': The Role of Religion in Nationalist Politics," in chapter 4.

[17]Cohen, pp. 14-15.

[18]Mojzes, *Yugoslavian Inferno*, p. 170.

unity of culture, nation and state, as Vrcan suggests. Bosnia is the prime example of this. Many Muslim and Catholic (and some Serbian Orthodox) leaders have rejected the ultranationalist's vision of culturally-homogenous societies, insisting instead that the future of their distinct cultural, religious and ethnic identities depends upon the success of a multi-cultural, multi-religious, multi-ethnic state in Bosnia. The increasing threat of a partition of Bosnia into ethnically-homogenous areas is evidence mostly of the success of extreme nationalists in using violence to kill any hopes of realizing a pluralist vision. Bosnia is not the paradigmatic case of a clash of civilizations, but of a clash between different kinds of nationalism. Religious and cultural differences have vastly complicated their efforts to counter the extremists in their midst, but religion and culture are less the cause of the conflict than its victim.

Finally, an excessive focus on religious and cultural differences tends to obscure other factors -- political, economic, and military. The roots of the war are better understood if one looks at the role of the Yugoslav military in seeking to maintain its power, the inherent difficulties involved in sorting out incompatible claims of self-determination after the collapse of the Yugoslav state, and especially the rise of extreme nationalisms, incited by former communists who sought a new ground of legitimacy. The war's barbarity and intractability have been due less to ancient civilizational hatreds than to the fears intentionally induced by warlords and criminals, the logic of extreme nationalisms, which thrive by inciting religious and cultural conflict, and the hatred and vengeance that feed on and intensify cycles of violence.

Religion, Nationalism and Human Rights

If there is a religious dimension to the conflict, it is found more in the integral link between religion and national identity than in religious-cultural differences. Paul Mojzes acknowledges that the war in the former Yugoslavia is primarily "ethno-national," not religious. But there is an "ethno-religious" dimension because leaders of each religious community have provided "enthusiastic and uncritical support of rising nationalism among their peoples."[19] Religious leaders have contributed to ethnic separatism and national chauvinism by encouraging ethnically-based politics, by sanctioning and sanctifying wars of national self-determination, and by showing little concern for the human rights and fears of other ethnic and religious groups.

In evaluating the extent to which the actions of the three major religious communities reflect this ethno-religious account of the war, several distinctions should be kept in mind. First, religious cultivation of cultural and national

---

[19]P. Mojzes, *Yugoslavian Inferno*, pp. 128, 126.

identity and religious support for national self-determination are not, in themselves, evidence of religious nationalism. They become so only when religion justifies chauvinistic forms of nationalism or illegitimate claims of self-determination. Jean Bethke Elshtain distinguishes between ethno-cultural nationalism, which tends to be insular, aggressive and intolerant, and civic nationalism, which is more open, democratic, and pluralistic. The former Yugoslavia, she believes, is a prime example of the former kind of nationalism: "a ruthless granulation of political entities in the name of a principle of the unimpeachable singularity of national, linguistic, cultural, even racial identities coupled with the dangers of 'mixing' any group with the other."[20]

The link between religion and national identity in the Balkans places religion on the side of some form of ethnocultural nationalism, but this kind of nationalism is not as uniformly chauvinistic and aggressive as Elshtain and Mojzes suggest. In the Balkans as elsewhere, there are strong and weak forms of ethnocultural nationalism, as well as hybrids of ethnocultural and civic nationalism. Few nations fit easily into one of Elshtain's two types. Weak forms of ethnocultural or ethnoreligious nationalism are not necessarily problematic; it is the strong, chauvinistic forms which rightly give one pause.

Similarly, some claims of self-determination in the former Yugoslavia are more legitimate than others. Whether religious support for independence or secession has contributed to the conflict in the former Yugoslavia depends upon the validity of the underlying claim. Maintaining Yugoslavia was not necessarily a preferred or a viable option by 1991. Support for an independent Croatia within its current borders is not necessarily as legitimate as support for a Greater Croatia.

Just as there is a difference between positive and negative forms of nationalism and legitimate and illegitimate claims of self-determination, so also there is a difference between legitimate and illegitimate approaches to defending the rights of one's own community. Religious leaders should not be faulted for boldly speaking out against "ethnic cleansing" of their people, for giving pastoral priority to serving the needs of their own community, and for reiterating traditional principles about the right and duty of self-defense. It is when this legitimate concern for the defense of the rights of one's own community is manipulated by ultranationalists or becomes exclusivist that religious leaders exacerbate conflicts.

The major religious bodies in the former Yugoslavia have been neither monolithic nor undifferentiated in their approaches to nationalism, self-

---

[20]Jean Bethke Elshtain, "Identity, Sovereignty, and Self-Determination," in G. Powers, D. Christiansen, R. Hennemeyer, *Peacemaking: Moral and Policy Challenges for a New World* (Washington, D.C.: U.S. Catholic Conference, 1994), p. 100.

determination, human rights, and the use of force. Postive and negative, legitimate and illegitimate actions have been evident in each religious community, though not to the same extent.

The Catholic Church

Croatian cultural and national identity is closely identified with Catholicism. In terms of effectiveness as a national symbol, the Catholic Church in Croatia ranks next to Poland.[21] In modern times, two strands of Croatian nationalism developed within Catholicism. Archbishop Josip Strossmayer (1815-1905) personified the Illyrian movement, the integrative strand, because of his support for union between Croatia and Serbia and between Serbian Orthodoxy and Croatian Catholicism.

The clearly dominant tradition in recent decades, however, has emphasized church support for the restoration of an independent Croatia that is religiously and culturally Catholic and Western.[22] This tradition was summarized in an account by the Catholic Press Agency in Zagreb of an interview with Cardinal Kuharić: "'The Church among the Croats has always represented the rights of the Croatian nation, like those of every other ethnic nation, to freedom and 'the guarantee of freedom for every ethnic nation is the state,' said Cardinal Kuharić."[23]

This linkage between religion, ethnicity, and national identity has led some to conclude that the Catholic Church bears considerable responsibility for the conflict.[24] Paul Mojzes points to several ways that the church has contributed to the rise of nationalism. It supported, especially in 1990-91, the nationalism of Tudjman's Croatian Democratic Union.[25] In Bosnia, the church supported the establishment of ethnic political parties, specifically the Croatian Democratic

---

[21]Peter F. Sugar, "The Historical Role of Religious Institutions in Eastern Europe and their Place in the Communist State," Pedro Ramet, ed., *Religion and Nationalism*, p. 52.

[22]P. Ramet, "Religion and Nationalism in Yugoslavia," in Ramet, ed., *Religion and Nationalism*, pp. 299, 305-308.

[23]Catholic Press Agency--Zagreb, account of interview with Catholic weekly, *Glas Concila*, January 3, 1996.

[24]See, e.g., Mojzes, *Yugoslavian Inferno*, pp. 129-135; Cohen, "Bosnia's 'Tribal Gods': The Role of Religion in Nationalist Politics," pp. 62-68.

[25]Studies of the first multi-party election in Croatia in 1990 support the thesis that national identity and religion, which were strongly linked, were the basic determinants for electoral orientation. Committed religious believers were far more likely to vote for the HDZ and far more likely to support Croatian autonomy. See I. Siber, "The Impact of Nationalism, Values, and Ideological Orientation in Multi-Party Elections in Croatia," in J. Seroka & V. Pavlović, eds. *The Tragedy of Yugoslavia: The Failure of Democratic Transformation* (Armonk, N.Y.: M.E. Sharpe, 1992), pp. 149-150.

Union (HDZ), which contributed to the political divisions that led to war there.[26] Moreover, the church embraced Slovenian, Croatian and Bosnian independence, without adequately taking into account the fears of Serb minorities in Croatia and Bosnia.

From the church's perspective, ethnic parties were the best hope to end communist rule in Croatia and Bosnia.[27] After fifty years of an antagonistic relationship with a Yugoslav government that regularly (and falsely) accused the church of clerical-fascism and clerical-nationalism, it was not surprising that the church would welcome an independent Croatian government that respected religious liberty and sought close relations with the church. Since then, the need to maintain national unity in a time of crisis, and the task of rebuilding society after communism and forging a newly-independent nation, have led to a certain amount of practical cooperation between church and state. Nevertheless, the church has made a conscious effort to free herself from the image of being too closely tied to the state, and has been increasingly critical of efforts of the Tudjman government and various other political parties to claim church sanction.[28] Reiterating the Pope's warnings, during his visit to Zagreb in September 1994, about idolizing the nation or the state, Cardinal Kuharić said recently, "If all those in authority had listened to him [the Pope], each in his place, ... we would have a far better reputation in the world, a clear conscience, and clean hands. As it is we have only demeaned ourselves."[29]

The church's position on self-determination derived from similar concerns. Its support for Croatian independence in 1991 had much to do with the church's experience under a Serbian-dominated Kingdom of Yugoslavia between the wars, followed by Tito's communist-dominated Yugoslavia in the post-war period. In its concrete manifestation, the Yugoslav idea connotes for the Church neither respect for Croatian cultural and national identity nor respect for democracy and basic human rights. Catholic leaders point especially to the persecution and intolerance of religion, symbolized by Cardinal Stepinac's imprisonment in 1946 after a show trial, as proof of the fundamental inadequacy of the Yugoslav experiment. By 1990, the militant nationalism and hard-line communism of the Serbian government under President Slobodan Milošević, the

---

[26]Mojzes, *Yugoslavian Inferno*, pp. 131-133.

[27]Živko Kustić, editor-in-chief, Catholic Press Agency -- Zagreb, quoted in "Church Keeps Distance of [sic] the Political Parties in Croatia," Catholic Press Agency -- Zagreb, October 25, 1995.

[28]Ilija Živković, "Religious Communities and Religious Freedom in Croatia," presentation at the Conference of Slavic Studies Annual Meeting, Washington, D.C., October 25-28, 1995.

[29]Account of interview with Cardinal Franjo Kuharić in the Catholic weekly, *Glas Concila*, Catholic Press Agency -- Zagreb, January 3, 1996.

continued power of Yugoslav communists in the military, and the revival of anti-Catholic propaganda in Serbia convinced the church that in Croatia and Slovenia the restoration of religious freedom, national identity, and integration with Western Europe promised by the transition to democracy in their republics were at risk.[30]   Given these concerns, a church historically identified with Croatian national identity "accepted and recognized," as a legitimate "expression of the will of the people," the May 1991 referendum and parliamentary vote in favor of exercising Croatia's constitutional right to secede from Yugoslavia.[31]

The Vatican's justification for its much-criticized decision, in January 1992, to recognize Croatia and Slovenia reflects how the war changed the moral and political calculus of secession. Even after the declaration of independence in June 1991, the Catholic bishops of Yugoslavia and the Vatican presumed that integrating the new independent republics with what remained of the Yugoslav constitutional system should be done through dialogue and negotiation. The Vatican considered it both politically possible and morally appropriate to maintain some form of confederation. But the intensity and brutality of what was considered an aggressive and unjust war against Croatia convinced the Vatican that negotiation of a new relationship between the Yugoslav republics was impossible short of full independence.   Consequently, by October 1991, the Vatican sought an international consensus in favor of *conditional* recognition of Croatia and Slovenia (and later Bosnia-Herzegovina and Macedonia). Among other things, conditional recognition was intended to respect the right of self-determination and the territorial integrity of the republics, to ensure respect for minorities, and to encourage the parties to abide by a cease-fire and permit a more lasting settlement to the conflict.[32]

The Vatican was one of the first states to recognize Bosnia-Herzegovina. Throughout the war, both the Vatican and the Catholic bishops in Bosnia-

---

[30]"Our Church and Our Nation: Letter from the Croatian Bishops to their Brother Bishops throughout the World," reprinted in *Catholic International*, Vol. 2, No. 16 (September 1991), pp. 760-762.

[31]Statement of the Bishops of Yugoslavia, June 27, 1991, reprinted in *Catholic International* Vol. 2, No. 16 (September 1991), p. 763. The Vatican especially emphasized this constitutional right to secede, see Vatican communique, "Holy See's Position on Yugoslav States," reprinted in *L'Osservatore Romano*, weekly english edition, 1-8 January 1992, p.2.

[32]"Holy See's Position on Yugoslav States," L'Oservatore Romano, English weekly edition, 1-8 January 1992, p. 2; "Vatican Sets Conditions for Recognizing Croatia and Slovenia," Catholic News Service, 20 December 1991, pp. 28-29; Letters of John Paul II to the Bishops of Croatia, October 10, 1991, and to Serbian Orthodox Patriarch Pavle, October 11, 1991, reprinted in *L'Osservatore Romano*, English weekly edition, 27 October 1991, pp. 1, 3; Cardinal Franjo Kuharić, Address to U.S. Bishops General Meeting, Washington, D.C., November 11, 1991, reprinted in *Origins* Vol. 21, No. 24 (November 21, 1991), pp. 381-83.

Herzegovina and Croatia have supported a united, multi-ethnic Bosnia and have opposed proposals to partition Bosnia along ethnic and religious lines. Cardinal Kuharić and Cardinal Puljić strongly condemned the extremism and violence of the Bosnian Croats during the Croat-Muslim fighting in 1993 and efforts to create a Greater Croatia. The church's position has placed it at odds with the Tudjman government and the Bosnian Croat leadership in Herzegovina, both of which have publicly denounced the church's position as unpatriotic and against the interests of Croatians.[33]

The church supported the establishment of the Croat-Muslim Federation in 1994 as a way to resolve the Croat-Muslim fighting. It has also supported the Dayton Agreement, as a potential step toward a lasting peace. Reflecting their commitment to a united Bosnia, Cardinal Puljić of Sarajevo and other church leaders have criticized aspects of the Dayton agreement, however, because they fear it will lead to the partition of Bosnia, given its ratification of "ethnic cleansing," its lack of adequate federal structures, and the unlikelihood that its provisions regarding the right of return, democratic elections, and other civilian matters will be implemented.[34]

Given the church's support for an independent Bosnia, Croatia, and Slovenia, it reiterated traditional Catholic teaching about the right and duty of these new states to defend themselves, respecting the laws of war, against aggression.[35] While some Catholic leaders have spoken of a sacred duty to defend the nation, Church support for the use of force in self-defense has been relatively restrained. Even during the worst of the ethnic cleansing in Bosnia, the bishops did not embrace lifting the arms embargo against Bosnia and Croatia for fear of widening and escalating the conflict. Rather, with Pope John Paul II, they appealed for "humanitarian intervention" by the international community "to disarm the aggressor" and begin a process of demilitarizing the region.[36]

---

[33]Paul Mojzes claims that Catholic leaders supported a united Bosnia only to protect Croat Catholics outside of Herzegovina, proof of a lack of concern for non-Croat Catholics. Mojzes, *Yugoslavian Inferno*, p. 135. For a detailed and, I think, more accurate analysis of the Catholic Church's strong support of a united, multi-ethnic Bosnia that does not assume cynical motives, see Branka Magas, "Croat Catholics Divided," *The Tablet*, July 17, 1993, p. 908.

[34]Cardinal Vinko Puljić, "Thoughts for the Assembly of the Representatives of the Council of Europe," Strasbourg, February 13, 1996. Available at the U.S. Catholic Conference, Washington,D.C.

[35]See, e.g., Croatian Catholic Bishops, "Urgent Appeal from the Bishops of Croatia," Zagreb, July 30, 1991.

[36]John Paul II, Address to the International Conference on Nutrition, *Origins* 22:28 (December 24, 1992): p. 475; Address to the Diplomatic Corps, January 16, 1993, *Origins* 22:34 (February 4, 1993): 587. Cardinal Vinko Puljić, Archbishop of Sarajevo, Address at

The church's reaction to Croatia's resort to force in August 1995 to retake the Serb-held Krajina area of Croatia typifies the ambiguity many religious leaders face in responding to violence and human rights abuses. Church leaders expressed joy and relief at what they saw as the liberation of a large part of Croatia, an area from which all Croats had been "cleansed" in 1991. In responding to reports of human rights abuses they did not want to give credence to Serbian allegations that they were being "ethnically cleansed" from the area, when Serb leaders themselves had orchestrated the exodus. They also gave the benefit-of-the-doubt to their government's claimed commitment to protect Serb rights. At the time of the military operation, the Church leaders urged Serbs to stay in Croatia and urged Croats to protect their rights. Once the extent of Croat abuses became clear, the church condemned them as "immoral" and a "stain" on the wider community.[37]

Overall, while the Catholic Church in the former Yugoslavia has shown some characteristics of Mojzes' ethno-religious nationalism, this description of its role in the current conflict is too undifferentiated. The church in Croatia embraces a weak form of ethno-nationalism which sees the "church among the Croats" as nurturing and protecting the spiritual values, historical memory, and culture of the Croatian people, but the church does not advocate a form of religious nationalism that equates national identity with adherence to the Catholic faith, and it has been outspoken in opposing efforts to create ethnically-homogenous societies.[38] The church's support for independence was motivated partly by ethnic nationalism, but moreso by legitimate concerns for democracy and human rights, especially religious liberty. The Vatican's recognition of Croatia and Slovenia was defensive in nature, a reaction to an already failed Yugoslavia and a destructive war in Croatia, not a cause of Yugoslavia's dissolution or the resulting conflict in Bosnia, which was inevitable given the failure of Yugoslavia. Catholic leaders justified the use of force in defending against Serb aggression and in appealing in particular to the international community to stop the slaughter of civilians in Bosnia. While these appeals represented a legitimate application of traditional just war principles, they were

---

the Center for Strategic and International Studies, March 30, 1995, quoted in Catholic News Service, April 3, 1995, p. 7.

[37]"Message from the Bishops of the Republic of Croatia," Catholic Press Agency (IKA) - - Zagreb, October 15, 1995; "Statement by the Croatian Commission on Justice and Peace," Catholic Press Agency (IKA) - Zagreb, September 12, 1995; "Catholic Agency Defends Croatian Church's Human Rights Record," Catholic News Service, March 15, 1996, p. 18.

[38]Pedro Ramet, "Religion and Nationalism in Yugoslavia," in P. Ramet, ed., in *Religion and Nationalism in Soviet and East European Politics* (Durham, N.C.: Duke University Press, 1989), p. 319, 322.

seen by the Serbian Orthodox as further proof of a Catholic campaign against them. The churches record on human rights was mixed. On the one hand, a consistent concern for human rigths was reflected in Cardinal Kuharić's frequent admonition: "If the opponent burns my house, I will guard his. If he demolishes my church, I will protect his. And if he kills my father, I will safeguard the life of his father."[39] On the other hand, church leaders were often preoccupied with their own community's suffering, and sometimes slow to condemn abuses by Croatian forces.

Bosnian Muslims

Bosnian Muslims are the only Muslims in the world officially designated as a national as well as religious group, yet, of the three main religious bodies in the Balkans, Bosnian Muslims have the least sense of national identity. Muslim was largely exclusively a religious or cultural identity until the 1960s, when the communist party began encouraging the idea of a Muslim ethnic group and, later, nationality. Designation of Muslims as a separate national group was designed to cut off the Muslims from Croatian Catholics and Serbian Orthodox, both of whom claimed that Bosnian Muslims were descendants of Catholics or Orthodox who converted during centuries of Turkish rule. The designation of Muslims as a nationality had the strong support of Muslim clerics, who claimed a role as communal leaders of their people, based on this link between religion and ethnicity.[40]

Nevertheless, most Bosnian Muslims remained highly secularized and largely supportive of the Yugoslav state. In a 1990 survey of adults in Yugoslavia, Bosnia had the highest percentage (29%) of any republic not declaring confessional orientation. A 1989 survey of children found that only 34% of Bosnian Muslims were religious believers. A 1991 survey found that more Bosnian Muslims (88%) valued their affinity with Yugoslavia than either Bosnia's Serbs (85%) or Bosnia's Croats (63%).[41]

Cohen argues that, largely in response to the mobilization of Serbian nationalists in Bosnia, Muslims (and Croats) became more nationalistic in the late 1980s. Pan-Islamic oriented clerics began mobilizing support for Muslims in Kosovo, which further hurt Muslim-Serb relations. The fact that distinct political parties, each linked to religious leadership, emerged to represent each of Bosnia's three main national communities further polarized the situation.

---

[39]Account of Interview with Cardinal Franjo Kuharic in the Catholic weekly, *Glas Concila*, Catholic Press Agency -- Zagreb, January 3, 1996.

[40]P. Ramet, "Religion and Nationalism in Yugoslavia," p. 323-25.

[41]Lenard J. Cohen, "Bosnia's 'Tribal Gods': the Role of Religion in Nationalist Politics," in chapter 4, pp. 45-46.

While most Bosnian Muslims were highly secularized, the founding members of the ruling Party of Democratic Action included most of the major representatives of the pan-Islamic current in the Islamic community in Bosnia. The party was headed by Alija Izetbegović, "a Muslim conservative," who Cohen argues, "if not accurately described as a religious fundamentalist, was definitely perceived by most members of the republic's other ethnoreligious communities as a religious nationalist and a man whose political mindset included devotion to Islamic principles."[42]

Izetbegović's *Islamic Declaration*, which offered a blueprint for an Islamic state in Bosnia once Muslims became a majority, has been the subject of considerable controversy. Many downplay the significance of a document written more than twenty years ago, interpreted by many to be a relatively benign attempt to link Islamic principles with a pluralistic modern state, and from which Izetbegović has since distanced himself. But the Declaration (and other actions of the Islamic leaders of the party) was perceived by many non-Muslims as proof of a latent Islamic fundamentalism.[43] Cohen concludes:

> The frequent observation by Western commentators that Bosnian Muslims have had a traditionally secular and European outlook, and have tended to 'wear their faith lightly,' is essentially correct. But those outside Bosnia often failed to recognize that, owing to the attitudes advanced by most nationalist and many religious leaders within the Muslim community during the 1980s and 1990s, and also in view of the modern history of Bosnia, most non-Muslims did not take the political aspirations of the Islamic faithful quite so lightly.[44]

Concerns about the actual intentions of Izetbegović and other Muslim leaders have increased during the war as Muslim religious leaders have become more radicalized and Bosnian politics have become more Islamicized, both developments largely a reaction to the inadequate international response to the plight of the Muslims. As in Croatia and the Serb Republics of Bosnia and Krajina, religion has been introduced into the schools. Religious indoctrination also has been introduced into the military. The appearance of several thousand Iranian, Afghan, and other foreign Islamic troops in Bosnia and Muslim units within the Bosnian army, such as the Black Swans and the 7th Muslim Brigade, exemplify this trend.[45] Mustafa Cerić, the *rais ul ulema* of Bosnia, has promoted bans on the sale of pork and mixed marriages. Izetbegović obtained a temporary amendment to the Bosnian constitution guaranteeing a Muslim

---

[42]Cohen, p. 58; Mojzes, *Yugoslavian Inferno*, p. 142.

[43]Cohen, p. 59.

[44]Cohen, p. 61.

[45]Editorial, "Islam a growing force in Bosnia military," *The Christian Century*, vol. 112, no. 29 (October 18, 1995), p. 955.

successor in the event of his death, and Muslims are increasingly favored in the distribution of jobs both within and outside the government.[46] These developments have led an aide to Cardinal Puljić to conclude that "Sarajevo is considered a Muslim canton, and the authorities act as such."[47]

The Bosnian Muslims largely share the Catholic view of the war as a legitimate defense against Serbian aggression. Even more than Catholic leaders, they have been committed to a united, multi-ethnic Bosnia, though the commitment to pluralism has waned under the pressures of the war. Also like their Catholic counterparts, Muslim leaders have appealed for international intervention to stop genocide, but they have been much stronger than the Catholics in condemning the arms embargo as immoral.[48] As the situation in Bosnia grew more desperate, some Muslims began to speak in terms of a *jihad*, which combined with the increasing visibility and power of specifically Islamic military units within the Bosnian military has contributed to a sense of holy war.[49]

The Muslim role in the emergence of nationalism is distinguishable from that of Catholic and Serbian Orthodox leaders in two important respects. First, while most Serb and Croat nationalist politicians are former communists who had no special commitment, if any, to religion, the Bosnian president and many leaders of the dominant party in Bosnia are strongly motivated by a version of political Islam. Second, whereas Catholicism and Serbian Orthodoxy long have been closely identified with their respective nations, the Islamicization of Bosnia has largely been a product of a war in which Muslims were targeted solely because of their identity. If Croatian and Serb fears of an Islamic state in Bosnia become a reality, it will be mostly a self-fulfilling prophecy.

Serbian Orthodox Church

Historically, the Serbian Orthodox Church has been the most uncritically nationalistic religious body in Yugoslavia, promoting a strong form of ethno-religious nationalism.[50] It sees itself as a defender of Orthodoxy at the frontier of Islam's assault on Europe and Roman Catholicism's assault on Eastern Orthodoxy. Like other Orthodox churches, it also considers itself to be the

---

[46]Cohen, pp. 42-45.

[47]Catholic News Service, March 21, 1996, p. 4.

[48]Meeting with Mustafa Cerić, U.S. Catholic Conference, October 1994.

[49]David Steele, "Former Yugoslavia: Religion as a Fount of Ethnic Hostility or an Agent of Reconciliation," *Religion in Eastern Europe*, vol. 14, no. 2 (October 1994), p. 16.

[50]Pedro Ramet, "The Interplay of Religious Policy and Nationalities Policy in the Soviet Union and Eastern Europe," in P. Ramet, ed., *Religion and Nationalism in Soviet and East European Politics* (Durham: Duke University Press, 1989), p. 23.

principal defender of authentic national identity. While Serbian Orthodox ecclesiology envisions a symphonic relationship of close cooperation between church and state, it is not a state church, but a national church.

The church's nationalist vision is rooted in two related concerns. First, the church defines the Serbian nation as a natural entity, an organic body that cannot survive and flourish if it is divided or if it is separated from its religious, specifically Orthodox, roots. There is a strong sense that one who is not Orthodox is not Serb, and that all Serbian Orthodox should live in the same state.[51] Second, the church shares with many Serbs a deep sense of insecurity growing out of a history of victimization: victimization by Turks during the Ottoman Empire, by Tito's communism in the post-War period, and especially, by the Ustashe during World War II. This sense of victimization has been an overriding factor in the church's response to the Yugoslav crisis.

Given its traditionally strong ethno-religious nationalism, the Serbian Orthodox Church, especially younger religiously--and politically--conservative clerics, was predisposed to look favorably on the rise of Serbian nationalism in the late 1980s, though it was neither the cause of this rise, nor did it embrace all its forms or proponents. The new Serbian nationalism seemed to offer freedom from a Titoist Yugoslavia that had suppressed and manipulated the church and had discriminated against Serbs. Of special concern were Serbian minorities in Albanian Muslim-dominated Kosovo (10-15%), in Croatia (12%) and in Bosnia (32%).[52] By 1990, the Serbian Orthodox Church was claiming that Serbs in both Kosovo and Croatia were suffering or threatened by genocide. In the case of Kosovo (and later Bosnia), the challenge was defined, in part, as defense against Islam; in Croatia, as defense against Catholicism and the rise of an allegedly neo-fascist state under President Franjo Tudjman.

The Serbian Orthodox perspectives on the nature of the Yugoslav conflict and self-determination, therefore, are diametrically opposed to that of Catholic and Muslim leaders. The war is not, as the Catholics and Muslims claim, an aggressive attempt to preserve Yugoslavia or to create a Greater Serbia. It is "an interethnic civil war" started by those intent on destroying Yugoslavia, which, despite its communist failings, had given the Serbian nation its state unity for the first time. Self-determination, according to the Orthodox Bishops, means allowing Serbs who have lived for centuries in Croatia and Bosnia to choose the state in which they will live. While Catholic and Muslim leaders consider the internal borders of the former Yugoslavia as historic and inviolable

---

[51]Gerald Shenk (with David Steele), "God With Us? The Roles of Religion and Conflicts in the Former Yugoslavia" (Uppsala: Life and Peace Institute, 1993), pp. 37-38.

[52]Cohen, "Bosnia's 'Tribal Gods': The Role of Religion in Nationalist Politics," pp. 54-55.

borders of their new states, the Orthodox dismiss them as merely "administrative," "imposed by a group of Marxist revolutionaries in the Second World War and by the post-war totalitarian communist system." "That is why," the bishops argue, "we cannot but understand why our people are unable to accept the forcefully imposed dissection of their living national organism or the unjust partition of territory."[53] In short, the Serbian Orthodox Bishops would have preferred maintaining a reformed Yugoslavia in which Serbians were given their rightful status; failing that, they believe the creation of a Greater Serbia is a legitimate expression of the right of self-determination, and is necessary to protect the rights of Serbian minorities in Croatia and Bosnia and to preserve the natural unity of the Serb nation.

This perspective on self-determination would be more credible if it were not tied to a strong, chauvinistic version of ethnic-religious nationalism. The exclusivist character of this religious nationalism is evident in a letter Serbian Orthodox Patriarch Pavle wrote to Lord Carrington during the war in Croatia in 1991:

> It is time it was understood that the victims of genocide and their previous and perhaps future executioners cannot live together any longer. After the Second World War nobody forced the Jews to live with the Germans in the same state. The Serbs, however, were forced to live with the Croats.[54]

This conviction that Serbs are threatened with genocide if they remain as minorities in Croatia or Bosnia (or Kosovo) combined with the belief in the organic unity of the Serb nation has led Orthodox leaders to cooperate with ultranationalist politicians in encouraging Serbs to flee areas not under Serb control. Unlike many of their Catholic and Muslim counterparts who stayed in Serb-held areas until they were forced out by "ethnic cleansing," most Orthodox bishops and priests fled areas under Croatian and Bosnian control early in the war. In August 1994, the Orthodox Bishop of Knin joined local military and political leaders in encouraging Serbs to flee Croatia en masse in advance of a Croatian military move to retake the Krajina. Bishop Hrizostom represented a minority view among Orthodox Bishops when he sharply rebuked Bosnian Serb leaders for encouraging Serbs to flee the Sarajevo suburbs before they were turned over to the control of the Muslim-Croat Federation in February 1995.

The Orthodox commitment to a Greater Serbia in which the Orthodox Church would have a central role has led to a close relationship between

---

[53]Message of the Holy Assembly of Bishops of the Serbian Orthodox Church from the extraordinary session in Banja Luka, November 1-4, 1994, reprinted in *The Path of Orthodoxy*, vol. 29, no. 12 (December 1994), pp. 1, 8.

[54]Patriarch Pavle, letter to Lord Carrington, quoted in van Dartel, "The Nations and the Churches in Yugoslavia," p. 284.

Orthodox leaders and ultranationalist politicians. Much has been made of the Serbian Orthodox Church's unusual and courageous show of resistance to state authority in moving from tacit support of the nationalist Milošević regime to open hostility, including leading massive demonstrations in 1992 that called for Milošević to step down in favor of a new government of national unity. But while the church has opposed the man most responsible for the rise of Serb nationalism, it has supported other, equally or more aggressive nationalist leaders, such as Radovan Karadžić.[55] Church leaders believe that the political leaders of the Bosnian and Croatian Serbs are more committed to the church's central role in the Serbian nation. The Serb Republic in Bosnia permits religious education in state schools, for example, and Karadžić has effectively appealed to the integral link between Serbian Orthodox and Serbian national destiny:

> We have a firm belief that we are on [the] right path of God and that this folk [Serbs and Russians] will pay their debt to Serbdom and Orthodoxy; our deaths, suffering, and endurance we accept as God's grace, that he gave us the gift of destiny to accomplish this and, if God permits, that we save Serbia and Montenegro from devastation.[56]

Karadžić and other ultranationalists also are more committed than Milošević to maintaining the essential unity of the Serb nation. The Serbian Orthodox Church strongly opposed Milošević's acquiescence in the international community's demands that Serbia end support for the Bosnian Serbs and give up the idea of a Greater Serbia. Significantly, the Synod declared as invalid Patriarch Pavle's witnessing to the August 29 agreement between Milošević and the Bosnian Serb leaders which gave Milošević authority to negotiate at Dayton on behalf of the Bosnian Serbs. Many bishops have called for the Patriarch's resignation because he failed to oppose the Dayton Agreement, which the

---

[55]An exception is Bishop Hrizostom, from northwest Bosnia, who criticized Bosnian Serbs' leaders in Pale for "cheating you when they tell you that they have solved our problems by giving us burnt and looted homes which belong to others, who are refugees just as we are.... The Serb politicians have used our trust against the interests of their people." Patrick Moore, Internet, quoting *Onasa*, February 21, 1996, which cited *Večernje Novosti*, Belgrade.

[56]"Vaskrsenje sčučurene duše: Razgovor s gospodinom Radovanom Karadžićem," *Svetigora*, vol. 4, nos. 35/36 (March 1995), p. 15; quoted in P. Mojzes, "The Religiosity of Radovan Karadžić," *Religion in Eastern Europe*, vol. 15, no. 4 (August 1995), p. 20. Karadžić claims that "Communism was used by non-Serbian peoples to keep the Serbs in subordination, while elsewhere the national and religious programs of the Roman Catholic Church and Islam were being promoted." *Ibid.*, p. 18.

Orthodox Assembly sees as an unmitigated defeat for Serbs because it forces Serbs to give up the idea of a Greater Serbia.[57]

The Serbian Orthodox have been most severely criticized (Swiss and German Protestants have sought their suspension from the World Council of Churches) for giving moral and religious legitimacy to, or at least remaining silent in the face of, Serb aggression and ethnic cleansing. Like Catholic and Muslim leaders, the mainstream leadership of the Serbian Orthodox Church, while strongly supporting Serb self-determination, insisted that, if Yugoslavia was to dissolve, it should do so by agreement and without violence.[58] Also like other religious leaders, since the outbreak of war they have defended the right and duty of their people to protect themselves and their homeland from what they considered "ethnic cleansing" and genocide against Serbs in Bosnia and Croatia. Some Serbian Orthodox statements have distinguished between legitimate self-defense and "wars of conquest,"[59] and there have been many general denunciations and a few specific condemnations of "ethnic cleansing."[60] But Orthodox leaders have supported Karadžić, dismissing his indictment for war crimes as simply another example of the bias of the international community.[61] Also, amidst widespread "ethnic cleansing" and a brutal siege of Sarajevo, they issued strong appeals for Serbs to defend themselves and their nation, while remaining silent about the crimes that were being committed in the name of this "defense." In July 1994, for example, they declared:

> With full responsibility before God and before our People and human history, we
> call the entire Serbian Nation to stand up in defense of their centuries-long rights

---

[57]Statement from the Special Session of the Holy Assembly of Bishops of the Serbian Orthodox Church, December 22, 1995, reprinted in *The Path of Orthodoxy* vol. 31, no. 1 (January 1996), p. 12.

[58]Cohen, "Bosnia's 'Tribal Gods': The Role of Religion in Nationalist Politics," p. 22.

[59]Patriarch Pavle, letter to Jakub Effendi Selimoski, head of the Islamic community in Bosnia, *Pravoslavlje*, May 1, 1992, p. 2; statement of Holy Assembly of Bishops, *Novosti*, November 8, 1991, p. 7, both quoted in Gordon Bardos, "The Serbian Church against Milošević," *RFE/RL Research Report*, vol. 1, no. 31 (31 July 1992), p.11.

[60]In May 1995, Patriarch Pavle condemned the killing of two Catholic priests, a nun, and an elderly couple, and the destruction of several Catholic churches in Banja Luka."Statement of the Holy Synod of Bishops," May 18, 1995, reprinted in *Religion in Eastern Europe*, vol. 15, no. 4 (August, 1995), p. 40.

[61]Other unhelpful acts included: Orthodox priests officiating at the very public wedding of Željko Ražnjatović (Arkan), one of the most notorious Serbian warlords, and Patriarch Pavle visiting Bosnian Serb troops besieging Goražde in the Spring of 1994. Jonathan Luxmoore, "When War Crimes Are Patriotic," *National Catholic Register*, March 12, 1995, p. 4.

and liberties, of their vital interests, necessary for physical and spiritual survival and right to remain in the land of their fathers and grandfathers.[62]

The inability of key Serbian Orthodox leaders to acknowledge the extremism of Karadžić and other Bosnian Serb leaders and the validity of most allegations of "ethnic cleansing" and human rights abuses is due in part to ubiquitous Serb propaganda and intimidation, but moreso to a deep mistrust of the international community and an abiding sense of siege. This mistrust and siege mentality were evident in an August 1995 statement:

> Our crucified Church sees that Her crucified people are threatened from within by the spiritual and moral consequences of fifty years of ideological atheism, and from without by the interests of heartless world political powers, with their inhuman sanctions, pressures, threats, slandering and even direct bombings of innocent Serbian people.[63]

This siege mentality has combined with a vision of a spiritually--and politically--strong and united Serbian nation to produce a strong version of ethnic-religious nationalism, which has played a mostly negative role in the current war. This is not to say that the church bears a significant responsibility for the rise of aggressive Serbian nationalism, for intellectuals, journalists and politicians have been far more influential. Yet secular nationalists sought and received support for their ultranationalism in Serbian Orthodoxy and have manipulated, with great effect, religious symbols and fears. The church has contributed to the war, therefore, not in creating aggressive and chauvinistic Serb nationalism but in validating its claims of national rights and myths of victimization, and giving it theological and religious legitimacy.[64]

Religious Legitimation of Nationalism

One conclusion we can draw from these brief descriptions of the actions of the three religious communities is that, to the extent they have had a role in the conflict, it has been in supporting and legitimating various kinds of nationalism. With the exception of some key Catholic leaders in Herzegovina, the Catholic Church has supported a weak form of ethnic-nationalism that is qualified by one important element of civic nationalism: support for a multi-ethnic, multi-religious state in Croatia and Bosnia. Many, if not most, ordinary Muslims and key Bosnian political figures, especially early in the war, have held to a vision of a secularized, multi-ethnic Bosnia, but Muslim religious leaders and Izetbegović's party have increasingly embraced a weak form of an Islamic state. Many Serbian Orthodox leaders, more than their Catholic and Muslim

---

[62]Serbian Orthodox Assembly, July 5, 1994.

[63]Message of the Holy Assembly of Bishops, Belgrade, August 17, 1995.

[64]van Dartel, "Nations and Churches in Yugoslavia," p. 283.

counterparts, have embraced a strong form of ethnic-religious nationalism in which a multi-ethnic, multi-religious state is seen as a threat to national and religious identity, except where Serbs and Orthodox are dominant.

For most nationalist politicians, nationalism has provided new scapegoats to fill a void left by the demise of communism.[65] But for religious leaders, nationalism is much more compelling than merely a reaction to the demise of communism; it has been a means to bring that about and to advance legitimate national, cultural and religious rights that were suppressed under communism. One reason religious groups supported ethnic political parties is that there were few viable non-communist alternatives in the immediate aftermath of the demise of the Yugoslav communist party. Even if alternatives had been available, the religious leaders would not have embraced political parties that promoted a highly secularized state and society in which religion was marginalized or privatized.

The religious dimension to the conflict has been exacerbated by the diametrically opposed views of the Orthodox, on the one hand, and the Catholics and Muslims, on the other, of the causes of the conflict and the meaning of self-determination. I believe that the Muslim and Croat understanding of the conflict and their claims of self-determination (excluding the Croat vision of a Greater Croatia) are more valid. Given that, by 1991, Yugoslavia had ceased to exist as a functioning state, in large part due to the rise of Serb nationalism, Catholic and Muslim support for an independent Slovenia, Croatia and Bosnia were reactions to, not the cause of, the descent of Yugoslavia into nationalist conflict. The links between religion and national identity were not the cause of the Yugoslav conflict, it was the almost inevitable destabilizing effect of these historic links once the federal government had lost its legitimacy.[66]

Where religious leaders have failed the most during this war is in not condemning, in unambiguous and clear terms, violence and human rights abuses committed by their own people. Religious leaders on all sides have provided excruciating details about the suffering of their own people, while paying relatively little attention to the harms inflicted by their own national group,

---

[65]Huntington, "The Clash of Civilizations?" pp. 38-39; E.J. Hobsbawm, *Nations and Nationalism Since 1780: Programme, Myth, Reality* (2d ed.) (Cambridge: Cambridge University Press, 1992), p. 174.

[66]Cf. P. Ramet, "The Interplay of Religious Policy and Nationalities Policy in the Soviet Union and Eastern Europe," Ramet, ed., *Religion and Nationalism in Soviet and East European Politics*, p. 41: "Multiethnic societies are not *necessarily* unstable; illegitimate regimes in multiethnic states *are*, because the illegitimacy of their rule reinforces the natural desire of peoples to live apart from those of other languages, religions, and cultures."

offering instead general condemnations of human rights violations by all sides and sometimes even categorical denials of well-documented atrocities.[67]

This failure to be a strong and consistent witness for human rights reflects an understandable pastoral priority given one's own flock, especially when confronted with threats to the very survival of one's religious community. It takes extraordinary courage during a genocidal conflict to criticize your defenders for abusing the rights of those from the community you believe threatens your own existence. Religious leaders in the former Yugoslavia also have felt that the world has ignored or been indifferent to the dramatic suffering of their people and that criticism of human rights abuses would further deflect attention from this suffering and play into the hands of the aggressors. The ubiquitous war propaganda spewed out by government-controlled media in each country and sometimes unsubstantiated allegations by international organizations and human rights groups led religious leaders, like many others in these countries, to disbelieve accusations of atrocities and to give their own governments the benefit of the doubt. The tendency of some church leaders to "rally around the flag" and to become enmeshed in the politics of atrocities, grossly exaggerating claims of genocide and other abuses, has further exacerbated the situation.[68] Fear and intimidation have also been factors. In most parts of the region, speaking out against violence and human rights abuses takes great courage. A Serbian Orthodox Bishop living in Banja Luka or a Catholic priest in Mostar put themselves at risk if they are too outspoken about "ethnic cleansing" by Serb or Croat warlords.

It would be inappropriate to adopt a false evenhandedness that aportions blame equally for the relative silence of religious leaders about specific acts of violence and war crimes. All sides in the war have committed gross abuses, but Serb forces have been responsible for the brunt of the "ethnic cleansing." Therefore, the Serbian Orthodox Church bears the heaviest responsibility for its

---

[67]For example, the Serbian Orthodox Bishops denied that there was a systematic campaign of rape in Bosnia (Communique of Holy Assembly of Bishops, December 8-10, 1992) and Cardinal Kuharić initially said he was unaware of any violence against civilians after the Croatian army retook Western Slavonia (Catholic News Service, May 8, 1995, p. 31).

[68]See, e.g., Serbian Orthodox charges that the Catholic Bishops had ignored the destruction of 340 Orthodox churches and monasteries during the war, the plight of Serbian refugees, the destruction of Serb villages, and other acts in Croatia and Bosnia that they claimed amounted to a new "genocide" against the Serbs. "Communique of Holy Synod," December 26, 1994. In response, Cardinal Kuharić, in turn, criticized the Serbian Orthodox Bishops for their silence in the face of Serb "ethnic cleansing" in Banja Luka and the siege of Sarajevo, and he questioned the validity of the claims regarding the destruction of Serb churches and villages. J. Luxmoore, "In Balkan war of words, churches turn up volume," *National Catholic Register*, February 5, 1995, p. 1.

failure to clearly speak out. To the extent that all three religious bodies have not shown a consistent and unequivocal commitment to human rights and a consistent opposition to violence, they have missed an important opportunity to mitigate the hatred and transcend the deep divide among their respective communities.

III. Religious Bridge Building and Reconciliation

Throughout the war, there have been innumerable initiatives designed to help the three religious communities play a peacemaking role in the Balkans. These expectations and initiatives have multiplied after the Dayton Agreement. They arise precisely because of the link between national and religious identity, and the respect and influence that some religious leaders enjoy. They are also based on an assumption that reconciliation after the past five years of bloodletting will require more than restoring tolerance, law and justice -- as important as these are.

In *An Ethic for Enemies*, Donald Shriver argues that what is needed in these situations is a political equivalent of the religious notion of forgiveness. In politics, forgiveness requires a four-step process of (1) moral judgment about past injustices, (2) forbearance from revenge, (3) empathy for the enemy, and (4) a commitment to repair broken social relationships. "Such a combination," he posits,

> calls for a collective turning from the past that neither ignores past evil nor excuses it, that neither overlooks justice nor reduces justice to revenge, that insists on the humanity of enemies even in their commission of dehumanizing deeds, and that values the justice that restores political community above the justice that destroys it.[69]

That the Balkans could use such a process to escape its cycle of violence and atrocities seems indisputable. The pain, the hatred, the fear, the mistrust, the vengefulness, the loss of a sense of solidarity with those of other communities are palpable. Religious leaders have not been as prominent as they should have been in moving forward the process Shriver outlines, but all religious leaders, and many courageous individuals have insisted on the urgent need for and a vision of forgiveness and reconciliation between religious, ethnic, and national groups--against overwhelming ideologies that insisted, at the point of a gun, that such a vision was impossible, unpatriotic, and even unnatural.

Perhaps the most visible symbol of this commitment to reconciliation were the series of high-profile meetings and statements by Serbian Orthodox, Roman

---

[69]Donald Shriver, *An Ethic for Enemies: Forgiveness in Politics* (New York: Oxford University Press, 1995), pp. 6, 9.

Catholic, and Muslim religious leaders before and during the war.[70] These wartime initiatives did not bear fruit, in part because of the deep differences between the three religious communities. Despite these differences, religious leaders seem to agree on the need for renewing genuine dialogue and for reconciliation between the religious bodies and between the three communities. In October, 1995, the Pope convened all the bishops of the former Yugoslavia in Rome to discuss the church's pastoral role in post-war reconstruction. Of the ten commitments for pastoral action coming out of the meeting, eight dealt solely or entirely with opposing "excessive nationalism," promoting interfaith and intercommunal reconciliation, and ensuring that church programs served people of all faiths and ethnic groups; the other two dealt with prayer and rebuilding churches.[71] Even in opposing the Dayton Accords, the Serbian Orthodox Assembly reiterated its previous pleas for healing: "[W]e call our people to mutual reconciliation and repentance, and to reconciliation with the peoples with whom we have lived together for centuries and with whom we will live in the future."[72]

The role of religion in catalyzing a process of reconciliation will have to overcome several challenges. There is not a recent history of deep interfaith collaboration. Despite their geographical proximity, interfaith relations in the former Yugoslavia have never been very close. The Serbian Orthodox Church has historically been extremely wary of Catholic ecumenical initiatives, which they see as a continuation of a centuries-long effort to extend its jurisdiction over the Balkans at the expense of Serbian Orthodoxy. Catholic enthusiasm for ecumenical dialogue has been limited as well, in part due to the opposition of the Orthodox and in part due to an image, strengthened by recent events, of a "Byzantine" church that is a servant of the state and antidemocratic.[73]

---

[70]Major statements and meetings of or including interfaith leaders from the Balkans included: "The Abyss of War," August 24, 1991, in *Origins* Vol. 21, No. 15 (September 19, 1991), pp, 235-236; Meeting of joint Serbian Orthodox-Catholic commission on dialogue, St. Gallen, Switzerland, January 21-23, 1992; "Message of Patriarch Pavle and Cardinal Kuharić," Geneva, September 23, 1992, reprinted in *Religion in Eastern Europe*, vol. 12, no. 5 (October 1992), p. 50; "Appeal for Peace in Bosnia and Herzegovina," Zurich, November 26, 1992; "The Bosphorus Declaration," Turkey, February 9, 1994; "The Sarajevo Declaration," May 17, 1994; "The Vienna Declaration," March 30, 1995; "Ecumenical Conference on Christian Faith and Human Enmity," Kecskemét, Hungary, August 21-27, 1995, statement and press release reprinted in *Religion in Eastern Europe*, vol. 15, no. 5 (October 1995), pp. 31ff; "An Appeal of Conscience," *Washington Post*, November 1, 1995, p. A3.

[71]"Communique: Pastoral Action After a Long War," October 17, 1995, reprinted in *Origins* vol. 25, no. 21 (November 9, 1995), p. 368.

[72]Special Session of Serbian Orthodox Assembly, December 22, 1995.

[73]Geert van Dartel, "The Nations and the Churches in Yugoslavia," *Religion, State and Society*, vol. 20, nos. 3 & 4 (1992), pp. 276-277.

What interfaith relations existed have been virtually destroyed by the war, especially those between the Serbian Orthodox, on the one hand, and the Catholics and Muslims, on the other. The gulf between the religious groups on the causes of and solutions to the conflict will be difficult to overcome. The religious communities each feel that the other bears a heavy burden for its actions or inactions in response to this and past conflicts, and each believes that future cooperation depends on a process of repentance. The senior Muslim leader in Bosnia-Herzegovina, Mustafa Cerić, has refused to meet with Serbian Orthodox leaders until they repent for failing to oppose genocide against Muslims. Catholic Church leaders feel similarly about the Serbian Orthodox support for aggression against Croatia and Bosnia and for their encouraging Croatian Serbs to leave Croatia in August 1995. The Serbian Orthodox concerns were evident in their opposition to a proposed visit of Pope John Paul II to Belgrade in September 1994. They cited the Catholic Church's role in the *Ustashe* genocide, the Vatican's contribution to the demise of Yugoslavia by recognizing Croatia and Slovenia, and the Pope's support for international intervention to "disarm the aggressor" in Bosnia. The Catholic Archishop of Belgrade recently suggested that a long period of time is needed before this and similar issues can be publicly discussed and condemned because up until now any condemnation would have been taken as an admission of guilt that justified revenge, thus making matters worse not better.[74] Other religious leaders have taken a similar position on public acts of repentance, noting the fear that such acts would be misused to impose collective guilt on the whole religion or nation. They insist that a way must be found to undertake an objective analysis of the multiple conflicts and injustices perpetrated over the decades and centuries as part of any move toward reconciliation. Several initiatives that are bringing local religious leaders together to promote interfaith dialogue, reconciliation, and cooperation could contribute to this process.[75]

The reconciliation process outlined by Shriver must begin now, but it will take many years to complete. In the short term, religion will play a constructive

---

[74]C. Wooden, "Croatian Bishops Propose Nation-Rebuilding Guidelines," Catholic News Service, October 17, 1995, p. 15. That a reexamination of the Church's relationship to the *Ustashe* is underway is evident from a recent conference, addressed by Cardinal Kuharić and other church and political leaders, as well as theologians. While highlighting the positive resistance to the *Ustashe* by Cardinal Stepinac and the church, many speakers concluded that the church was too closed in on itself and thus did not adequately support the resistance to it and other totalitarian regimes during the Twentieth Century. Catholic Press Agency -- Zagreb, November 25, 1995.

[75]A notable example is the Project on Religion and Conflict Resolution of the Center for Strategic and International Studies in Washington, which has been convening local interfaith groups in the Balkans since 1993.

role in more immediate and practical ways. Throughout the war, many religious leaders have insisted that the average people, freed from war hysteria, violence, and intimidation, would return to living together in peace in a multi-ethnic, multi-religious society. The appeals by these leaders for people to stay in or return to their homes, even if they will be a minority, is a direct challenge to nationalist politicians (and some religious leaders) who are encouraging voluntary "ethnic cleansing." If there is to be any possibility of healing the wounds of war and rebuilding a multi-ethnic, multi-religious society, refugees must be able to return to their homes and resume a normal existence. Interfaith cooperation will likely be most fruitful in this practical task of rebuilding.[76]

The most important work of healing will come, not just or even mainly through interfaith reconciliation, however necessary that is, but from within the religious bodies themselves. Religious institutions, from schools to independent media, will play an important part in building a civic society that had only begun to emerge at the time the war broke out. More important, healing traumatized individuals and communities poses a daunting pastoral challenge, which economic and political reconstruction, even if successful, will leave unaddressed, but which religious bodies are uniquely suited to address.

Conclusion

The war in the former Yugoslavia confirms one of Douglas Johnston's conclusions about religious conflicts in *Religion: The Missing Dimension of Statecraft*: namely that, "[t]he political, economic, and security dimensions of most social confrontations usually outweigh the religious, even when the conflict is superficially about religion."[77] The war also confirms a tendency to overestimate what religion and religious leaders can do to prevent or mitigate these conflicts, especially when they involve the kind and scale of political extremism and violence found in this conflict. Religion is too readily dismissed as part of the problem in the former Yugoslavia, because religious identity is, at least on the surface, a distinguishing characteristic of the opposing sides, and because the link between religious and national identity is often described in exclusively negative terms and as a source of conflict.

---

[76]The Pope has committed some of the proceeds from his best-selling book, *Crossing the Threshold of Hope*, to rebuild churches, including Orthodox churches and mosques. C. Wooden, "Church Leaders Hold Peace Council as Balkan Cease-Fire Continues," Catholic News Service, October 23, 1995, p. 14.

[77]Johnston, "Review of the Findings," in Douglas Johnston & Cynthia Sampson, eds, *Religion: The Missing Dimension of Statecraft (New York: Oxford University Press, 1994)*, p. 263.

Religion has contributed to the conflict, but mostly indirectly. Weak and marginalized at the time of the collapse of Yugoslav communism, religion has been susceptible to manipulation by communists-turned-nationalists who harbor mostly disdain for things religious, but cynically enlist religion in the cause of their virulent nationalisms. Unfortunately, there have been ready recruits among all three religious groups, most notably among Serbian Orthodox leaders, Croatian Catholics in Herzegovina, and the ruling Muslim-dominated Party of Democratic Action in Bosnia-Herzegovina. The majority of religious leaders, however, have not subscribed to this religious nationalism, yet their legitimate cultivation of national identity and defense of communal rights has sometimes exacerbated divisions, especially among religious groups, played into the hands of the political extremists, and diverted them from finding ways to bridge the ethnic-nationalist chasms in the Balkans. Nevertheless, many religious figures have taken positive, even heroic, steps to minimize the conflict and have remained lonely voices for moderation and tolerance amidst the extremism that surrounds them.[78]

It would be tempting to seek a solution to this and similar conflicts in decoupling religion and national identity, secularizing society, and replacing communal commitments with a more individualistic ethic. The better and more realistic approach would be to find within the rich cultural and religious traditions of the Balkans the moral norms and basic beliefs that are consistent with and reinforce a vision of society in which religious, ethnic and national differences are less a source of conflict than a reason for coexistence. The best way to counter religious extremism or manipulation of religion is with strengthened, more authentic religion, not weakened religion. The challenge for religious leaders in the Balkans is to show that religion can be a counter to extreme nationalism and a source of peace because of, not in spite of, its close link with culture and national identity.

---

[78]Catholic Bishop Franjo Komarica of Banja Luka, who urged nonviolence in the face of ethnic cleansing and lived under house arrest for eight months rather than succumb to Serb pressures to abandon his diocese, is one of these heroes. See Diane Paul, "A cry for human rights in a 'cleansed' Banja Luka," *The Christian Century,* vol. 112, no. 27 (September 27-October 4, 1995), p. 898.

16

CONFLICT RESOLUTION AMONG RELIGIOUS PEOPLE IN BOSNIA AND CROATIA

David A. Steele

On May 19, 1993, the bodies of a Serb man and a Muslim woman lay in a no-man's-land between the warring sides in Sarajevo. Boško and Admira had been promised safe passage by both sides, but the promise of a future was cut short by sniper's fire. Their attempt to escape the ravages of war had failed. But as their bodies lay in an embrace for almost a week while each side fought for possession, they became a symbol of tolerance and togetherness.[1] Their love could not overcome all the obstacles of the moment, but perhaps it could point the way to a reconciled future.

How does one begin to walk the difficult road to reconciliation when the tragedy of the past four years in Bosnia and Herzegovina has far surpassed the woes of Job? A complete answer to this question is certainly very complex. What follows in this chapter are some guidelines to help begin the process of building reconciliation and creating a climate for constructive resolution of conflict. They have been developed from my own experience of the past few years in leading conflict resolution training seminars for religious people in Bosnia and Croatia.

The purpose of these seminars has not been to end the war. Instead, they have been designed to encourage middle level and grass-roots religious leadership to work together to overcome the stranglehold of ethnic division on both the individual and collective spirit. The aim is to encourage the development of a critical mass of support for peacebuilding by rebuilding community and developing constructive ways of handling grievances and

---

[1]Slavenka Drakulić, *The Balkan Express: Fragments from the Other Side of War* (New York: W.W. Norton & Company, 1993), 151-56.

differences. Without such efforts to heal the wounds of war and prepare for a collaborative future, no peace proposal stands a chance of lasting success.

Based on my own experience, as well as that of many courageous Muslims, Croats, and Serbs from the former Yugoslavia, I suggest five guidelines to use in pursuit of true reconciliation and constructive conflict resolution: (1) Expression and acknowledgement of grievance; (2) Clarification of perception; (3) Acceptance of basic needs and concerns; (4) Encouragement of self-critical honesty; and (5) Creation of alternative approaches for resolving particular disputes. These guidelines are explored in the order listed since there is a logical progression to the various points. In actual practice, however, the process will inevitably not be a linear one and may well include steps not mentioned here. In no way can this list be said to be exhaustive. It is suggestive of the kind of interactive process which I have found feasible and useful in situations of deep-seated conflict.

Expression and Acknowledgment of Grievance

First, it is important to acknowledge all suffering and the resulting grievances, even though it may seem divisive to give too much credence to complaints. When human beings, or whole societies, have been traumatized, they must know that their hurts are taken seriously by others. This requires one to listen carefully to, and identify with, the suffering of all--the Muslim refugee who has lost 94 members of his extended family, the Serb refugee who witnessed the killing of his children in front of his eyes, the Croat who escaped from Serb-controlled detention into a society on the brink of Muslim-Croat fighting, the priest or *imam* who no longer has any congregation because of ethnic cleansing and genocide, the residents of Sarajevo (of all ethnic groups) who suffered through years of siege and who have seen loved ones killed at funerals, in food lines, and while playing in the snow. To be in solidarity with all sufferers does not mean that all suffering is equal. Nor does it mean that all groups are equally guilty. Such things are hardly ever equal. Furthermore, it does not mean accepting all the diagnoses, conclusions, perceptions, strategies, or positions of the sufferer. It does not entail agreeing with all the means by which the sufferer proposes that his or her hurts be redressed. Instead, it involves giving sensitive, compassionate attention to legitimate emotions of grief, anger, and fear.

Such an engaged presence requires active listening as well as guidance through the stages of grief. The primary modus operandi is story telling, coupled with brief interpretive information that can help the sufferer move to the next step of healing or assist others to more fully understand. This requires the creation of a "safe space," a place where one feels secure enough to share deep pain and to explore the redemptive possibilities in its wake.

At a seminar in Bizovac, Croatia, in February 1995, a Croatian Baptist pastor shared his experience of being stabbed by Serbian troops. The anger was still visible in his voice as he showed us the scars on his body. Yet, we also heard the testimony of faith in God that he gave to his attackers on that horrible day. It was not hard to believe that they did not know what to make of his strength of spirit.[2] His story was followed by that of a Serbian Orthodox priest who told of being shot three times by Croatian troops, once in the head. Again, the story was coupled with faith as this man of God later gave assurance of his forgiveness to one of the soldiers and invited him to turn to God. When asked what enabled him to respond with faith in the midst of such pain, he simply referred to his training in tranquility in an Orthodox monastery.[3] At a seminar in Visoko, Bosnia, in October 1995, a Croatian laywoman told of being held prisoner, along with her two children, in a Croatian concentration camp where she was subjected to torture and used as a human shield. Yet, she spoke of her faith providing the support by which she was able to keep fear from controlling her. Though she was determined to tell the world of the horror she had witnessed and experienced, she also stressed the need to forgive.[4] In each seminar, the acceptance of these people and their stories helped create an atmosphere of trust and hope that enabled others to then share their grief and pain.

Clarification of Perception

Conflict always involves some degree of misunderstanding. Perceptual problems may account for a large or a small part of the total problem, but they always exist. In some cases, it is the situation itself that is misperceived.

The problem of unfounded rumor abounds in situations of conflict, especially when communication has been severed. I have encountered many partial truths that have been distorted beyond recognition by the other side who have little chance to verify the things they hear. One person hears that his former friend is now fighting on the other side when in reality the friend has deserted the enemy army for moral reasons. Another person reads that a church or mosque has been destroyed by the opposing army when in fact it was the

---

[2]Božidar Karlović, pastor of Baptist Church in Pakrac, Croatia, as told during seminar in Bizovac, Croatia, February 6, 1995.

[3]Andjelko Sajlović, Orthodox priest in Kučanci, Croatia, as told during seminar in Bizovac, Croatia, February 6, 1995.

[4]Jagoda Basalić, Catholic laywoman from Zenica, Bosnia, as told during seminar in Visoko, Bosnia, October 10, 1995.

shells fired by one's own army that damaged the building. Someone hears that all the residents of a particular village have been either ethnically cleansed or killed when, in fact, it is a different area that has suffered this tragedy.

When it is difficult for anyone to go to the other side to hear or see what is actually happening, it is at least important to recognize that one's source of information is one-sided. I find myself frequently asking people for their source of information and pointing out that it comes only from their own side of the conflict. In December 1993, while attending an "Ecumenical and Inter-religious Round-table on the Former Yugoslavia" sponsored by the Conference of European Churches in Pecs, Hungary, it was refreshing to see religious leaders from all sides of the conflict recognizing the severity of this problem. During the round-table, a commitment was made by several representatives that the churches and other religious communities should take the lead in rebuilding broken communication links. It was proposed that a joint information center be established through which inter-faith teams could together investigate the veracity of disputed claims. This kind of honest cooperative effort is needed to rectify the problem of rumors.

A second type of perceptual problem involves misunderstanding of the intentions or meanings behind another party's words or actions. For example, intentions are frequently misunderstood when one people insist on distinguishing their language from that of another ethnic group. This kind of misperception tends to evoke very strong reactions because it is experienced as a threat to group identity on both sides. Conflict over such issues often leads to stereotyping, prejudice, and bias. The challenge is to assist people to form a healthy group identity, one that recognizes but does not glorify one's own history, and one that does not delegitimize, demonize, or distort the image of another group. Such misunderstandings can even occur through an attempt on the part of one group to clarify its identity. For example, in the seminar in Visoko, the use of the term "*Boshniak*" to define group identity was hotly debated by a Muslim and a Croat participant. As the discussion progressed, it became clear that while Muslim fears of extinction were prompting a very inclusive use of the term, Croat fears of assimilation were forcing a rejection of it as a part of their identity. Mutual experience of victimization had, in fact, contributed to such a threatened sense of group identity that bias and misperception were the inevitable result.

One exercise I have used to address the problem of stereotyping is to ask the people in a mixed ethnic group to switch roles. The Serb is to take the part of a Muslim, the Muslim to take the part of a Croat, and the Croat to take the part of a Serb. They are then asked to represent their adopted persona in a presentation about conflict in the former Yugoslavia. During the ensuing role play, participants may share historical perspectives, specific incidents, or fears of future oppression, all of which have been formative in the perceptions of those they are representing. At one such round-table discussion in Vienna in May 1993, participants shared that the role play was beneficial even though they had no problem performing it.[5] The act of actually stepping into the other's shoes helps to make one's behavior, not just one's horizons, more inclusive.

Acceptance of Basic Needs and Concerns

There is a difference between the positions someone takes on an issue in dispute and his or her basic needs or concerns. While a group's demands may be questionable, it is always important to express solidarity with basic interests as well as any legitimate pursuit of them. The most basic concerns of any group involve essential human needs such as recognition, well-being, security, belonging, and control over one's life. Fear of the loss of these needs creates the kind of desperation which leads not only to intransigence, but sometimes violence. Therefore, it is of utmost importance to meet people at the point of their most basic concerns and to help persons in the midst of conflict to do so with one another. In the seminar in Visoko, we approached this through small discussion groups focused around four categories of fears: personal safety, social disintegration, economic collapse, and political manipulation. Mixed ethno-religious groups proceeded to identify a kaleidoscope of common fears and needs, a sharing which helped lay the foundation for later consideration of collaborative projects.

During a seminar in Sarajevo in April 1995, a small group of mixed ethnic background did an analysis of the needs and fears that underlay conflicts within the Muslim-Croat Federation. They not only identified fears and needs that characterize particular ethnic groups, but examined distinctions within each group. In this way, they were able to identify many needs and fears held in common by supposedly "incompatible groups." Discovery of such compatibility where it is not expected can create understanding and openness which builds relationships between adversaries and which, in turn, can lead to breakthroughs in the resolution of a dispute.

One example of the transformative power of such openness was demonstrated by an *imam* at the Sarajevo seminar. While living in Žepa at an earlier point in the war, he and his people had been literally starving. In the midst of such tragedy, he began to ask what could possibly bring healing to his

---

[5]David Steele, "Account and Evaluation of a Roundtable Discussion, 'The Role of Religion in the Conflicts in Serbia, Croatia, and Bosnia and Herzegovina," Appendix A in *God With Us? The Roles of Religion in Conflicts in the Former Yugoslavia* by Gerald Shenk, with contributions by David Steele (Uppsala: Life & Peace Institute, December 1993), 58-59.

people. He found himself, then, thinking about the Serbs surrounding the city and realized that they were afraid of the same thing--death! This realization made him examine the reasons for their survival anxiety. As he enumerated for us, in front of Serb participants, some of the historical reasons why Serbs might be afraid, the door was further opened for creative dialogue on the problems currently facing the ethnically mixed residents of Sarajevo.[6]

Encouragement of Self-Critical Honesty

Self-critical honesty requires looking at the past in its entirety. Such an inquiry must be made with the understanding that guilt is usually not one-sided. All sides share, even if unequally, some responsibility for what has happened. In the same way, God's grace is not limited to one side.

Confession and forgiveness are difficult to practice in situations of deep-seated conflict. Because group identity is often battered, one must approach these tasks carefully, ensuring that one is not admitting too much or too quickly, absolving another party of its responsibility. As one Bosnian Croat recently said to me, "We are swimming in blood here. How can we look at possible past misdeeds by Croatian people?" When the sins committed against one's people seem to far outweigh those committed by one's people, it is difficult to be the first to admit anything. Yet, recognition of one's own need for another's confession or forgiveness can sometimes help even very hurt people overcome their internal obstacles.

When making confession, it is important to be clear about what we are admitting. If our apology is for sins committed by others in our ethnic group, it is important to recognize the harm that has been done, but not to assume full responsibility for it with all the concomitant feelings of personal guilt. At the same time, acknowledgement of collective guilt may involve the individual in a thorough examination of his or her attitudes toward the "other" group. Such self-examination can, itself, be a catalyst for healing, but attitudes of exclusion should not be confused with actions which exclude (e.g. policies of ethnic cleansing). The latter warrants a tribunal while the former warrants sober reflection and the desire to change.

One powerful example of the healing power of confession and forgiveness took place in a seminar in Vienna in May 1993. Many of the participants came to see the way in which newly-awakened nationalism had drawn on religious symbols to reinforce its appeal to its own constituency. Of particular significance was the admission by a Serb that his government had propagated a policy resulting in much suffering. Recognition of these tendencies on the part

---

[6]Name withheld to protect the anonymity of the person.

of all groups led to warnings about the development of too close a relationship between any religious community and the state.[7]

Creation of Alternative Approaches

Once people have addressed many of the relational problems mentioned above, they are often ready to take a new look at the problems they face. Hopefully, this can be done in a cooperative fashion with people working together on the issues rather than against each other. At this stage in the process, it is helpful to encourage people to brainstorm ideas without regard to feasibility. Although the initial ideas may not be practical, their expression tends to stimulate creativity so that more realistic new ideas can emerge.

In each seminar I have conducted, such a brainstorming process has generated numerous potential future actions. For example, at the end of the seminar in Bizovac, a list of possible projects was enumerated which included developing an inter-faith newsletter, assisting in the resettlement of refugees, planning of ecumenical prayer services, assisting with a telephone support network for war trauma victims, organizing public meetings to promote inter-ethnic coexistence, influencing government officials to avoid war-making policies, establishing working relationships with religious communities in Vojvodina, Serbia, organizing inter-ethnic friendship camps or bus tours, developing an inter-faith program of religious education for the schools, and encouraging parishioners not to seek revenge. Six months after the seminar there was a small committee still functioning to implement some of the projects. Despite the renewal of war in the region, they had built a small inter-faith community of people. This group had been able to develop some of the more typically religious activities as well as work on refugee resettlement on an ecumenical level. They had let go of the more ambitious projects for the moment, but were still hoping to expand their work into more social service projects.

Conclusion

The possibilities for creative conflict resolution by indigenous people are limitless. There is much courage, openness, and hospitality among the people of Bosnia and Herzegovina. There are many who have the ability to acknowledge grievance, clarify perceptions, recognize basic needs, confess and forgive sins, and create new options for peacemaking. I close this chapter with

---

[7]Steele, "Account and Evaluation of a Roundtable Discussion, 'The Role of Religion in the Conflicts in Serbia, Croatia, and Bosnia and Herzegovina,'" 61-62.

one account of peacemaking in central Bosnia, a story which illustrates that just a few people can effect major change.

At the outbreak of fighting between Croats and Muslims in Central Bosnia, two Franciscan priests from Guča Gora decided to try to stop the fighting from spreading into their region. Despite threats to their lives, they walked through both Croatian and Muslim army lines in order to find the *imam* from the neighboring village. They proposed bringing together the two local Muslim and Croat commanders to see if they could prevent violence from erupting among these troops. Even though one of the Croats volunteered to remain in the Muslim village as a guarantee of good will, the *imam* insisted there should be no hostages. All three religious leaders then met with the two commanders at a cafe where they negotiated an agreement that the two armies would not fight. Although the region was later overrun by other troops, these commanders and their troops did not take part in the hostilities.[8] This small victory for peace may look insignificant in the light of the violence that ensued. Like the story of Boško and Admira, however, it can be a beacon of light and hope to those who believe that small deeds do count.

---

[8]Ivo Marković, Franciscan priest from Guča Gora, Bosnia, as told during seminar in Vienna, May 17, 1993.

17

REVENGE OF FORGIVENESS

Miroslav Kiš

Humans are tragic instances in the flow of history. This is a statement of fact, not a statement of truth. Christian truth about human nature revolts against the reduction of humans to the level of instance.

Guilt

Sitting comfortably in my hotel room, protected by my passport, my citizenship, by thousands of miles, I watch them. The long columns of them, the evicted, the "ethnically cleansed" ones as they roam the countryside. Uprooted from their homes, wrenched away from their doorstep, their dishes, their aprons, their cattle, they have become nobody. No identity, but a sense of becoming a surplus, a nuisance, a tragic instance. Just enough critical mass to wear a label of ethnicity or religion, but not enough of it for a price tag.

Then a close up view, and all my intentions to write an academic, dispassionate essay vanish. I stare into faces, into permanent wrinkles on a fourteen year old's expression of terror--a vague, foggy stare out of focus; faces tired of hunger, starving for rest. There is no way forward, no back, no left, no right. It's all the same. They are not lost, not misplaced, not homeless; they are obsolete, forgotten, leftovers.

They don't seem real. The only real thing is an echo of a gun and in an instant another instance is gone. Really gone. Just like that! Hopefully gone into some statistic. Hopefully, I say because hundreds and thousands of them lay in a mass, unaccounted for, a nameless mass. "They" just put a big invisible label of ethnicity or religion on them. Those who still walk in a daze carry within them, deep somewhere where the bullet cannot reach, huddled in a fetal position, their own tiny, human self in a coma.

Once upon a time these were all human beings. It was at the time of birth before they were labeled ethnically and religiously. Then, they were girls or boys, sons or daughters. Wrapped in swaddling clothes, nursed, baptized in love, they grew.

One day the adults took them somewhere important. Solemn and grave was the ceremony when they gave them a name: the religious and ethnic name giving them a sense of belonging. With time, most of them outgrew those names and became neighbors, friends, sweethearts, wives, and husbands. Marriages and friendships transcended ethnicity and religion, and so they lived happily . . . but not ever after.

But why? Who saddled this innocent population with such hatred and wounds of violence? They are not to blame, those who opted to transcend human labels. Neither is ethnicity *per se* nor religion, as such, at fault. It is most certainly the hybrid, sometimes called "ethnic religion," devised by "those" whose sense of belonging stalled at the national-nationalistic level, who turned religion into a private, exclusivist "club" to which you belong by birth or you become a tragic instance of human history. You either act as a bigot, or must be gone at once.

Identity

As maturation advances, the sense of self expands in depth and breadth. This development occurs in the context of a group formed of accepting and nurturing humans who adopt each member and define their role. Heidegger uses the expression "belonging together" for such a milieu.[1] The home and family is a natural locus where the sense of identity emerges from the shadows of merely being in time to the light of belonging. Here the basic needs and wishes build preferences which ultimately create a value system. Words compose a particular vocabulary for the communication of ideas and opinions, thus forming a concept of self and reality. What is funny may identify who is funny, what is good determines who is good, and what is important may decide who is important. When in a dilemma, the individual usually follows what the group (sense of "we") knows to be the best. To venture out on a limb is a risky option to one's very identity. In the past centuries, disowning a member of a clan proved to be a formidable punishment. You cannot fail to conform and expect to belong at the same time.

With a concept of self securely lodged, the individual can reach out into society. Church and school serve as the first step out. When the sense of belonging is strong, the individual will confront divergent ways of being and belonging with greater ease and adroitness. If the feeling of connectedness is weak, each discovery of alternative options creates a fear of dissolution of

---

[1]Martin Heidegger, *Being and Time* (New York: Harper and Row, 1962), 29-39.

weak, each discovery of alternative options creates a fear of dissolution of identity, the fear of oblivion. However, through an extended period of time spent in a nurturing environment of the home, church, or school; a new, richer and broader sense of belonging becomes apparent. The discovery that my way of seeing things is not the only way opens the vistas and new opportunities. The individual now yearns for larger spheres of belonging: ethnicity.

A more abundant, but still limited arsenal of cultural norms, now shepherd human behavior much like a script prescribes the words, moods, and actions of a player in the theater. National dishes, national heroes, national flags, and national teams inspire a feeling of national pride. Loyalty, allegiance, and patriotism are important positive virtues. Humans suffer in an amorphous and unstructured context. Affiliation with home, church, or ethnic values and identity is an essential ingredient of a healthy personality. It provides human life with a framework.

However, identification with a particular lifestyle creates distinction and partiality as well. I was 25 when for the first time outside of Yugoslavia my survival depended on French cuisine, which knew nothing of cabbage rolls and Ukrainian pyrogies. Only a conscious effort made me admit that Italian pizza actually tasted okay. "When in Rome do as the Romans do" is not an easy assignment, especially if Romans insist on it. Cultural or ethnic bias becomes arrogance and prejudice when the claim is made that Rome is wherever one Roman lives. A Roman may behave as in Rome at any place, but he should not insist that the non-Romans give up their uniqueness or freedom in order to create a Rome for him. There can be no absolute Rome, even in Rome itself, as soon as just one non-Roman enters the "Eternal City's" gate. In a modern cosmopolitan civilization and in an advanced Christian consciousness, absolute Rome can survive only as a fantasy in the Roman's mind.

Such a realization is not only possible, it is mandatory. Higher loyalties claim the Christian human identity. Not only because *cosmos* is our *polis*, but more importantly because *uranos* is the home for all humans. Eden is our port of origin, and there is our destiny. A patriotism which discovers "Our Father who art in heaven," cannot remain attached to ethnicity and nationality to the point of ethnocentrism and bigotry. A religion which worships and obeys the non-ethnic God of heaven is apt and able to transcend intolerance and hatred. Any other god is an idol, and any other religion is idolatry. The Bible insists that Yahweh is God, Lord of Israel (Exodus 6:7), but He is also the only God there is (Deuteronomy 6:4), and, therefore, the God of all nations (Acts 17:26, 27; Romans 15:9-12). His temple is the house of prayer for all people (Isaiah 56:7; Matthew 21:13).

The Hybrid

Sad and painful is the descent of humans into the realm of tragic instances of history. Such a descent is always coerced by violent and brutal events. History records many inhuman atrocities perpetrated by religious and ethnic wars. So Ottoman and Crusaders' exploits shattered the religious and ethnic identity of their victims with speed and ferocity. Whether forced Islamization or imposed Christianization, these fanatics carried out crimes against humanity in the name of serving a god. But God was not involved in those horrors. His methods to win the human race to Himself or to defend His truth stand in a sharp contrast to swords and guns. To all who reach for knives in defense of their religion, Jesus addressses a stern command, "Put your sword back into its place; for all who take the sword will perish by the sword" (Matthew 26:52). This means that the religion of Jesus has no need of bombs for its promotion because violence always initiates a vicious cycle of revenge. More importantly, a true religion has other, more superior methods at its disposal (Matthew 26:53; 28:18-20).

Consequences of Ottoman tyranny followed almost inevitably. The oppressed nations faced total annihilation on several fronts simultaneously. First, its oppressor took away religious freedom with implications that Allah triumphed over the Balkans and Islamization proceeded with torture, brainwashing, and killings. At the same time, the invaders forced their culture upon the conquered territories. Ethnicity also faced extinction. Just a casual look at the poetry and literature during the Ottoman domination will register the pain and horror as well as the bravery and heroism of the subjugated nations, who refused to give up their identity for a promise of peace. Where realistic victories could not be won, the imaginary, almost mythical bravery of legendary heroes, filled their hearts with pride. Clandestine oral or written epic poetry remained one of the few reliable sources of comfort through long centuries of savagery (recall the abduction of 12 to 16 year old boys for Draconian brainwashing and military training, the impailings, the rapes, the burning of villages).

The end of World War I in 1918 and the liberation of the Balkans from the Turks left deep-seated scars in the identity of the oppressed. For our purposes here, we will mention only a few.

First, a deep gulf divided the citizenry. On one side, there were those who caved in under the enormous pressure of Islamization and acculturation and, consequently, enjoyed relative prosperity during the centuries of occupation. The majority, though, endured the hardship and could not tolerate the traitors. When the Turks left for Asia Minor in 1918, these defectors remained behind and bore the brunt of revenge for decisions and actions made by their distant ancestors.

Second, a long-term threat by Ottoman oppression to both ethnicity and religion caused these two aspects of individual and corporate identity to become united. To be a Serb meant to be an Orthodox, but not just any Orthodox (Greek or Russian for example). It meant to be a Serbian Orthodox. A marriage with another Christian of a different tradition or with a Muslim brought an intolerable, double disgrace: apostasy, and treason. Self-defense, for many centuries, implied a defense of religion and ethnicity and created a very intense sensitivity to these matters. Reconciliation or tolerance appeared as tantamount to the loss of honor and identity. Revenge, not forgiveness, played the role of catharsis. Affirmation of the religious and ethnic singularities and traditions consumed the entire soul of the liberated peoples. Literature, music, dances, cultural events, and paintings paid tributes to unsung heroes and called heaven's curse on atrocities and injustices.

But history does not allow enough time to heal the wounds, to still the anger, in order to deal with memories which cripple the growth--at least not on the Balkan peninsula. Only twenty years later another nationalistic invasion engulfed the troubled region: World War II. New bloodshed added new wounds, and new betrayals deepened and widened the rift. The situation offered an easy victory to Communism. Discerning rightly the evils of nationalism, Communism claimed international credentials and sought to lift the consciousness of the masses toward the ideal of brotherhood and unity. In addition, it claimed to have evidences pointing to the fact that genocide and atrocities should be placed at the door of churches. These allegations unleashed and "justified" Communist natural aversion to religion and national religion in particular.

But good intentions cannot justify any means. The strong control and powerful propaganda did not deliver brotherhood and unity. Many of us watched with amazement the emergence of various factions prior to the tragic events of 1991. It appears that history can teach us several lessons.

First, any attempt at transcending the nationalistic-religious fanaticism through violent and coercive means will most likely fail. This is true at least for the Balkan people. Just as over five hundred years of Ottoman oppression could not quench the sense of ethnic-religious identity, but instead kept it alive, so the forty years of Communism provided a lid which temporarily contained the overt violence and intolerance, but could not prevent internally brewing restlessness.

The second lesson points to the fact that repression begets reprisal. "All who take the sword will perish by the sword." As the iron curtain lifted, some of the old and some new debts reappeared and a handful of citizens began affirming their rights over the rights of others. Violence and manipulation of power were the only methods used by oppressors for centuries, and democratic processes appeared weak and sadly inadequate for settlement purposes. The thirst for revenge tipped the scale in favor of those same methods and inter-ethnic animosities, and violence flared out of control.

The third, and most important lesson, is that repressive control arrests the growth of identity into the higher spheres. As Marxist ideology enforced by Communism passed from the scene, religio-ethnic elements of society filled the vacuum in the ranks of leadership. A government with no unified ideology displayed aimlessness, having no charisma so vitally needed for hegemony. National and religious zeal with a carefully orchestrated propaganda successfully galvanized social forces, focusing attention back to national and religious identity. The new zealots endeavored to safeguard their own cultural and religious tradition, at any price. Nationalist Messianism promised salvation and restoration of national pride and dignity.

As Reinhold Niebuhr shows, particularization of the universal messianic hopes to national Messianism appears as a subject of concern dating back as far as the time of the prophet Amos.[2] An entire worldview can be constructed around a nationalistic agenda, and the whole of religious life devoted solely to the advancement of ethnic aspirations. The liturgy, the saints, the holidays, as well as political, economic, and cultural activities become nation-centered. What begins with self-defense can easily become self-centeredness, soon to end up as self-sufficiency and national narcissism. And when several nations become involved in the same pursuits with violent means, then the sight of transcendent and universal goals is lost and sacrificed to the concerns of immediate self-affirmation. Buber's claim that personal dialogue between "I" and "thou" can be preserved from descent to "I-it" level through the dialogue of "I" with "Eternal Thou" may be applicable on the social scale as well. Social relations need the ultimate point of reference for which nationality cannot qualify.

In the midst of this turmoil and fermentation, many, maybe most of those born after 1940, wanted to see the old legacy of hatred and revenge to cease. A new concept of self, brotherhood, and unity where embrace is possible with all humans filled their dreams. Not an impossible dream when looked at from a Christian and a more advanced, civilized perspective.

---

[2]Reinhold Niebuhr, *Nature and Destiny of Man.* Vol. II. (New York: Charles Scribner's Sons, 1964.)

Forgiveness

Once upon a time, at the time of birth, they gave us our names. They did not take us somewhere very important in order to make us into religio-ethnic beings. They took us somewhere important because some One very important was worshipped there. Of nationality, of a name day, of godfathers, of holidays, there was only casual talk. We were told that our primary citizenship is in heaven and that our lineage proceeds from God. Christmas? No, we do not celebrate Christmas when others do. Not because we do not believe in it. Far from it! It would be great to celebrate it with our neighbors. Seventh-day Adventists (SDA) in other countries do celebrate that holiday with the rest of the people. Our concern in Yugoslavia is that we do not know what date to choose: December 25 or January 6. One same Jesus can not have two birthdays. So in view of not offending anyone, we celebrate the New Year and Christmas together on January 1. Religious traditions are man-made institutions, and we were assured that they are not worth fighting for, except if the Bible teaches it.

Besides, hatred and animosity among humans are the very antidote to Christianity. Different cultures, languages, scripts, or traditions make for variety and richness of human life. In Christ, there is neither Jew nor Greek, and in our relations in school, the street, or in the church, we must not discriminate against those who are different as if they were inferior or superior. To affirm our worth by berating others makes us dependent on them, and this is self-contradictory. At home, in our Sabbath School, lessons in the church, hearing and reading about missions, our horizons and our identity sensed the immenseness of the great human family and our place in it under the same God.

We were instructed very clearly and disciplined very diligently whenever prejudice or nationalistic bias entered our childish minds. The gospel and nationalistic exclusivism do not mix. Thus Niebuhr affirms:

> One of the most perfect disavowals of nationalism in the gospels is to be found in the words of John the Baptist: 'And think not to say within yourselves, we have Abraham to our father; for I say unto you, that God is able of these stones to raise up children unto Abraham.' Here the freedom of God over the instruments of His will, very specifically over the one chosen instrument, the nation of Israel, is asserted according to highest insights of prophetic universalism, as against the lower level of nationalistic Messianism.[3]

In the context of the SDA church, no religious rite, ceremony, or holiday has any ethnic affiliation or meaning. The kingdom of God as a true Christian culture has preeminence over every other custom. And when national or cultural events do take place, participation in them stands in a category separate from religious doctrine and devotion.

---

[3]Niebuhr, *op.cit.*, 42.

This kind of self-understanding fueled the Seventh-day Adventist service to humanity during the recent conflict on the Balkan Peninsula. ADRA (Adventist Development and Relief Agency) crossed borders and demarcation lines distributing food, medicine, clothing, and care. There is no need to report the data which would quantify the involvement in humanitarian work. "Do not let your left hand know what your right hand is doing," advises Jesus, the greatest of humanitarian benefactors. Accountability, however, can be documented. For instance, during the long periods of time the mail between displaced, separated families crossed the lines, thanks to the sacrificial work of ADRA. When stopped at any check point, ADRA workers were recognized by all sides for what they are, an international, interfaith, humanitarian organization, and the packages and mail could proceed unharmed. Frequent controls and cross-examinations only confirmed their commitment to unbiased service.

Dreamers never die. Sometime ago the echo of the last "real thing"- - a gun shot --hushed over the forests and mountains of Bosnia. The instances of human history, stirred up by the silence, timidly, but hopefully, examine the air around them. Deep somewhere, where the bullet cannot reach, huddled in a fetal position, their own tiny, human selves in coma begin to awaken. Each moment of consciousness brings a memory of nightmares, of wounds of fear, of killings, of hopelessness. Unaborted fruits of rape which roam the streets, in whose veins streams a blood that some abhor as "mixed," paradoxically incarnate the only true reality. They shout that NO HUMAN BLOOD IS EVER "MIXED." The color of skin, the name tag, the religion, the ancestry, the inherited shame or guilt, are not blood pollutants. A "Christian sperm" likes a "non-Christian ovum," but also a "Christian womb" is well suited to cradle a "non-Christian" fetus. These children of atrocities are not atrocious. They are the most beautiful evidence of unity in the human race under God. Their greatest enemies are those adults whose identity stalled at the nationalistic-religious level, who compulsively try to drag civilization down by their utter inability to forgive, live, and let live.

A few years from now some of these "children of hatred" might show us how to love across the borders, ethnic lines, and religious divisions. They should teach us that no one needs to feel as a homeless nobody, that our homeland and our lineage is above the highest Bosnian mountain. Since the wheels of time cannot be turned back, since the dead cannot resurrect just yet, and since the consequences threaten the silence of peace, their presence on the streets of Bosnia plead for the only true and effective revenge: revenge of forgiveness.

18

MULTIRELIGIOUS AND INTERCULTURAL CENTER "ZAYEDNO"

Marko Oršolić

The International Center for Promoting Interreligious Dialogue, Justice, and Peace, "Zayedno" [Together], Sarajevo, B&H, was founded on the United Nations Day of Human Rights in the Jewish Community center in Sarajevo, December 10, 1991. At the organizing meeting, there were about fifty influential people from the public and religious sphere, including the mayor, Muhammed Krešeljaković, the president of the Bosnian Academy of Sciences and Arts, Seid Huković, the rector of the Sarajevo University Mulić, the Franciscan provincial, Petar Andjelković, the only rabbi in Yugoslavia, representatives of the Islamic Religious Community and the Serbian Orthodox Church. A professor of Sarajevo University, Mišo Kulić, gave the introductory lecture about the philosophical prerequisites of interreligious dialogue, although according to his own admission he is an agnostic. At the founding meeting were present also representatives of the European Franciscan peace movement, the German Pax Christi movement and peace movements of five European countries.[1]

An American reader may be surprised at the listing of names and institutions, but this is necessary in order to counter the many manipulations with entire nations and institutions when careless and illegitimate decisions of certain individuals are spread through the media as if they were the positions of local and even world-wide churches and religious communities, as well as entire nations. That is why we specified people and their functions although we are eager to stress that they represented only themselves and not their institutions.

---

[1]The International Center "Zajedno" in *Frieden und Wissenschaft* by Dr. Rudolf Dustenberg, 1994, 203.

The Center, like all peace movements of religious inspiration, wants to clearly counter the religious separation of people based on an erroneous notion of God, who undoubtedly in Judaism, Christianity (Orthodox, Catholic, and Protestant) and Islam is one and the same. However, "Zayedno" differs methodologically from all other European peace movements, because it is a grassroots movement and keeps the same distance toward all religious communities. It maintains a difference for the simple reason that the established religious communities of southeastern and eastern Europe, at this time, are not capable of nurturing sincere and open dialogue because of the burdens from the time of Fascism and Bolshevik Communism.[2] Likewise, they are still encumbered by century-long traditionalism. Namely, both the Catholic and Serbian Orthodox churches in southeastern Europe organized commissions for ecumenism and interreligious dialogue, but they functioned only at the top or were blocked by political-national petrification. Protestant churches are present to a smaller degree in northern Serbia (Vojvodina) and in eastern Croatia (Slavonia). In those regions they contribute to inter-Christian ecumenism. But they are not present in B&H, and they themselves are not sufficiently open to Judaism and Islam. On the other hand, the Islamic Community in the Slavic south, despite some international efforts, did not form committees for dialogue with Christians or other non-Muslims. For this additional reason, the Center "Zayedno" leaves it up to the religious communities in the Slavic south to organize themselves ecumenically on their own while "Zayedno" is a completely independent organization with people from all three monotheistic revealed religions (Judaism, Christianity, and Islam) and includes people of good will (agnostics) who take religion seriously and who are aware of their great role in creating understanding between people and nations. Religions and churches in southeastern Europe correspond to nations, and hence Bosniac-Muslim people are adherents of Islam, Serbs of Orthodoxy, and Croats of Catholicism.

The multireligious and intercultural center "Zayedno" was established in Sarajevo, the capital city of B&H, exactly because in this city, literally within several hundred square meters, there are worship places of all three monotheistic faiths of Islam and Judaism as well as Christianity in its Orthodox, Catholic, and Evangelical forms. Therefore, Sarajevo is the European Jerusalem, according to Khaled Duran.

"Zayedno" does not merely mean that we are a togetherness of people who are Jews, Christians, or Muslims, but stands more for the nurture of religious roots and affirmation of common truths, among them the following:

---

[2]Thomas Bremer, "Die Kirchen in ehemahligen Jugoslawien" in *Der Krieg auf Balkan*, ed. by Idstein, s.a.

1. There is only one God although different names are used; 2. immortality of the soul; 3. temporality of this world; 4. God is good who rewards good and punishes evil; 5. one can please God by reverence and good deeds. All three monotheistic religions have through the centuries suppressed their common essence and have mutually alienated themselves. Therefore, it is necessary to use an objective contextual hermeneutics which is more important than the continuous affirmations of religious hierarchies about things that belong to the essence of all religions. This can be done in a similar manner.

1. The Holy Scriptures in Judaism, Christianity (in its Orthodox, Catholic, and Protestant forms) and Islam, when taken in their entirety and not literally interpreted or partially extracted and one-sidedly interpreted, do not recognize enemy perceptions based on their religious affiliation. To the contrary, Holy Scriptures could become a wonderful means to combat enemy pictures that were created in the secular realm.

2. When in the fourth century during the Constantinian era Christianity became a state religion, and three hundred years later when Islam emerged as a state religion, the preconditions were created for an instrumentalization of religion to provide an *a priori* legitimation of all state power as God-given. These processes came so far during the centuries, that prior to World War I, there were in Europe four empires. One was Catholic (Austria-Hungary), one was Protestant (Germany), one Orthodox (Russia) and one Islamic (Ottoman Turkish). All four collapsed during WWI, but the role of religion in daily religious consciousness, at least among Catholics, remained the same until the Second Vatican Council (1962-1965). Vatican II was a radical turn to the Bible, of what religion really means.

Many enemy pictures from that time (Crusades, religious wars, *jihads*, etc.) are still present in the minds of many and result in much ignorance and misunderstanding. Many Christians forget that from a global perspective Christians are also a minority today. Many, at least in Europe, are not taking Islam seriously.

Cardinal Koening expressed this idea powerfully at a Christian-Muslim conference in Vienna:

> Those who sought world-wide dominance burdened all of humanity with misunderstandings that the three monotheistic religions--Judaism, Christianity and Islam--became enemies of each other through historical misunderstandings and prejudices, in conflict with each other and due to various factual and historical reasons are full of mistrust that goes to their core. It is tragic and hard to grasp that despite the fundamental unity of faith in God, the God of Abraham, these three religious communities set themselves against each other. It is tragic that these three strictly monotheistic religions for which there is no parallel in world religious history still do not see their

common religious basis. Because they should be the ones who should jointly support the understanding among nations, justice, and peace.[3]

Many people still perceive themselves as if Christians had no joint basis with Jews and Muslims, or otherwise, they would always invite to their meetings at least Jewish and Muslim observers.

Many enemy pictures exist because we are observing Islam as it is concretely lived today rather than turning to the Holy Scriptures of Judaism and Islam. Christians in the West are often unconscious of Hegel's absoluteness of Christianity. Namely, Hegel in his grandiose synthesis of the philosophy of the West understands Judaism as "the religion of sublimity which is dialectic self-discipline of the Spirit and is the early stepping stone of the Greek 'Religion of Beauty' and the Roman 'Religion as Purposiveness' necessary for Christianity as the only 'Absolute Religion' into which they are lifted up." Islam, the "grandiose Revolution of the Orient," according to Hegel, had for a long time exhausted itself and was removed from the ground of world history into the Oriental past and is thus to be dealt with only peripherally.[4] In Hegel's time, there was no oil industry, or otherwise, he would have had to philosophize differently as it seems that wherever Allah is worshipped, there is oil, only not in Bosnia.

Johann Wolfgang Goethe criticized the major Christian misunderstandings of Islam in his poetic and theologically inadequate manner:

Narrisch, dass jeder in seinem Falle,
Seine besondere Meining preist!
Wenn ISLAM Gott ergeben heisst,
In Islam leben und starben wir alle.[5]

More pointedly than Goethe, the *Qur'an*, the Muslim Holy Scripture, deals with the Muslim view of the Christian revelation in Sura 137:

"We believe in Allah and in that which he gave us and Abraham and Ishmael and Isaac and Jacob and the tribes revealed, and in that which Moses, Jesus, and the (other) Prophets were given by their Lord. We do not know any difference among them. We remain dedicated to Allah."

In Sura 29, verse 47, the *Qur'an* is even clearer:

"With those who have the book (i.e. Jews and Christians) argue only in a proper manner, only the few among them are excluded and say, 'We believe

---

[3]Andreas Bsteh, ed. *Friede für die Menschheit.* (Moedling, 1994), 64.

[4]Hegel, *Weltgeschichte* and Hans Kung, *Projekt Weltethos* (Munchen, 1991), 114.

[5]Cited in Maria Haarmann, ed. *Der Islam: Ein historisches Lesebuch* (Munchen, 1995), 36.

in that which was to us and to you revealed. Allah, our God and your God, is only one, and we have completely surrendered to God.'"[6]

The Catholic Church had after fifteen centuries used the same thought in *Nostra Aetate*. In the meantime, Christians have fought against "unbelieving Muslims" and for this struggle used an entire arsenal of enemy pictures which until this day plays a great role in Christian consciousness.

The Jews, Christians, and Muslims have great, far-reaching developments in the understanding of God as Karen Armstrong noted in detail in her book, *The History of God: The 4000 Years of Judaism, Christianity, and Islam*[7]

Only on April 13, 1986, did the Pope John Paul II visit for the first time in centuries the synagogue in Rome, and only on the founding day of the International Center for the Promotion of Interreligious Dialogue, Justice, and Peace, "Zayedno," in Sarajevo, did Orthodox, Evangelical, Catholic, and Muslim theologians join with Jews in the synagogue and pray, although within easy reach in the same vicinity are worship places of the above named religions.

When we do not regard our Holy Scriptures from a global-universal perspective, there comes to exist terrible mutual alienation and enemy pictures, and our faith is misused as a tribal religion. Thus, we easily have Serbian New Year, a Croatian Christmas, etc.

The worst misuse of the Christian religion of the Nazi period still did not bring about the official condemnation by the religious communities of Southeast and Eastern Europe (the exception is the Bosnian Franciscan Catalogue). Therefore, "Zayedno" believes that it is impossible to ask Serbian Orthodox dignitaries to understand who are the war criminals of the present time if the Islamic and Catholic dignitaries did not publicly condemn the war criminals of World War II. Therefore, "Zayedno" will attempt to urge all religious communities in Europe to attend the Second Ecumenical Gathering in Graz in June 1997 to bring about a joint document in which there would be a clear rejection of the misuse of faith and of religious communities for political purposes in the twentieth century in Europe. Only then will it be possible to talk of the peace-making role of our monotheistic religions.

"Zayedno" opposes mixing religion and politics and considers itself a "politics-free zone." No matter what politics, i.e. in convenient and inconvenient times, faith must be a faith of peace and reconciliation. It must stand for all-encompassing justice, affirming the dignity of each human being and affirming all-encompassing brotherhood and sisterhood of all people. Jesus Christ in his

---

[6]The citations from the *Qur'an,* translated from the German edition published in Munich by Orbis Verlag, 1993, 325 and 34.

[7](New York: Alfred A. Knopf, 1993).

Sermon on the Mount speaks of peace-makers who with their activity become divinized in a spacial manner, although in that given time his earthly homeland was occupied by Romans. This commitment by Christ our contemporary nationalists would proclaim as support of the Roman occupation, or at least, as insufficient resistance, which would be tantamount to betrayal.

On October 25-26, 1994, "Zayedno" and the Bosnian Academy of Science and Arts organized a symposium in order to stimulate the dialogue in Sarajevo. The foreign guests were mostly from Bavaria, Germany, where earlier that year a "Zayedno" Center had been established with the support of the Bavarian Council of Churches. The guests were Dr. Gerhard Voss, O.S.B., the editor of the ecumenical periodical, *Una Sancta*, Dr. Hermann Probst, a Lutheran minister of the student congregation in Munich, and Peter Lorenz, a Quaker. The theme was about the role of the Ecumene in interreligious dialogue and the beginnings of the Jewish-Christian-Muslim dialogue. The foreign guests also had the chance to meet with the Roman Catholic Archbishop, Vinko Puljić, and other religious leaders. A description of this symposium and the main papers were published in 1995 under the title "Za medjureligijski i medjukulturalni dijalog u Sarajevu."[8]

About a year later on December 8-9, 1995, another symposium was held with the theme "Religion and Statecraft" also in the Academy of Arts and Sciences building. The foreign guests this time were two American professors from the Philadelphia area, Dr. Leonard Swidler of Temple University and Dr. Paul Mojzes of Rosemont College, who are the editors of the *Journal of Ecumenical Studies*.

At this meeting, in addition to the numerous presentations by the Bosnian and American professors about the role of religions engaged in dialogue for the sustenance of multinational, multicultural, and multireligious states, there was discussion on how to support the establishment of a department of interreligious dialogue at the University of Sarajevo after the end of the war and support for an interreligious periodical. The foreign guests also had the opportunity to speak with various academics, with the *Reis-ul-ulema*, Dr. Mustafa Cerić, Vinko Cardinal Puljić, the Roman Catholic Archbishop of Sarajevo as well as with Fr. Krstan Bijeljac, a Serbian Orthodox priest. The latter felt that the Serbian Orthodox bishops who had fled their dioceses during the war do not represent the best interests of Serbian Orthodox believers, having lost their moral authority as leaders who stay with their people.

---

[8]Published by the Academy of Science and Arts of Bosnia and Herzegovina and "Zajedno" in Sarajevo.

It is very clear that the chances for dialogue become increasingly difficult with every day of continued war and ethnic separation. The prospects for the future are not bright, but they are not hopeless. This only reinforces the need, the urgency, and the imperative for promoting a Bosnia and Herzegovina in which the various nations, religions, and cultures will cooperate and be in dialogue and mutual respect. In order for this to succeed, in addition to local efforts, it is necessary that those from abroad who espouse the dialogue assist in the process intellectually, spiritually, and financially, because the alternative is separation and the ultimate dismemberment of Bosnia and Herzegovina into rival ethnoreligious states that will always oscillate between war and uneasy, temporary cease-fires.

Translated from Croatian and German by Paul Mojzes

19

EXCLUSION AND EMBRACE: THEOLOGICAL REFLECTIONS IN THE WAKE OF "ETHNIC CLEANSING"[1]

Miroslav Volf

There is a need to make an attempt to make sense of the demonic aggression in the Balkans today. The practice of "ethnic cleansing" is taken as an occasion to suggest that we place the problem of otherness at the center of theological reflection on social realities. As the ghettos and battlefields throughout the world testify indisputably, the future not only of the Balkans but of the whole world depends on how we deal with ethnic, religious, and gender otherness. The author's response to the problem of otherness is a "theology of embrace" in which the dominant categories of "oppression and liberation" are replaced by categories of "exclusion and embrace."

In the Gospels, Jesus tells a puzzling story about the unclean spirit who leaves a person only to return with seven other spirits of an even more wicked character. The new state of the person is even worse than the old (see Matt. 12:45ff). I am sometimes tempted to apply this story to the situation in Eastern Europe after the 1989 revolution. The demon of totalitarian communism has

---

[1]This essay was originally a paper presented at a joint conference of the Gesellschaft für Evangelische Theologie and Arbeitskreis für Evangelische Theologie in Potsdam, Germany, February 15-17, 1993. The theme of the conference was "God's Spirit and God's People in the Social and Cultural Upheavals in Europe," with my assigned topic being "The Tasks of the Christian Community in the Social and Cultural Upheavals in Europe." Jayakumar Christian and Dr. Young-Lee Hertig have read a previous version of the paper and helped me to see some issues from Indian and feminine Korean perspectives, respectively. Suggestions of my colleagues and/or friends, Professors David Augsburger, Phillip Clayton, and James Wm. McClendon, Jr., have helped me a great deal.

The paper was published in the *Journal of Ecumenical Studies*, Vol. 29, No. 2, pp. 230-248 and is reprinted here by permission of the author and the publisher.

just been or is being exorcised, but worse demons seem to be rushing in to fill
the empty house.[2]

This is how I introduced a paper in April, 1991, on the tasks of the churches in
Eastern Europe following the 1989 revolution. It was at a conference of Third
World theologians in Osijek, Croatia. Some six months later, the Evangelical
Theological Faculty, which hosted the conference, had to flee to neighboring
Slovenia; Osijek was being shelled day in and day out by Serbian forces. What
during the conference had only *seemed* about to happen has now in fact taken
place. New demons have possessed the Balkan house, preparing their vandalistic
and bloody feast, first in Croatia and then in Bosnia. Signs of their presence in
other parts of Eastern Europe are less tangible but real, nonetheless.

The task for Eastern European churches remains the same today as it was
in 1991--to ward off the onrush of both the old and the new demons. What has
changed is the complexity of the task. I intend, however, neither to repeat nor
to supplement my previous analysis and recommendations. Instead of asking a
primarily missiologically oriented question about what churches in Eastern
Europe today should do, I will discuss a more fundamental issue involving the
challenge that being caught between the old and new demons presents for
theological reflection--reflection that, of course, must always take place under
the horizon of the mission of God in the world.

What are some of the key theological issues facing Christians in Eastern
Europe, particularly in the Balkans? When the heat of the battle subsides and
attention is focused neither on killing nor on surviving, two issues are at the
forefront of peoples' minds. The first is *evil and sin*: How does one make sense
of the vicious circle of hell-deep hatred and the baffling network of small and
great evils that people inflict on each other? The second is *reconciliation*: How
do we stop the killing and learn to live together after so much mutual hatred and
bloodshed have shaped our common history? These issues coalesce in the more
abstract but fundamental question of *otherness*--of ethnic, religious, and cultural
difference. In Eastern Europe this question is seldom posed in such abstract
terms and often is not asked consciously at all, but it frames all the other
questions with which people are grappling existentially.

Those whose theological palates long for some exotic fruit from foreign
soil might be disappointed with my list. Are not these same issues surfacing
everywhere in the world today? Am I not offering staple foods that can be found
anywhere? My answer is, yes, probably, but as a theological chef I do not think
this should bother me. My responsibility is not to tickle the palates of (Western)

---

[2]Miroslav Volf, "When the Unclean Spirit Leaves: Tasks of the Eastern European
Churches after the 1989 Revolution," *Occasional Papers on Religion in Eastern Europe*, Vol.
XI, No. 1 (February 1991), 11.

theological connoisseurs dulled by abundance and variety but to fill the empty stomachs of people engaged in a bloody conflict. I have to prepare the food *they* need. Opinions of connoisseurs might be interesting and instructive, but nutritious value for the hungry is what matters. This is what it means to do contextualized theology. So my question will be: How do the issues of otherness, sin, and reconciliation look from the perspective of the social upheaval and ethnic conflict in the Balkans?

Much of my reflection on these issues took place as I was living and teaching in Osijek during the fall of 1992. By that time, the war in Croatia was over (or at least its first phase was,[3] but its traces were everywhere--broken windows, scarred facades, destroyed roofs, burned and desolated houses, a ruined economy, and, above all, many deep wounds in the hearts of the people. Meanwhile, the war was continuing with even greater brutality in the neighbors' courtyard. As Croatians were watching the unabated Serbian aggression in Bosnia and trying to cope with the never-ending stream of refugees, they were reliving their own war inferno. There was much pride over their newly won statehood, even if it had had to be paid in blood, but there was even more trepidation about the future: When would the powerful aggressor be stopped and brought to justice? Would Croatians ever regain the lost territories and return to their villages and cities? If they did, how would they rebuild them? The feeling of helplessness and frustration, of anger and hatred was ubiquitous.

From the beginning of the conflict, I was sharing in the destiny of my people--first from afar, from Slovenia and from my home in California, then first-hand, when I arrived in Osijek for a prolonged stay. It was then that I was forced to start making sense of what I encountered. What I present here can best be described as a "preliminary account of an exploration." This exploration would never have been undertaken and would have long since been given up had it not been for the powerful experience of the complex and conflicting social realities brought on by revolution and war. Experience goaded me to explore, so I will not shy away from appealing to it here.

The Other

I was crossing the Croatian border for the first time since Croatia had declared independence. State insignia and flags that were displayed prominently at the "gate to Croatia" were merely visible signs of what I could sense like an electrical charge in the air: I was leaving Hungary and entering Croatian space. I felt relief. In what used to be Yugoslavia one was almost expected to apologize for being a Croat. Now I was free to be who I ethnically am. Yet, the

---

[3]This article was completed in January, 1993.

longer I was in the country, the more hemmed in I felt. For instance, I sensed an unexpressed expectation to explain why as a Croat I still had friends in Serbia and did not talk with disgust about the backwardness of Byzantine-Orthodox culture. I am used to the colorful surrounding of multi-ethnicity. A child of a "mixed marriage," I grew up in a city that the old Habsburg Empire had made into a meeting place of many ethnic groups, and I now live in the (tension-filled) multicultural city of Los Angeles. However, the new Croatia, like some jealous goddess, wanted all my love and loyalty and wanted to possess every part of my being. I must be Croat through and through, or I was not a good Croat, I could read between the lines of the large-lettered ethnic text that met my eyes wherever I looked. "Croatia," I thought to myself, "will not be satisfied until it permeates everything in Croatia."

It is easy to explain this tendential *omnipresentia Croatiae* in Croatia. After forced assimilation under Communist rule, it was predictable that the feeling of ethnic belonging would vigorously reassert itself. Moreover, the need to stand firm against a powerful and destructive enemy leaves little room for the luxury of divided loyalties. The explanations make sense, yet the unsettling question remains: Does one not discover in Croatia's face some despised Serbian features? Has the enemy not captured Croatia's soul along with Croatia's soil? Serbian aggression has enriched the already oversized vocabulary of evil with the term "ethnic cleansing": Ethnic otherness is filth that needs to be washed away from the ethnic body, pollution that threatens the ecology of ethnic space. But, not unlike many other countries, Croatia wants to be clean, too--at least clean of its enemies, the Serbs! There is, of course, a world of difference between whether one suppresses otherness by social pressure to conform and emigrate or even by discriminatory legislation and whether one works to eliminate it with the destructive power of guns and fire. Is not the goal the same--a monochrome world, a world without the other?

During my stay in Croatia I read Jacques Derrida's recent comments on today's Europe, reflecting on his own European identity:

> I am European, I am no doubt a European intellectual, and I like to recall this, I like to recall this to myself, and why would I deny it? In the name of what? But I am not, nor do I feel, European in every part, that is, European through and through. . . . Being a part, belonging as `fully a part,' should be incompatible with belonging `in every part.' My cultural identity, that in the name of which I speak, is not only European, it is not identical to itself, and I am not `cultural' through and through, `cultural' in every part.[4]

---

[4]Jacques Derrida, *The Other Heading: Reflections on Today's Europe*, tr. Pascale-Anne Brault and Michael B. Naas (Bloomington, IN: Indiana University Press, 1992), 82-83.

The identity of Europe with itself, Derrida went on to say, is totalitarian. Indeed, Europe's past is full of the worst of violences committed in the name of European identity. Europe colonialized and oppressed, destroyed cultures, and imposed its religion--all in the name of its identity with itself. It was not too long ago that Germany sought to conquer and exterminate in the name of its identity with itself (and Croatia participated in the project its own way). Today, the Balkans are aflame in the name of Serbia's identity with itself. Identity without otherness--this is our curse!

The practice of ethnic and other kinds of "cleansing" in the Balkans forces us *to place otherness at the center of theological reflection*. The problem, of course, is not specific to the Balkans. The processes of integration in Europe place otherness high on the agenda. So do, for instance, the disintegration of the Soviet empire and the fragility of multi-ethnic and multireligious nations such as India. The large framework for the problem is set by developments of planetary proportions. Modern means of communication and the emerging world economy have transformed our world from a set of self-contained tribes and nations into a global city. The unity of the human race is no longer an abstract notion. The closer humanity's unity, the more powerfully we experience its diversity. The "others"--persons of another culture, another religion, another economic status, and so on--are not people we read about from distant lands; we see them daily on the screens in our living rooms, pass by them on our streets. They are our colleagues and neighbors, some of them even our spouses. The others are among us; they are part of us, yet they remain others, often pushed to the margins. How should we relate to them? Should we celebrate their difference and support it, or should we bemoan and suppress it? The issue is urgent. The ghettos and battlefields throughout the world testify indisputably to its importance.[5] It is not too much to claim that the future of not only the Balkans but of the whole world depends on how we deal with ethnic, religious, and gender otherness.

Liberation theologians have taught us to place the themes of oppression and liberation at the center of theological reflection. They have drawn our attention to the God who is on the side of the poor and the oppressed, as well as the demands that God's people be on the same side.[6] Nothing should make

---

[5]For a short analysis of the political and cultural, but mainly philosophical, importance of the "difference," see Mark C. Taylor, *Altarity* (Chicago: The University of Chicago Press, 1987), xxi. See also Tzvetan Todorov's classic treatment of the problem of otherness in the account of the encounter between European and American civilizations, *The Conquest of America: The Question of the Other*, tr. Richard Howard (New York: Harper, 1984).

[6]See the classic work by Gustavo Gutiérrez, *A Theology of Liberation: History, Politics, and Salvation*, tr. Sr. Caridad Inda and John Eagleson (Maryknoll, NY: Orbis Books, 1973).

us forget these lessons, for the "preferential option for the poor" is rooted deeply in biblical traditions. Nevertheless, the categories of oppression and liberation are by themselves inadequate to address the Balkan conflict--or, indeed, the problems in the world at large today. The categories are, of course, almost tailor-made for both Croats and Serbs: each side perceives itself as oppressed by the other, and both are engaged in what they believe to be the struggle for liberation. Unless one is prepared to say that one side is completely right and the other wrong, this is precisely where the problem lies.

Categories of oppression and liberation provide combat gear, not a pinstriped suit or a dinner dress; they are good for fighting, but not for negotiating or celebrating. Even assuming that one side is right and the other wrong, what happens when the fight is over and (we hope) the right side wins? One still faces the question of how the liberated oppressed can live together with their conquered oppressors. "Liberation of the oppressors" is the answer that the "oppression-liberation" schema suggests. But, is it persuasive? Victors are known for never taking off their soldiers' suits; liberation through violence breeds new conflicts. The categories of oppression and liberation seem ill-suited to bring about the resolution of conflicts between people and groups. I suggest that the categories of "exclusion and embrace" as two paradigm responses to otherness can do a better job. They need to be placed at the center of a theological reflection on otherness, an endeavor I will call a "theology of embrace."

A "theology of embrace" would, however, amount to a betrayal of both God and oppressed people if it were pursued in such a way as to marginalize the problems of oppression and liberation. Rather, we need to see oppression and liberation as essential dimensions of exclusion and embrace, respectively. Those who are oppressed and in the need of liberation are always "the others." Indeed, almost invariably, the oppressed do not belong to the dominant culture of the oppressors but are persons or groups of another race, gender, or religion. To embrace others in their otherness must mean to free them from oppression and give them space to be themselves. Anything else is either a hypocritical tap on the shoulders or a deadly "bear hug." Thus, the question must never be whether one should struggle against oppression but what theological categories are most adequate to accomplish the task.

I will address the issue of otherness by looking first at the nature of Christian identity. This will provide a platform from which to talk about sin as exclusion and about salvation as embrace. However, within the confines of a single essay, I am able neither to ground the "theology of embrace" sufficiently in the work of Christ nor to reflect extensively on its concrete implications. Nor can I work out the differences in the way exclusion and embrace take place on individual and group levels.

Aliens

In his reminiscences, *From the Kingdom of Memory*, Elie Wiesel defined the stranger as

> someone who suggests the unknown, the prohibited, the beyond; he seduces, he attracts, he wounds--and leaves . . . The stranger represents what you are not, what you cannot be, simply because you are not he. . . . The stranger is the other. He is not bound by your laws, by your memories; his language is not yours, nor his silence.[7]

How should we respond to the strange world of the other? In answering this question, Christians will have to reflect on their *own identity as strangers.*

From the inception of the Christian church, otherness was integral to Christian ethnic and cultural identity.[8] Toward the end of the New Testament period, Christians came to designate themselves explicitly as "aliens and exiles" (1 Pet. 2:11).[9] By the second century these metaphors became central to their self-understanding. They saw themselves as heirs to the Hebrew Bible people of God: Abraham was called to go from his country, his kindred, and his father's house (Gen 12:1); his grandchildren and their children became "aliens in the land of Egypt" (Lev 19:34). The nation of which he and Sarah were foreparents lived as exiles in the Babylonian captivity, and, even when they lived securely in their own land, Yahweh their God expected them to be different from the nations that surrounded them. However, at the root of Christian self-understanding as aliens and exiles lies not so much the story of Abraham and his posterity as the destiny of Jesus Christ, his mission, and his rejection, which brought him to the cross. "He came to what was his own, and his own people did not accept him" (Jn 1:11). He was a stranger to the world because the world into which he came was estranged from God, and so it is with his followers: "When a person becomes a believer, then he moves from the far country to the vicinity of God. . . . There now arises a relation of reciprocal foreignness and

---

[7] Elie Wiesel, *From the Kingdom of Memory: Reminiscences* (New York: Summit Books, 1990), 59-60.

[8] See Reinhard Feldmeier, *Die Christen als Fremde: Die Metaphor der Fremde in der antiken Welt, im Urchristentum und im 1. Petrusbrief*, Wissenschaftliche Untersuchungen zum Neuen Testament 64 (Tübingen: J. C. B. Mohr [Paul Siebeck], 1992).

[9] Gustav Stählin, "xénos ktl," in Gerhard Kittel, ed., *Theological Dictionary of the New Testament,* vol. 5, tr. and ed. Geoffrey W. Bromiley (Grand Rapids, MI: Wm. B. Eerdmans Publishing Co., 1967), 30. Biblical quotations are from the *New Revised Standard Version* (©1989 by the Division of Christian Education of the National Council of the Churches of Christ in the U.S.A.).

estrangement between Christians and the world."[10] Christians are born of the Spirit (Jn 3:8) and are, therefore, not "from the world" but, like Jesus Christ, "from God" (see Jn 15:19). It is not at the disposal of Christians whether to be alien in their own culture. The "difference" from one's own culture--from the concrete "world" one inhabits--is essential to the Christian's cultural identity.

Why be "different"? Simply for the sake of difference? Even that is progress in a world without the other. Belonging without distance destroys: I affirm my identity as Croatian and want either to shape everyone in my own image or eliminate them from my world. So, why not dirty the walls of a monochrome culture with some spiteful, colorful graffiti? There is a value in difference even simply as difference, yet the difference will remain sterile if it is nothing but a protest gesture. It might also turn into its very opposite. If belonging without distance destroys, distance without belonging isolates: I deny my cultural identity as Croatian and draw back from my own culture, but, more often than not, I become trapped in the snares of counter-dependence. I deny my Croatian identity only to affirm even more forcefully my identity as a member of this or that anti-Croatian sect. As the "positive fusion" is substituted by "negative fusion," an isolationist "distance without belonging" slips into a destructive "belonging without distance." Difference from a culture must never degenerate into a simple flight from that culture. Rather, to be an alien and an exile must be a way of living *in* and *for* a culture. In biblical terminology, the realm and reign of God are not *of* this world, but they are *in* and *for* this world. Distance must involve belonging, as belonging must involve distance.

Given, then, the need for interpenetration of distance and belonging, what is the positive purpose of the distance? The category of "new creation" sets us on the trail leading to an answer. In a key passage about the nature of Christian existence, Paul declared: "So if anyone is in Christ, there is a new creation" (2 Cor 5:17). The rebirth of a person by the Spirit is nothing less than an anticipation of the eschatological new creation of God, a gathering of the whole people of God and of all the cultural treasures that have been dispersed among the nations. By the Spirit, that future universal event becomes a concrete reality in each believer.

One consequence of the re-creation of a person by the Spirit is that she or he can no longer be thought of apart from the rich and complex reality of the new creation. The Spirit sets a person on the road toward becoming what one might call a "catholic personality," a personal microcosm of the eschatological new creation. Catholic personality is a personality enriched by otherness, a personality that is what it is only because all differentiated otherness of the new

---

[10]*Ibid.*, 29.

creation has been reflected in it in a particular way. The distance from my own culture that results from being born by the Spirit does not isolate me but *creates space in me for the other*. Only in distance can I be enriched, so that I, in turn, can enrich the culture to which I belong.

Because everything belongs partly to a catholic personality, a person with catholic personality cannot belong totally to any one thing. The only way to belong is with distance. This distance from any particular reality, from any particular person and culture--which exists for the sake of transcending the exclusion of all other reality from that person's identity--might be called "catholic foreignness." Christians are not simply aliens to their own culture; they are aliens who are at home in every culture, because they are open to every culture. Something of this catholic foreignness might have been in the mind of the anonymous author of the Epistle to Diognetus when he wrote, "Every foreign land is their fatherland, and every fatherland a foreign land."[11]

The notion of the catholic personality avoids exclusivism because each person has became a particular reflection of the totality of others. At the same time it transcends indifferent relativism. Each does not simply affirm the otherness as otherness but seeks to be enriched by it. But, should a catholic personality integrate all otherness? Can one feel at home with everything in every culture? With murder, rape, and destruction? With nationalistic idolatry and "ethnic cleansing"? Any notion of catholic personality that was capable only of integrating but not of discriminating would be grotesque. For, there are incommensurable perspectives that stubbornly refuse to be dissolved in a peaceful synthesis, and there are evil things that we should stubbornly resist integrating into our personalities.[12] The practice of exclusion cannot be given up. The biblical category for it is "judgment." This brings us to the second positive purpose of the distance.

Distance that results from being born by the Spirit--"catholic foreignness"--entails a judgment not only against a monochrome character of one's own culture but also against evil in every culture. The new creation that an authentic *catholic* personality should anticipate is not an indiscriminate affirmation of the present world. Such an affirmation would be the cheapest of all graces and, hence, no grace at all--neither toward the perpetrators of evil nor, of course, toward their many victims. There can be no new creation without judgment, without the expulsion of the devil and the beast and the false prophet (Rev

---

[11]The Epistle to Diognetus 5:5, in Henry G. Meecham, *The Epistle to Diognetus: The Greek Text with Introduction, Translation, and Notes* (Manchester: University of Manchester Press, 1949), 81.

[12]See Richard J. Mouw, "Christian Philosophy and Cultural Diversity," *Christian Scholar's Review* 17 (December, 1987): 114ff.

20:10), without the swallowing up of the night by the light and of death by life (Rev 21:4, 22:5).[13] The notion of "catholic foreignness," therefore, necessarily involves a conflict with the world: the struggle between truth and falsehood, between justice and arbitrariness, between life and death.[14] Distance from a culture that rebirth by the Spirit creates is a judgment against the evils of a culture. It creates space for the struggle against the various demons that assault it. A truly catholic personality must be an *evangelical* personality--a personality transformed by the Spirit of the new creation and engaged in the transformation of the world.

Does not talk about demons and darkness return us to the exclusion that the notion of the "catholic personality" should have overcome? Indeed, does not the notion of catholic personality presuppose exclusion, because it rests not only on belonging but also on distance? The best way to tackle these questions is to look at the significance of "centrality." It seems rather obvious that, when talking about identity, one cannot do without a center; otherwise, the talk of difference and its being internal to oneself makes no sense. To what is the difference internal? Derrida, who is not known to be graceful toward what he calls "hegemonic centrality," recognizes as much when he insists that self-difference "would gather this center [the human center of an individual], relating it to itself, only to the extent that it would open it up to" the divergence from itself.[15] Derrida cannot give up the center, for then the difference would remain everywhere and nowhere. The center seems to function, however, only as a precondition for openness for the other, as a contentless container of difference.

But, if the self is not a center organizing the difference but merely a container of the difference, does one not end up--exactly contrary to Derrida's intention--with a "melting-pot" (or some chaotic "salad-bowl")? The lesser trouble with the melting-pot is that it never existed. The greater trouble is that it dissolves the difference. The identity with oneself--a personal centeredness--must be preserved for the sake of difference.[16] My being centered in distance

---

[13]See Miroslav Volf, *Work in the Spirit: Toward a Theology of Work* (New York: Oxford University Press, 1991), 120-121.

[14]See Jürgen Moltmann, *Der Weg Jesu Christi: Christologie in messianischen Dimensionen* (Munich: Kaiser, 1989), 226. Cf. idem, "Dient die `pluralistische Theologie' dem Dialog der Weltreligionen?" *Evangelische Theologie* 49 (December, 1989): 528-536.

[15]Derrida, *The Other Heading*, 10. He says as much when he speaks of the contradictory demand that the European cultural identity not be dispersed but that, at the same time, it not accept "the capital of a centralizing authority" (ibid., 38-39).

[16]In his Gifford lectures, Paul Ricoeur distinguished categorically between *idem*-identity and *ipse*-identity. In the circle of *idem*-identity, the other is "distinct" or "diverse," and it functions as the antonym of "same." In the circle of *ipse*-identity, the otherness is constitutive of sameness; here the selfhood of oneself "implies otherness to such an intimate degree that

from the other is not a negative act of exclusion but a creative act of separation. The Book of Genesis rightly describes creation as successive divine acts of separation (see 1:3ff.). Because the other and I can be constituted in our mutual otherness only by separation, no genuine openness to the other is possible without it. This is why the encounter with a stranger is creative only if, as Wiesel has put it, you "know when to step back."[17]

In the case of Christians, superimposed on the center that creates their human identity is another center that creates their *Christian* identity. Emergence of this new center is also an act of creation--the new creation--and it takes place through separation. Why this new center? Why the additional separation? It is because a human center is not an impersonal axis but a personal self--a heart-- that cannot exist without a "god," without a framework of meaning and value. The god of the self is the doorkeeper who decides about the fate of the otherness at the doorstep of the heart. To embrace a Christian God does not mean to place a doorkeeper at the entrance of one's heart that was without one before but to replace one doorkeeper with another. One cannot get rid of one's gods; one can only change them. When one thinks one has gotten rid of them, a restless demon who wanders through waterless regions looking for a resting place but finds none has already taken their place (see Mt 12:43). So, the question is not whether one has a doorkeeper but who the doorkeeper is and how the doorkeeper relates to otherness. Does the Christian doorkeeper prohibit anything non-Christian from entering?

There are two injunctions that surface persistently in the Bible. One is to have no strange gods; the other is to love strangers. The two injunctions are interrelated: one should love strangers in the name of the one triune God, who loves strangers. This triune God is the center that regulates a Christian's relationship to otherness, a doorkeeper who opens and closes the door of the self.[18] To be a Christian does not mean to close oneself off in one's own identity

---

one cannot be thought of without the other" (Paul Ricoeur, *Oneself as Another*, tr. Kathleen Blamey [Chicago: The University of Chicago Press, 1992], 3). So, when we speak of the loss of identity--of *Ichlosigkeit*--then the "I" of which the subject says that it is nothing is "a self deprived of the help of sameness" (*ibid.*, 166).

[17]Wiesel, *From the Kingdom*, 73. On p. 65, he noted that a stranger "can be of help only as a stranger--lest you are ready to become his caricature. And your own."

[18]The metaphor of the door is helpful insofar as it implies a necessary demarcation, but it is also misleading insofar as it suggests a sharp and static boundary. In analyzing the category "Christian," missiologist Paul Hiebert has suggested that we make use of the mathematical categories of "bounded sets," "fuzzy sets," and "centered sets." Bounded sets function on the principle "either/or"; an apple is either an apple or not; it cannot be partly an apple and partly a pear. Fuzzy sets, by contrast, have no sharp boundaries; things are fluid with no stable point of reference and with various degrees of inclusion--as when a mountain

and advance oneself in an exemplary way toward what one is not. It means, rather, to be centered on this God--the God of the other--and to participate in *God's* advance toward where God and God's reign are not yet. Without such centeredness, it would be impossible either to denounce the practice of exclusion or to demand the practice of embrace.

Exclusion

What strikes one immediately in the Balkan war is the naked hate, a hate without enough decency--or, shall we say, hypocrisy?--to cover itself up. Not that hate is unique to this conflict: Most wars feed on hate, and the masters of war know how to manufacture it well. It is the proportions of the Balkan hate and its rawness right there on the fringes of what some thought to be civilized Europe that cause us to stagger. Think of the stories of soldiers making necklaces out of the fingers of little children! Never mind whether they are true or not--that they are being told and believed suffices. The hate that gives rise to such stories and wants to believe them is the driving force behind the ruthless and relentless pursuit of exclusion known as "ethnic cleansing." This is precisely what hate is: an unflinching will to exclude, a revulsion for the other.

It might be that the most basic sin is pride, though this way of defining sin does not seem to capture with precision the experiences of most women.[19] However, I doubt that it is helpful to go about reducing all sins to their common root;[20] the Bible at any rate does not seem to be interested in such a business. I will not pursue here the search for the one basic sin but will indicate a fundamental way of conceiving of sin: *sin as exclusion*.[21] For those who are

---

merges into the plains. A centered set is defined by a center and the relationship of things to that center, by a *movement* toward it or away from it. For Hiebert, the category of "Christian" should be understood as a centered set. While a demarcation line exists, the focus is not on "maintaining the boundary" but "on reaffirming the center" (Paul G. Hiebert, "The Category `Christian' in the Mission Task," *International Review of Mission* 72 [July, 1983]: 421-427; see esp. 424). The center of a person who is a new creation in Christ is constituted by separation, but around the center there is space for otherness.

[19]See Judith Plaskow, *Sex, Sin, and Grace: Women's Experience and the Theologies of Reinhold Niebuhr and Paul Tillich* (Washington, DC: University Press of America, 1980); and Daphine Hampson, "Reinhold Niebuhr on Sin: A Critique," in Richard Harries, ed. and intro., *Reinhold Niebuhr and the Issues of Our Time* (London: Mowbray; Grand Rapids, MI: Wm. B. Eerdmans Publishing Co., 1986), 46-60.

[20]So, also, Jürgen Moltmann, *The Spirit of Life: A Universal Affirmation*, tr. Margaret Kohl (Minneapolis, MN: Fortress Press, 1992), 127.

[21]Exclusion," as I am using the term here, should not be confused with "separation." Separation, as I noted earlier, is a creative act through which otherness is constituted. If one speaks of sin as separation (see, e.g., Barry Ulanov's reflections on sin as separation ["The Rages of Sin," *Union Seminary Quarterly Review*, vol. 44, nos. 1-2 (1990), 137-150]), one

interested in exploring the connection between exclusion and pride, one could point out that exclusion, which is a form of contempt toward the other, might be considered "the reverse side of pride and its necessary concomitant in a world in which self-esteem is constantly challenged by the achievements of others."[22]

One of the advantages of conceiving of sin as exclusion is that it names as sin what often passes as virtue, especially in religious circles. In the Palestine of Jesus' day, "sinners" were primarily social outcasts, people who practiced despised trades, those who failed to keep the Law as interpreted by the religious establishment, and gentiles and Samaritans. A pious person had to separate from them; their presence defiled, because they were defiled. Jesus' table fellowship with social outcasts, a fellowship that belonged to the central features of his ministry, turned this conception of sin on its head: *The real sinner is not the outcast but the one who casts the other out.* As Walter Wink has written, "Jesus distinguishes between those falsely called sinners--who are in fact victims of an oppressive system of exclusion--and true sinners, whose evil is not ascribed to them by others, but who have sinned from the heart (Mk 7:21)."[23] Sin is not so much a defilement but a certain form of *purity*: the exclusion of the other from one's heart and one's world. In the story of the prodigal son, the sinner was not only the younger brother but also the elder brother--the one who withheld an embrace and expected exclusion. Sin is a refusal to embrace the other in her otherness, a desire to purge him from one's world, by ostracism or oppression, deportation or liquidation.

The exclusion of the other is an exclusion of *God*. This is what one can read between the lines of the story of the prodigal son. The departure of the younger brother from the father's home was an act of exclusion. He wanted his father--and maybe his brother, too--out of his world. Yet, in his life of exclusion, in the far country, he was closer to the father than was his older brother who remained at home. For, like the father, he longed for an embrace. His older brother kept the father in his world but excluded him from his heart. For the older brother an act of exclusion demanded retaliatory exclusion. For the father an act of exclusion called for an embrace. By excluding his younger brother, the older brother excluded the father who longed for an embrace. But, did not <u>both</u> brothers exclude the father? Are they not *both sinners*? Are not both *equally* sinners? This brings us to the problem of the universality of sin.

---

should think of it as a second-order separation--a rendering asunder of things that in their otherness belong together.

[22]Reinhold Niebuhr, *The Nature and Destiny of Man: A Christian Interpretation.* Vol. 1: *Human Nature* (New York: Charles Scribner's Sons, 1961), 211.

[23]Walter Wink, *Engaging the Powers: Discernment and Resistance in a World of Domination* (Minneapolis, MN: Fortress Press, 1992), 115-116.

From a distance, things look fairly simple in the Balkan war: Croatians and especially Muslims are the victims, and Serbians are the aggressors. Has any city in Serbia been destroyed, any of its territories occupied? The macro-picture of the conflict is clear, and it does not seem likely that anything will ever change it. I approached the clear contours of this picture with a pre-reflective expectation that the victim is innocent and the oppressor guilty. This natural presumption was aided by my belonging to the victimized group. I had, of course, never doubted that Croatians share some blame for the outbreak of the war (just as I never doubted that only Croatia's renunciation of sovereignty would have prevented the conflict from breaking out in the first place), but I expected Croatians to be more humane victims. At night in Osijek, I would hear explosions go off and know that another house or shop of a Serb who did not emigrate had been destroyed, and rarely was anyone brought to justice. Refugees, those who were victimized the most, looted trucks that brought them help; they were at war with *each other*. Are these simply necessary accompaniments of a war? If so, they prove my point: the more closely one looks at the picture, the more the line between the guilty and the innocent blurs, and all one sees is an intractable maze of small and large brutalities. I was tempted to exclaim: "All are evil, equally evil!" Then I heard those same words broadcast by the Serbian propaganda machine. The logic was simple: If evildoers are everywhere, then the violence of the aggressor is no worse than the violence of the victim. All are aggressors, and all are victims. Placing the micro-picture of the maze of evil so close to our eyes was calculated to remove the macro-picture of aggression and suffering from our field of vision.

Christian theology has traditionally underlined the universality of sin. "[A]ll have sinned and fall short of the glory of God," said the Apostle Paul (Rom 3:23), echoing some central Hebrew Bible passages. In the bright light of the divine glory, stains of injustice appear on all human righteousness, and blemishes of narcissism, indifference, and sometimes hate appear on all human love. In addition to freeing us "from delusions about the perfectibility of ourselves and our institutions,"[24] the doctrine of the universality of sin pricks the thin balloons of self-righteousness of aggressor and victim alike and binds them in the solidarity of sin, thus preparing the way for reconciliation. This is why the doctrine of the universality of sin should not be given up.

If all are sinners, then are all sins equal? Reinhold Niebuhr, who in our century most powerfully restated the doctrine of the universality of sin, thought so. However, he sought to balance the equality of sin with the inequality of

---

[24]*Ibid.*, 71.

guilt.[25] If one affirms the equality of sin, such a balancing act becomes unavoidable. But, why assert the equality of sin in the first place? From "all are sinners" it *does not* follow that "all sins are equal."[26] Aggressors' destruction of a village and refugees' looting a truck equally sin, but they are not equal sins. The equality of sins dissolves all concrete sins in an ocean of undifferentiated sinfulness. This is precisely what the prophets and Jesus did not do. Their judgments are not general but specific; they do not condemn anyone and everyone, just the rich and mighty who oppress the poor and crush the needy. The sin of driving out the other from her possession, from her work, from her means of livelihood--the sin of pushing him to the margins of society and beyond--weighs high on their scales. How could there be universal solidarity in *this* sin? The mighty are the sinners, and the weak are the sinned against. Even if all people sin, not all sin equally. To deny this would be to insult all those nameless heroes who refused to participate in power-acts of exclusion and had the courage to embrace the other, even at the risk of being ostracized or imprisoned. The uprightness of these people demands that we talk about sin concretely.[27]

But, if we always speak of sin concretely--if we speak of it only in the plural--do we not reduce sin to sinful acts and intentions? Is this not too shallow a view of sin, and does it not lead to unhealthy and oppressive moralizing? The answer would be yes, if it were not for the *transpersonal dimension of sin and evil.*

"Eruption" might be a good word to describe the conflict in the Balkans. I am thinking here less of the suddenness by which it broke out than of its insuppressible power. It does not seem that anybody is in control. Of course, the big and strategic moves that started the conflict and keep it going are made in the centers of intellectual, political, and military power, but there is far too much will for brutality among the common people. Once the conflict started, it seemed to trigger an uncontrollable chain reaction.[28] These were decent people, helpful neighbors. They did not, strictly speaking, *choose* to plunder and burn, rape and

---

[25]Niebuhr, *Nature and Destiny,* 222ff.

[26]So, already, William John Wolf, "Reinhold Niebuhr's Doctrine of Man," in Charles W. Kegley and Robert W. Bretall, eds., *Reinhold Niebuhr: His Religious, Social, and Political Thought,* Library of Living Theology 2 (New York: Macmillan, 1956), 240.

[27]See Moltmann, *Spirit of Life,* 126.

[28]On the eve of World War II, Carl Gustav Jung wrote: "The impressive thing about the German phenomenon is that one man, who is obviously `possessed,' has infected a whole nation to such an extent that everything is set in motion and has started rolling on its course towards perdition" ("Wotan," in Herbert Read et al., eds., *Collected Works of C. G. Jung,* tr. R. F. C. Hull, Bollingen Series 20 (New York: Pantheon Books, 1964), 185.

torture--or secretly enjoy these acts. A dormant beast in them was awakened from its uneasy slumber--and not only in them: the motives of those who set to fight against the brutal aggressors were self-defense and justice, but the beast in others enraged the beast in them. The moral barriers holding it in check were broken, and the beast went after revenge. In resisting evil, people were trapped by it. After World War II, Carl Gustav Jung wrote, "It is a fact that cannot be denied: the wickedness of others becomes our own wickedness because it kindles something evil in our own hearts."[29] Evil engenders evil, and, like pyroclastic debris from the mouth of a volcano, it erupts out of aggressor and victim alike.

In a fascinating book, *Engaging the Powers*, Walter Wink accessed the problem of the power of evil by looking at the "Powers" and their perversion into the "Domination System." The Powers, he claimed, are neither simply human institutions and structures nor an order of angelic (or demonic) beings. They are both institutional and spiritual; they "possess an outer, physical manifestation . . . and an inner spirituality or corporate culture."[30] The Powers are essentially good, but when they became "hell-bent on control," according to Wink, they degenerate into the Domination System. This system itself is neither only institutional nor spiritual; rather, the "powers of this present darkness" (see Eph 6:12) are the interiority of warped institutions, structures, and systems that oppress people. I will modify Wink's terminology and substitute the "Exclusion System" for his "Domination System," for as a rule the purpose of domination is to exclude others from scarce goods, whether economic, social, or psychological. Wink is right, however, that it is through the operation of the *system* that the power of evil imposes itself so irresistibly on people. Caught in the system of exclusion, as if in some invisible snare, people begin to behave according to its perverted logic. Should we call this anything else but "possession"?

Yet, persons cannot be reduced to the system. The system needs persons to make it "breathe" with the spirit of evil, and persons can escape the logic of the system, as the noble history of resistance demonstrates. So, if people do acquiesce, it is not because the system forces them to acquiesce but because there is something in their souls that resonates with the logic of exclusion. Could the culprit be the desire for identity--the instinctive will to be oneself-- that is written into the very structure of our selves, as Wolfhart Pannenberg

---

[29]Carl Gustav Jung, "After the Catastrophe," in ibid., 198.

[30]Walter Wink, "All Will Be Redeemed," *The Other Side* 28 (November-December, 1992): 17. See Wink, *Engaging the Powers*, 33-104.

recently suggested?[31] The will to be oneself is essentially healthy, of course, yet it always carries within it the germs of its own illness. To remain healthy, the will to be oneself needs to make the will to be the other part of itself. So, because the other must become part of who we are as we will to be ourselves, a tension is built into the desire for identity. It is the antipodal nature of the will to be oneself that makes the slippage into exclusion so easy. The power of sin from without--the Exclusion System--thrives on both the power and the powerlessness from within, the irresistible power of the will to be oneself and the powerlessness to resist the slippage into exclusion of the other.

The desire for identity could also explain why so many people let themselves be sinned against so passively--why they let themselves be excluded. It is not because they do not have the will to be themselves, but because one can satisfy that will *by surrendering to the other*. Their problem is not so much exclusion of the other from their will to be oneself but a paradoxical exclusion of their *own* self from the will to be oneself (what in feminist theology is called "diffusion of the self"). I call this exclusion a "problem," not a "sin," for it often comes about as a result of introjected acts of exclusion that we suffer.[32] Sin "is lurking at the door" when the introjected exclusion of ourselves by others starts crying after our exclusion of the others--when we begin looking for everything dark, inferior, and culpable in them. Like Cain, we then become ready to kill the otherness of the other.

Embrace

What do we do against the terrible sin of exclusion that lurks at our door or has already entered our soul? How do we master it? Is there a way out of the circle of exclusion to an embrace? The tragedy of the Balkan situation is that very few people seem to be asking these questions. Vengeance is on everybody's mind. Serbs want to avenge the slaughter of their compatriots in World War II and to repay others for their injured sense of national pride during the post-War years. Croatians and Muslims want revenge for Serbian atrocities, some from the present war and some from the previous one, and for their economic exploitation. The greater their success at revenging themselves, the more Serbs feel justified in their aggression. An evil deed will not be owed for long; it demands an instant repayment in kind. Vengeance, as Hannah Arendt wrote in *The Human Condition*,

---

[31]See Wolfhart Pannenberg, *Systematische Theologie II* (Göttingen: Vandenhoeck & Ruprecht, 1991), 298-299.

[32]Such introjection is possible, of course, because our will to be one with ourselves can be satisfied in part by giving ourselves to others.

acts in the form of re-acting against an original trespassing, whereby far from putting an end to the consequences of the first misdeed, everybody remains bound to the process, permitting the chain reaction contained in every action to take its unhindered course. . . . [Vengeance] incloses both doer and sufferer in the relentless automatism of the action process, which by itself need never come to an end.[33]

The endless spinning of the spiral of vengeance has its own good reasons that are built into the very structure of our world. If our deeds and their consequences could be undone, revenge would not be necessary. The undoing, if there were will for it, would suffice. Our actions are irreversible, however. Even God cannot change them. Therefore, the urge for vengeance or for punishment seems irrepressible. Arendt called this "the predicament of irreversibility."[34] The only way out of it, she insisted, was through an act of *forgiveness*.

Yet, forgiveness is precisely what seems impossible. Deep within the heart of every victim, hate swells up against the perpetrator. The Imprecatory Psalms seem to come upon their lips much more easily than the prayer of Jesus on the cross. If anything, they would rather pray, "Forgive them not, Father, for they knew what they did" (Abe Rosenthal). If the perpetrators were repentant, forgiveness would come more easily. However, repentance seems as difficult as forgiveness. It is not just that we do not like being wrong but that, almost invariably, the other side has not been completely right either. Most confessions, then, come as a mixture of repentance and aggressive defense or even lust for revenge.[35] Both the victim and the perpetrator are imprisoned in the automatism of exclusion, unable to forgive or repent, and united in a perverse communion of mutual hate.

In the Imprecatory Psalms, the torrents of rage have been allowed to flow freely, channeled only by the robust structure of a ritual prayer.[36] Strangely enough, it is they that point to a way out of the slavery of hate to the freedom of forgiveness. For the followers of the crucified Messiah, their main message is that hate belongs before God--not in a reflectively managed and manicured form of a confession but as a pre-reflective outburst from the depths of our being. Hidden in the dark chambers of our hearts and nourished by the system

---

[33]Hannah Arendt, *The Human Condition* (Chicago: The University of Chicago Press, 1958), pp. 240-241.

[34]*Ibid.*, p. 237.

[35]See Carl Gustav Jung, "Epilogue to `Essay on Contemporary Events,'" in Read, *Collected Works,* pp. 240-241.

[36]See Christoph Barth, *Introduction to the Psalms* (New York: Scribners, 1966), pp. 43ff.; Erhard S. Gerstenberger, "Enemies and Evildoers in the Psalms: A Challenge to Christian Preaching," *Horizons in Biblical Theology,* vol. 4, no. 2 (1983), pp. 61-77.

of darkness, hate grows and seeks to infect everything with its hellish will to exclusion. In light of the justice and love of God, however, hate recedes and the seed is planted for the miracle of forgiveness. Forgiveness flounders because I exclude the enemy from the community of humans and exclude myself from the community of sinners. However, no one can be in the presence of God for long without overcoming this double exclusion, without transposing the enemy from a sphere of monstrous inhumanity into the sphere of common humanity and oneself from the sphere of proud innocence into the sphere of common sinfulness. When one knows that the torturer will not eternally triumph over the victim, one is freed to rediscover one's humanity and imitate God's love for oneself. When one knows that the love of God is greater than all sin, one is free to see oneself in light of the justice of God and, so, to rediscover one's own sinfulness.

Yet, even when the obstacles are removed, forgiveness cannot simply be presumed.[37] It always comes as a surprise--at least to those who are not ignorant of the ways of men and women. Forgiveness *is* an outrage, not only against the logic of the Exclusion System but also "against straight-line dues-paying morality," as Lewis Smedes has suggested.[38] The perpetrator *deserves* unforgiveness. When forgiveness happens, there is always a strange, almost irrational, otherness at its very heart, even when we are aware that, given the nature of our world, it is wiser to forgive than to withhold forgiveness. Could it be that the word of forgiveness that must be uttered in the depths of our being, if it is uttered at all, is an echo of Another's voice?

Forgiveness is the boundary between exclusion and embrace. It heals the wounds that the power-acts of exclusion have inflicted and breaks down the dividing wall of hostility. It leaves a distance, however, an empty space between people that allows them either to go their separate ways in what is called "peace" or to fall into each other's arms.

"Going one's own way"--a civilized form of exclusion--is what the majority of the people in the Balkans contemplate in their most benevolent and optimistic moments. "Too much blood was shed for us to live together," I heard almost every time I participated in conversations about what might happen after the clamor of battle dies down. Never mind geographic proximity, never mind the communication lines that connect us, our similar languages, our common history, our interdependent economies, the complex network of friendships and relations created by the years of living with each other and making love to each other!

---

[37]See James Wm. McClendon, *Systematic Theology I: Ethics* (Nashville, TN: Abingdon Press, 1986), 224ff.

[38]Lewis B. Smedes, *Forgive and Forget: Healing the Hurts We Don't Deserve* (San Francisco, CA: Harper & Row, 1984), 124.

A clear line will separate "them" from "us." They will remain "they" and we will remain "we," and we will never include "them" when we speak of "us." We will each be clean of the other and identical with ourselves, and so there will be peace among us. What muddies this clean calculation is the fact that the war broke out in the name of Serbian identity with itself. By what magic does one hope to transform exclusion from a cause of war into an instrument of peace?

The only way to peace is through embrace--that is, after the parties have forgiven and repented, for without forgiveness and repentance embrace is a masquerade. An embrace always involves a double movement of *aperture* and *closure*. I open my arms to create space in myself for the other. The open arms are a sign both of discontent at being myself only and of desire to include the other. They are an invitation to the other to come in and feel at home with me, to belong to me. In an embrace I also close my arms around the other--not tightly, so as to crush her and assimilate her forcefully into myself--for that would not be an embrace but a concealed power-act of exclusion--but gently, so as to tell her that I do not want to be without her in her otherness. I want her to remain independent and true to her genuine self, to maintain her identity and, as such, to become part of me so that she can enrich me with what she has and I do not.[39] An embrace is a "sacrament" of a catholic personality. It mediates and affirms the interiority of the other in me, my complex identity that includes the other, a unity with the other that is both maternal (substantial) and paternal (symbolic)[40]--and still something other than either.[41]

Why should I embrace the other? The answer is simple: because the others *are* part of my own true identity. I cannot live authentically without welcoming the others--the other gender, other persons, or other cultures--into the very structure of my being, for I am created to reflect the personality of the triune God. The Johannine Jesus says that "the Father is in me and I am in the Father" (Jn 10:38). The one divine person is not that person only but includes the other divine persons in itself; it is what it is only through the indwelling of the other. The Son is the Son because the Father and the Spirit indwell him; without this interiority of the Father and the Spirit, there would be no Son. Every divine person *is* the other persons, but each is the other persons in their own particular

---

[39]See Wiesel, *From the Kingdom*, 61.

[40]For the categories, see Julia Kristeva, *Au commencement était l'amour: Psychoanalyse et foi*, Textes du xxe siècle (Paris: Hachette, 1988), 35ff.

[41]This rather schematic analysis of embrace needs to be fleshed out concretely, of course. The identity of a person or a social group cannot be abstracted from its history. An embrace must include both individual histories and a common history, which is often a history of pain. The mutual inclusion of histories and of common memory is therefore essential to a genuine embrace.

way. Analogously, the same is true of human persons created in the image of God. Their identity as persons is conditioned by the characteristics of other persons in their social relations. The others--other persons or cultures--are not filth that we collect as we travel these earthly roads. Filth is rather our own monochrome identity, which is nothing else but the sin of exclusion at cognitive and voluntative levels--a refusal to recognize that the others have *already* broken in through the enclosure of our selves and an unwillingness to make a "movement of effacement by which the self makes itself available to others."[42] In the presence of the divine Trinity, we need to strip down the drab gray of our own self-enclosed selves and cultures and embrace others so that their bright colors, painted on our very selves, will begin to shine.

But, how do the bright colors shine when the Exclusion System is dirtying us incessantly with its drab gray paint? How do we overcome our powerlessness to resist the slippage into exclusion? We need the energies of the *Spirit of embrace*--the Spirit who "issues from the essential inward community of the triune God, in all the richness of its relationships," who lures people into fellowship with the triune God and opens them up for one another and for the whole creation of God.[43] The Spirit of embrace creates communities of embrace--places where the power of the Exclusion System has been broken and from whence the divine energies of embrace can flow, forging rich identities that include the other.

---

[42]Riceour, *Oneself as Another*, 168.
[43]Moltmann, *Spirit of Life*, 219.

BIOGRAPHICAL NOTES ABOUT AUTHORS

Dr. Esad Ćimić is a native of Mostar, Herzegovina. He studied philosophy at Sarajevo University and completed his doctorate in 1964. Subsequently he became a professor at the Universities of Sarajevo, Zadar, Belgrade and Zagreb. Some of the academic moves were necessitated by the political conditions of the time. Since 1995 he is professor of systematic sociology and sociology of religion at the University of Zadar in Croatia. He is the author of nine books and over 200 articles.

Dr. Lenard Cohen is a professor in the Department of Political Science at Simon Fraser University in British Columbia. He received his PhD. degree from Columbia University. His main area of specialization is East European politics, with a special focus on the Balkans. Dr. Cohen's published books and articles concerning the politics of the former Yugoslavia and post-Yugoslavia include: *Political Cohesion in a Fragile Mosaic: The Yugoslav Experience* (1983), and *The Socialist Pyramid: Elites and Power in Yugoslavia* (1989) as well as his most recent book, *Broken Bonds: Yugoslavia's Disintegration and Balkan Politics in Transition* (1995). His current research work includes forthcoming studies of political development in Serbia (*Serpent in the Bosom: Slobodan Milošević and Serbian Nationalism*) and Croatia (*Embattled Democracy: Post-Communist Croatia in Transition*).

Dr. Dragoljub B. Djordjević is a Professor of Sociology and of the Philosophy of Natural Sciences at the Mechanical Engineering Faculty, University of Niš, Serbia. He received his Ph.D. in Sociology of Religion in 1983 from the University of Niš. He has published twelve books including *From Magic to Science* (1994), *The Return of the Sacred* (1995), *Sociology Forever* (1996), and *Temptations of Atheism* (1997). He is Founder and President of the Yugoslav Society for the Scientific Study of Religion.

Dr. John P. Dourley is Professor of Religion in the Department of Religion, Faculty of Arts, Carleton University, Ottawa, Ontario, Canada. He is also a Jungian analyst, a graduate of the Zürich/Kusnacht Institute (1980), and a Roman Catholic priest. He has written extensively on the religious implications of Jungian psychology and has four titles in this area with Inner City Press, Toronto, Ontario.

Dr. Francine Friedman is Associate Professor of Political Science and Director of the Office of European Studies at Ball State University. Her most recent publications include *The Bosnian Muslims: Denial of a Nation* (Westview Press, 1996) and "To Fight or Not to Fight: The Decision to Settle the Croat-Serb Conflict," *International Interactions*, Vol. 27 (1997).

Dr. Dimitrije Kalezić is Professor and Dean of the Orthodox Theological Faculty in Belgrade. Born in Danilovgrad, Montenegro, Yugoslavia, he completed his theological studies at the Orthodox Theological School in Sremski Karlovci. He also studied Catholic theology in Vienna, Austria. An ordained Orthodox priest since 1971 he was elevated to the rank of *protojerej* in 1982. His scholarly work is in religious philosophy, systematic theology, philosophy of culture, literature, and language as related to religion. He published *The Ethics of the Mountain Wreath, St. Basil of Ostrog in His Time, St. Sava, History of Antique Philosophy*, and numerous articles.

Dr. Miroslav Mirko Kiš is chair of the department of theology and Christian philosophy in the Seventh-day Adventist Theological Seminary at Andrews University, Berrien Springs, Michigan, since 1983. Born in the village of Miklušcvci, Yugoslavia, Kiš completed his bachelor's degree in theology at the Seminaire Adventist at Collonges, France, in 1973. In 1983, he earned his doctorate in philosophical ethics from McGill University, Montreal, Canada. He has written articles on religious ethics for several denominational magazines and journals.

Dr. Sulejman Mašović graduated and received his doctorate from Zagreb University School of Law and thereupon completed post-graduate studies in social, pedagogical, and economic sciences. Since 1960 he is a professor of defectology at the Zagreb University, but he also lectured at schools of sociology, pedagogy, and theology in Zagreb, Rijeka, Sarajevo, etc. He participated in numerous international meetings of the U.N., European Community, and similar. He is a member of Meshihat of the Islamic Community of Croatia and of several international organizations.

Dr. Paul Mojzes is the Academic Dean and Professor of Religious Studies at Rosemont College, Rosemont, Pennsylvania. Born in Osijek, Croatia, he grew up in Novi Sad, Vojvodina, Serbia, where he finished the high school and attended Belgrade University Law School from 1955 to 1957. He received the A.B. degree from Florida Southern College in religion in 1959, and Ph.D. from Boston University in church history in 1965. He is the co-editor of the *Journal of Ecumenical Studies* and the editor of *Religion in Eastern Europe*. He is the author of *Christian-Marxist Dialogue in Eastern Europe* (1980), *Religious Liberty in Eastern Europe and the USSR: Before and After the Great Transformation* (1992) and *Yugoslavian Inferno: Ethnoreligious Warfare in the*

Balkans (1994). In addition he is the editor or co-editor of several books and the author of numerous articles.

Marko Oršolić, a native Bosnia, received his diploma in theology, political science, and history. He received masters degrees in ecumenical theology and dialogue in Ljubljana and in philosophy in Zabreb. He wrote a book, *A Christian in the Service of the Revolution.* In his country he is a pioneer of Christian-Marxist dialogue as well as inter-religious (Judaism, Christianity, and Islam) dialogue. He is the founder of the International Interreligions, Intercultural Center "Together" and professor of Franciscan theology in Sarajevo. He is the receipient of the foremost cultural recognition of Sarajevo in 1991 and the Abbot Emmanuel Henfelder grant for the development of Catholic-Orthodox relations (1996). For twenty years he was the editor of the Yugoslav philosophical-theological review, *Nova et Vetera.*

Gerard F. Powers has been a foreign policy advisor for the U.S. Catholic Conference in Washington, D.C. since 1987. He is responsible for European affairs and security matters. He is an adjunct faculty member at the National Law Center of George Washington University. Recent articles have examined the use of force in the Gulf Water, the right to self-determination, and the role of religion in the conflicts in Northern Ireland and the former Yugoslavia. He is co-editor of *Peacemaking: Moral and Policy Challenges for a New World.*

Dr. Radmila Radić (Belgrade, 1958), received her masters degree and Ph.D. in historical science from University of Belgrade, Philosophical Faculty. She is a research fellow at the Institute for Recent History of Serbia, Belgrade. She published several articles and the book *Faith Against Faith*: *The State and Religious Organizations in Serbia 1945-1953* (Belgrade, 1995). She is one of the authors of *The Serbian Side of the War* (Belgrade, 1996).

Dr. Michael Sells is the Emily Judson Baugh and John Marshall Gest Professor of Comparative Religions at Haverford College in Pennsylvania. He is author of *The Bridge Betrayed: Religion and Genocide in Bosnia* (University of California Press, 1996), as well as a number of articles on the religious dimensions of genocide in Bosnia. He is the founder and president of "The Community of Bosnia Foundation," which supports a multireligious Bosnia and seeks to help Bosnian survivors of genocide in tangible ways. Among his earlier books is *Mystical Languages of Unsaying* (University of Chicago Press, 1994).

Dr. Gerald Shenk is professor of Church and Society at Eastern Mennonite University, Harrisonburg, Virginia. He received his B.S. degree from Eastern Mennonite University, M.A. degree from Fuller Theological Seminary, and Ph.D. from Northwestern University. He spent nine years in the lands of former

Yugoslavia where he studied sociology of religion at the University of Zagreb and Sarajevo. He is the author of *God With Us? The Roles of Religion in Conflicts with the Former Yugoslavia.* (Uppsala, Sweden: Life & Peace Institute, 1993). His research interests include the religious contributions to peacemaking and he promotes this concern by frequent trips to the Balkans.

Dr. David Steele is a fellow at the Center for Strategic and International Studies in Washington, DC where he directs a project on religion and conflict resolution which primarily involves conducting conflict resolution training seminars for religious leaders from the former Yugoslavia. He holds a Ph.D. in Christian Ethics and Practical Theology from University of Edinburgh. He is the author of numerous articles on religion and conflict resolution, including "At the Front Lines of the Revolution: East Germany's Churches Give Sanctuary and Succor to the Purveyors of Change," in *Religion: The Missing Dimension of Statecraft,* Oxford University Press, 1994.

Dr. Mitja Velikonja obtained the Ph.D. in sociology from the Faculty of Social Sciences, University of Ljubljana, Slovenia. He is currently an assistant at this faculty and a research fellow of the Centre for Religious and Cultural Studies. He has published several articles on contemporary national, social, political, and religious mythologies in Slovenian and British social science journals. His first book is entitled *Masade duha - Razpotja sodobnih mitologij* [Masadas of Mind - The Crossroads of Contemporary Mythologies], published in 1996 in Ljubljana. Main areas of his research interest are socio-historical changes and myths of ancient and present-day societies in Central and Eastern Europe.

Dr. Miroslav Volf, who teaches theology at Fuller Theological Seminary, Pasadena, California, and the Evangelical Theological School in Osijek, Croatia, was born in Croatia and educated in Croatia, USA, and Germany. He has published a number of books and scholarly articles and lectured widely in Asia, Europe, and the United States. Most of his work has been on the borderline between theology and the social sciences (such as the relationship between Christian faith and economics). His most recent book, *Exclusion and Embrace: A Theological Exploration of Identity, Otherness, and Reconciliation* (Nashville: Abingdon, 1996) offers theological perspectives on the relation between cultures.

Dr. Srdjan Vrcan is a professor emeritus of the Law School of University of Split in Croatia. He is a former dean of the school and his speciality is sociology of religion. As a Fulbright scholar he spent a year in the United States. He has attended numerous conferences and is widely published in the field of Eastern European religious developments. During the last few years his articles on the war in the former Yugoslavia were published in Slovenia, Italy, France, Great Britain and the U.S.A.

Dr. Mato Zovkić is the general vicar of the Sarajevo archdiocese of the Catholic Church and professor of New Testament at the Catholic Theological Seminary in Sarajevo. He was born in Bosnia and received his theological education in Zagreb and Rome. He represents the Sarajevo Archdiocese in matters of interreligious relations and has attended numerous conferences to promote interreligious cooperation. He lived in Sarajevo during part of the war and then taught in Bol na Braču, Croatia, where the Catholic Seminary was termporarily moved until 1996.

DATE DUE